IC³® Internet Core and Computing Certification Study Guide

Ron Gilster

New York   Chicago   San Francisco   Lisbon   London   Madrid
Mexico City   Milan   New Delhi   San Juan   Seoul   Singapore   Sydney   Toronto

Cataloging-in-Publication Data is on file with the Library of Congress

McGraw-Hill books are available at special quantity discounts to use as premiums and sales promotions, or for use in corporate training programs. To contact a representative, please e-mail us at bulksales@mcgraw-hill.com.

IC³® Internet Core and Computing Certification Study Guide

1234567890   DOC DOC   019

ISBN: Book p/n 978-0-07-163808-1 and CD p/n 978-0-07-163809-8
of set 978-0-07-163811-1

MHID: Book p/n 0-07-163808-3 and CD p/n 0-07-163809-1
of set 0-07-163811-3

Sponsoring Editor Megg Morin	**Acquisitions Coordinator** Meghan Riley	**Indexer** Jack Lewis	**Illustration** Glyph International
Editorial Supervisor Jody McKenzie	**Copy Editor** Robert Campbell	**Production Supervisor** Jim Kussow	**Art Director, Cover** Jeff Weeks
Project Manager Vipra Fauzdar, Glyph International	**Proofreader** Paul Tyler	**Composition** Glyph International	**Cover Designer** Peter Grame

This book is dedicated to those readers for whom earning a first certification is just the first step in a successful career.

Ron Gilster (MBA, A+, Network+, i-Net+, CCNA, & AAGG) is a best-selling author with over 40 titles in print, with the majority of his books on information technology (IT) certifications. Ron has held a variety of IT-related positions, ranging from computer operator to senior manager. He has worked in consulting, manufacturing, software development, telecommunications, and higher education. His books include the *CEA-CompTIA DHTI+ Digital Home Technology Integrator All-in-One Exam Guide*, *CCNA for Dummies*, *A+ Certification for Dummies*, *Microsoft Office SharePoint Server 2007: A Beginner's Guide*, and *PC Hardware: A Beginner's Guide*.

About LearnKey

LearnKey provides self-paced learning content and multimedia delivery solutions to enhance personal skills and business productivity. LearnKey claims the largest library of rich streaming-media training content that engages learners in dynamic media-rich instruction complete with video clips, audio, full motion graphics, and animated illustrations. LearnKey can be found on the Web at www.LearnKey.com.

CONTENTS

v

ACKNOWLEDGMENTS

I'd like to acknowledge the wonderful, talented, and oh-so-patient professionals at McGraw-Hill Technical who were instrumental in giving birth to this book: Megg Morin, Meghan Riley, Jody McKenzie, Bob Campbell, and Vipra Fauzdar of Glyph International.

I'd also like to express my thanks to the wonderful and supportive companies, schools, organizations, and individuals who contributed graphics, photographs, and other art to this project.

Thank you all so much!

The objective of this study guide is to prepare you for the three IC³ exams by familiarizing you with the technology or body of knowledge this exam measures. Because the primary focus of the book is to help you pass the test, I have covered every major topic and subtopic listed in the official objectives of the IC³ exams along with additional information on the related technology. Some aspects of the technology are only covered to the extent necessary to help you understand what you need to know to pass the exam, but I hope this book will continue to serve you as a valuable professional resource well after you have passed the exams and earned your IC³ certification.

In This Book

This book is organized in such a way as to serve as an in-depth review for the IC³ exams, Computing Fundamentals, Key Applications, and Living Online, for entry-level computer and Internet users. Each part of this book focuses on one of the three IC³ exams, and each chapter within a part then covers one or more of the objectives of that exam, with an emphasis on the "why," "when," and "how to" of working with operating systems, application software, computer hardware, and the Internet and World Wide Web.

On the CD

For more information on the CD-ROM, please see the Appendix "About the CD-ROM" at the back of the book.

Exam Readiness Checklist

At the end of the Introduction, you will find an Exam Readiness Checklist. This table has been constructed to allow you to cross-reference the official exam objectives with the objectives as they are presented and covered in this book. The checklist also allows you to gauge your level of expertise on each objective at the outset of your studies. This should allow you to check your progress and make sure you spend the time you need on more difficult or unfamiliar sections. References have been provided for the objective exactly as the vendor presents it, the section of the study guide that covers that objective, and a chapter and page reference.

In Every Chapter

We've created a set of chapter components that call your attention to important items, reinforce important points, and provide helpful exam-taking hints. Take a look at what you'll find in every chapter:

- Every chapter begins with **Certification Objectives**—what you need to know in order to pass the section on the exam dealing with the chapter topic. The Objective headings identify the objectives within the chapter, so you'll always know an objective when you see it!

- **Exam Watch** notes call attention to information about, and potential pitfalls in, the exam. These helpful hints are written by authors who have taken the exams and received their certification—who better to tell you what to worry about? They know what you're about to go through!

e x a m

ⓦ a t c h

The IC³-1 exam uses the terms CPU and microprocessor interchangeably, which is essentially true. In fact, though, emerging microprocessors can include more than just a CPU. However, for purposes of the exam, they are essentially the same thing.

**on the
ⓙob**

- **On the Job** notes describe the issues that come up most often in real-world settings. They provide a valuable perspective on certification- and product-related topics. They point out common mistakes and address questions that have arisen from on the job discussions and experience.

- **Inside the Exam** sidebars highlight some of the most common and confusing problems that students encounter when taking a live exam. Designed to anticipate the what the exam will emphasize, getting inside the exam will help ensure you know what you need to know to pass the exam. You can get a leg up on how to respond to those difficult-to-understand questions by focusing extra attention on these sidebars.

■ The **Certification Summary** is a succinct review of the chapter and a restatement of salient points regarding the exam.

✓ ■ The **Two-Minute Drill** at the end of every chapter is a checklist of the main points of the chapter. It can be used for last-minute review.

Q&A ■ The **Self Test** offers questions similar to those found on the certification exams. The answers to these questions, as well as explanations of the answers, can be found at the end of each chapter. By taking the Self Test after completing each chapter, you'll reinforce what you've learned from that chapter while becoming familiar with the structure of the exam questions.

Some Pointers

Once you've finished reading this book, set aside some time to do a thorough review. You might want to return to the book several times and make use of all the methods it offers for reviewing the material:

1. *Re-read all the Two-Minute Drills,* or have someone quiz you. You also can use the drills as a way to do a quick cram before the exam. You might want to make some flash cards out of 3 × 5 index cards that have the Two-Minute Drill material on them.

2. *Re-read all the Exam Watch notes and Inside the Exam elements.* Remember that these notes are written by authors who have taken the exam and passed. They know what you should expect—and what you should be on the lookout for.

3. *Re-take the Self Tests.* Taking the tests right after you've read the chapter is a good idea, because the questions help reinforce what you've just learned. However, it's an even better idea to go back later and do all the questions in the book in one sitting. Pretend that you're taking the live exam. When you go through the questions the first time, you should mark your answers on a separate piece of paper. That way, you can run through the questions as many times as you need to until you feel comfortable with the material.

4. *Take and re-take the MasterExams on the CD.* The CD that accompanies this book includes 150 multiple-choice questions that cover every of the IC³ exams and objectives. Use this valuable tool to acquaint yourself with the topics and subject matter that you'll likely encounter on the exams.

The Internet and Computing Core Certification (IC³) program from Certiport, Inc., is a standards-based certification program that measures a candidate's knowledge and understanding of basic computing and Internet usage. Passing the IC³ exam means that you have demonstrated that you possess the knowledge and skills generally accepted as necessary for required for basic use of computer hardware, software, networks, and the Internet.

Who Should Take the IC³ Exams?

IC³ is intended for anyone, regardless of career goals, who wishes to demonstrate his or her knowledge of computer and Internet basics. Having an IC³ certification gives you not only recognition in the job market or education, but the confidence that you have verified your knowledge of the computer, its application, and support.

The individuals who are most likely to benefit from gaining the IC³ certification are students in junior high and middle school, high school, GED programs, and continuing education students, as well as Job Corps participants and working adults who wish to certify that they have a working knowledge of computers and the Internet. Because IC³ is an international certification, its value provides a global recognition of the individual's skills and knowledge.

What Knowledge Is Tested on the IC³ Exams?

The three IC³ exams, Computing Fundamentals, Key Applications, and Living Online, each test a basic component of what has been established as the essential knowledge of basic computer hardware and software, the use of application software, and the resources available and use of the Internet, respectively.

The Computing Fundamentals exam tests an individual's knowledge of computer hardware, application software, and operating systems. This exam covers such areas as the candidate's ability to identify types of computers, how the hardware and software of a computer works, and how a computer fits into a network.

The Key Applications exam tests an individual's knowledge of word processing, electronic spreadsheets, and presentation software. The exam covers how each type of application software is used to create, edit, and share documents.

The Living Online exam measures an individual's knowledge of computer networks, the Internet, the World Wide Web, and e-mail, as well as the accepted courtesy and ethical guidelines that users should practice. This exam also covers the impact the Internet has on society, especially at home, school, and work.

Why Take the IC³ Exams?

If just earning the IC³ certification isn't enough, the IC³ offers a few additional perks. Perhaps the most valuable reason to earn the IC³ certification, especially for college-bound students, is the fact that the American Council on Education (ACE) has recommended that anyone holding the IC³ certification should be granted general education or computer or information literacy. Nearly two thousand colleges, universities, and other institutions of higher education can grant this credit to a student. However, whether or not a college actually awards this credit is up to each individual school, so you should check with the college administration before assuming you'll get this credit.

Another reason to take the IC³ exams and become certified is that it is a valuable first step toward other higher-level certifications, such as the Computing Technology Industry Association's (CompTIA) A+ and Network+ certifications and others.

College credit and a gateway to other certifications are perhaps the two most important reasons to take the IC³ exams, but as mentioned earlier, there are several other reasons as well. Perhaps the most important of these is that the IC³ exam is a globally recognized standard of certification that measures your knowledge and skills as a computer user. Over 250 experts from almost 20 countries have worked together to develop the exam objectives and the tests that measure the individual's knowledge in each objective area.

What Types of Questions are on the IC³ Exams?

The IC³ exams combine knowledge-based question types, including multiple-choice, multiple-answer, matching, and true/false, with performance-based simulations to truly and effective measure an individual's knowledge and ability to complete simple computing tasks in an application or user interface environment.

Multiple-Choice Questions

The most common question format on the IC³ exam is the multiple-choice question. I'm sure you've seen this type of question many times before. A question is asked or a statement is made, and three, four, or more answers or responses are listed below it from which you are to choose the one that best answers or completes the question or statement. The following is an example of a multiple-choice question like those you'll find on the IC³ exams:

7. Which of the following is not a primary group of PC software?
   - ○ A. Application software
   - ○ B. Simulation software
   - ○ C. System software
   - ○ D. Utility software

To answer a multiple-choice question, one that has only one correct answer, you'd click the circle of the answer you believe to be correct. When the circle option is shown on the answers of a multiple-choice question, there is only one correct answer and they are mutually exclusive. This means that if after choosing one answer, you were to click another, the selection for the first would be turned off and the second answer then highlighted.

Just so you know, the answer for the preceding sample question is B.

Multiple-Answer Questions

At first glance, multiple-answer questions appear to be multiple-choice questions. What's the difference? Your first clue that a question may have more than one answer is that in place of the circle options there are now little squares or check boxes. Another clue should have been that in the wording of the question, you were advised to pick a certain number (as in the example shown next) or to "choose all that apply," which means there could be potentially one, two, three, or four (or more) correct answers to the question. An example of a multiple-answer question is

48. Which of the following are steps in a CPU's instruction cycle?
    - ☐ A. Decode
    - ☐ B. Execute
    - ☐ C. Fetch
    - ☐ D. Recycle

To answer a multiple-answer question, one that could have multiple correct answers, you click the check box for each answer you believe to be correct. When the check box option is shown on the answers of a multiple-answer question, there may be multiple correct answers and they can all be selected.

Just so you know, the answers for the preceding sample question are A, B, and C, which should all be selected to properly answer the question.

Matching Questions

Matching questions ask you to match a set of terms or items to a list of definitions or results. On the IC³ exam, matching questions are typically animated. For the matching question shown in Figure 1, the terms on the left are dragged into the empty box adjacent to its matching definition on the right using the mouse. Other matching questions may ask you to enter the number or letter of a term into a box adjacent to its matching information.

True/False Questions

True/false questions are another type with which you are probably quite familiar. A statement is given, and you must decide whether the statement is true or false. It sounds simple enough, but you have to beware of semantic and wording traps that may be embedded in the statement. You should be especially wary of statements that

FIGURE 1

An example of a matching question like the ones included on the IC³ exams

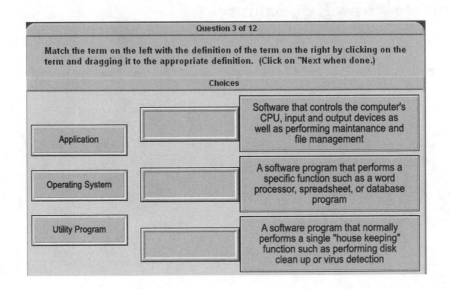

include words like "all," "always," "never," or "not." If the statement isn't totally true in every situation or instance, then the statement is false.

Performance-Based Questions

Performance-based questions ask you to perform a task that simulates something you'd do when working with a particular application. You will likely encounter this type of question in the areas that cover operating system actions, like creating a folder or a shortcut, application actions, like changing the width of an Excel 2007 column (see Figure 2), or editing a document.

One of the drawbacks of a book with words printed on a page is that I am unable to show you an example of a performance-based question like those you're likely to encounter on the exams. However, by practicing each of the actions and procedures outlined in this book, the candidate will have the knowledge and skills to execute the requested steps easily.

FIGURE 2

An example of a performance-based question you'll encounter on the IC³ exams

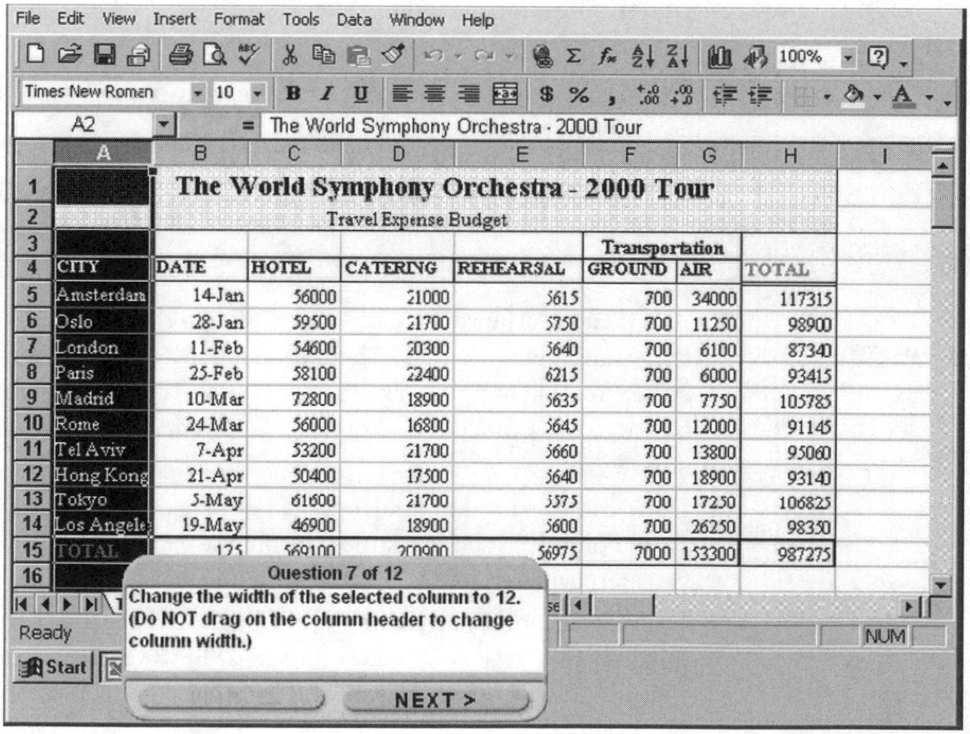

Study and Testing Strategies

Preparing for the IC³ exams involves studying, practicing, and practice testing. Studying involves reading and re-reading the information in this book that explains the practices, policies, and basic knowledge involved in using computer hardware, software, and the Internet. Be sure you know which hardware component does what, how the different components work together, and the types of problems each can have or cause. You also need to practice each of the processes detailed in this book until you are able to do them automatically when asked to perform a certain process or task.

1. Read each chapter of the book and understand the exam objective and the information and processes you should know to achieve the goal of each objective.

2. Use the questions and answers at the end of each chapter to see if you have gained the knowledge and understanding needed for the exam.

3. Use the practice exams on the CD that accompanies this book to measure your readiness for the exam.

4. Right before you take the exams, read through the Two-Minute Drills at the end of each chapter to refresh your knowledge of the information covered for each objective.

Right before you go into the testing center to begin the exams, read through the Two-Minute drills one more time for a last-minute refresher. Here are some tips on how to perform your best on the exams:

■ Allow enough time during and after your refresher to relax. How you do on the exams is important, but should you fail, it's not the end of the world, either. You can always retake the test, which, of course, is somewhat of a fallback, but if you are tense or nervous, you may not do well on the exams anyway.

■ Don't eat a big meal or drink a lot of liquid right before the exam. In fact, you should probably use the restroom before the exam. Once you begin the exam, you aren't allowed to take a break until you have finished it.

■ The testing center will provide you with scratch paper and a pen that you can use during the exams. You must turn these in when you are finished, but you can use them for whatever you wish during the test. I recommend that before you begin an exam, you do a brain dump onto the paper, writing down any lists, diagrams, or process sequences you're trying to remember. This clears them from your mind and allows you to relax a bit more.

■ Because the exams are timed, you shouldn't waste too much time on any one question. For most people, you are allowed 45 minutes for each of the three exams, which should be more than enough time if you are well prepared. Don't hurry or get into a panic, just steadily progress through the questions calmly.

■ Read each question completely, perhaps even twice, and, in your mind, answer the question or envision the process required as best you can. Then read each of the answers and rule out those that are definitely incorrect. Then analyze each of the possible correct answers to determine the best answer available. If you are asked to complete a task, run through the steps in your mind before you start moving the mouse. The test is looking for a specific sequence of events.

■ Be sure you answer every question. An unanswered question is counted as an incorrect response. If you wish to return to a question later, use the Mark feature to indicate that you wish to identify the question as one you'll come back to.

Registering to Take the IC³ Exams

As you near the point where you believe you are ready to take the IC3 exams, you should visit the Certiport, Inc., Web site (www.certiport.com) to register. On the Certiport Web site, purchase an exam voucher, which costs, at the time this was written, $33. You can then schedule an appointment at a testing center to take the exams. There should be at least one testing center in your vicinity. However, you may need to travel a short distance to a nearby city, if a testing center is not in your immediate area.

When you arrive at the testing center to take your exams, be sure you have two forms of identification. Any two of a driver's license, state-issued identification card, Social Security card, or passport are sufficient. You can't take anything into the testing area, except the scratch paper and pen or pencil that the test administrator provided, so don't bring along cheat sheets, this book, or any other materials, except as last-minute study aids.

When you complete the test, your score and how you did on each particular exam is displayed for you. Of course, you'll have passed; I have complete confidence in you. However, as a courtesy to anyone else that may be in the testing area, keep the cheering and fist-pumping to a minimum.

The IC³ Computing Fundamentals Exam

Exam Readiness Checklist

Official Objective	Study Guide Coverage	Ch #	Pg #	Beginner	Intermediate	Expert
Identify different types of computer devices and applications	Different Types of Computer Devices	1	4			
Identify the role of the CPU, including how the speed of a microprocessor is measured	The Role of the CPU	2	42			
Identify concepts related to computer memory (measurement of memory, RAM, ROM)	Concepts Related to Computer Memory	2	48			
Identify the features and benefits (storage capacity, shelf-life, etc.) of different storage media	Features of Storage Media	2	55			
Identify the types and purposes of standard input and output devices on desktop or laptop computers	Standard Input and Output Devices	1	12			
Identify the types and purposes of specialized input devices (e.g., cameras, scanners, game controllers, etc.)	Specialized Input Devices	1	19			
Identify the types and purposes of specialized output devices (e.g., printers, projectors, etc.)	Specialized Output Devices	1	23			
Identify how hardware devices are connected to and installed on a computer system	How Hardware Is Connected and Installed	1	25			
Identify factors that affect computer performance	Factors That Affect Computer Performance	2	63			

Exam Readiness Checklist

Official Objective	Study Guide Coverage	Ch #	Pg #	Beginner	Intermediate	Expert
Identify the importance of protecting computer hardware from theft or damage	Protecting Computer Hardware from Theft or Damage	3	80			
Identify factors that can cause damage to computer hardware or media (e.g., environmental factors, magnetic fields, etc.)	Factors That Can Damage a Computer	3	82			
Identify how to protect computer hardware from fluctuations in the power supply, power outages, and other electrical issues (such as use of computers on different electrical systems)	How to Protect Computer Hardware from Power Issues	3	84			
Identify common problems associated with computer hardware	Common Hardware-Related PC Problems	4	100			
Identify problems that can occur if hardware is not maintained properly	Hardware Issues Caused by Poor Maintenance	4	101			
Identify maintenance that can be performed routinely by users	Preventive Maintenance by Users	4	103			
Identify maintenance that should ONLY be performed by experienced professionals, including replacing or upgrading internal hardware (especially electrical) components (such as processors or drives) that are not designed to be user accessible	Maintenance by Computer Professionals	4	104			
Identify the steps required to solve computer-related problems	General Troubleshooting Steps	4	105			
Identify consumer issues related to buying, maintaining, and repairing a computer	Buying, Maintaining, and Repairing a Computer	4	112			
Identify how software and hardware work together to perform computing tasks and how software is developed and upgraded	Hardware and Software Integration and Software Development	5	128			

Exam Readiness Checklist

The IC³ Computing Fundamentals Exam *(continued)*

Official Objective	Study Guide Coverage	Ch #	Pg #	Beginner	Intermediate	Expert
Identify fundamental concepts relating to word processing and common uses for word-processing applications (e.g., reviewing, editing, formatting, etc.)	Word-Processing Applications	6	153			
Identify fundamental concepts relating to spreadsheets and common uses for spreadsheet applications (e.g., worksheets, data sorting, formulas, and functions, etc.)	Spreadsheet Applications	6	162			
Identify fundamental concepts relating to presentation software and common uses for presentation applications (e.g., slides, speaker notes, graphics, etc.)	Presentation Applications	6	169			
Identify fundamental concepts relating to databases and common uses for database applications (e.g., fields, tables, queries, reports, etc.)	Database Applications	6	173			
Identify fundamental concepts relating to graphic and multimedia programs and common uses for graphic or multimedia software (e.g., drawing, painting, animation tools, etc.)	Graphics or Multimedia Applications	6	176			
Identify other types of software	Software for Specific Applications	6	181			
Identify fundamental concepts relating to education and entertainment programs (e.g., computer-based training (CBT), video, audio, etc.)	Education and Entertainment Software	7	204			
Identify the types and purposes of different utility programs (e.g., virus, adware and spyware detection programs, etc.)	Utility Programs	7	198			
Identify other types of software (e.g., chat, messaging, web conferencing, accounting software, etc.)	Other Software Types	7	205			

Exam Readiness Checklist

Official Objective	Study Guide Coverage	Ch #	Pg #	Beginner	Intermediate	Expert
Identify how to select the appropriate application(s) for a particular purpose, and problems that can arise if the wrong software product is used for a particular purpose	Choosing the Right Application	7	207			
Identify how applications interact and share data	Application Interactions	6	182			
Identify what an operating system is and how it works, and solve common problems related to operating systems	Operating Systems	8	220			
Use an operating system to manipulate a computer's desktop, files, and disks	Manipulate a Desktop and Files and Disks	9	250			
Identify how to change system settings, install and remove software	Change System Settings	9	266			

Key Applications Exam

Exam Readiness Checklist

Official Objective	Study Guide Coverage	Ch #	Pg #	Beginner	Intermediate	Expert
Be able to start and exit an application, identify and modify interface elements, and utilize sources of online help	Start, Work with, and Exit an Application	10	284			
Perform common file-management functions	Common File-Management Functions	11	310			
Perform common editing and formatting functions	Common Editing and Formatting Functions	11	315			
Perform common printing/outputting functions	Common Printing and Outputting Functions	11	323			

Exam Readiness Checklist

Key Applications Exam *(continued)*

Official Objective	Study Guide Coverage	Ch #	Pg #	Beginner	Intermediate	Expert
Be able to format text and documents, including the ability to use automatic formatting tools	Formatting Documents	12	336			
Identify common uses for word processing (such as creating short documents like letters and memos, long documents like reports and books, and specialized documents such as Web pages and blog entries) and identify elements of a well-organized document	Common Uses of Word Processing	12	360			
Be able to use word-processing tools to automate processes such as document review, security, and collaboration	Reviewing, Securing, and Collaborating on Word Processing Documents	13	372			
Be able to modify worksheet data and structure and format data in a worksheet	Working with the Data, Format, and Structure of a Worksheet	14	388			
Be able to sort data, manipulate data using formulas and functions, and create simple charts	Using Formulas and Functions and Creating Charts	15	410			
Be able to create and format simple presentations	Creating Slide Presentations	16	434			

Living Online Exam

Exam Readiness Checklist

Official Objective	Study Guide Coverage	Ch #	Pg #	Beginner	Intermediate	Expert
Identify that networks (including computer networks and other networks such as the telephone network) transmit different types of data	Transmitting Data	17	468			

Exam Readiness Checklist

Official Objective	Study Guide Coverage	Ch #	Pg #	Beginner	Intermediate	Expert
Identify concepts related to network communication (e.g., high speed, broadband, wireless [wifi], etc.)	Communicating on a Network	17	469			
Identify fundamental principles of security on a network including authorization, authentication, and wireless security issues	Securing a Network	17	480			
Identify benefits of networked computing	Identifying the Benefits of Networking	18	507			
Identify the risks of networked computing	Identifying the Risks of Networking	18	508			
Identify the roles of clients and servers in a network	Identifying the Roles of Clients and Servers	18	505			
Identify networks by size and type	Identifying Networks by Size and Type	18	496			
Identify how to use an electronic mail application	Using an Electronic Mail Application	19	518			
Identify different types of electronic communication/collaboration and how they work	Identifying Types of Electronic Communication	20	540			
Identify the appropriate use of different types of communication/collaboration tools and the "rules of the road" regarding online communication ("netiquette")	Identifying Appropriate Uses for Electronic Communication	20	546			
Identity information about the Internet, the World Wide Web and Web sites and be able to use a Web browsing application	The Internet, the World Wide Web, and Web Browsers	21	558			
Understand how content is created, located, and evaluated on the World Wide Web	Creating Content on the Web	22	586			
Identify how computers are used in different areas of work, school, and home	Computers at Work, School, and Home	23	606			
Identify the risks of using computer hardware and software and how to use computers and the Internet safely, ethically, and legally	Using Computers Safely and Ethically	24	618			

Part I

The IC³ Computing Fundamentals Exam

Objectives Map: The IC³ Computing Fundamentals Exam

Official Objective	Study Guide Coverage	Chapter number
Identify different types of computer devices and applications	Different Types of Computer Devices	1
Identify the role of the CPU including how the speed of a microprocessor is measured	The Role of the CPU	2
Identify concepts related to computer memory (measurement of memory, RAM, ROM)	Concepts Related to Computer Memory	2
Identify the features and benefits (storage capacity, shelf-life, etc.) of different storage media	Features of Storage Media	2
Identify the types and purposes of standard input and output devices on desktop or laptop computers	Standard Input and Output Devices	1
Identify the types and purposes of specialized input devices	Specialized Input Devices	1
Identify the types and purposes of specialized output devices	Specialized Output Devices	1
Identify how hardware devices are connected to and installed on a computer system	How Hardware Is Connected and Installed	1
Identify factors that affect computer performance	Factors That Affect Computer Performance	2
Identify the importance of protecting computer hardware from theft or damage	Protecting Computer Hardware from Theft or Damage	3
Identify factors that can cause damage to computer hardware or media	Factors That Can Damage a Computer	3
Identify how to protect computer hardware from fluctuations in the power supply, power outages and other electrical issues	How to Protect Computer Hardware from Power Issues	3
Identify common problems associated with computer hardware	Common Hardware-Related PC Problems	4
Identify problems that can occur if hardware is not maintained properly	Hardware Issues Caused by Poor Maintenance	4
Identify maintenance that can be performed routinely by users	Preventative Maintenance by Users	4
Identify maintenance that should ONLY be performed by experienced professionals, including replacing or upgrading internal hardware (especially electrical) components (such as processors or drives) that are not designed to be user accessible	Maintenance by Computer Professionals	4
Identify the steps required to solve computer-related problems	General Troubleshooting Steps	4
Identify consumer issues related to buying, maintaining and repairing a computer	Buying, Maintaining, and Repairing a Computer	4
Identify how software and hardware work together to perform computing tasks and how software is developed and upgraded	Hardware and Software Integration and Software Development	5
Identify fundamental concepts relating to word processing and common uses for word-processing applications	Word Processing Applications	6
Identify fundamental concepts relating to spreadsheets and common uses for spreadsheet applications	Spreadsheet Applications	6
Identify fundamental concepts relating to presentation software and common uses for presentation applications (e.g. slides, speaker notes, graphics, etc.)	Presentation Applications	6
Identify fundamental concepts relating to databases and common uses for database applications	Database Applications	6
Identify fundamental concepts relating to graphic and multimedia programs and common uses for graphic or multimedia software	Graphics and Multimedia Applications	6
Identify other types of software	Software for Specific Applications	6
Identify fundamental concepts relating to education and entertainment programs	Education and Entertainment Software	7
Identify the types and purposes of different utility programs	Utility Programs	7
Identify other types of software	Other Software Types	7
Identify how to select the appropriate application(s) for a particular purpose, and problems that can arise if the wrong software product is used for a particular purpose	Choosing the Right Application	7
Identify how applications interact and share data	Application Interactions	6
Identify what an operating system is and how it works, and solve common problems related to operating systems	Operating Systems	8
Use an operating system to manipulate a computer's desktop, files and disks	Manipulate the Desktop, Files, and Disks	9
Identify how to change system settings, install and remove software	Change System Settings	9

1

Computer Hardware and Peripherals

One of the major components of any computer system, along with computer software, data, a user, and documentation, is, of course, the computer hardware. The IC^3 exam measures your knowledge of the hardware components typically found in the computer systems commonly used in both business enterprises and academic institutions. This chapter, and Chapters 2–4, discuss and explain the basic computer types, the basic and specialized input and output peripheral devices of the typical computer system, and the methods used to install new or replace old peripheral devices on or into a computer.

CERTIFICATION OBJECTIVE

Different Types of Computer Devices

1.1.1   Identify different types of computer devices.

If there were only one type of computer system, the world would be perhaps a simpler place. However, this would mean that certain computer applications would not be nearly as effective or efficient. As the use of computers has evolved since the late 1970s, computers have become specialized in their application and use. In today's world, computer systems have been generally categorized into four primary groups:

- Desktop computers
- Portable computers
- Servers
- Embedded computers

More than any other characteristic, these four categories refer more to the size of the overall computer and its more common usage. Desktop computers are typically larger and less portable. Portable computers are smaller than a desktop system and designed to be easily carried from one point to another. Handheld computers are small enough to be held and operated in the human hand, hence their name. An embedded computer is a part of the circuitry and operating components of another device. In the sections that follow, each of these computer system categories is discussed.

Desktop Computers

The *desktop* computer, commonly known as the personal computer or "PC," is by far the most frequently used computer system. Its name is derived from the fact that it started out designed to sit on the top of a desk or table. A desktop computer is specifically not designed for portability, primarily because of the size and number of its major components and the connections between them.

The desktop computers available today are almost all stand-up vertical designs known as towers, in contrast to the horizontal lay-flat designs common in the past. While you can still purchase a horizontally oriented desktop PC, they are getting harder to find. The advantage of the tower-style case over a horizontal desktop case is that the tower doesn't necessarily have to be placed on the desktop; it could be placed on the floor or a mounting bracket or stand to open additional desktop space.

A desktop computer consists of four major component groups, as illustrated in Figure 1-1:

- System unit
- Monitor or display
- Keyboard and mouse
- Peripheral devices

The following sections provide an overview of the PC system unit and its contents. The other major components groups (monitor, display, keyboard, mouse, and peripherals) are covered individually later in the chapter.

Desktop PC System Unit

The *system unit* of a desktop PC is what most people call the "computer." Actually, the computer is the microprocessor inside the system unit along with virtually all of the electronic components related to the primary functions of the computer system,

The major components of a desktop computer

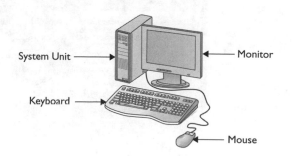

such as the microprocessor, power supply, memory, and connecting circuitry, as shown in Figure 1-2.

The components that make up the desktop computer's system unit are

- Computer case
- Motherboard
- Central processing unit (CPU)
- Memory
- Cooling system
- Power supply
- Storage devices

Computer Case Of course, when you purchase a new PC, it comes with a computer *case*, or as they are called by the manufacturers, a chassis. A computer case isn't a one-size-fits-all thing; cases come in a wide array of sizes, styles, designs, and colors. There are full towers, mid-towers, and horizontally oriented cases.

When you purchase a computer case, it can include everything but the peripheral devices and the motherboard or be just a bare-bones case. The computer cases available at a local computer outlet are likely to include only a power supply and a cooling fan module (more on power supplies and cooling fans in Chapter 3).

Motherboard The *motherboard* is the main circuit board of a PC that contains the circuitry and connection mountings for many of the components and devices that are installed inside the system unit. The motherboard, also known as the mainboard, system board, logic board (in Apple computers), or the "mobo" for short, provides the electronic interconnections for the CPU, memory, internal storage devices, expansion cards, and other critical devices of the computer. Figure 1-3 shows an example of a PC motherboard. Motherboards are discussed in more detail in Chapter 2.

Central Processing Unit The *central processing unit (CPU)*, like the one shown in Figure 1-4, is a single all-in-one circuit that includes the microprocessor. As its name defines, the CPU is the device that controls and manages the logical execution of the programmatic instructions of the system software. The role and makeup of the CPU are discussed in more detail in Chapter 2.

FIGURE 1-3

A PC motherboard (Photo courtesy of EVGA Corporation.)

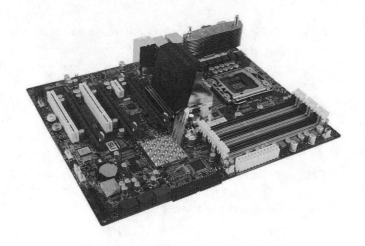

Memory   Computer *memory* is an electronic device installed in the system unit
to store information in support of the activities of the CPU and the components
installed on the computer system. In the context of a computer system, memory is a
generic term for a variety of different memory technologies, purposes, applications,
and forms. Memory systems are either volatile or nonvolatile, which translates to the
method used to store data and the length of time the data is retained. The different
types of memory and their respective uses are discussed in more detail in Chapter 2.

Cooling System   The purpose of the computer's *cooling system* is to remove heat
from the CPU and the interior of the system unit. Because they are electronic, all of
the systems and circuits inside the system unit emit heat. Heat is the enemy of electronic components, because heat can shorten their lives. For this reason, a system is
needed to cool the CPU, memory, motherboard, and the other circuits and boards
inside the system unit. In most PCs, the main component in the cooling system is
a fan. Chapter 3 discusses the cooling system in more detail.

Power Supply   The voltage available at most household and business electrical
outlets is either 110 or 240 volts (V) of alternating current (AC), and the power
used by the circuits inside the computer generally ranges from 3.3 V to 12 V of direct
current (DC). This means that the power source must be converted by the power
supply unit (PSU) of a PC. Computer power supplies are rated by the wattage (the
rate at which the power is transferred), with low wattage (200 to 300 watts) to high
wattage (500 to 1,300 watts). Chapter 3 discusses the cooling system in more detail.

Storage Devices   Most PC system units also enclose one or more *storage devices*
that are either permanent or removable. In a typical PC, the system unit includes
one or more of the following storage devices: hard disk drives, CD-ROM or DVD

drives, and perhaps even a floppy disk drive (although this particular device is slowly becoming extinct). In addition, the system unit may also provide a variety of input/output ports for compact flash (CF) cards, PC cards, universal serial bus (USB), or IEEE 1394 (commonly known as FireWire) connections.

The hard disk drive and the CD-ROM or DVD drives are essentially self-contained devices that are mounted into the system unit in a case bay designed specifically for these devices. They are then connected to the motherboard and power supply for communications and power, respectively. Chapter 2 provides more information on storage devices installed inside the system unit. For more information on USB, IEEE 1394, and CF devices, see "Specialized Input/Output Devices" later in this chapter.

Portable Computers

A portable computer is designed to be—portable. In the early days of portable computers, they were along the lines of relatively heavy small suitcases. However, today's portables are about the size of a notebook, which is what most people call them. The earliest portables had separate keyboards, which were often a part of the computer's enclosure, but today's portable computers integrate virtually all of their components into the computer system.

Developments in battery technology and wireless networking have made the portable computer increasingly more popular. Users can move about as they wish, taking their computer with them. A variety of computer types are classified as portable computers, including:

- **Laptop computers**   This computer type is designed to be used in a seated position with the computer placed on a table or desk, or your lap. Laptop computers include what we call notebook computers, although some of the newer notebook computers can be operated without sitting down. For the most part, a laptop or notebook computer integrates a display, a keyboard, and a touchpad mouse.

- **Tablet PCs**   This computer type is a variation of the laptop or notebook computer, but in place of a keyboard and mouse is a touch-sensitive display that can be used to both operate the computer and enter text or other data.

- **Personal digital assistants (PDAs)**   This type of portable computer, which is also called a palmtop or handheld computer, has advanced from its beginnings as an electronic day-book into what is now called a Smartphone, which includes a mobile telephone, Web browser, e-mail client, text message communicator, media player, video camera, and more.

- **Subnotebook computer**   This type of portable computer, which is also referred to as a netbook, generally has a display smaller than 13 inches and a full keyboard and touchpad mouse; its size is relatively between a PDA and a laptop or notebook computer. Netbooks are used primarily to browse the Internet and to receive or send e-mail.

- **Wearable computers**   This type of portable computer is worn on the body, on an arm or wrist, for instance (see Figure 1-5), and typically includes voice-recognition and speech synthesis capabilities powered by an embedded computer (discussed in the section that follows). Generally, this type of portable computer is designed for a specific purpose, such as parts or goods inventory and other data collection activities.

- **Calculators**   Although most handheld calculators cannot be considered to be computers of any kind, due to their limited input, output, and user interface capabilities, some higher-end calculators contain enhanced computation capabilities and can retrieve and run programming stored inside the device on read-only memory (ROM). The line between a calculator and a computer continues to blur, but without the capability to multitask, calculators are likely to remain calculators, especially as operating systems and programming for handheld communications and computers continue to evolve.

FIGURE 1-5

A wearable computer, like this Zypad WL 11xx by Eurotech S.p.A., which is worn on a wrist, is typically used for specialized purposes. Photo courtesy of Eurotech S.p.A.

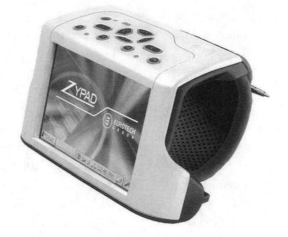

Servers

Although a server is actually a piece of software that services requests sent to it by other computers (clients) connected to the same network, the term *server* is also used to denote a computer dedicated to running server software. In the context of information technology, a server is any combination of hardware and software that provides services to other network nodes. Typically, a server is a centralized computer on which the network operating system (NOS) and centrally stored data and program resources are located.

Embedded Computers

Many computerized devices, such as MP3 players, video players, PDAs, cellular telephones, and some digital watches, contain an embedded computer. An embedded computer is typically self-contained, with its hardware and electromechanical parts integrated into a single device.

on the

Oob

The term "embedded computer" is not defined by an industry standard. Manufacturers can, and do, use this term for a variety of devices and applications. However, in general, the definition you need to remember is that of the processor being integrated into a single circuit with supporting components.

Embedded computers, which are also referred to as single-board computers (SBCs) and small form factor (SFF) computers, can range from single-purpose, single-function devices to multitasking and multithreaded systems. Some examples of embedded computer applications are touchscreen displays and terminal systems, toys, automobiles, digital photograph frames, geo-physical systems (GPSs), handheld digital recorders, Bluetooth interfaces, wireless local area network (WLAN) interfaces, traffic signal controls, household appliances, and a wide variety of industrial control and monitoring systems. Many of the more sophisticated SBCs and SFF devices can be bundled into multiprocessor units, interface with an array of peripherals, load and run different operating systems and applications, and connect to a network.

An emerging application for SBC and SFF embedded computer systems is in subnotebook or netbook computers (see "Portable Computers" earlier in this chapter). Because the embedded computer system affords a smaller size, the overall dimensions of the computer can remain small, creating a truly portable device. Smaller computer forms are also finding their way to the desktop. Although somewhat restricted in their power and capabilities, though not by much, fanless, small form factor devices can solve a space problem in many computing applications, such as home automation.

CERTIFICATION OBJECTIVE

Standard Input and Output Devices

1.1.5   Identify the types and purposes of standard input and output devices on desktop or laptop computers.

Without input and output devices, the computer would be useless. Either a human (the user) or another computer must be able to enter data or commands to the computer and then receive, as a display, a data stream, or a sound, the results of the operation the computer was instructed to perform. Computers with human interfaces have standard input and output devices that can be categorized into two general groups: input devices and output devices.

Standard Input Devices

Input devices serve two distinct purposes on a PC. One, they provide a means for the user to command and control what the PC does; and two, they provide the user and other devices a means to enter data and capture data.

A PC's output devices are adapted to the senses of sight and sound; input devices can be used to gather data from a number of sources. For example, the user manipulates the keys of a keyboard using a combination of sight and touch to enter text and numeric data. Likewise, a mouse senses the movements of a hand to point, select, and execute objects on the PC's visual display. Scanners convert captured images and text into computer-readable forms. Video capture cards convert analog video into digital data. There are devices to capture sound and special devices to capture data used to control the temperature in a building or automate a home. Output devices are limited to sight and sound (so far), but the options for input devices are virtually limitless, as more devices are adapted to capture data where and in the form it exists naturally.

The standard input devices used with most PC systems are the keyboard and the mouse. Each of these devices is discussed in the sections that follow.

Keyboards

The most common input device is the *keyboard*. The keyboard allows a user to communicate with the PC through keystrokes that represent character data and commands. Virtually every PC sold has a keyboard included as a part of its standard package. Virtually all keyboards have a standard keyboard layout; they connect to a PC with primarily one connector; and for the most part they are interchangeable, even between manufacturers.

For the most part, the layout of a keyboard's keys is still a variation on the key layout of its predecessor, the typewriter, at least for its alphabetic, numbers, and special character keys. Keyboards have a core set of keys, with variations for a particular continent (North America, Europe, etc.), country (France), or language (Chinese). However, keyboards also include a variety of other keys either dedicated by the hardware or assigned by software.

All keyboards follow some fairly basic layout patterns. It is logical that a keyboard with only 83 keys can be much smaller and more simply laid out than one with 108 keys. The style and layout of a keyboard is a direct function of the number of keys it has. The most basic standard PC keyboard has 83 keys. However, the keyboard layout used most today is called an *enhanced* keyboard that typically has from 101 to 108 keys, depending on the manufacturer. The current standard for keyboard layout is the Windows keyboard that features 104 keys.

The laptop, notebook, or palmtop PC manufacturer is faced with a size and space problem. The result is that portable PC keyboards are small and cramped and the arrangement of the keys, which can vary from manufacturer to manufacturer or even from model to model, is commonly nonstandard, outside of the alphabetic key placements.

Keyboards are connected to a desktop PC (and laptops and notebooks, if desired) through a serial port, a USB connection, or a wireless radio frequency (RF) or infrared (IR) interface. A wireless keyboard enlarges the workspace of the user beyond the length of the cord on a corded keyboard.

The Mouse

A *mouse* translates the motion of the user's hand into electrical signals that the PC converts into movement to track a pointer across the monitor's display. Two types of mouse units are used with PCs:

- **Optomechanical mouse**   The process used by this type of mouse to convert movement into light pulses (and eventually binary data) is called optomechanical. The ball, rollers, and disk move mechanically, and LEDs and sensor are used to sense the movement.

- **Optical mouse**   The optical mouse eliminates the use of mechanical devices (balls, rollers, and wheels) and uses optical scanning to detect the movement of the mouse over virtually any surface. The optical mouse captures images of the surface underneath the mouse at a rate of up to 2,000 images per second. A digital signal processor (DSP) then analyzes these images and detects the movement. The optical system of the mouse eliminates the need for a mouse pad and works on virtually any flat, textured surface except those that are very shiny.

The PC mouse has one, two, or three buttons, with two being the most common for PC mouse units. Apple Mac systems use a single mouse button. UNIX and Linux systems have functions that require the use of a third mouse button. The buttons on a mouse are typically on the top, but some models have buttons on the side and elsewhere, which require special device drivers to function. (See Chapter 5 for more information on device drivers.)

The majority of corded mouse units sold today use either a Universal Serial Bus (USB) or a six-pin mini-DIN (PS/2) connector to connect to a PC. However, wireless mouse units are available with infrared (IrDA) and radio frequency (RF) connections as well.

Another common type of PC mouse unit is the wheel mouse. The wheel mouse has a finger wheel located on its top between the two buttons. The user can spin the wheel to scroll forward and backward through a document instead of clicking a window's scroll bar or using the PAGE UP and PAGE DOWN keys or buttons or the cursor control arrow keys.

Other Pointing Devices

Many types of pointing devices exist, but the three that have some popularity beyond the mouse are the touchpad, the trackball, and the joystick (for more on joysticks, see the later section "Game Controllers").

Touchpad   A *touchpad* is a fixed-place pointing device that is very common on notebook computers, on some desktop computer keyboards, or as a standalone device used in place of a mouse. A touchpad is a small, flat, square or rectangular surface on which you slide (touch) your finger to move the cursor on the display. When coupled with a pair of "mouse" buttons as on most laptop and notebook models, a touchpad essentially provides the same action and control as a mouse through the touch of a finger on the pad. Touchpads can also be standalone devices that connect to the PC through a serial or USB port. Newer models of standalone touchpads are now available with a wireless interface.

Trackball   A *trackball* is a mouse-like tool that has two or more buttons and a ball on top of the device. The ball, which can be located on the top or side of the trackball, is manipulated with either a thumb or finger to move the cursor on the screen.

A trackball, which is typically a corded device, uses essentially the same technology as an optomechanical mouse to communicate its movements to the PC and connects through either a PS/2 or USB connection. The trackball pointing device itself does not move, only its ball, which means a trackball requires less space on the desktop.

Standard Output Devices

Where PC input devices can be adapted to collect data from virtually any data source, output devices are limited by the human senses of sight and hearing (although some game controllers do involve the human sense of feel). Our primary sensory inputs are our eyes and ears; a PC's outputs must conform to our inputs. The standard output devices on a PC can then be grouped as either sight (visual) or sound (auditory) devices. Sight devices include the video monitor and a printer, and the sound device on a PC is one or more audio speakers.

Monitors

A PC would be essentially useless without some form of display device. While you can still use a PC that has no sound output, not much would get done without the ability to see what you or the PC is doing. A monitor is the only part of the PC that actually holds its value and has durability. A quality monitor can last for years and, based on the past, remain usable through several generations of PC systems.

There are basically two types of monitors used with most PC systems: the older, legacy cathode ray tube (CRT) and the newer flat-panel monitors. While the CRT-type monitor has been the mainstay of displays since the introduction of the PC back in the early 1980s, the flat-panel monitor has become the accepted standard for today's PC.

CRT Monitors A CRT display uses essentially the same technology as a tube-type television set. The CRT is a funnel-shaped glass tube that uses electron guns to light up phosphor elements on the back of the display glass. The lighted phosphors blend to form images and movements that show through the display of the CRT for the user to view. The user is viewing the phosphors through a single pane of glass, which is why the display is so bright and easily viewed from an angle.

Flat-Panel Monitors The primary advantage of a flat-panel monitor over a CRT monitor is its footprint. If you have limited space on a desk or worktable, a flat-panel monitor is probably your best option. A typical CRT display is at least 12 inches or more from front to back, which can take up a considerable amount of workspace on a desk. A flat-panel monitor (like the one shown in Figure 1-6) is typically only

FIGURE 1-6

A flat-panel
computer
monitor (Photo
courtesy of
ViewSonic
Corporation.)

a few inches deep, including its foot. The computer systems sold today, those that
include a monitor, generally include a flat-panel monitor.

The primary technology used in flat-panel monitors is *liquid crystal diode (LCD)*.
LCDs don't emit light, which is why flat-panel displays are backlit. The image the
viewer sees is the result of the light source shining through several layers of filters
and glass. LCD displays appear to be less bright than CRT-style displays and are
generally less legible from an angle. However, LCD displays are digital, which means
they are able to reproduce images more accurately, especially colors.

on the
job

*Many people confuse the terms flat-screen and flat-panel. Flat-panel displays
use LCD technology to reproduce images on a flat screen. A flat-screen
display is a type of CRT that has a flat square screen as opposed to the more
standard curved glass screen.*

Pixels and Resolution   The images displayed on a PC's monitor are created from
a pattern of dots in much the same way as the photographs in a newspaper. Dots are
shaded lighter or darker so that your eyes can form a visual image from them. Monitors
create these dots from phosphor using masking methods that isolate each dot so that
it can be illuminated. The image produced on a color monitor is created by illuminated
small triangles of phosphor dots called picture elements, or pixels. One-third of the
dots are red dots; one-third are green dots; and one-third are blue dots. These different-
colored dots are grouped in a triangular pattern to form a pixel.

A color CRT has three electron guns that are used to light up the phosphors in each pixel. The electron guns sweep over the pixels from side to side, one row at a time, to create or refresh the displayed image. LCD displays are of two different types: passive matrix and active matrix. A passive matrix display has a layer of LCD elements on a grid (matrix) of wires. When current is applied to the wire intersections, the diodes (pixels) are lighted. A passive matrix refreshes the display by applying current to the pixels at a fixed refresh rate. Active matrix displays control each LCD element (diode) individually with one or more transistors that continually refresh each element of the display.

The number of pixels on a monitor determines the detail that can be produced on its screen. The greater the number of pixels, the better the image a monitor can produce. The number of pixels on a monitor is its resolution, which is expressed as the number of pixels on each row of the display and the number of rows of pixels on the display. For example, a monitor that supports 1024 × 768 resolution has 1024 pixels arranged horizontally on each pixel row and 768 vertical rows of pixels, which means the monitor has a total of 786,432 pixels to use to produce a display.

Refresh Rate　　A key setting on a video system is its refresh rate, or the number of times per second that the screen is entirely redrawn. The refresh rate is actually a function of the video card and indicates how many times per second the data used by the monitor to refresh the displayed image is sent.

On CRT monitors, the phosphor on the CRT's screen begins to dim almost immediately, so the electron gun must sweep back over each pixel a number of times per second to keep the display sharp and bright. A low refresh rate can make the CRT screen flicker, causing eye fatigue, and possibly headaches as well. You definitely want a monitor that supports a refresh rate of 75 Hz (hertz) or faster, especially at higher resolutions and color depths. LCD displays do not have refresh rate issues. Because of the way LCD technology works, it can provide stable images at 60 Hz, and sometimes less.

Integrated PC and Monitors　　Many new systems integrate a flat-panel monitor and the PC into a single device. These PCs are the ultimate in desktop space efficiency, with the keyboard being the largest single piece of the PC. PCs integrated with flat-panel monitors have been a mainstay in many industrial applications for a few years, but now the technology has moved to the desktop. This PC configuration, which employs the embedded computer or SFF technology discussed earlier (see "Embedded Computers"), integrates the motherboard, disk drive, and CD-ROM or DVD drive into the housing of a flat-panel monitor. However, because of their tight packaging, there isn't much room for expansion cards, disk drives, or other internal devices. Any additional peripheral devices that the user wishes to add must be done through either a USB or an IEEE 1394 (FireWire) connector.

Networking

An installed expansion card (commonly referred to as a network interface card or NIC) or an onboard network system (integrated into the motherboard) provides the connection between a PC and a network. In effect, the network interface serves as a go-between to connect the PC to the network media and sends and receives signals to and from other devices connected to the same network.

Whether you consider a PC's network interface to be an input or an output device is relative to the task it performs at any given moment. When you send a request for a network resource or a Web page, the network interface is an output device. However, when you receive the information you requested, the network interface becomes an input device. We'll discuss the role of the network interface and its configuration in more detail in Part 3 of this book.

Audio Devices

The primary audio output device on PC systems is either the internal speaker or a set of speakers connected to either an audio expansion card or a sound system incorporated into the motherboard of the PC. PC speakers are available for a variety of purposes and quality levels.

Internal PC Speaker   Nearly all PC systems include an internal speaker that is intended primarily for warning and alerting sounds. The internal speaker has never been intended for the reproduction of recorded audio, such as music, audio/video multimedia, or the like. The low sound quality of the internal speaker is also a problem on laptops and notebooks because space limitations restrict the size of the internal speakers.

Speaker Systems   Computer speakers are external speaker systems that add a sound reproduction system to a PC. Because no sound amplification capabilities are included in the basic PC circuitry, computer speakers include an amplifier and possibly a woofer (to enhance bass sounds).

Computer speakers typically connect to a PC through a PC 99 (the standard that controls the color-coding on PC jacks and connectors) lime-green 3.5 millimeter (mm) stereo jack. Another, less common, connection type used for PC speakers, especially to high-end audio expansion cards, is the RCA connection, which uses a yellow connector for video, a white connector for monaural sound or the left channel of stereo sound, and a red connector for the right channel of stereo sound. Still other speaker systems are available that connect to the PC using a USB connection. Speaker systems, which include headphones as well, are also available with a wireless connection to a PC.

CERTIFICATION OBJECTIVE

Specialized Input Devices

1.1.6   Identify the types and purposes of specialized input devices (e.g., cameras, scanners, game controllers).

In addition to the conventional and standard input device, a variety of special-purpose devices can also be used as inputs to a computer system. These devices include such items as digital cameras, image scanners, joysticks, and game controllers, among others. These devices interface to a computer system using technologies that have become standard on most newer computers, including Universal Serial Bus (USB), the Institute of Electrical and Electronics Engineers (IEEE) 1394 standard (also known as FireWire), and the standard PS2 interface.

Digital Cameras

Digital cameras, both still cameras and video cameras, connect to a PC through a variety of media and interface technologies, and some support multiple interface types. The more common interface among newer digital cameras is some form of a compact flash (CF) card. USB and FireWire technology are also common interfaces.

Although all CF cards are relatively small in size, the largest of this type of media is the PC Card (also referred to as a Personal Computer Memory Card International Association, or PCMCIA, card). A PC Card is a form of permanent storage device that fits into a computer's PC Card slot, which is a common interface on most laptop and notebook computers. Figure 1-7 shows the PC Card slot on a notebook computer.

Flash memory cards come in a variety of shapes, sizes, and form factors. The devices that fall under the flash memory umbrella include thumb drives or jump

FIGURE 1-7

A PC Card in a PC Card interface on a notebook computer (Photo courtesy of the Personal Computer Memory Card International Association.)

drives, which use the USB interface to interface to a host device, memory sticks, CF cards, and micro CF cards.

A CF card is a common storage device for many digital cameras. When you wish to transfer the contents of the CF card into a PC, the card is installed in a compatible interface slot on the PC or in a peripheral reader and transferred to the PC memory or hard disk using software specific to the interface type of the card.

Video cameras commonly interface to a PC through either a USB or a FireWire cable using specialized software that is commonly specific to the camera's manufacturer or using standard operating system video camera interface software.

Scanners

The most commonly used type of image scanner is the *flatbed scanner* that uses either the charge-coupled device (CCD) or contact image scanner (CIS) technology to capture the two-dimensional image of a document or image. The scanner then produces a digitized image of the scanned object (in a BMP, GIF, JPEG, PNG, or TIFF format) and sends it to a PC using a TWAIN interface.

e x a m

ⓦ a t c h

The term TWAIN actually has no meaning. It is alleged to stand for "Technology Without an Interesting Name." However, those who wish a more sophisticated meaning attribute the name to Rudyard Kipling, who wrote "... and never the twain shall meet ...," which was adapted to describe the difficulty of interfacing PCs and digital image devices back in the day.

Scanners can be used to capture documents using optical character recognition (OCR) software that produces an editable document. OCR software interprets the image captured by the scanner into text that is saved in a standard text document.

Game Controllers

Some of the more popular computer software applications are computer games. Because games are much more interesting and fun when played with something other than just a keyboard or mouse, specialized game controllers have emerged to provide users with a high degree of interactivity. There are essentially two types of game controllers for PCs: joysticks and full-featured game controllers.

Joysticks

A *joystick* is a type of pointing device that is used primarily with game software on a PC. Joysticks are available as corded and wireless devices. A joystick consists of a handle that is connected to a yoke inside its base. The yoke is set on a pivoting mechanism that allows the joystick to move in any direction from a center point. Sensors are attached to the yoke that detect the movement of the handle and yoke on an X- or Y-axis and send data signals to the adapter card to which the joystick is attached. Most joysticks attach to a game port located on a game, video, or sound card; to a USB connection; or (in the case of some high-end models) even to a wireless (but less responsive) interface.

PC Game Controllers

With the popularity of game consoles from Sony, Nintendo, and Microsoft, which all include a game controller or game pad to control and interact with their games, users soon demanded similar devices for games played on the PC. A variety of game controllers and game pads have emerged that can be connected to the computer through either a USB connector or a wireless interface. These devices include such features as control button sets, joystick controls, or perhaps even a steering wheel (for racing games).

Barcode Readers

Barcodes have been used to uniquely identify items since the early 1960s, with the most common use as the means to identify a product though a Universal Product Code (UPC) printed on its packaging. A *barcode* consists of printed parallel bars of varying widths and spacing to represent alphabetic and numeric characters. A barcode reader, which can be handheld or stationary, uses a light source, such as a light-emitting diode (LED) or a laser. The light source is projected onto the barcode, and a sensor captures and decodes the pattern of the light reflecting back to the reader. Barcodes can also be printed as squares, dots, and other shapes to create two-dimensional symbols. Barcode systems remain less expensive than other forms of identity capture, such as radio frequency identification (RFID).

Remote Controls

Like a barcode reader, a *remote control* displays a light source that has been modulated into a command code. The light beam emitted by the light source is detected by a remote device, such as a computer or a television, which decodes the command and performs its function. A remote control can be used for many different devices, provided that the devices are equipped with a compatible receiver and decoder.

Access Control Devices

Another type of specialized input device takes the form of the security devices that control access to a computer or perhaps even a doorway. There are two basic types of access control devices used to control access to computers and the areas in which computers are located: biometric devices and access card readers.

A *biometric* device uses a body feature of the person seeking access to identify and authorize that person. A commonly used biometric device on personal computers is a fingerprint scanner, which matches the print on a person's finger to a digital image of the fingerprint on file in the computer. If the prints match, access is granted. In some systems, the fingerprint match can be used in lieu of a login and password to gain access to the computer or any of its folders or files. Another type of biometric device available for PCs is an iris-scan and recognition system. Just as fingerprints are unique to an individual, so are the patterns in the human eye's iris. An iris recognition camera scans the patterns in a human eye's iris to detect a match with the digital image of the authorized iris scan stored on a PC.

An *access card reader* system reads the information from an encoded card or from an RFID card to determine if the card holder is authorized access to a system or a location. An access card may have a strip of film attached to one side of the card, much like a credit card, or have a radio frequency transmitter that holds, hides, or broadcasts information identifying the card holder. When the card is swiped through a reader or moved to close proximity of an RF receiver, the card holder's identity is received and if access to the computer or location is authorized, the system allows the access.

Specialized Output Devices

1.1.7   Identify the types and purposes of specialized output devices (e.g., printers, projectors).

Although printers have been a part of most computer systems from the start, printers can be specialized to a particular application. Dot matrix printers are good for multipart forms; inkjets are good quality, inexpensive printers for document processing and photographic prints; and laser printers provide a high-quality result for a variety of applications.

Another type of specialized output device is projector systems. These devices, which interface to the PC through its video output port, can be used to project an image for group presentations, classroom lectures, and a variety of sales and marketing uses.

Printers

From the beginning of the PC, a *printer* has been the de facto output device for PC systems, especially those used primarily for document preparation. Over the years, printer technology has evolved from the typewriter to dot matrix printers to inkjet printers to laser printers and still other specialized types of printers, including photograph printers, and large document printers and plotters. Each of these types of printers has one or more specific applications for which it is best suited.

Dot Matrix Printers

A *dot matrix* printer gets its name from its printing mechanism, which typically consists of from nine to fourteen small print heads that are struck into an inked ribbon to produce a character consisting of a pattern of dots. Figure 1-8 shows an example of

FIGURE 1-8

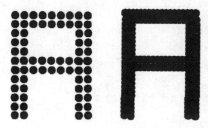

Examples of dot matrix printing. The character on the left is printed in what is called draft quality, and the character on the right is near-letter quality.

a character produced on a dot matrix printer. Because a dot matrix printer is a form of an impact printer, it is still in use to print multipage carbon set forms in some industrial settings.

Inkjet Printers

Inkjet printers create a printed image by spraying small droplets of very quick-drying ink through tiny nozzles (jets) onto the paper. The print quality of the inkjet is measured in dots per inch (dpi). The greater the number of dots of ink used in a square inch of paper, the higher the print quality will be.

Inkjet printers produce a better-quality print than a dot matrix printer at roughly the same cost. Inkjets are also less expensive and usually physically smaller than most laser printers, which appeals to most home and small office users.

A more specialized form of inkjet printer is a photo printer. These devices produce higher image resolutions than a standard inkjet printer and typically require special photographic paper to achieve a quality result.

Laser Printers

Laser printers use dry toner and electrical charges to create an image on a printed page. Most of the mechanisms used to print a document on a laser printer are located inside a removable cartridge; they are the photosensitive drum, a charging mechanism that's used to condition the drum, a developing roller used to deposit toner on the drum, and, of course, the toner.

The process used to print a color document in a laser printer is essentially the same as that of a monochrome printer, but a color laser printer goes through a few more steps. Before a document is printed by a color laser printer, its raster image processor (RIP) computes the position of each dot on the page and creates an image of the document in the printer's memory.

A color laser printer must apply each of its colors separately using the CMYK (cyan, magenta, yellow, and black) color scheme. For each color to be applied, a complete print cycle occurs: the drum is written, the controller directs the correct color toner to be applied, the partial image is transferred to the paper, and the excess toner is removed. The paper actually makes as many as four passes around the drum to collect each color layer of the image. The fusing process is performed only once on the page, after all of the colors have been applied.

Photograph Printers

Photograph printers, which are also known as photo printers and snapshot printers, are generally one of two types of printers: inkjet or dye-sublimation. An *inkjet* printer sprays very tiny drops of ink onto the paper at rate of about 30,000 drops per second.

A *dye-sublimation*, or *dye-sub*, printer uses a thermal process to transfer a dye from a ribbon that has several colored panels. The dye is transferred onto specially treated thermal paper to reproduce the image of the photo.

Large Document Printers

Many higher-end printers, such as some inkjets and lasers, have the capability to print documents requiring large-sized paper. The standard paper size throughout the world is the A4 standard, which is roughly 8.5 inches by 11 inches. However, some documents may be sized to A3, A2, or lower. An A2 document requires paper that is about 16.5 inches by 23.5 inches. While each of the paper size standards is standard around the world, not all printers are capable of printing documents on the larger paper.

Large documents, such as posters, banners, and computer-aided drafting drawings, cannot be reasonably printed on a standard printer. About the largest paper size they can handle is 11 inches by 17 inches without additional hardware or upgrades. A *plotter* is a type of printer that is designed specifically to deal with the problems of printing documents requiring larger paper size. A typical plotter is able to handle paper as wide as 3 to 4 feet in width.

Control Devices

Computers are also used to provide control and commands to a wide variety of manufacturing, assembling, and precision machinery, to mixers, heaters, coolers, and robotic systems, as well as many home systems, including the heating and ventilation, security, and even lawn sprinklers. Computer-controlled devices have a built-in interface that connects the control device to a computer through which it receives commands as simple as on or off or as complex as adjusting the thickness of raw paper being milled, a robot welding the chassis of an automobile, or an embroidery machine stitching a logo on a shirt.

CERTIFICATION OBJECTIVE

How Hardware Is Connected and Installed

1.1.8   Identify how hardware devices are connected to and installed on a computer system.

Peripheral devices don't just magically connect to a PC. Each different type of peripheral device has a specific interface or connection type and can only be connected to a PC that supports that particular type of connection.

Installing Peripheral Devices

Peripheral devices are connected to the PC through a system-specific interface. In some cases, the interface devices must be installed inside the system unit, and in other situations, they are connected to an interface port integrated into the PC system and its motherboard. Many peripheral devices are now designed to connect to both desktop and portable PCs, but some still require the installation of an internal controller.

Installing Internal Peripheral Devices

When we speak of internal peripheral devices, memory, hard disk drives, CD-ROM/DVD drives, and other devices mounted inside the system case are included. However, since these systems are covered in detail in Chapter 2, let's focus on the installation of expansion cards in this section.

Expansion Bus   On most new PCs, the need to add further controller and interface devices is almost nonexistent. In the past, expansion cards were used to add basic functions to a PC, including memory, hard disk and floppy disk controllers, video controllers, serial and parallel ports, modems, and even the clock and calendar functions. However, today's PCs have most of these capabilities built into the motherboard or chipset. For the most part, expansion cards are now used to improve or add to the capabilities of a PC, such as controllers and adapters for special-purpose hardware and network interfaces. Through expansion cards, a PC can become a sound system, a graphics workstation, a movie theater, or a member of a global network.

Every expansion card, whether it is a video adapter, modem, or network interface card, is designed to communicate with the motherboard and CPU over a single communications and interface standard, referred to as a *bus*. An expansion bus defines a specific interface that consists of how much data it carries, how fast it transfers it, how it connects to the motherboard, and how it interacts with the CPU or memory.

Expansion cards, so called because they expand the capabilities of the PC, are inserted into a compatible bus architecture expansion slot. These are the expansion buses common to most PCs:

- **ISA (Industry Standard Architecture) and EISA (Extended ISA)**   The ISA expansion bus is generally obsolete, but most motherboards still have at least one ISA slot to provide backward compatibility for older hardware. ISA bus expansion slots are 16-bit but will also support 8-bit cards. The EISA bus extends the ISA bus to 32 bits and is backward compatible to ISA cards.

For the most part, EISA has been replaced by the PCI bus, but it is still available on some motherboard designs.

■ **PCI (Peripheral Component Interconnect)** The PCI bus has become the de facto standard for expansion cards on PC motherboards and is found on both PCs and Apple Macs. The PCI bus supports 32-bit and 64-bit interfaces and full Plug-and-Play capability.

■ **AGP (Accelerated Graphics Port)** While the AGP bus is an expansion bus like the PCI bus, it is used only for video cards, primarily to improve 3-D graphics. AGP runs at faster speeds than the PCI bus and can transfer video data at 264 Mbps to 1 Gbps.

Expansion Cards There are a variety of expansion card types that can be installed inside a system unit into slots on the motherboard. Not all systems require an expansion card, but some users desire a higher performance level than an integrated system provides and install an expansion card to boost the PC's performance. The different types of expansion cards include

■ **Controller cards** A controller card contains the circuitry and components needed to control the operations of a certain peripheral device, such as a disk drive, CD-ROM/DVD, or the like. A controller card connects to the peripheral device through a flat 40-wire ribbon cable. On new PCs, the device controllers are built into the motherboard and chipset, but some devices, such as some scanners, require their own controller card.

■ **Input/output (I/O) cards** I/O expansion cards add interface ports, such as serial and parallel ports, to a PC. While once quite common, this type of expansion card is rarely used because the ports it would add are typically included in the PC as a part of the motherboard.

■ **Modem cards** A modem (short for modulator/demodulator) allows you to connect to and communicate with other computers over the public telephone network. A modem can be either an internal or an external device. An internal modem can be an expansion card or be integrated into the motherboard and chipset. See Chapter 17 for more information on data communications.

■ **Sound cards** Sound cards are fairly standard in their basic function: reproducing sound. Adding a sound card to a PC can upgrade the quality of the sound reproduction of the PC.

■ **Video cards**   A video card can improve the quality of the video image displayed on your monitor as well as speed up the graphic rendering, something usually quite important for PC games. The video card must be matched to the monitor it drives.

PC Cards   Portable PC systems, such as laptops, notebooks, and some handheld systems, can have additional resources or devices installed through a PC Card (PCMCIA) or ExpressCard slot.

The use of the USB interface has reduced the role of the PC Card for adding additional peripheral device controllers, but one use has maintained its popularity: network interface cards, especially wireless network interfaces. Another popular use of the PC Card interface is to add memory to a portable PC. A PC Card memory card is a credit card–sized or smaller module that contains flash memory.

Installing External Peripheral Devices

Connecting or installing an external peripheral device, such as an external hard disk drive, keyboard, mouse, printer, or network interface, is a relatively simple matter. Really, the only hard part of connecting the interface jack to a port on a PC system is to match the jack and the port by type and then check the orientation of the jack to the port. As shown in Figure 1-9, the common connection ports on a PC include USB, FireWire, sound, network, modem, and memory cards. In addition to the ports shown in Figure 1-9, a desktop system may also include what is typically called a five-in-one interface that includes a slot for the most popular CF cards.

To install an external peripheral device, orient the jack (the connector to be plugged into the PC) to the port (the connector on the PC) and gently push the connectors together until you have a snug fit.

FIGURE 1-9   The interface ports on a notebook computer, left to right: headphones, microphone, USB, FireWire, modem, and network (Photo courtesy of Lenovo.)

Device Drivers

Because it would be impractical for the developers of operating systems to try to include support software for every peripheral device that could possibly be attached to a PC, specialized software is required for most peripheral devices. This software is referred to as a device driver.

A *device driver*, which is also called a software driver, is software that acts as an intermediary between a hardware device and the operating system. Some device drivers also provide an interface for higher-end software applications and some types of peripheral devices, such as printers. When the operating system or an application calls for a specific action from the driver, the device driver issues the corresponding commands to the device requested. When it's finished or in need of addition data, the device requests the data from the device driver, which in turn communicates to the calling program. Virtually all device drivers are hardware and operating system specific. Without the appropriate device drivers, most hardware systems don't function properly.

CERTIFICATION SUMMARY

On the IC^3 exams, you may find questions that specifically address the types of computers, peripherals, and applications commonly used. However, it's more likely that you'd encounter these areas as supposed knowledge in questions on other parts of this book.

This chapter provided a relatively detailed overview on the following objective areas of the IC^3 exams:

- ■ The different computer types and applications
- ■ Peripheral devices used for inputting data and outputting information
- ■ The process used to install or connect a peripheral device to a computer

Be sure that you have a good understanding of the information in this chapter; it will serve you well on the exams.

✓ TWO-MINUTE DRILL

Different Types of Computer Devices

❑ Computer systems are generally categorized into four primary groups: desktop computers, portable computers, handheld computers, and embedded computers.

❑ A desktop computer or personal computer (PC) is the most frequently used computer system.

❑ A desktop computer consists of four major component groups: system unit, monitor, keyboard and mouse, and peripheral devices.

❑ The components inside the system unit are: computer case, motherboard, CPU, memory, cooling system, power supply, and storage devices.

❑ Portable computers include a variety of lightweight transportable PCs. The most common of the portable PCs are: notebook PCs, laptop PCs, tablet PCs, PDAs, subnotebook PCs, and wearable computers.

❑ An embedded computer is a self-contained system with its hardware and electromechanical parts integrated into a single device.

Standard Input and Output Devices

❑ Input devices serve two distinct purposes on a PC: they provide a means for the user to command and control the PC, and they serve as the vehicle for a user to capture and enter data. The standard input devices used with most PC systems are the keyboard and mouse.

❑ A mouse translates the motion of the user's hand into electrical signals that are converted to track a pointer across the monitor's display. Two types of mouse units are used with PCs: optomechanical and optical.

❑ Other types of point devices include touchpads, trackballs, and joysticks.

❑ Standard output devices include monitors (displays), networking devices, and audio systems.

❑ There are two types of monitors used with PC systems: the CRT monitor and the flat-panel monitor. A CRT is a funnel-shaped glass tube that uses electron guns to light up phosphor elements on the back of the display glass. A flat-panel monitor uses LCD elements to produce its image.

❑ Computer speakers provide for better sound reproduction than the internal speaker of a PC.

Specialized Input Devices

❑ Special-purpose devices that can be used as input sources are: digital cameras, image scanners, joysticks, and game controllers.

❑ Digital cameras interface with a PC directly through a USB or FireWire technology and indirectly through CF cards.

❑ Flatbed scanners can be used to capture two-dimensional images and produce a digitized image of the scanned object as a BMP, GIF, JPEG, PNG, or TIFF file format.

❑ There are two types of game controllers for PCs: joysticks and game controllers. A joystick is a type of pointing device that consists of a handle attached to a yoke or a pivoting mechanism that tracks movement from a center point. The use of a game controller provides a better level of control and interaction for some PC games.

Specialized Output Devices

❑ Printers can be specialized to a particular PC application: dot matrix printers are good for multipart forms; inkjets provide a good quality, inexpensive option for document processing and photographic prints; and laser printers provide a high-quality result for a variety of applications.

How Hardware Is Connected and Installed

❑ Peripheral devices connect to a PC using a system-specific interface. Internal peripheral devices often connect through an expansion card and a communications bus that defines a specific interface type and standard.

❑ Portable PC systems can install additional resources or devices through a PC Card slot.

❑ External peripheral devices connect through a jack on the device's cable and a compatible port on the PC. To install an external peripheral device, orient the jack to the port and snug up the connection.

❑ A device driver is software that acts as an intermediary between a hardware device and the operating system.

SELF TEST

The following questions are intended to help you be sure that you understand the material included in this chapter. Read the questions and the answer choices carefully.

Different Types of Computer Devices

1. Which of the following is not considered a type of personal computer?

    A. Desktop computer

    B. Notebook computer

    C. Laptop computer

    D. Mainframe computer

2. True or False: All desktop PCs are configured as tower units.

    A. True

    B. False

3. The four major component groups of a desktop PC system include

    A. System unit

    B. Monitor or display

    C. Keyboard and mouse

    D. Peripheral devices

    E. Wireless interface

    F. Sound input devices

4. Which of the following component(s) is/are not commonly installed as an external device?

    A. Motherboard

    B. Central processing unit (CPU)

    C. Memory

    D. Power supply

    E. Choices A through D are all internal devices

    F. Choices A through D are all external devices

5. Sequence the following portable computers by size, smallest to largest, by entering a number (from 1 to 4) in the space provided.

A. _____ Handheld computer

B. _____ Notebook computer

C. _____ Laptop computer

D. _____ Subnotebook computer

6. A computerized device, such as an MP3 player, digital watch, or a Tablet PC, commonly includes what type of CPU system?

A. Pentium microprocessor

B. Dual-core microprocessor

C. Embedded computer

D. No microprocessor is included in these types of systems.

Standard Input and Output Devices

7. Which two of the following are considered to be the standard input devices for virtually all PC systems?

A. Monitor

B. Keyboard

C. Mouse

D. Printer

8. Which of the following interface types is not commonly used to connect a mouse to a PC?

A. USB

B. PS/2

C. IrDA

D. Parallel

9. A touchpad is a common device on which type of PC system?

A. Desktop PC

B. Notebook PC

C. Handheld PC

D. Embedded computer

10. What does the abbreviation CRT stand for?

    A. Color ray terminal

    B. Color raster tube

    C. Cathode ray tube

    D. Cathode raster terminal

11. The number of pixels on a computer monitor defines its

    A. Resolution

    B. Aspect ratio

    C. Refresh rate

    D. Video standard

12. What device provides the interface between a PC and the network media?

    A. Serial port

    B. USB port

    C. Network interface

    D. Network adapter

13. External speaker systems commonly connect to a PC through a single jack that conforms to what PC standard?

    A. PCMCIA

    B. PC99

    C. IEEE 1394

    D. There is no standard for audio connections on a PC.

14. What type of storage device can be inserted into a digital camera and then used to transfer the captured images to a PC?

    A. USB connector

    B. CF card

    C. FireWire connector

    D. ExpressCard

Specialized Input Devices

15. What external peripheral devices can be used to capture the image of a document for use in a PC?

    A. Scanner

    B. Joystick

    C. Printer

    D. Flat-panel monitor

16. What type of PC application is a joystick best suited for?

    A. Word processing

    B. Printing

    C. Gaming

    D. Data entry

Specialized Output Devices

17. According to the information in this chapter, what two device types can be considered specialized output devices?

    A. Monitors

    B. Printers

    C. Projectors

    D. Audio systems

18. Which of the following is not a type of printer associated with PC systems?

    A. Dot matrix

    B. Ink-jet

    C. Laser

    D. Chain

19. What is the last step in the laser printing process?

    A. Cleaning

    B. Conditioning

    C. Developing

    D. Fusing

How Hardware Is Connected and Installed

20. What expansion bus has become the de facto standard for modern PC systems?

   A. ISA

   B. EISA

   C. PCI

   D. AGP

21. To add an external wireless network interface card to a notebook PC, what card standard is commonly used?

   A. PCI

   B. PC Card

   C. USB

   D. FireWire

22. True or False: A notebook PC is a poor replacement for a desktop computer because it cannot support the same interface and connection types as the desktop computer.

   A. True

   B. False

23. What is the special-purpose software that serves an intermediary between a peripheral device and the system or application software?

   A. Expansion card

   B. Device manager

   C. Device driver

   D. Network interface

SELF TEST ANSWERS

Different Types of Computer Devices

1. ☑ **D.** Mainframe computers are large, enterprise-level computer systems.
   ☒ **A, B,** and **C** are incorrect. They are each a type of PC.

2. ☑ **B.** Not all desktop PCs are in tower cases; some are available for a horizontal orientation.
   ☒ **A** is incorrect. The statement is false.

3. ☑ **A, B, C,** and **D.** These four component groups are common to virtually every PC system.
   ☒ **E** and **F** are incorrect. Neither is required on a PC to utilize its basic functions.

4. ☑ **E.** Answers **A** through **D** are all internal devices on a PC, so **E** is the most correct answer.
   ☒ **F** is incorrect. The devices listed aren't external devices in common use.

5. ☑ 1 – Handheld computer (**A**); 2 – Subnotebook computer (**D**); 3 – Notebook computer (**B**); and 4 – Laptop computer (**C**).

6. ☑ **C.** Small form factor devices, such as an MP3 player or a wearable computer, use the embedded computer technology to reduce the overall size of the system.
   ☒ **A** and **B** are incorrect. Each is too large to serve this purpose. **D** is just wrong!

Standard Input and Output Devices

7. ☑ **B** and **C.** A keyboard and a mouse are the standard input devices for nearly all PC systems sold today.
   ☒ **A** and **D** are incorrect. These devices are output devices.

8. ☑ **D.** A mouse is not connected to a PC through a parallel port, rather it is connected to a PC through a PS/2, a USB, or an infrared (IrDA) connection.
   ☒ **A, B,** and **C** are incorrect. A PS/2, USB, or IrDA connection can be used to connect a mouse to a PC. A parallel port could be used, but it would be custom and extremely rare.

9. ☑ **B.** A touchpad built into the PC near the keyboard is a very common configuration for notebook PCs. While specialized keyboards are available with a touchpad that can be used with a desktop system, this is not a common feature.
   ☒ **A, C,** and **D** are incorrect. Handheld and embedded computers typically interface through a touchscreen.

10. ☑ **C.** That's it, cathode ray tube.
    ☒ **A, B,** and **D** are incorrect. These are made-up answers and therefore incorrect.

11. ☑ **A.** The resolution of a display is stated as the number of pixels on each horizontal line by the number of vertical lines of pixels in the display.
    ☒ **B, C,** and **D** are incorrect. The choices given in **B, C,** and **D** have nothing to do with resolution.

12. ☑ **D.** Okay, maybe **C** as well, but the adapter is the actual device.
    ☒ **A, B,** and **C** are incorrect. A serial port is not used for a network connection, so **A** is incorrect. However, **B** is something like answer **C**; the USB port is an interface and not the actual networking device.

13. ☑ **B.** The lime-green jack used to connect speakers to a PC conforms to the PC99 standard.
    ☒ **A, C,** and **D** are incorrect. None of the choices given in these answers are standards that specifically apply to audio connections.

14. ☑ **B.** A compact flash (CF) card can be inserted into a digital camera, and then removed and inserted into a compatible slot on the PC. While some cameras do support a USB connection, it is not exactly a device.
    ☒ **A, C,** and **D** are incorrect. None of these answers have the characteristics given in the question. USB and FireWire are connection standards. The ExpressCard technology has not been adapted for other than computers.

Specialized Input Devices

15. ☑ **A.** A scanner can be used to capture the image of a document sheet or anything that fits on its flatbed.
    ☒ **B, C,** and **D** are incorrect It may be totally obvious, but **B, C,** and **D** are not image capture devices, which makes them wrong.

16. ☑ **C.** A joystick, which enjoys a great deal of popularity among flight simulator gamers, was developed specifically for gaming.
    ☒ **A, B,** and **D** are incorrect. These choices are not applications that can effectively work with a joystick.

Specialized Output Devices

17. ☑ **B and C.** Printers are commonly adapted to a particular application, and a projection system is also a special-purpose device.
    ☒ **A and D** are incorrect. A monitor and an audio system are not so specialized.

18. ☑ **D.** A chain printer, which is something you've probably never heard of before (hint, hint), is not typically associated with a PC. This type of printer is used by the government to print IRS refunds and the like.
    ☒ **A, B,** and **C** are incorrect These choices are each a PC-level printing system.

19. ☑ **A.** The last step cleans the drum and the rollers before starting on the next sheet.
☒ **B** is the first step; **C** is the third step; and **D** is the fifth step.

How Hardware Is Connected and Installed

20. ☑ **C.** The PCI bus is essentially the de facto standard bus architecture for modern PC systems.
☒ **A, B,** and **D** are incorrect. The ISA and EISA buses (answers **A** and **B**) are for the most part obsolete, and AGP (answer **D**) is a video standard only.

21. ☑ **B.** It doesn't matter really if the network is wired or wireless. The PC Card slot is the most frequently used external port interface for networking. A notebook with a built-in wireless interface would not require this interface.
☒ **A, C,** and **D** are incorrect. **A** and **C** could be used to connect an external network adapter and **D** is less commonly used.

22. ☑ **B.** Most notebook computers have at least some subset of the ports and interfaces found on a desktop PC.
☒ **A** is incorrect. The statement is false.

23. ☑ **C.** The device driver is the intermediary agent between a peripheral device and the system or application software. An expansion card may still require a device driver.
☒ **A, B,** and **D** are incorrect. An expansion card, first of all, is not software and is used only to physically install a connection or controller card into a PC. The Device manager is a software utility on a Windows operating system. The network interface also requires a Device manager to operate properly.

2

Internal Hardware Systems

The performance of a computer system is directly related to a specific set of components and how well matched they are. The CPU, memory, storage devices, and other parts of the computer system must work together to achieve the level of performance that you, like all other users, desire and expect.

This chapter discusses the role each of these components plays in the overall performance of a computer system at the level of knowledge you should have to pass the IC³-1 exam. Understanding each of the components that make up the internal hardware of a PC and how they must work together is very important to success on the exams.

CERTIFICATION OBJECTIVE

The Role of the CPU

1.1.2   Identify the role of the central processing unit (CPU), including how the speed of a microprocessor is measured.

Everything a computer does is controlled by a microprocessor, which contains the *central processing unit (CPU)* of the computer. This includes all of the arithmetic, logic, and other basic computing steps behind all of the actions of a PC. What you may see as an application is in fact hundreds, even thousands, of instructions that the CPU executes one at a time to carry out the actions of each software program. The CPU is a piece of electronic circuitry that uses digital logic to perform these instructions.

exam
ⓦatch
The IC³-1 exam uses the terms CPU and microprocessor interchangeably, which is essentially true. In fact, though, emerging microprocessors can include more than just a CPU. However, for purposes of the exam, they are essentially the same thing.

The Microprocessor

A microprocessor, like the one shown in Figure 2-1, is constructed of multiple layers of silicon electronic circuits. Silicon is the primary building material used in manufacturing electronic integrated circuits, including those used to construct the microprocessor, because it's an excellent semiconductor.

A *semiconductor* is a material that is neither a conductor nor an insulator but can be chemically altered to be either one. A conductor allows electrical current to pass through it, such as copper, aluminum, or gold. A material that doesn't allow an electrical current to pass through it is called an insulator. Insulators are materials like rubber, wood, or glass.

on the **job**

The creation of a microchip is a very involved chemical process. If you want an excellent explanation and look at how an integrated circuit is manufactured, visit the "How a Microprocessor Is Made" Web site provided by Intel Corporation at www.intel.com/pressroom/archive/backgrnd/making_a_chip.htm?iid=tech_man+made.

For more information on how a microprocessor (CPU) is manufactured, plus some other very good information about the history of integrated circuits, visit the http://en.wikipedia.org/wiki/Microprocessor or www.howstuffworks.com/microprocessor.htm Web sites.

FIGURE 2-1

A PC microprocessor (Photo courtesy of Advanced Micro Devices, Inc.)

The CPU

The *CPU* is a multifunction integrated circuit that is essentially the computer. The CPU is made up of several parts that work together to carry out the instructions and actions that translate to a word processing system or a game on your PC. The CPU integrates several special-purpose components (see Figure 2-2), which are

- **Control Unit (CU)**   The control unit directs the functions of the CPU. It tells the other parts of the CPU how to operate, what data to use, and where to put the results.
- **Protection Test Unit (PTU)**   The PTU works with the CU to ensure that functions are carried out correctly. It generates an error signal if an action is not performed properly.
- **Arithmetic and Logic Unit (ALU)**   The ALU performs all of the calculations and comparative logic functions for the CPU, including all add, subtract, divide, multiply, equal to, greater than, less than, and other arithmetic and logic operations.
- **Floating Point Unit (FPU)**   The FPU goes by several other names, including the math coprocessor, the numerical processing unit (NPU), and the numerical data processor (NDP). It handles all floating point operations for the ALU and CU. Floating point operations involve numbers with decimal places and high math operations like trigonometry and logarithms.

FIGURE 2-2

The components incorporated into the CPU

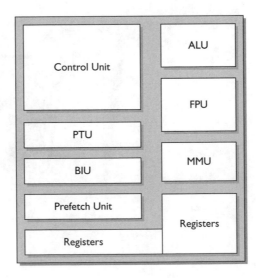

- **Memory Management Unit (MMU)**   The MMU handles the addressing and cataloging of where data is stored in system memory. Whenever the CPU needs something from memory, it requests it from the MMU. The MMU manages memory segmentation and paging allocations and translates all logical addressing into physical addressing.

- **Bus Interface Unit (BIU)**   The BIU supervises the transfer of data over the bus system between the other components of the computer and the CPU. It also serves as the interface point for the CPU and its external bus, as well as handling all data transfers out of the control unit.

- **The Prefetch Unit**   This unit preloads the instruction registers of the CPU with instructions from memory whenever the BIU is idle. This allows the CPU to look ahead at future instructions. The prefetch unit does not analyze instructions, so on occasion it may bring in an unnecessary instruction because it assumes that the instructions will be carried out one after the other without branching or jumps.

- **Decode Unit**   The decode unit decodes incoming instructions to their simplest form to get them ready for the control unit.

- **Registers**   Built into the CPU are a number of holding areas and buffers (registers) that are used to temporarily hold the data, addresses, and instructions being passed around among the CPU's components.

CPU's Bus System

The *bus system* carries the various signals, addresses, and data that are transferred around the computer among its components, including the components of the CPU. A bus structure is a group of electronic transmission lines that connect the various components of the CPU, motherboard, I/O ports, and expansion cards to one other. Bus structures have different sizes, ranging from 16 to 64 bits on modern CPUs, and their size determines the amount of data that can be transmitted. Obviously, a 64-bit bus carries more data than a 16-bit bus.

In a typical PC, there are several bus structures; the most important are

- **Data bus**   Carries information to and from the CPU.

- **Address bus**   Carries the address from where data is to be read to where data is to be written.

■ **Control bus**   Carries the signals used by the CPU and the other components of the computer to communicate with each other, including when data is ready to be read, when another device wishes to use the bus, and the type of operation to be performed (read, write, interrupt).

Cooling the Microprocessor

Beginning with the 80486 processor and into the present day, microprocessors are cooled with a heat sink, a cooling fan, or both, that is attached directly to the surface of the processor. In addition, the system fan was reversed to extract the heated air from inside the computer case and force it out.

Microprocessors operate at temperatures upward of 185 degrees Fahrenheit (85 degrees Celsius). It is very important that a processor's cooling system is kept at or near its designed operating temperature. When a microprocessor gets too hot, it begins to perform poorly, shut down, or become permanently damaged. Heat sinks and fans are designed to draw the heat up and out of the processor's packaging and carry it away on the tines of the heat sink and the airflow of the fan.

Microprocessor Mountings

Microprocessors are mounted on the motherboard of the computer. There are two general types of mountings used to connect the processor on the motherboard: slots and sockets. Sockets have evolved as the most popular, primarily due to special cooling requirements of the newest microprocessors. Microprocessor sockets use two primary mounting types to connect to the motherboard: pin grid arrays (PGAs) and land grid arrays (LGAs). PGAs have tiny holes into which the pins of the processor fit, and LGAs have pins that contact the pins of the processor. Table 2-1 lists the sockets most commonly used on new motherboards.

Chipsets

The *chipset* on the motherboard of a PC provides much of a PC's ability to accept, display, and move data. The chipset also assists in the movement of data and instructions on the system buses between the CPU, cache memory, and peripherals. The chipset only contains enough instructions to operate at the most rudimentary level because most of the interaction that occurs between the chipset and a device is actually provided by the device's device driver reacting to the basic commands communicated to it from the chipset.

TABLE 2-1	Commonly Used Microprocessor Sockets	

Socket/Slot Name	PGA/LGA	CPUs Using This Slot/Socket
Socket 462/Socket A	PGA	AMD Athlon, Duron Sempron
Socket 479	PGA	Intel Pentium M, Celeron M
Socket 754	PGA	AMD Athlon 64, K8 Sempron, Turion 64
Socket 775/Socket T	LGA	Intel Celeron D, Core 2 Duo, Core 2 Quad, Core 2 Extreme
Socket 939	PGA	AMD Athlon 64 X2, Dual-Core Opteron
Socket 1366/Socket B	LGA	Intel Core i7
Socket AM2	PGA	Phenom X3, Phenom X4, 2G Opteron
Socket M	PGA	Intel Core Solo, Core Duo
Socket P	PGA	Intel Core 2 Duo, Intel Core 2 Quad

The chipset controls the flow of data, instructions, and control signals between the CPU and system memory, and over the motherboard's bus, as well as data transfers between the CPU, memory, and peripheral devices. It also supports the expansion bus and any power management features of the system. Some expansion cards and even some peripheral devices also have chipsets to assist in their interoperability and compatibility to certain systems.

A characteristic that differentiates one type of chipset from another is the number of integrated circuits (chips) used in the set. The two-chip chipset contains separate components for what are called the north bridge and the south bridge, but these components are also integrated into single-chip chipsets.

The *north bridge* is the major bus circuitry that provides support and control for the main memory, cache memory, and the PCI bus controllers. The north bridge is typically a single chip (usually the larger of a chipset of two or more chips), but it can be more than one chip. The *south bridge* includes the controllers for the peripheral devices and any controllers not essential to the PC's basic functions, such as the EIDE (Enhanced Integrated Device Electronics) controller and the serial port controllers.

In addition to its chipset, there are at least two, and possibly more, controllers mounted directly on the motherboard. At minimum, the motherboard has a keyboard controller and an I/O controller. Some video adapters, sound cards, network interface cards (NICs), and Small Computer System Interface (SCSI) adapters have built-in controller chips.

CERTIFICATION OBJECTIVE

Concepts Related to Computer Memory

1.1.3   Identify concepts related to computer memory (measurement of memory, RAM, ROM).

Memory is where a PC temporarily stores data and instructions before and after use by the CPU. In the PC, memory typically refers to primary storage, which is also called system memory, temporary storage, or random access memory (RAM). With the exception of read-only memory (ROM), other forms of storage (hard disk, floppy disk, CD-ROM/DVD, and the like) are secondary storage.

ROM

Read-only memory (ROM) is nonvolatile, which means that it retains its contents without a power source and that its contents can't be readily changed by the user. ROM is used for storing the PC's startup instructions and the system basic input/output system (BIOS).

There are three variations of ROM used in the PC:

- **PROM (programmable read-only memory)**   This type of ROM chip is encoded with its instruction and data set during manufacturing. A PROM chip cannot be reused and is thrown out when it becomes obsolete.

- **EPROM (erasable programmable read-only memory)**   This type of ROM is erasable and can be reprogrammed using a special programming device. However, it cannot be changed by the user.

- **EEPROM (electronically erasable programmable read-only memory)**   Most new PCs now include an EEPROM that can be reprogrammed like an EPROM but, unlike the EPROM, doesn't need to be removed from the PC to be reprogrammed.

on the
job

An EEPROM can be reprogrammed through a process called flashing that uses specialized software running on your PC to apply a downloaded file. Flashing lets you upgrade your computer's BIOS easily without removing and replacing the ROM chip.

RAM

The terms *RAM* and primary memory are synonymous on a PC. RAM is volatile memory, meaning that it can only store its contents as long as its power source is constantly maintained. When RAM's power source is interrupted for longer than a few milliseconds, the contents of RAM are lost.

RAM is much faster than a hard disk, CD-ROM/DVD, or other forms of secondary storage. On the average, accessing data from a hard disk drive takes from 8 to 16 milliseconds (ms). To access the same data from RAM takes only 50 to 80 nanoseconds (ns). There are one thousand milliseconds and one billion nanoseconds in one second. What this works out to is that RAM at 50 ns is over a million times faster than a hard disk. Other secondary storage devices, such as a CD-ROM/DVD or a floppy disk, are even slower.

RAM is a component that can be upgraded on most PCs, including laptops and notebooks. However, replacement RAM must be matched to the PC's CPU and bus speeds. Most of the electronic circuit speeds of a PC are measured in megahertz, or one million CPU cycles per second. The rule of thumb for matching RAM to a CPU is that the closer the RAM's speed is relatively matched to the data bus and CPU, the more data will be transferred from RAM to the CPU and other components of the PC. Most RAM manufacturers include online guides on their Web sites to help match RAM speeds to bus and CPU speeds.

You may have heard that adding RAM to a slow PC will speed it up. This may be true, but only because the processor was able to perform faster input/output (I/O) operations as a result of the added or upgraded RAM. Having more RAM in the PC doesn't improve the overall speed of the processor, but it does improve how much data the processor can access without the need to go to slower secondary storage devices.

on the job

To download an excellent tutorial on memory systems, visit Kingston Technologies' Web site at www.kingston.com/tools/umg/ and download their "Ultimate Memory Guide."

DRAM

The most commonly referenced form of RAM is dynamic RAM, or DRAM. Compared to the other RAM technologies, DRAM is inexpensive and stores the largest number of bits in the smallest amount of physical space.

A DRAM cell, which stores one bit, is made up of a single capacitor. A capacitor stores either a positive or negative voltage value that is used to represent 1 or 0 binary values. DRAM must be refreshed every two milliseconds. This is done when the contents of every single DRAM cell (capacitor) are read and then rewritten by a refresh logic circuit. This constant refreshing contributes to the fact that DRAM is the slowest type of RAM.

SDRAM

RAM technology, along with motherboard, chipset, and CPU technology, has advanced to include the capability to transfer more data across the system, data, and address bus structures. Most of today's PCs use synchronous DRAM (SDRAM) that operates in synchronization to the clock cycles. Using its synchronous interface, SDRAM is able to push or pull more data to and from the bus structure. This is a method of data transfer called *pipelining*.

SDRAM's capabilities are expanded using double-data-rate (DDR) technology. DDR boosts SDRAM speeds by "double-pumping" data onto the bus twice per cycle (as opposed to once per cycle of single-data-rate [SDR] DRAM), thereby achieving twice the data rate without the need to increase the clock rate.

Typically, data is transferred on the bus structure at 64 bits (or 8 bytes) at a time in a parallel fashion. Basic DDR SDRAM (now referred to as DDR1) can nominally transfer 2,128 megabytes (MB) per second across a 133 megahertz (MHz) bus structure, double the nominal transfer rate of standard SDRAM.

Further developments in DDR technology have yielded DDR2 and DDR3, which double and double again the transfer rate of DDR, respectively. Where DDR doubles the transfer rate of standard SDRAM, DDR2 doubles the DDR rate, and DDR3 doubles that of DDR2. By 2012, DDR4 is expected that will raise the data transfer rate to approximately 2 gigabits per second.

Static RAM

The primary difference between SRAM and DRAM is that SRAM doesn't require the constant refreshing required of DRAM, which must be electrically refreshed about every two milliseconds. SRAM is only refreshed when data is written to it. SRAM is also faster than DRAM, but it is much more expensive and requires a much larger physical space to store the same amount of data as DRAM. Because of these characteristic differences, SRAM is most commonly used for cache memory and DRAM for common system memory.

Memory Operations

Many of the actions of a PC are synchronized to one or more "clocks." These clocks provide electronic timings by which the components of the PC can synchronize their actions to those of the CPU and other devices. For example, the CPU's internal clock speed controls the timing of electronic signals and data transfers to and from the CPU.

The CPU's clock is the system clock and sets the length and number of electronic cycles available in one second. The system clock's cycles are measured in megahertz (MHz), or one million hertz (a hertz is the completion of one electronic cycle). A CPU with a clock speed of 2.0 gigahertz (GHz) operates at 2 billion cycles per second. To put this in terms of instructions, a single computer instruction, such as adding two binary numbers that are already in the CPU's registers, generally takes one CPU cycle. Therefore, theoretically, the 2.0 GHz processor is capable of completing 2 billion instructions per second. However, most processors can't translate their clock speed rating directly into the number of instructions per second because data must be moved in and out of the CPU's registers to RAM, the hard disk, and other destinations, and these actions also require additional clock cycles to complete. To accommodate these actions, the CPU goes into what is called a wait state, meaning the CPU is idle and waiting.

For example, to read data from RAM, the CPU may use three or more wait states. The CPU issues the request for data along with an address. Receiving the address and transferring it to the memory controller uses about one wait state. Finding the data in memory also takes about one wait state. Transferring the data to the CPU's registers uses another wait state. The significance is that more data can be transferred from RAM to the CPU's registers on each cycle if the RAM's speed is matched to that of the CPU clock, minimizing the number of CPU wait states.

Simply installing more RAM in a PC does not improve the overall speed of the processor, but it does improve how much data the processor can access without the need to go to the slower hard disk drive. You may have heard that adding RAM to a slow PC will speed it up. Yes, but only because the processor was able to perform faster input/output (I/O) operations.

on the *Job*

Any particular motherboard typically accepts only one RAM type. Before adding new RAM of any size (matched to the CPU and FSB speeds), read the documentation of your computer or motherboard to determine the memory type and technology your motherboard supports. Memory manufacturers, such as Crucial (www.crucial.com) and Kingston (www.kingston.com), have online tools that you can use to match the brand and model of your PC to the memory that it supports.

Memory Measurements

Nearly everything the PC connects to is measured in bits these days, especially any movement of data, including both internal or external communications, but RAM is still measured in bytes—actually, kilobytes, megabytes, or gigabytes. Table 2-2 lists the various data units commonly associated with RAM (and secondary storage as well).

Memory modules are available in three primary package types: single-inline memory modules (SIMMs), double-inline memory modules (DIMMs), and small outline DIMMs (SODIMMs). SIMMs are legacy devices used in older PCs that incorporates memory chips on one side of a circuit card. DIMMs are the current standard for memory modules and incorporate memory chips on both sides of a circuit card. SODIMMs are smaller DIMMs designed for use in notebook computers.

Not only must you consider the amount of memory you wish to install, but you must also consider the package type, the memory technology, and the compatible speeds of the RAM, CPU, and bus structures. Different memory technologies (DDR, DDR2, DDR3, etc.) have unique module characteristics that can make them incompatible with each other and their mounting systems.

Another consideration is the amount of physical RAM the operating system can support, which, as shown in Table 2-3, can vary by the operating system version.

Memory Speeds

RAM is much faster than the CPU, and a hard disk, floppy disk, CD-ROM, or any other form of secondary storage. On the average, accessing data from a hard disk drive takes from 8 to 16 milliseconds (ms). Accessing the same data from RAM

TABLE 2-2	Unit	Size	Capacity
RAM Units of Measure	Bit	One binary digit	Stores either a binary 0 or 1
	Byte	Eight bits	One character
	Word	16 to 64 bits	Numeric values and addresses
	Kilobyte (KB)	1,024 bytes	About one page of double-spaced text
	Megabyte (MB)	1,024 KB	About the size of a short book
	Gigabyte (GB)	1,024 MB	1,000 short books
	Terabyte (TB)	1,024 GB	An entire library
	Petabyte (PB)	1,024 TB	Just about all the libraries in the U.S.

TABLE 2-3

Microsoft
Windows RAM
Limitations

Windows Version	Physical RAM Limit
Windows Vista (32-bit)	4GB
Windows Vista (64-bit)	128GB
Windows Vista Home Basic (32-bit)	4GB
Windows Vista Ultimate (32-bit)	4GB
Windows Vista Ultimate (64-bit)	128GB
Windows XP Pro (32-bit)	4GB
Windows XP Pro (64-bit)	128GB

takes only from 5 to 10 nanoseconds (ns). What this works out to is that RAM at 5 ns is over a million times faster than a hard disk. Other secondary storage devices, such as the CD-ROM/DVD or floppy disk, are even slower.

Another speed in the PC that must be considered is the speed of the data and address buses. Like the CPU speed, the bus transfer speed is in megahertz, which represents the speed used to move data and instructions between structures, such as the CPU and memory. Most RAM manufacturers include online guides on their Web sites to help match RAM and RAM speeds to bus and CPU speeds. One of the system components that figures into the speeds at which data can be transferred between RAM and the CPU is the front side bus (FSB), which is also known as the processor bus, memory bus, and system bus.

The FSB is a data pathway that runs between the CPU and essentially all the other major components of the computer, including RAM, device controllers, and the expansion bus structures. Because the bidirectional FSB carries a significant amount of the data flowing to or from the CPU, much of the actual performance of the computer is determined somewhat by the characteristics of the FSB, including its width and the amount of data it can transfer per cycle.

The bus speed of the FSB ranges from 66 MHz to 400 MHz and higher on newer computers. The speed of the FSB should be considered when you want to upgrade a motherboard or purchase a new computer. The bottom line is essentially that you should match the speed of the memory, CPU, and FSB as closely as possible to realize the best performance from a computer.

Caching

The two components of a PC that must work the closest together are the CPU and RAM. RAM is faster than the CPU, which tends to defeat the design goal to have the CPU idle as little as possible. If the CPU requests data from RAM, the data must be located and then transferred over the data bus to the CPU. Regardless of how fast RAM is, the CPU must wait while these actions are carried out, which is where cache memory becomes important.

Cache memory is very fast memory used to hold frequently requested data and instructions. In other words, cache memory holds data and instructions from a slower device or process at the ready for a faster device. On today's PCs, you commonly find cache memory logically located between RAM and the CPU or perhaps between the hard disk and RAM. A cache is any buffer storage used to improve computer performance by reducing its access time. A cache holds instructions and data likely to be requested by the CPU for its next operation.

Cache memory is a small amount of SRAM that has access speeds of 2 ns or faster. Data and instructions stored in SRAM-based cache memory are transferred to the CPU many times faster than if the data were transferred from the PC's main memory.

Caching operates on the principle of locality of reference that makes the assumption that the next data or instructions to be requested are very likely to be located immediately following the last data or instructions requested by the CPU. Under this principle, caching copies data or instructions just beyond the data requested into the cache memory in anticipation of the CPU asking for them.

How successful the caching system is at making its assumptions determines the effectiveness of the caching operation. As iffy as this may sound, caching systems surprisingly have a cache hit ratio (with a hit being a correct guess) of about 90 to 95 percent. Each time the caching system is correct in anticipating the data or instructions to be requested by the CPU and already has them in cache, it counts as a cache hit, which is tallied by the caching system. Of course, if the CPU asks for data that is not in cache, the data must be requested from RAM and a cache miss is tallied.

There are two types of cache memory:

- **Internal cache** (primary cache)   Internal cache is also called Level 1 (L1) cache because it is placed internally on the microprocessor chip.
- **External cache** (secondary cache)   External cache is also called Level 2 (L2) cache because at one time it was placed on the motherboard near the CPU. Several microprocessors now include L2 cache inside the microprocessor.

CERTIFICATION OBJECTIVE

Features of Storage Media

1.1.4   Identify the features and benefits (storage capacity, shelf-life, etc.) of different storage media.

Virtually every PC sold today has at least one hard disk drive installed inside its system case. A *hard disk drive* is a type of secondary storage. RAM, or primary storage, stores data temporarily while it's in use; secondary storage holds data, programs, and other digital objects permanently. In fact, RAM is also referred to as temporary storage, and the hard disk and other forms of secondary storage are considered permanent storage. The data is not permanent in the sense that it is etched in stone. However, compared to the volatility of RAM, it is far more enduring. Permanent storage on a disk drive means that the data is still available even after the primary power source is removed.

Hard Disk Drives

There are many different types and styles of hard disk drives available, all of which have roughly the same physical components, as illustrated in Figure 2-3. The differences among the different drive styles and types are usually in the components—the materials

FIGURE 2-3

The major components of a hard disk drive (Original image courtesy of Western Digital Corporation.)

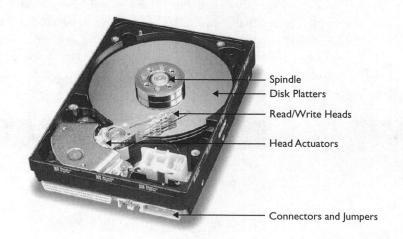

Spindle
Disk Platters
Read/Write Heads
Head Actuators
Connectors and Jumpers

used and the way they are put together. However, one disk drive essentially operates like all others.

The following sections provide an overview of each of the hard disk's components.

Disk Platters

The *platters*, or disks, as they are more commonly called, are the storage media in a hard disk drive. Disks are made from a number of different materials, each with its own performance and storage characteristics.

The primary two materials used in disks are aluminum alloys and glass. Aluminum alloy is the traditional material for platters. This material provides strength without weight. However, because aluminum disks tend to flex by expanding when heated, many disk drives now use a glass-ceramic composite material for their disk platters. The glass platters are more rigid and as such can be less than half as thick as the aluminum disks. A glass disk doesn't expand or contract with changes in temperature, resulting in a more stable hard disk drive. Glass materials have become the standard for hard disk platters as the drives continue to get smaller, store more data, and operate at higher speeds.

Most PC hard drives generally have two platters. There are those with more (as many as 10), and many have less (one platter), especially the smaller form-factor drives. The number of platters included in a disk drive is a function of design and capacity, which is controlled primarily by the overall size of the disk drive. The form factor of a disk is essentially the size of its platters, although it has also come to mean the size of the drive bay into which the drive can be installed. The more common form factors and their actual platter sizes are listed in Table 2-4.

Of the form factors listed in Table 2-4, the 3.5-inch drive is currently the most popular, having replaced the 5.25-inch drive in desktop and tower-type PCs. The 2.5-inch drives and 1.8-inch drives are popular in notebook computers.

Each platter is mounted on the disk spindle with a spacer inserted between the platters, if more than one, so that each side of the disk can be accessed with

TABLE 2-4	Form Factor	Platter Size
Hard Disk Drive Form Factors	5.25 inches	5.12 inches (130 millimeters [mm])
	3.5 inches	3.74 inches (95 mm)
	2.5 inches	2.5 inches (63.5 mm)
	1.8 inches	1.8 inches (45.7 mm)

a read/write head. The surface of each disk platter is polished and then covered with a layer of magnetic material, on which data is stored.

Data is stored on a platter using electromagnetic principles. A magnetic field is generated from a magnetic core wrapped or surrounded by an electrical wire through which an electrical current is passed to control the polarity of a magnetic field. As this magnetic field is passed over the disk, it influences the magnetic polarity of a certain area of the recording media. Reversing the direction of the flow of the electrical current reverses the polarity of the magnetic field, which reverses the influence it has on the recording media.

The material used to coat hard disk platters is a thin film medium. Virtually all disk drives manufactured today use thin film media, which are an extremely thin layer of metals placed on the disk's surface. The thin metal film is put on the disk using a process called sputtering. Despite its unusual name, sputtering is a very complicated way of plating a platter that electrically binds the metal media to the disk in a vacuum.

Read/Write Heads

Each side of a disk platter has media applied to it that allows it to store data. Accordingly, each side of a disk platter also has at least one *read/write head*. A disk drive that has two platters has four read/write heads. There are exceptions to this rule, but generally a disk drive has two heads for each platter, one to read and write data to the top side and one for the bottom side.

The read/write heads are all connected to the same actuator mechanism that moves the heads in unison in and out, from the spindle to the edge of the platter. Remember that the disk itself is spinning rapidly and that when the read/write head for the top platter is over track 29, all of the other read/write heads are over track 29 on each of the other disks.

The read/write head uses magnetic flux to record data on the disk media. Flux refers to a magnetic field that has a single and specific polarity. As the disk surface rotates under it, the read/write head senses or creates a flux reversal, a change in the alignment of magnetic particles on the disk surface, to read or write from the disk. In a read operation, an encoder/decoder (endec) interprets the read/write head signals, converting them into binary data. During a write operation, the endec focuses on creating a signal pattern for the read/write head.

Encoding Method   Depending on the disk media and head technology in use on a disk drive, a variety of methods are used to encode data. The encoding method used maximizes the data storage capacity of the disk drive using a particular scheme for arranging magnetic particles. The primary encoding method in use is run length limited (RLL). RLL yields high data density by spacing 1-bits farther apart and specially encoding groups of bits that are to be accessed together. RLL introduced data compression techniques. Most current disk drive technologies (including IDE, ATA, and SCSI) use a form of RLL encoding.

Connectors and Jumpers

There are two primary types of connectors on a hard disk drive: data and power. The data connector, which is also called an interface connector, carries both the data and command signals from the controller and CPU to and from the disk drive. Some drives use only a single cable for data and control signals, such as SCSI, IDE, and SATA. These systems also allow more than one drive to be connected to the cable.

The source of the disk's power connector is the PC's power supply. The power supply provides the disk with 5 VDC and 12 VDC power. The logic board and other electronics of the drive use 5 V, and the spindle motor and head actuator use 12 V power.

The jumpers on the disk drive are used to configure the drive as a master or slave on a shared interface, as well as other configuration settings. See your disk drive documentation for the correct position for the jumpers, as they differ among manufacturers and even models. However, many drives have an illustration of the jumper settings on the drive.

Data Interface Methods

The mechanism that controls the transmission of data between the CPU and other devices on the PC is an interface. Disk storage devices, such as hard disk drives, floppy disk drives, tape drives, and CD-ROM/DVD drives, all use a transfer interface to move data to and from themselves and the rest of the PC. The interface used for a particular storage device is defined in the device controller and the drive electronics. The interface standards that are the most commonly used are IDE, SCSI, and SATA.

IDE

The *IDE (Integrated Drive Electronics)* interface, also known as the AT Attachment (ATA) interface, was originally developed as an alternative to the expensive SCSI technology. IDE technology integrates the disk controller into the disk drive, which allows IDE devices to be connected directly to the motherboard or through a passthrough board. IDE interface cards are usually multifunction cards that support not only the hard disk, but a floppy drive, a game port, and possibly a CD or DVD drive.

The standard IDE interface supports up to two 528MB drives. EIDE (Enhanced IDE), also called ATA-2, increases the capacity of the interface to eight multigigabyte drives. Another standard closely related to the EIDE interface standard is the ATAPI (ATA Packet Interface), an interface standard for CD-ROMs, DVDs, and tape drives that connect to common ATA (IDE) connectors.

In the past few years, the ATA interface (also known as the parallel ATA) has given way to the Serial ATA (SATA) interface. This interface is designed to connect to host bus adapters or the device interfaces integrated into the motherboards of both portable and desktop computers. Whereas the ATA/IDE interface connected to a device controller using a 40-pin data cable, the SATA interface connects directly to the motherboard using an 8-pin connector.

SCSI Interface

The *Small Computer Systems Interface (SCSI)* is not an interface standard in the way that IDE is. It is a system standard that is made up of a collection of interface standards covering a range of peripheral devices, including hard disks, tape drives, optical drives, CD-ROM/DVDs, and disk arrays. Up to eight SCSI devices can connect to a single SCSI controller by sharing a common interface, called a SCSI bus or SCSI chain.

Like IDE devices, SCSI controllers are built into the devices. As SCSI devices are added to the SCSI bus, each device is assigned a unique device number to differentiate it from the other devices. The SCSI controller communicates with the devices on the bus by sending a message encoded with the unit's device number, which is also included in any reply sent by the device. A SCSI bus must be electrically terminated to prevent unclaimed or misdirected messages from bouncing back onto the bus.

Input/Output Standards

In addition to a particular encoding method and interface, a hard disk drive uses a specific input/output standard, which is also referred to as a transfer protocol. Data is transferred from the disk drive to system memory using one of two transfer modes: Programmed I/O (PIO) or Direct Memory Access (DMA). PIO is a legacy data transfer protocol and I/O standard used by many older disk drives that uses the CPU to execute the instructions that move data from the disk drive to RAM or the CPU. DMA transfers data directly to or from memory without involving the CPU in the transfer, freeing the CPU to perform other tasks.

Data Addressing

While there is a certain amount of randomness to the organization of data on a hard disk drive, the data is addressed and indexed so that it can be retrieved when requested. Data is addressed on the disk using two methods: cylinder-head-sector (CHS) or logical block address (LBA).

CHS Addressing

CHS addressing is used on most IDE drives. It locates data on the disk by the cylinder (track), head (meaning platter side), and sector on the track of its placement. For example, a file could begin on cylinder 250, head 4, and sector 33.

Each disk is organized into the following logical building blocks:

- **Tracks**   A *track* is a concentric area, one circumference of the disk in length, on a disk. On a hard disk, there can be 1,000 tracks or more. The first track, which is where data is usually written first, is along the outermost edge of the disk.

- **Sectors**   *Sectors* divide a disk into a number of cross-sections that intersect all of the disk's tracks. Sectors break tracks into addressable pieces. A sector is typically 512 bytes in length, and disk drives have from 100 to 300 sectors per track. Without a sector division, a track could only be addressed at its beginning. Sectors provide segment beginning points on the tracks as well as the disk as a whole.

- **Cylinders**   A *cylinder* is the logical grouping of the same number track on each disk surface. For example, if a hard disk drive has three platters, it has six disk surfaces and six track 52s. All six of the track 52s are vertically aligned and are logically combined to create cylinder 52. Data is written vertically between disks following the track and cylinder path, which eliminates the need to move the read/write heads.

- **Clusters**   A *cluster* is formed from groups of sectors. This logical grouping is used by operating systems to track data on the disk. There are normally around 64 sectors to a cluster, but the size of the disk drive and the operating system in use determine the actual number of sectors in a cluster.

LBA

In this method of data addressing, each sector on the disk is assigned a sequential logical block number. LBA addressing simply lists a single logical location for each file. LBA is used on SCSI and EIDE drives.

Removable Storage Devices

In addition to the hard disk drive for mass secondary storage on a PC, additional storage can be added to the system using its external port interfaces, primarily USB, FireWire (IEEE 1394), or eSATA (External Serial ATA) connections.

USB Removable Storage

The USB standard defines the USB mass storage device class (MSC) that supports flash drives of ever-expanding capacities. In addition, external portable hard disk drives (see Figure 2-4) and enclosures are available that can translate the interface technology of an internal hard disk drive (IDE, ATA, SATA, or SCSI) to the USB interface. A primary feature of the MSC devices is that they are hot-swappable, meaning that they can be added or removed from the computer as needed.

IEEE 1394 Removable Storage

The IEEE 1394 standard, implemented primarily as FireWire, also provides support for external mass storage devices that are designed specifically for the FireWire interface. Some of these devices support multiple interface standards, including USB and the eSATA standards.

FIGURE 2-4

An external hard disk drive that supports both USB and IEEE 1394 interfaces (Photo courtesy of LaCie.)

eSATA External Hard Disks

On systems that have either an integrated eSATA port or an eSATA expansion card, an eSATA external disk drive can be connected. The advantage that the eSATA interface has over the USB and IEEE 1394 interface standards is its speed (up to three times faster) and the elimination of the need to translate the internal interface to another interface standard for transmission into the PC.

CD and DVD Recordable Media

CD and DVD recordable and rewritable media drives can be connected to a PC through a USB or IEEE 1394 interface. While either of these media types is perhaps the slowest form of external storage that can be used on a PC, their portability and their ease of physical storage and organization can overcome their inconvenience of use.

Network and Online Data Storage

Data storage can be distributed to dedicated network and remote online services. The former is typically a local area network service used to manage, organize, and share data resources, and the latter is used more for backup purposes.

Network Attached Storage

Hard disk storage space can also be available on a networked device called a *network attached storage (NAS)* unit. A NAS is a dedicated computer with expanded storage capacity that provides access to shared data resources to the entire network. The benefit of a NAS to a network is that file management is offloaded to a networked device designed specifically and dedicated to file management.

The alternative to NAS is to include a file server on the network. A file server, while specifically purposed to service data and file requests, is a general server that can, if needed, perform other computing or network functions.

Online Data Storage

Online data storage, which is also called Internet or Web data storage, allows users to transmit data to a remote storage service for general backup or archiving purposes. Although the general public has been slow to trust these services, the cost of additional storage space for a local computer or a network and the improvements in Internet security have made these services more attractive.

Most online data storage services provide access to uploaded data through password protection. Once a user has been authenticated, the user can interact with the data and files in much the same way local data are accessed. The use of online data storage also satisfies the requirement of offsite data storage inherent to most disaster recovery plans and data security policies.

CERTIFICATION OBJECTIVE

Factors That Affect Computer Performance

1.1.9   Identify factors that affect computer performance.

Gilster's Law says that when it comes to determining what you should do to improve the performance of a PC, "You never can tell—and it all depends." What affects the performance of one computer may be totally different than why another PC is running slow or performing erratically—other than the user, that is. However, there are some tried-and-true troubleshooting steps you can take on any PC to determine if the PC is realizing its optimal performance levels.

To really give a PC a careful examination to identify any potential performance issues, you need to use a three-step process: internal hardware systems, software systems, and external hardware systems.

Internal Hardware System Performance

As discussed earlier in this chapter, how well the CPU, memory, and bus structures are aligned can definitely impact the system's performance, good or bad. However, one thing we didn't discuss earlier is that to achieve the highest possible performance of a PC may require some investment in higher-end components with cutting-edge compatibilities.

To improve the performance of the bus structure, you need to separate the data and address buses. However, to do so may require the purchase of a high-end motherboard and chipset. Otherwise, you may need to stay with a lower-cost solution that multiplexes the data and addresses onto the FSB. Here are other performance versus cost trade-offs that can be considered to improve the operations of a PC:

■   Install a motherboard with a wider (more bits) data bus structure to speed data transfers instead of working with a data bus with a lower number of bits; for instance, use a 64-bit data bus instead of a 32-bit data bus.

- Install a motherboard that supports multiple words of data instead of using a less expensive one with single-word transfer.

- Install a motherboard, chipset, caching, RAM, and processor that use synchronous clocking, which also improves data I/O operations, instead of a less costly set that uses asynchronous clocking.

- Use the manufacturer's recommendations for the best memory size and technology to install on a particular motherboard, matching the speeds of the CPU, cache, FSB, and RAM.

- Some RAM modules can suffer from chip creep that causes the memory module to oil-can itself out of its mounting slot, especially if the side locks weren't properly engaged. Check the side locks on the memory modules and verify that they are snuggly seated in their slots. You may also want to check the expansion boards for the same condition, since you'll have the system case open.

- Run defragmentation software on your hard disk drives and any other active mass storage devices to free up necessary disk space and to better arrange the stored data for faster retrieval. You may also want to remove any unnecessary files. As the disk drive fills up, it begins to work slower and slower, especially on write operations.

System Software Performance

Although it can sound like subtraction by addition, you should install a reputable and proven computer virus scanning software system that also looks for and prevents incoming viruses, spyware, adware, and other forms of malware. You should also remove any services or other unnecessary installed programs that start running when the PC is booted. Too many programs running in background mode can slow an entire system as they compete for system resources. Monitor the Windows Task Manager's CPU and RAM utilization graphics and verify which of the running programs are using the available CPU cycles and RAM. You may find a program you knew nothing about taking up your system resources.

You may want to consider running PC diagnostics software, especially on a Windows system, to identify potential problems that could impact performance in the future, such as registry issues, virtual memory sizing, and more.

Too often a performance issue that is tied to the system software is based on a faulty configuration of the operating system. Search out information on how to properly tune your operating system. For information on Windows XP or Windows Vista, visit www.microsoft.com/Downloads.

Video Performance

Another area where the performance of a PC can be noticed is the video display. Because it's visual, the performance of the video display is readily noticed by users. The two areas in which video performance can be impacted are video memory and the refresh rate of the monitor.

Video Memory

The amount of video memory actually needed is dependent on the type of video display in use on the PC. While the type of memory included on a video card can be a major factor in the video performance, most quality video cards are configured and tuned to provide a specific level of performance using an appropriate type of memory. When the speed of the memory on the video controller card is faster, the entire video card is faster, which provides for better video performance on the whole. Video memory can also impact the resolution and color of the display and facilitate better display refresh rates.

The one area where the amount of video memory can have an impact is in 3-D accelerator video cards. Three-dimensional video is generated through a series of mathematical calculations. If more memory is provided to the video processor and control system, these calculations can be made faster. However, there is a point at which adding more memory to a video system will no longer improve the video speed. More memory doesn't reduce the number of calculations that need to be made, but it can help to improve the resolution and color depth of the display.

Refresh Rate

Cathode ray tube (CRT) monitors must be continuously refreshed to retain the image being displayed. This condition is unique to CRTs and, for the most part, isn't an issue with liquid-crystal displays (LCDs) or light-emitting diode (LED) displays.

The refresh rate of a CRT monitor indicates the number of times per second that the monitor redraws the displayed image. Depending on the age and type of the monitor, its recommended refresh rate, which is measured in Hertz (cycles per second) and abbreviated as Hz, can range between 60 and 85 Hz, with settings in the 70s or 80s common. If a monitor is configured to a 75 Hz refresh rate, the monitor redraws the displayed image 75 times each second.

Increasing the refresh rate on a CRT can reduce the amount of flicker of the screen, which makes it easier on the user's eyes. However, if the refresh rate is set too high, it can damage the monitor and reduce its life span. Each monitor has a recommended refresh rate that takes both of these factors into consideration.

CERTIFICATION SUMMARY

You should encounter one or two questions on the IC[3] exams that specifically address the information in this chapter. Be sure you understand these concepts:

- The purpose and use of the components that make up the CPU
- How primary memory is used in the storage of data and in the execution of program instructions
- The different types of storage media
- The components, features, and configuration settings that can impact the performance of a computer.

Especially study this last item and the effect a combination of factors can have on how a computer performs.

✓ TWO-MINUTE DRILL

The Role of the CPU

❑ Everything a computer does is controlled by a microprocessor, which contains the central processing unit (CPU). The CPU is a multifunction integrated circuit that is made up of several special-purpose components, including the control unit (CU), arithmetic and logic unit (ALU), memory management unit (MMU), and a number of registers.

❑ The bus system carries the various signals, addresses, and data that are transferred among the CPU, motherboard, I/O ports, and expansion cards of the PC. In a PC, there are several bus structures: the data bus, the address bus, and the control bus.

❑ It is very important that a processor be kept at or near its designed operating temperature. When a microprocessor gets too hot, it performs poorly, shuts down, or becomes permanently damaged. Heat sinks and fans are designed to aid in the cooling of the processor.

❑ Microprocessors are attached to the motherboard of the computer in a mounting socket. Microprocessor sockets use two primary form factors: PGA and LGA.

❑ The chipset provides much of a PC's ability to accept, display, and move data. The chipset also assists in the movement of data and instructions on the system buses among the CPU, cache memory, and peripherals. The north bridge provides support and control for the main memory, cache memory, and the PCI bus controllers.

Concepts Related to Computer Memory

❑ ROM is nonvolatile and retains its contents without a power source. ROM is used for storing the PC's startup instructions and the system BIOS. The types of ROM used in the PC are PROM, EPROM, and EEPROM.

❑ RAM is volatile memory that can only store data as long as its power source is constantly maintained. When RAM's power source is interrupted for longer than a few milliseconds, the contents of RAM are lost.

❑ Replacement RAM must be matched to the PC's CPU and bus speeds.

❑ The most common form of RAM is DRAM. DRAM must be refreshed every two milliseconds.

❑ Today's PCs use SDRAM that operates in synchronization to clock cycles. SDRAM has been expanded using DDR technology.

❑ SRAM is refreshed only when data is written to it. SRAM is faster than DRAM. SRAM is most commonly used for cache memory and DRAM for common system memory.

❑ The CPU's internal clock speed controls the timing of electronic signals and data transfers to and from the CPU.

❑ Memory modules are available in three package types: SIMMs, DIMMs, and SODIMMs. DIMMs are the current standard for memory modules. SODIMMs are smaller DIMMs designed for use in notebook computers.

❑ The FSB is a data path that connects the CPU and RAM, the device controllers, and the expansion bus structures.

❑ Cache memory is very fast memory that holds frequently requested data and instructions. Cache memory is logically located between RAM and the CPU and buffers data retrieval to improve computer performance by reducing its access time. There are two types of cache memory: internal cache (L1) and external cache (L2).

Features of Storage Media

❑ A hard disk drive is secondary storage that holds data, programs, and other digital objects permanently.

❑ Platters are the storage media in a hard disk drive. The two materials used in disks are aluminum alloys and glass. Most hard drives have two platters. Each platter is mounted on a spindle so that each side of the platter can be accessed by a read/write head. The material used to coat hard disk platters is a thin film medium.

❑ Each side of a disk platter has at least one read/write head. The read/write heads are connected to the same actuator mechanism that moves the heads in unison. The read/write head uses magnetic flux to record data on the disk media. An endec interprets the read/write head signals, converting them into binary data.

❑ The primary encoding method, RLL, yields high data density by spacing 1-bits farther apart and specially encoding groups of bits that are to be accessed together.

❑ There are two primary types of connectors on a hard disk drive: data and power. The data connector carries both the data and command signals from the controller and CPU to and from the disk drive.

❑ The interface method used by a storage device is defined by the device controller and the drive electronics. The interface standards that are the most commonly used are IDE, SCSI, and SATA.

❑ The IDE interface, also known as the ATA interface, integrates the disk controller into the disk drive, which allows IDE devices to connect directly to the motherboard.

❑ The ATA interface has given way to the SATA interface. The SATA interface connects directly to the motherboard using an eight-pin connector.

❑ SCSI is a system standard made up of a set of interface standards covering a range of peripheral devices, including hard disks, tape drives, optical drives, CD-ROM/DVDs, and disk arrays.

❑ Data is transferred from the disk drive to system memory using one of two transfer modes: PIO or DMA. PIO uses the CPU to execute its instructions. DMA transfers data directly to or from memory without involving the CPU.

❑ Hard disk data is addressed using two methods: CHS or LBA. CHS addressing is used on IDE drives and locates data on the disk by a cylinder, head, and sector number. LBA addressing simply lists a single logical location for location on the disk. LBA is used on SCSI and EIDE drives.

❑ External storage devices can be connected to a PC through a USB, IEEE 1394, or eSATA connections.

Factors That Affect Computer Performance

❑ How well the CPU, memory, and bus structures are aligned can definitely impact the system's performance.

❑ To improve the performance of the bus structure, you need to separate the data and address buses, which may require the purchase of a high-end motherboard and chipset.

❑ A wider data bus structure can speed up data transfers.

❑ Multiple words of data transfer can improve data throughput rates.

❑ Install a motherboard, chipset, caching, RAM, and processor that use synchronous clocking, which also improve data I/O operations.

❑ Use the manufacturer's recommendations for the best memory size and technology to install on a particular motherboard, matching the speeds of the CPU, cache, FSB, and RAM.

❑ Run defragmentation software on your hard disk drives and any other active mass storage devices to free up necessary disk space and to better arrange the stored data for faster retrieval.

❑ Install a reputable and proven computer virus scanning software system that also looks for and prevents incoming viruses, spyware, adware, and other forms of malware.

❑ Monitor the Windows Task Manager's CPU and RAM utilization graphics and verify which of the running programs are using the available CPU cycles and RAM.

❑ A performance issue may be based in a faulty configuration of the operating system.

SELF TEST

The following questions are intended to help you be sure that you understand the material included in this chapter. Read the questions and the answer choices carefully.

The Role of the CPU

1. All of the following are components of the CPU, except
  A. CU
  B. ALU
  C. FSB
  D. MMU

2. The circuitry that carries signals, addresses, and data among the internal components of the computer is the
  A. RAM
  B. Bus
  C. ROM
  D. CPU

3. Into what device is the microprocessor on the motherboard of a PC mounted?
  A. FSB
  B. Heat sink
  C. Chipset
  D. Socket

4. What devices are attached to the microprocessor to prevent it from overheating?
  A. Heat sink
  B. Socket
  C. ROM
  D. Fan

5. What component of the microprocessor provides the instructions that allow the PC's primary components to accept, display, and move data?
  A. Chipset
  B. Bus
  C. FSB
  D. Registers

Concepts Related to Computer Memory

6. Which of the following is not a characteristic of ROM?
   A. Nonvolatile
   B. Read-only
   C. Rewritable
   D. Contains the BIOS

7. Which of the following is not a characteristic of RAM?
   A. Volatile
   B. Random access
   C. Read-only
   D. Rewritable

8. Which of the following is the most commonly used form of RAM?
   A. SRAM
   B. Level 1 cache
   C. SDRAM
   D. Level 2 cache

9. Which of the following is the fastest form of memory?
   A. SRAM
   B. DRAM
   C. SDRAM
   D. EEPROM

10. What is the memory form factor commonly used on notebook computers?
    A. SIMM
    B. DIMM
    C. SODIMM
    D. EEPROM

11. What is the cache memory that is located the closest logically to the CPU?
    A. L1 cache
    B. L2 cache
    C. L3 cache
    D. Disk cache

Features of Storage Media

12. What type of storage is a PC's hard disk drive considered to be?

   A. Primary storage

   B. Secondary storage

   C. Temporary storage

   D. Permanent storage

13. How many read/write heads are associated with each platter in a hard disk drive?

   A. One

   B. Two

   C. Four

   D. Eight

14. What internal device provides electrical power to the hard disk drive?

   A. Motherboard

   B. Power supply

   C. Battery power

   D. Hard disk controller

15. Which of the addressing methods used with hard disk drives uses a combination of cylinder, head, and sector numbers to form an address?

   A. CHS

   B. LBA

   C. DMA

   D. PIO

16. An external storage device can be connected to a PC using all of the following standards, except

   A. USB

   B. IEEE 1394

   C. eSATA

   D. PS/2

Factors That Affect Computer Performance

17. What components of the PC should be as compatible as possible to ensure PC performance?

   A. CPU

   B. Memory

    C. Bus

    D. External devices

    E. All of the above

    F. None of the above

18. Which authority should be consulted first when determining the best memory size and technology to install in a PC?

    A. General help Web site

    B. Operating system manufacturer

    C. Computer manufacturer

    D. Memory manufacturer

19. Performance issues related to the software of a PC are typically related to what component of a PC?

    A. Memory

    B. CPU

    C. Operating system configuration

    D. Hard disk drive

SELF TEST ANSWERS

The Role of the CPU

1. ☑ **C.** The FSB is a data pathway that runs between the CPU and the other major components of the computer.
   ☒ **A, B,** and **D** are incorrect. The control unit (CU), the arithmetic and logic unit (ALU), and the memory management unit (MMU) are all parts of the CPU.

2. ☑ **B.** The bus structures of a PC motherboard carry signals, addresses, and data among the internal components of the computer.
   ☒ **A, C,** and **D** are incorrect. Random access memory (RAM) and read-only memory (ROM) are types of temporary storage. The CPU is the main component of a PC.

3. ☑ **D.** Microprocessors are mounted on the motherboard in a socket.
   ☒ **A, B,** and **C** are incorrect. The front-side bus is the main connection between the components on the motherboard. A heat sink is a device that is attached to a component to draw off excess heat. The chipset contains support utilities and drivers for the CPU and operating system.

4. ☑ **A** and **D.** Heat sinks and fans are used to draw off excess heat from and cool the CPU.
   ☒ **B** and **C** are incorrect. A socket is the mounting for the microprocessor, and read-only memory contains firmware.

5. ☑ **A.** The chipset contains instructions that allow primary components to accept, display, and move data.
   ☒ **B, C,** and **D** are incorrect. The bus structure is the connection system between components on the motherboard. The front-side bus (FSB) is the main connection between the components on the motherboard. The registers are temporary storage components in the CPU.

Concepts Related to Computer Memory

6. ☑ **C.** ROM is not rewritable; it is read-only.
   ☒ **A, B,** and **D** are incorrect. ROM is nonvolatile, is read-only, and can contain the BIOS.

7. ☑ **C.** RAM is not read-only.
   ☒ **A, B,** and **D** are incorrect. RAM is volatile, random accessible, and rewritable.

8. ☑ **C.** SDRAM is the most commonly used form of RAM.
   ☒ **A, B,** and **D** are incorrect. SRAM is a form of RAM, but it is too expensive and physically large to be used for primary memory. Level 1 cache and Level 2 cache are temporary storage devices used in support of the CPU.

9. ☑ **A.** SRAM, which is used for cache memory, is typically the fastest form of memory used in a PC.
☒ **B, C,** and **D** are incorrect. DRAM and SDRAM must be constantly refreshed, which makes them slower than SRAM. The EEPROM is commonly used for ROM.

10. ☑ **C.** SODIMM is the memory form factor used on notebook computers.
☒ **A, B,** and **D** are incorrect. SIMMs and DIMMs are memory modules used in a large-case PC. The EEPROM is commonly used for ROM.

11. ☑ **A.** Level 1 is the cache memory located closest to the CPU.
☒ **B, C,** and **D** are incorrect. L2 and L3 are logically a further distance from the CPU than L1 cache. Disk cache is associated with a hard disk drive.

Features of Storage Media

12. ☑ **B and D.** A PC's hard disk drive is considered to be secondary storage, which is also called permanent storage.
☒ **A and C** are incorrect. RAM is both primary storage and temporary storage.

13. ☑ **B.** Each platter has two read/write heads, one for each surface of the platter.
☒ **A, B,** and **D** are incorrect. In high-end disk drives, found on mainframes and the like, a disk may have four or eight read/write heads, but this would be highly unusual for a PC disk drive.

14. ☑ **B.** The central power supply unit of a PC supplies power directly to a disk drive.
☒ **A, C,** and **D** are incorrect. The motherboard and hard disk controller also receive power directly from the power supply unit. The disk drive doesn't operate directly from battery power.

15. ☑ **A.** CHS stands for cylinder, head, and sector.
☒ **B, C,** and **D** are incorrect. LBA is long-block addressing, which is another form of disk addressing. Direct-memory access (DMA) and programmed input-output (PIO) are disk interface methods.

16. ☑ **D.** PS/2 is a connector type used to connect input devices, like a mouse or keyboard.
☒ **A, B,** and **C** are incorrect. USB, IEEE 1394 (FireWire), and eSATA are disk interface standards.

Factors That Affect Computer Performance

17. ☑ **A, B,** and **C.** All of the internal components on a PC should be compatible and interoperable for the PC to perform at its best.
☒ **D, E,** and **F** are incorrect. External devices must be compatible with the connections on the PC and the device driver suited to the operating system.

18. ☑ **C.** The computer manufacturer generally has the best overall information concerning a particular model of a PC.

    ☒ **A, B,** and **D** are incorrect. While these are good sources of information, they should be checked after the manufacturer's information.

19. ☑ **C.** The configuration of an operating system can have a big impact on how well a PC performs.

    ☒ **A, B,** and **D** are incorrect. The PC's memory, CPU, and hard disk drive are typically tuned by the manufacturer for optimal performance, which leaves the operating system.

3

Power and Environmental Protection

A PC system, including its internal and external components and peripheral devices, gains in value and importance as it's used, especially as data and programs are added to its storage. Regardless of whether a PC sits in a home or at a business, the loss of the PC through theft or environmental damage can be quite serious and costly in terms of activity interruption and the data resources lost.

Protecting a PC against loss or damage requires proactive solutions, including securing its physical space and protecting it from environmental and power source problems. These protective actions are too often overlooked or dismissed as trivial but when implemented can help to avert the loss of a very valuable tool and resource.

CERTIFICATION OBJECTIVE

Protecting Computer Hardware from Theft or Damage

1.2.1   Identify the importance of protecting computer hardware from theft or damage.

A PC is a relatively major investment that needs to be protected from theft or damage. Not only is the investment in hardware and software relatively significant, but the value of the data and information stored on a computer system can often greatly increase the overall worth of a PC. Projecting a PC from physical threats is important, but protecting it from environmental hazards can be just as important.

Physical Protection for a PC

Any scheme to secure a PC—its components, peripherals, and contents—must begin with the physical security of the area in which the PC sits. Beyond just locking a door or two, physical security involves restricting physical access to the PC, limiting what those who have access are able to do, and physically restricting the portability of the PC itself. Physical security is the first line of defense in any security scheme, but just how elaborate and restrictive a particular security scheme can or must be is typically defined by the situation and the size of the available budget.

Securing the Room

Unless you live alone, totally securing the room in your home in which a PC sits is likely not very practical, especially if the PC is shared by two or more people. However, you can secure the PC from tampering or theft. In an office setting, you may need to secure a PC anytime you are away from your workstation.

The most obvious, and perhaps most overlooked, step to securing a PC in either a home or an office is to lock doors and restrict who has access to the locked space. You can also secure the PC to its table or desk using security cables or computer locks. You could go so far as to keep the PC in a lockable cabinet, install video surveillance, and more. But, for what you need to know for the IC³ exam, let's focus on the simpler steps you can take.

Computer Locks   In addition to the lock on the door of the room in which a PC is located, a computer can also have a lock attached to prevent it from theft or use. Many PCs have a key lock on the front bezel that can lock the system and prevent anyone from using the keyboard or mouse. Cable locks can also be attached to the computer case to secure it to the table or desk on which it sits. Cable locks are especially useful for securing a portable computer to a desk or table surface. Some PC cases also include a dongle or tab on the rear of the case to which a key or combination lock can be attached to prevent any unauthorized access inside the system case. Figure 3-1 shows a computer cable lock kit that can be used to physically secure both desktop and notebook computers to a table or desk.

Most new notebook computers have a slot or opening on one side or on the back of the base portion of their case. This case feature is for external locking and security products that can consist of only a cable and a lock or a more sophisticated locking system that includes plates that are glued to the case for more secure attachments

and perhaps even a motion detector and an alarm. The more sophisticated locking systems are typically available for desktop systems as well.

Software Locks   In addition to the physical security of a PC that protects it from damage or theft, you can also protect a PC from unauthorized access or maliciousness by using a variety of software locks that are most likely already available on your PC. These protections include BIOS locks, system locks, and the like.

A *BIOS lock* is perhaps the lowest level of software protection you can set on a PC. It is engaged as a password assigned to the BIOS (System Setup). The bad news is that you absolutely must remember this password should you ever wish to access the BIOS configuration of your PC again, but the password must be robust enough that it can't be easily hacked.

Windows operating systems include features that allow you to lock a workstation manually or on a time-out clock. The process used to lock the system is slightly different in different Windows versions. On a Windows XP or Windows Vista system, you can lock the system by pressing the WINDOWS logo key on a Windows keyboard and the L (lock) key together; this displays the Unlock Computer Password dialog box, into which you can enter the password to be used to unlock the system. On a Windows XP or Windows Vista system without a Windows keyboard, you can enter the following command in the Start | Run box:

```
rundll32.exe user32.dll, LockWorkStation
```

You can also enter this command string in a new shortcut on the Desktop so that it's available when needed.

On a Windows Vista system, you can click the Lock icon on the Start menu or press the CTRL-ALT-DEL key combination and click the Lock This Computer option.

CERTIFICATION OBJECTIVE

Factors That Can Damage a Computer

1.2.2   Identify factors that can cause damage to computer hardware or media (e.g., environmental factors, magnetic fields).

The cleanliness, heating, cooling, and stability of the environment in which a PC operates can have a potentially serious impact on the operations and longevity of the computer and its peripherals. You should be aware of the environmental threats and dangers that can damage a PC, many of which are often overlooked.

Environmental Hazards

In addition to physical threats to the security of your PC, the environment in which it operates can also pose a threat to its electronics, stored data, and longevity. There is a long list of natural disasters that could pose a physical threat to your PC, which includes such things as floods, earthquakes, electrical storms, hurricanes, and tornados. However, these events are probably a bigger threat to the building and all of its contents as well as the humans who occupy the building. If a catastrophic event does impact the space in which a PC is installed, chances are that, unless some data integrity procedures are in place, the system and its data are a total loss.

Smoke and fire can also be a serious threat to a PC. Beyond actually burning up, a PC can be heavily damaged by the heat and smoke of a fire or the water, foam, or other fire suppressants used to put the fire out. Smoke, which contains tiny particles of burnt material, from a large fire can get inside the electronics, such as the hard disk drive, and damage or corrupt the system. Extreme heat from a fire can damage a PC by melting its plastic and soft metal components. Extreme cold can damage a PC by forming ice on the electronic circuits that can later melt and create electrical shorts. PCs have a normal operating temperature range outside of which, hot or cold, the system can be damaged.

In some environments, dust, debris, and other effluents that can be in the air of the space in which a PC is installed can pose a serious threat to the PC and its internal components. On some newer computer cases, one or more of the cooling fans are intake fans that can bring airborne particles inside the system case. Dust can clog up the fan and coat the motherboard and its components. Minute metal particles can create electrical shorts, a buildup of static electricity, and other electrical problems inside the system case.

Another environmental issue that is often overlooked is humidity. Computers are designed to operate in moderately humid environments. In a very humid environment, a computer can condense moisture from the air that can cause serious damage to the PC's electronics, since water is an excellent electrical conductor. In dry environments, static electricity can build up on a PC's electronics and cause serious damage to these components. In fact, in a dry environment, the user poses a major threat to the system simply because he or she can build up a static electricity charge and inadvertently discharge it to the PC. This threat, known as electrostatic discharge (ESD), is perhaps one of the more common threats to the PC.

How to Protect Computer Hardware from Power Issues

1.2.3   Identify how to protect computer hardware from fluctuations in the power supply, power outages and other electrical issues (such as use of computers on different electrical systems).

One of the main threats to a computer system can be the very thing it must have to operate, electrical power. The electrical power available to homes and businesses can damage the electronic circuits of a computer slowly over time unless some relatively simple steps are taken to protect the system.

Electrical Supply Hazards

Perhaps the PC's biggest enemy is the electricity it gets from the public power system. The public power system is an imperfect source of electricity that has intermittent periods of high, low, or no voltage. High-voltage periods, called over-voltage spikes, or surges, can burn up a PC's power supply and maybe even the motherboard and anything attached to it. Low-voltage periods, called under-voltage and brownouts, can damage the power supply and other parts of the PC. A sudden loss of power, a blackout, can cause the loss of data and processing time.

Electrical power fluctuations can cause catastrophic damage or degradation to a PC. Catastrophic damage occurs when a component or device is destroyed by a single event, such as a direct lightning strike on a building. Degradation occurs when a device is damaged slowly over a period of time. Catastrophic failures are very serious, but most of the damage done to a PC is through degradation, which can be the result of small electrical events over an extended period of time.

Common Electrical Events

Six general types of electrical events occur on an electrical power line and reach your PC:

- Electromagnetic interference (EMI)/radio frequency interference (RFI)
- Power surges
- Power spikes

- Power sags
- Brownouts
- Blackouts

Each of these events has its own varying level of impact on a PC, but the PC can be protected from each successfully. It's mostly a matter of how much you want to spend to protect your system.

The PC component that takes the brunt of electrical power events is the PC's power supply. The power supply receives the alternating current (AC) of the electrical source and converts it to direct current (DC) for use within the electronic components of the PC. The electrical power source is typically either 120 volts AC (VAC) or 220 VAC, and the internal components use from 1.5 VDC to 18 VDC. Fluctuations on the AC power source can be passed through to the PC electronics, causing immediate destruction or accumulating damage.

EMI and RFI   Every electrical circuit has a certain amount of electrical line noise, which is more commonly referred to as *electromagnetic interference (EMI)*. EMI is caused by a variety of sources, both in nature and electrical equipment. For the most part, EMI in a home or business comes from other electrical equipment, such as electrical motors, fluorescent lighting, or perhaps a nearby radio transmitter. An electrical supply line that is shared with other electrical equipment very often carries a significant amount of electrical noise (a power stream that radically fluctuates on the line over and above the normal electrical stream) over the power line to other devices connected to the same electrical circuit. An example is the noise you hear or see on an AM radio or the TV set when a vacuum cleaner is operated on the same electrical circuit. The static you hear is electrical noise. Nature can also cause EMI; a nearby electrical storm can be picked up by the electric supply and transmit EMI over the power lines of a building.

Nearly all PC power supplies are built to handle a certain amount of EMI, but excessive levels of EMI can pass through the power supply to the motherboard, disk drives, and other internal components of a PC. The problems that can develop from EMI and electrical line noise include memory errors, data loss, circuit connection loss, data transmission problems, and frequent system lockups.

Another closely related interference that can cause damage to a PC is *radio frequency interference (RFI)*. Exposure to a strong radio frequency (RF) broadcast, such as from a very close television or radio transmission tower, can result in damage to the electrical components of a PC as they absorb the energy field of the RFI. RFI can also be absorbed by the electrical power lines and create fluctuations on the power line similar to those caused by EMI.

Power Surges   The nominal voltage of the AC electrical outlets in a home or business throughout North America is 110 volts. However, the actual voltage can vary between 85 and 135 volts, and most PC power supplies have a strong enough operating range to handle power fluctuations within that range. Systems designed to operate on 220 volts AC (outside of North America), including those that can be switched between 110 volt service and 220 volt service, typically have an operating range of 180 to 270 volts AC.

Certain electrical disturbances, such as a lightning storm, distant lightning strikes, or problems on the electrical power supply grid (such as a major factory shutting down all at once or a sudden drop in the load on the supply lines), can cause the line voltage to suddenly increase. This sharp increase in voltage is called an over-voltage event, which is commonly known as a power *surge*. A surge is a short and temporary increase of voltage on the power grid that is something like a rogue wave of electricity that can raise the voltage on the line to as much as 1,000 volts. While a surge typically lasts for only few thousandths of a second, that's plenty of time to damage anything in its path. Power surges are also very common when the power returns from a power outage.

PC power supplies are designed to withstand a certain number of voltage surges. However, even the best power supply will degrade a bit from each surge it suffers and begin to lose its capability to withstand surges until it either fails or starts passing the surge on to internal PC devices. It is also common for power surges to happen in clusters or swarms, which can be fatal for an unprotected system.

Power Spikes   A power *spike* is a sudden, isolated, extremely high over-voltage event on an electrical line. The primary cause of a power spike is lightning striking within a few miles. Lightning carries millions of volts, and if a home or office takes a direct hit, a PC, along with all of the other electrical devices in the building, is very likely to be heavily damaged. Lightning directly striking a building is a fairly rare event, but a strike within several miles can create a sudden spike in the electrical currents near the strike. This means that any wires or cables in the area can pick up an electrical spike and pass it to whatever is connected to it. The wire or cable could be a power cable on a PC, a telephone wire, the electricity lines to a house or building, and so on.

Power Sags   Sudden demands for power on the power grid can create a wave of low voltage on the electrical supply system, which is called a *sag* or a *dip*. As the name suggests, a power sag is the opposite of a power surge—it's a temporary dip in the voltage on the supply line that usually lasts only a fraction of a second. Power sags that extend below the normal operating voltage range of a system are rare, but they can happen.

The components of a PC are not designed to operate at very low voltages, even for a very short time. The PC's power supply has some power in reserve to pull up short power sags, but a series of power sags in a short time can affect the power supply's ability to provide the correct voltages to internal PC components and can weaken, damage, or destroy them.

Brownouts   When the demand for electrical power exceeds the capability of the electrical supply system, the result is reduced voltage for everyone, or what is called a *brownout*. A brownout is meant to indicate that while there is enough power on the grid to prevent a blackout, or a total loss of power, there isn't enough power to meet the current electrical demand. Brownouts frequently occur during extreme weather conditions, such as a sudden abnormally cold or hot spell, when everyone is running their heat or air conditioning.

A brownout occurs when the voltage on the electrical grid is less than 105 volts AC for an extended time, which could be minutes or hours. A brownout strains the PC in the same way as a power sag, but because a brownout lasts longer, the result can be immediate failure of some components, a burned-out power supply, or in an extreme case, the corruption or loss of data. Unfortunately, brownouts are a tool employed by the power companies to shift supply around the grid to meet the demands in specific areas on a rolling basis, or what are called rolling brownouts.

The damage caused by a brownout to a PC is often not noticeable right away. However, the strain on a PC's components accumulates and eventually results in a failure that is nearly impossible to troubleshoot. Brownouts are far harder on computer equipment than blackouts.

Blackouts   A *blackout* is a complete loss of a PC's electrical source. Typically, you think of a blackout as a failure of the power supply grid over an entire area, but a blackout can occur in just a part of a building, an entire building, a block, a section of a city, or an even larger area. A blackout event is a sudden complete drop-off of the power source, which can cause a wide range of problems on a PC or a network. At minimum, all of the data in RAM is usually lost, but depending on the applications or utilities running on the PC, much worse could happen.

Blackouts are caused by electrical storms; traffic accidents involving utility poles; the electrical utility company being unable to meet user demands; or a total collapse of the power system due to demand overload.

In addition to a blackout, a series of surges and spikes can occur both before and after the blackout event. The damage to a PC is not only from the power failing but from the power surge on the power supply system when the power is restored.

Protecting Against Power Problems

There are several devices you can use to protect your PC and its peripheral devices. At the low-end range in cost are plug strips that include a fuse, and on the extremely high end are standby generators and line conditioners. Most people protect individual PCs with products toward the lower end of the cost scale, and enterprise networks and Internet service providers (ISPs) tend to implement more expensive power protection equipment.

The power protection equipment used in a home or small office doesn't need to be very sophisticated or costly to provide the level of protection required for most situations. Depending on a number of factors, such as the quality and reliability of the local electrical service, most PCs can usually get by with surge protection or a small uninterruptible power supply (UPS).

Power protection equipment must be viewed as an insurance policy against the almost certain power-related problems on your PC. The cost of the lowest-end protection is usually less than $20, which is a small price to pay to protect your investment in your PC, printer, and other peripheral devices.

Surge Suppressors   The most commonly used power protection device is a *surge suppressor*. This device, which provides protection that ranges from mostly psychological to good, is generally available and sold in virtually any store that also sells extension cords, including drug, grocery, hardware, and computer stores.

A surge suppressor, like the one shown in Figure 3-2, uses a component called a metal-oxide varistor (MOV) to suppress power surges on the electrical line. Anytime the voltage gets above a specified level, even if only for a millionth of a second, the MOV redirects the current to the ground circuit and not to the devices plugged into the suppressor. The specified level of the surge or spike that the varistor can handle is somewhat limited (a surge suppressor is not designed to handle the surge caused by a lightning strike), and if the voltage level is exceeded, the MOV is destroyed. Following a major electrical event, a surge suppressor can become only an expensive plug strip and all spikes and surges are passed on to the PC's power supply.

A good selection of surge suppressor strips is available that provide some level of protection. However, after any severe power event, such as lightning nearby or a power surge strong enough to affect your house or office lighting, be sure to check its fuse or circuit breaker for damage.

FIGURE 3-2

A high-end surge suppressor also includes line conditioning capabilities. (Photo courtesy of American Power Conversion Corporation.)

Surge suppressors that also include some line conditioning capabilities provide good overall protection. Line conditioning smoothes out EMI and other electrical noise on a circuit, but not all surge suppressors include line conditioning. No surge suppressor includes the level of line conditioning performed by a separate line conditioning unit, but a high-end surge suppressor should be able to handle most of the normal line noise that can be found on virtually every electrical line.

A surge suppressor is rated by the amount of energy it absorbs, which is stated in a quantity of joules. The higher the number of joules the surge suppressor is rated at, the better the unit. The rule of thumb is that 200 joules is the minimum protection, 400 joules is average protection, and 600 or more is excellent protection.

Line Conditioners   *Line conditioners*, also called power conditioners, filter the electrical stream to control surges and spikes and to eliminate any line electrical noise on the line. Because they are typically expensive, few PC users use a true line conditioner; most use the line conditioning capabilities of a surge suppressor or UPS instead. Most line conditioners also provide surge suppression, but they are not designed to provide standby power like a UPS (see the next section, "Uninterruptible Power Supply (UPS)").

EMI, RFI, and electric motor noise are the primary electrical interferences from which you need to protect your PC. If there is an excessive amount of electrical noise on the power supply, you can often hear it on a TV, radio, or stereo. The good news is that nearly all surge suppressors and UPS units filter out certain levels of line noise. However, if your system is located near a generator or compressor, like those found in a soda pop vending machine, it is unlikely that your surge suppressor or UPS is able to filter all of the electrical noise on the circuit, unless it is a very high-end model. In this environment, it may be wise to invest in a line conditioner and use it in place of a surge suppressor to protect your PC and peripheral devices.

Uninterruptible Power Supply (UPS)   Although its name perhaps promises more than the unit is actually able to deliver, an *uninterruptible power supply (UPS)* is designed to provide a number of power-related services to the devices connected to it:

- **Power source**   The UPS unit is placed between the devices you wish to protect from blackouts, brownouts, and other power line events and the electrical outlet from the normal AC electrical service.
- **Line conditioning**   Virtually all but the very least expensive UPS units provide line conditioning to filter line noise from the electrical supply.
- **Surge suppression**   UPS units provide protection from power surges and spikes on the electrical line.
- **Brownout and sag protection**   UPS units fill in the power loss during a power sag or a brownout. Most UPS units cannot make up the power loss of a brownout indefinitely, but unless the brownout is severe they can replace most of the power loss for a short period.
- **Backup power**   The primary purpose of a UPS is to provide backup electricity to the devices plugged into it for a certain amount of time.

The basic design of a UPS consists of an incoming AC power source, an electronic switch that detects the incoming power level, a battery that is constantly being recharged for use should the power source fail, and an AC outlet into which the power cord of a PC or a peripheral device can be connected.

There are three basic UPS technologies used to protect against or solve different types of power issues:

- **Standby power supply (SPS)**   An SPS is a pass-through unit that remains inactive until the power fails. It shares the incoming power with its devices to charge its batteries, and as long as the electrical power source is available, power is passed through the unit to its outlets and the devices plugged into them. Because of their lower cost, SPS units are often used to protect desktop workstations.
- **Line-interactive UPS**   A line-interactive UPS unit is well suited to environments where surges, spikes, or sags are common but few brownouts and blackouts occur. When the power supply is available, the line-interactive UPS provides line conditioning and produces a steady level of output voltage from a fluctuating input voltage level. This type of UPS also provides good protection from EMI, RFI, and other forms of line noise.

■ **Online UPS** This type of UPS provides all of the services of a surge suppressor, a line conditioner, and a battery backup in a single package. Online UPS units provide the best protection of all of the UPS technologies but also cost more than the other technologies. An online UPS continuously supplies a near-perfect DC power stream from an AC-to-DC power inverter. An online UPS handles over- and under-voltage events without using its battery.

CERTIFICATION SUMMARY

This chapter covered the physical risks and threats to a computer, including

■ Theft or malicious damage
■ Environmental issues
■ Electrical power risks

Some of this information is relatively common sense, but be sure you understand the threats and preventive measures that can be used to protect a computer from electrical power problems.

TWO-MINUTE DRILL

Protecting Computer Hardware from Theft or Damage

❑ To secure a PC, its components, peripherals, and contents, begin with the physical security of the area in which the PC sits. Limiting who has access and physically restricting the portability of the PC is the first line of defense in any security scheme.

❑ A computer can have a lock attached to protect it from theft or improper use. Many PCs have a key lock that locks the system and prevents anyone from using the keyboard or mouse. Cable locks can also be attached to the computer case to secure it to the table or desk on which it sits.

❑ BIOS locks and software locks can protect a PC from unauthorized access or maliciousness. A BIOS lock is the lowest-level software protection on a PC and is engaged as a password assigned to the BIOS System Setup.

❑ On a Windows XP or Windows Vista system, the system is locked by pressing the WINDOWS logo key on a Windows keyboard and the L (lock) key. On these systems, you can enter a command in the Start | Run box to lock the system.

Factors That Can Damage a Computer

❑ The environment of a PC can pose a threat to its electronics, stored data, and longevity. Smoke and fire are serious threats to a PC: the heat of a fire; the water, foam, or other fire suppressants; and the smoke and tiny particles of burnt material can damage or corrupt the system.

❑ Dust, debris, and other effluents that can be in the air pose a threat to a PC and its internal components because the cooling fan brings airborne particles inside the system case. Dust can clog up the fan and coat the motherboard and its components. Minute metal particles can create electrical shorts, a buildup of static electricity, and other electrical problems inside the system case.

❑ In a humid environment, a computer can condense moisture from the air that can cause serious damage to the PC's electronics, since water is an excellent electrical conductor. In dry environments, static electricity can build up on a PC's electronics and cause serious damage to these components.

How to Protect Computer Hardware from Power Issues

❑ The public power system is an imperfect source of electricity that has intermittent periods of high, low, or no voltage. High-voltage periods, called over-voltage spikes, or surges, can burn up a PC's power supply and maybe even the motherboard and anything attached to it. Low-voltage periods, called under-voltage and brownouts, can cause catastrophic damage or degradation to a PC and its power supply.

❑ Six general types of electrical events occur on an electrical power line: EMI and RFI, power surges, power spikes, power sags, brownouts, and blackouts.

❑ EMI is caused by a variety of sources, both in nature and electrical equipment. EMI in a home or business comes from other electrical equipment, such as electrical motors, fluorescent lighting, or perhaps a nearby radio transmitter.

❑ RFI is caused by a strong RF broadcast in the immediate vicinity. RFI is absorbed by the electrical power lines and creates fluctuations on the power line.

❑ A lightning storm, a distant lightning strike, or issues on the electrical power supply grid can cause the line voltage to suddenly increase, causing an over-voltage event or power surge. A surge is a short and temporary increase of voltage on the power grid that can raise the voltage on the line to as much as 1,000 volts. A power spike is a sudden, isolated, extremely high over-voltage event on an electrical line. A power sag is a temporary dip in the voltage on the supply line that usually lasts only a fraction of a second.

❑ A brownout occurs when demand for electrical power exceeds the capability of the electrical supply system and the voltage of the system is reduced. A blackout is a total loss of power on the electrical supply system.

❑ Several devices can be used to protect your PC and its peripheral devices: a surge suppressor that includes an MOV to suppress power surges on the electrical line; a line conditioner that filters the electrical stream to control surges and spikes and to eliminate any line electrical noise; and a UPS that protects against blackouts, brownouts, and other events.

SELF TEST

The following questions are intended to help you be sure that you understand the material included in this chapter. Read the questions and the answer choices carefully.

Protecting Computer Hardware from Theft or Damage

1. What is the first step that should be taken to secure a PC, its components, peripherals, and contents?
   A. Physical security
   B. Software security
   C. Network security
   D. Fire protection

2. To limit the portability of a desktop or notebook computer, what device can be installed and attached to the computer?
   A. Bezel lock
   B. Cable lock
   C. Biometric access
   D. Infrared motion detector

3. Which of the following provides the lowest-level software lock on a PC?
   A. Document password
   B. Login password
   C. BIOS password
   D. Network password

4. Which of the following options can be used on a Windows XP or Windows Vista system to lock the system?
   A. CTRL-ALT-DEL
   B. WINDOWS logo key and L
   C. rundll32.exe user32.dll, LockWorkStation
   D. Start Run Lockup

Factors That Can Damage a Computer

5. Which of the following can pose a threat to or damage a PC?
   A. Smoke and fire
   B. Airborne effluents
   C. High or low humidity
   D. All of the above

6. Airborne effluents can include which of the following?
   A. Dust
   B. Airborne particles
   C. Chemical mist
   D. All of the above

7. What environmental condition(s) can potentially damage a PC system when it exists in a high or low extreme?
   A. Humidity
   B. Heat/Cold
   C. Static electricity
   D. Air flow

How to Protect Computer Hardware from Power Issues

8. What is/are the common name(s) of an over-voltage electrical event?
   A. Brownout
   B. Blackout
   C. Power surge
   D. Power spike

9. Line noise on an electrical line is most likely caused by
   A. EMI or RFI
   B. Electrical equipment on the same circuit
   C. Fluorescent lighting
   D. Under-demand for electricity on a circuit

10. An intentional reduction in voltage across an entire electrical grid is commonly known as a
    A. Blackout
    B. Brownout
    C. Power sag
    D. Power surge

11. Power protection devices that can be used with a PC to protect against electrical events include which of the following?
    A. Surge suppressor
    B. Line conditioner
    C. UPS
    D. All of the above

SELF TEST ANSWERS

Protecting Computer Hardware from Theft or Damage

1. ☑ **A.** Securing the room and the environment in which a PC is located is the first step that should be taken to protect the PC.

☒ **B, C,** and **D** are incorrect. Software security provides protection, but only if access to the PC is limited typically. Network security is typically not a local station issue. Fire protection is part of the physical security of a space, so while it is partially correct, **D** is not the best answer.

2. ☑ **B.** A cable lock can be affixed to the case of a computer and locked to secure it to a table or desktop.

☒ **A, C,** and **D** are incorrect. A bezel lock typically only locks out the keyboard and mouse. A biometric access device can be used to gain access to a PC, but it cannot, on its own, limit the portability of the PC. An IR motion detector may be used to secure a room but really can't do much to limit the mobility of a PC.

3. ☑ **C.** Setting a password on the BIOS system setup provides the lowest-level software lock to a PC.

☒ **A, B,** and **D** are incorrect. Passwords on individual documents and those used to gain access to the PC or the network it's connected to can provide protection, but at a higher level.

4. ☑ **A, B,** and **C.** These are options that can be used to lock a PC system.

☒ **D** is incorrect. There is no "Lockup" command on a Windows system.

Factors That Can Damage a Computer

5. ☑ **D.** Answers A, B, and C are each a protection threat to a PC.

☒ **A, B,** and **C** are incorrect. All of those answers are included in D.

6. ☑ **D.** Dust, airborne particles, and any chemical effluents in the air can potentially damage or destroy a PC.

☒ **A, B,** and **C** are incorrect. These answers are included in D.

7. ☑ **A, B,** and **C.** Humidity, heat, cold, and static electricity are all potential threats to a PC. High humidity can create moisture, extreme heat or cold can damage the electronic circuits, and static electricity can degrade or destroy components.

☒ **D** is incorrect. Air flow is a necessity for the PC and its cooling system.

How to Protect Computer Hardware from Power Issues

8. ☑ **C and D.** Over-voltage can take the form of a power surge or a power spike.

    ☒ **A** and **B** are incorrect. Brownouts and blackouts are types of under-voltage events.

9. ☑ **A, B,** and **C.** Line noise is caused by EMI, RFI, electrical motors, and fluorescent lighting, among other causes.

    ☒ **D** is incorrect. Reduced demand for electricity doesn't cause line noise or any other electrical event directly.

10. ☑ **B.** When the voltage on a power grid is intentionally reduced, a brownout occurs.

    ☒ **A, C,** and **D** are incorrect. A blackout is a total loss of power; a power sag is a short reduction in voltage that occurs inadvertently; and a power surge is a short-term over-voltage event.

11. ☑ **D.** The devices listed in A, B, and C are power protection devices that can be used to protect a PC against electrical events.

    ☒ **A, B,** and **C** are incorrect. These answers are covered by D.

4

Maintaining and Troubleshooting Computer Systems

When a PC starts to malfunction, the source of the problem may not always be obvious. If the problem is with a mouse or keyboard, resolving the problem can be as easy as installing a new one. However, if the hard disk drive is intermittently producing read or write errors, the problem could be in the hard disk, power supply, memory, motherboard, cables, or software. Troubleshooting is the process used to isolate and identify the source of a PC problem, and that's what this chapter is all about.

For the IC³ exam, you need to know the processes used to troubleshoot and diagnose a problem on a PC, and not just hardware problems. Many of the more commonly occurring problems on a PC are software-related, which can be easily solved by reconfiguring or reinstalling the software. However, some problems can appear to be software issues initially but may actually be caused by hardware incompatibilities with the software installed.

No magic formula exists for solving all of the problems that can occur on a PC, but the general troubleshooting procedure can be used to isolate the cause of a problem. This chapter outlines the troubleshooting procedure and includes some helpful tips and hints that can make troubleshooting more effective and efficient.

CERTIFICATION OBJECTIVE

Common Hardware-Related PC Problems

1.2.4   Identify common problems associated with computer hardware.

Hardware problems are uncommon on new computer systems. What appears to be a hardware problem is most likely to occur immediately after a change has been made to the system, such as installing new hardware devices, installing new software, or making changes to the hardware or software configuration.

There are hardware-related problems that occur, unfortunately, on a fairly regular basis, especially to new computer users. Luckily, none of these problems are especially hard to correct. The more common of these problems are

- **Electrical power source**   Electrical connections are typically the source of the problem when a computer won't power up. In this situation, the first troubleshooting question that should be asked or the first thing that should be checked is whether or not the PC's power cord is snugly connected to the back of the PC and into a working AC power outlet. This problem can also happen with monitors, printers, or any other external peripheral device that plugs directly into a power source. If the power cord is plugged into a plug strip or a surge suppression strip, be sure that the strip itself is turned on.

- **On/off switch** Even computers that are left powered up all of the time can occasionally be powered off by a power failure, by an incomplete reboot after an automatic update, or by someone other than the primary user. Users who are used to the PC being on all the time may not think to check the power buttons on a PC or peripheral to see if they are switched on.

- **Device connections** In addition to or in place of their power connections, just about every installable device in a PC has some form of a communications, data, or command connection. If a device is failing to operate properly, check the connections on the device, such as the video cable on a monitor, the cable on a printer, or the data cable on an internal device.

- **Device configuration** If a newly installed device isn't working as it should, ensure that the device was properly configured using the installation or configuration disc that came with the device. Some devices—although this is fairly rare on most new devices—may have jumpers or switches that need to be set to the proper settings for compatibility with your hardware or operating system. On a Windows system, you may need to check the device's compatibility in the Device Manager.

- **Device drivers** It is likely that the default Windows driver for a device or the device driver that was shipped with the device (on the installation disk) is not the latest version available. If a device isn't working properly, check on the manufacturer's Web site for an updated device driver for the device.

CERTIFICATION OBJECTIVE

Hardware Issues Caused by Poor Maintenance

1.2.5   Identify problems that can occur if hardware is not maintained properly.

A regular scheme of preventive maintenance is recommended to keep a computer working properly and efficiently. If preventive maintenance is not performed regularly, some devices and components of a computer system can develop performance issues or fail.

Above all else, cleanliness is the best prevention for hardware problems followed closely by a regular preventive maintenance program. If a computer is not properly maintained, a variety of hardware issues, which can translate into what may appear to be software issues, can develop. The more common hardware issues that can develop as a result of poor maintenance procedures are

- **Poor system case cooling and ventilation**   Dust and debris can be pulled into the system case by the power supply fan and in particularly dirty areas. The accumulation of dust and other airborne particles on the internal components of a PC can degrade the effectiveness of the air flow inside the system case to properly cool these components. Heat can be destructive to the electronic components inside the PC if they are subjected to high temperatures for extended periods. In addition, dust and other particles can store static electricity or create a circuit issue that could degrade or destroy motherboard components.

- **Slow hard disk performance**   The hard disk drives should be regularly maintained to keep their performance up. This maintenance should include regular defragmentation, virus scanning, and operation checks. It's recommended that hard disks be defragged weekly or as needed. The disk should be scanned for read errors on a weekly basis. Unused or unnecessary files should be removed to keep adequate space available on the drives. Virus scanning software should be used daily to ensure that the system doesn't become infected. The disks should be checked quarterly, or anytime the system case is open, for unusual vibrations or operating temperatures.

- **Power supply degradation**   Surge suppressors and UPS devices should be checked weekly, or immediately after a severe electrical event, to ensure they are properly protecting the PC and its power supply.

- **Keyboard and mouse issues**   The keyboard and mouse should be cleaned quarterly to prevent the buildup of dust and other particles from degrading their performance.

- **Printer issues**   Printers must be regularly cleaned to avoid paper jams and toner or ink smears on printed pages. Small bits of paper, dust, and perhaps other debris can accumulate in the paper feed area and cause paper to misfeed or jam. Ink or toner can build up on the print head or on the drum of a laser printer, which can then smear onto pages being printed. Virtually every printer comes with a cleaning and maintenance guide to help prevent these problems.

CERTIFICATION OBJECTIVE

Preventive Maintenance by Users

1.2.6   Identify maintenance that can be performed routinely by users.

Many of the maintenance processes listed in the preceding sections should be performed as a part of a regular preventive maintenance program by a PC's user. Depending on the skill and knowledge of the user, some of the processes that require the system case to be opened should likely be performed by a computer technician.

The preventive maintenance processes that can be performed by a PC's user include much of the cleaning, checking, and scanning activities. The specific actions that a user can perform to keep the PC operating properly are

- **Virus scanning**   Most virus protection software can be configured to run a complete virus scan of a PC on a regular basis. While daily scanning is recommended, the system should be scanned completely at least once per week.

- **Cleaning the PC exterior**   Depending on the environment of the PC, the monitor screen, the exterior of the system case (especially its vents), and the keyboard and mouse should be cleaned at least once a month. Care should be taken not to use excessive liquid to avoid getting the electronics wet.

- **Disk drive scanning**   The hard disk drives should be scanned for read errors, using disk utility software or the CHKDSK command, each time the PC is started up, and the drives should be defragged at least once per week.

- **Power protection checks**   Surge suppressors and UPS units should be checked to ensure that their fuses, MOVs, and readiness are intact. Some of the higher-end UPS units provide diagnostic software that can be used to check the UPS's readiness.

- **Replacing or upgrading broken or expended components**   There are several components of a PC and its peripherals that regularly require replacement: empty printer ink or toner cartridges, keyboards with sticking keys or missing key caps, or mouse units. Memory should be upgraded, when appropriate, to maintain PC performance.

CERTIFICATION OBJECTIVE

Maintenance by Computer Professionals

1.2.7 Identify maintenance that should ONLY be performed by experienced professionals, including replacing or upgrading internal hardware (especially electrical) components (such as processors or drives) that are not designed to be user accessible.

There are some devices and components on a PC that a user should never attempt to maintain, including the internal components of a monitor, the power supply, the microprocessor, memory, and the electrical connections inside the system case.

Unless a user has the knowledge, training, and experience at the level of a computer technician, it's highly recommended that certain maintenance activities be performed only by a professional. While the voltages at which a PC operates internally aren't especially high, the risks for harm to both the user and the PC are much too high. An untrained or unsuspecting user could innocently fry an internal component of a PC with only the ambient amount of electrostatic discharge (ESD) he or she has stored from just walking across a carpet.

For these reasons and to ensure that the internal components of the PC and its peripherals continue to operate properly, only a professional computer technician should perform certain maintenance tasks:

- **Cleaning inside the system case**   This involves special equipment, such as non-static-generating vacuum cleaners, compressed air, and ESD protection straps.

- **Checking cables and expansion cards inside the system case**   The communications, power, and data cables that connect internal devices to expansion cards or the motherboard often have specific connection patterns that should be checked only by a PC professional. Expansion cards can become unseated and should be checked and reseated, if needed.

- **Checking or replacing the power supply**   The power supply should never be opened, even by a computer professional. However, performance problems in many storage or peripheral devices could be caused by power supply problems. A computer technician can check the power output of the power supply and, if required, replace the power supply.

- **Installation or major upgrades to components inside the system case** Replacing or upgrading storage devices, memory, a microprocessor, or a motherboard should only be performed by a computer professional in a location designed to protect the PC and its components.
- **Upgrading the BIOS** Many device problems may be linked to an out-of-date BIOS. Updating the BIOS should only be considered when the need is verified by a computer professional. The BIOS should only be upgraded to solve a specific (and documented) compatibility or performance issue on the PC.

CERTIFICATION OBJECTIVE

General Troubleshooting Steps

1.2.8 Identify the steps required to solve computer-related problems.

General PC troubleshooting involves a five-step process that seeks to identify, replicate, evaluate, diagnose, and resolve computer-related problems. Working through this sequence of steps provides you with a structured approached to finding and fixing a computer problem.

The general troubleshooting steps that should be used to identify and resolve computer problems are

- Identify the symptoms of the problem.
- Replicate the problem.
- Evaluate all possible causes for the problem.
- Diagnose each of the possible causes and isolate the likely cause.
- Apply a correction, configuration, repair, or replacement to solve the problem.

Using these steps as a general guide makes sure that the problem that is occurring is fully understood and that all possible causes and remedies are considered. In the sections that follow, the specific troubleshooting steps that should be followed are outlined.

General Troubleshooting Questions

A written record of past problems, troubleshooting, installations, upgrades, and repairs that have been made on a PC can be a valuable source of information, if for no other reason than to let you know that a problem has happened before and what was done to troubleshoot it. This record could be only a notebook or copies of past trouble tickets that show the activities of each troubleshooting or repair action taken in the past. The maintenance log can come in handy when dealing with warranty issues.

The information in the maintenance log can help you to answer a number of troubleshooting questions, such as

- **When did the problem first happen?** It is important to note when a problem happens: during the boot or startup, when the PC is up and running, or during shutdown.

- **Is this the first time this problem has happened?** If a problem has happened before, is there anything different about it this time?

- **What activity was being performed when the problem first showed up?** The problem could be caused by a particular application or file.

- **Can you re-create the problem?** As any PC user knows, sometimes stuff just happens that never shows up again. If you are unable to re-create a problem, make a note of it, just in case it does happen again in the future.

- **Did you add hardware or software to the PC right before the problem appeared?** This is when most problems occur. If you have just added new hardware or software, you can be sure the problem is related to this action in some way. Even if everything to do with the new hardware component or software program is perfect, you may have inadvertently dislodged a connector or power cable or installed a different version of a system file used by other software.

- **Is anything happening in the environment?** It may be, for example, a blackout, brownout, or lightning storms.

- **Did smoke come out of the PC or monitor?** If the answer is yes, it probably will not be difficult to find the problem. If the smoke came from the monitor, especially a CRT monitor, take it to a repair shop. If the smoke came from inside the case, put on your ESD protection, open the case, and carefully examine the motherboard, power supply, and expansion cards for smoke or burned marks. If none are apparent, the best advice is to take it to a repair shop. Don't power it up again to see if you can re-create the smoke. You may just fry the next component down the line.

Power Supply Issues

Some problems, especially the electrical setup of a PC, are caused by the operating environment of the PC. Perhaps the best place to start troubleshooting an unidentified PC problem is at the power source. Here are some questions that you should answer to possibly identify the source of the problem:

- **Is the PC plugged in and switched on?** This may seem like a silly question, but it's not if it is really the problem.
- **What is the PC's power source?**
    - If the PC is plugged directly into a wall socket, is the electrical plug snugly connected at each end of the power cord?
    - If the PC is plugged into a UPS, check that the UPS is working properly. A bad UPS can do more harm than good.
- **How many devices are sharing the electrical supply?** It could be that too many devices are sharing a plug strip, surge suppressor, or UPS. If this is the situation, it may be likely that the damage is already done, but try removing a few devices from the power source to see if the problem goes away. If the problem persists, check out the power supply.

Problems with the power source will usually show up as power supply problems. The power supply is the cause for a majority of PC hardware problems. If the power supply begins going bad, it can pass along power surges, spikes, and low-voltage conditions directly to the devices connected to it.

Environmental Issues

Even when a PC is properly protected against power source issues, its environment can cause problems. The conditions in the PC's environment can strain its cooling system and eventually affect the power supply. As a part of your troubleshooting processes, check out the PC's environment by asking these questions:

- **Is the environment dust-free and otherwise clean?** Airborne dust and particles are pulled into the PC's case, where they accumulate on the fan, air grills, motherboard components, processor, and expansion cards and clog up the air flow, defeat the cooling system, and directly affect the functions of the internal devices.

■ **Is the environment humid or overly dry?** Too much humidity can cause moisture to condense inside the PC and cause electrical problems. If the air is too dry, static electricity can be produced, which can affect the operations of the electronics inside the system case.

Troubleshooting the CPU

If a computer professional determines that a PC's processor has failed, the only remedy is to replace it. However, most problems that appear to be processor problems are usually a problem with another component. What may show up as a processor problem is more likely a problem with the cooling of the processor or the system, the power supply, or a compatibility issue between the motherboard and chipset (which would show up immediately after the processor is upgraded).

Here are the most common symptoms that a processor is about to fail:

■ The PC will not boot.

■ The PC does boot but will not start the operating system.

■ The PC crashes during startup, and if it does boot, it crashes frequently when running applications.

■ The PC suddenly has parity error problems in many devices.

■ The PC locks up after a few minutes of operation.

If a PC boots without problems but consistently halts or freezes after only a few minutes of operation, it is likely that the processor is overheating and shutting itself down. To test for this condition, shut down the PC and power it off. After a few minutes (long enough for the processor to cool down), cold-start the PC. If the same problem occurs, it is likely the processor is not being cooled sufficiently. You may need to add a fan or heat sink to the processor or add supplemental cooling fans to the system case.

If you experience any of these symptoms, contact a computer professional to check the cooling on the processor and on the system, clean the inside of the case, and check the motherboard's power connection.

Troubleshooting Hard Disk Drives

When a hard disk error occurs, it is usually a cause for real concern. Not only will the PC not boot, but there is the threat that all your data and programs could be lost. A hard disk problem can be caused by the hard disk drive, the hard disk controller, a SCSI host adapter, cabling, and in many situations, the power supply.

There is always the risk when troubleshooting a hard disk drive that any data stored on it could be destroyed. This is why you should always create and verify a full backup of the hard disk before you begin to work. To verify a disk backup, restore a few random files from it. All of this assumes that you can access the disk drive to make a backup or to perform troubleshooting.

Common problems that may occur with a hard disk drive are

- **Drive jumpers**   The drive jumpers on the disk drive must be set appropriately, with at least one master and, if more drives are present, the others set as slaves or select.
- **The configuration is incorrect**   The BIOS's setup configuration is not consistent with what the boot process is finding. The BIOS configuration of each hard disk drive installed in the system should be verified and, if need be, corrected.
- **Hardware resource conflicts**   Resource conflict issues typically stem from an IRQ (interrupt request) conflict. The Windows Device Manager can be used to verify that a resource conflict has been created for the hard disk drive controllers by the installation of a new piece of hardware.
- **Boot partition is corrupted**   If the system files on the boot partition are corrupted, the system cannot boot properly. Use the SYS C: command (from a command-line prompt) to transfer the system files to the hard drive. If this doesn't solve the problem, use the ScanDisk command to check for media defects and file problems and then reformat the boot partition and reinstall the operating system. Also verify that the boot partition has not been accidentally removed.
- **The hard disk may have a virus infection**   Another reason the system may not be able to find a boot sector is that the boot disk is infected with a computer virus. Many viruses can corrupt the master boot record on the hard drive and cause errors that show up as hard disk errors. If an antivirus program is not installed on the PC, install one and scan the hard disk.
- **The hard disk cable may be bad or not connected properly**   If a message displays during the boot process that is along the lines of "No hard disk," the hard disk is not installed incorrectly. If the front panel hard drive light stays on constantly, the drive data cable is not properly connected. Both ends of the data cable should be checked, as well as power supply connectors.

Troubleshooting Memory

Typically three general types of memory (RAM) problems on a PC require troubleshooting, and for the most part, these problems happen just after new memory has been installed. Memory problems also occur because of electrical problems on the motherboard. Troubleshooting memory problems is complicated because many devices can demonstrate symptoms that appear to be memory problems. If a PC appears to be having memory problems, the following should be checked:

- **Configuration**   If you have just added new or additional memory to a PC, the amount of memory installed may be more than the PC or operating system is able to support, or the BIOS settings may be incorrect.
- **Hardware**   All of the memory installed must be compatible and installed in complete banks. If slower memory is installed in one bank, all of the memory will operate at the slower speed. The problem could also be that at least one memory module is defective.
- **Installation**   Most memory problems are caused by the memory modules that are improperly installed. It could also be that a socket is bad, has a bent or broken lead, or just needs cleaning.

Knowing when a memory problem happens is very valuable information. A memory problem that happens during startup is a much different problem than one that happens while an application is running, and each is resolved quite differently. Memory problems can occur in these situations:

- **The first time a new PC is started**   This common problem is caused by the rigors of shipping a PC. The memory module may need to be reseated. A problem that appears to be memory-related could also be a bad motherboard. Check with the manufacturer or the vendor.
- **Immediately after new memory is installed**   Check the part numbers and speed of both the new and the old memory modules. You should also verify that the memory is appropriate for the motherboard, chipset, and processor.

Troubleshooting the Video System

Most video system problems are easily detected because they are visual and show up on the monitor. While the monitor can have problems itself, the video card is the cause of most video problems. When troubleshooting a video system, remember that no matter how high-end the video card may be, its performance is limited by the capabilities of the monitor.

- **Dark screen**   If the screen is blank or dark, check that the monitor is plugged into a power source, the power cord is connected to the monitor, and the monitor cable is connected to the PC. Many monitors use a double-ended VGA cable that has an HD-15 connector at the monitor end as well as the video card end. If the cables are okay, reseat the video card.
- **Video configuration**   The most common video problems are caused by the refresh rate, resolution, and color depth settings in the operating system. These problems are easily solved through the Display Properties on Windows systems.
- **Monitor compatibility**   If the monitor's display is scrambled, is distorted, or has multiple layers of the same images, the monitor is unable to handle the video card's output. Check the documentation for the monitor and the video card to determine the recommended color depth, resolution, and refresh rate settings.
- **Device driver**   The device driver provided by Windows or the driver shipped with a video card may be out-of-date. Visit the manufacturer's Web site for a current device driver for the video card.

Troubleshooting the Power Supply

A weak or faulty power supply can create a number of problems for the peripheral devices installed inside the system unit, especially the motherboard and disk drives. Unexplained or intermittent memory or hard disk errors are commonly caused by a faulty or failing power supply.

To troubleshoot a PC's power supply, each of the power connectors should be checked for their proper voltages using a multimeter. Check the power supply's documentation for information on the proper voltage levels of the connectors. If the power supply is not providing the correct voltage levels, the power supply should be replaced.

Troubleshooting the Sound System

It can be very difficult to isolate the source of a sound system problem. Here are some troubleshooting steps to use to track down an audio problem:

- **Resource conflicts**   Determine if there are resource conflicts between the sound controller and other devices. If a conflict exists, reassign the conflicting device or the sound card. The most common conflict is an IRQ.

■ **Speakers** Troubleshooting speakers is a fairly straightforward process:

1. Make sure the speakers are plugged into the correct jack on the sound connectors. Match up the color-coded plugs to the jacks or look carefully at the little pictures on the jacks.

2. Make sure the volume is set properly in the operating system and on the speakers.

3. Make sure that the speaker wires are not crimped or broken and that all of the jacks are seated in the appropriate plugs.

■ **Device drivers** Sound systems are completely dependent on their device drivers. Verify that the latest version of the sound system's device driver is installed by checking the manufacturer's Web site.

CERTIFICATION OBJECTIVE

Buying, Maintaining, and Repairing a Computer

1.2.9 Identify consumer issues related to buying, maintaining, and repairing a computer.

When purchasing a computer or choosing the best products or computer professionals to maintain or repair a PC, there are some issues that should be considered to ensure that you get what you need and the assurance that your choices prove to be dependable, reliable, and competent.

Purchasing a PC

Much like buying a car, a house, or any other major purchase, the more information you have, the more you're likely to buy the system you need or desire. There are myriad choices available, and it's hard to know exactly which combination of components is right for your needs and budget. The following sections discuss each of the major features or components that should be considered when purchasing a PC.

CPUs

Computer manufacturers, with the exception of Apple Computer, list the processor as the first and foremost component of a computer system. The make, model, and speed of the processor are right out front and used to identify the computer and its general capabilities. To know when a computer system is appropriate to your needs, state-of-the-art, and reliable, you need to understand that there are generally three categories of computers available, each categorized by their processors.

Older-Generation Processors   You can find many PC systems available, both in stores and online, that have a processor that is an older processor model or version from any of the major microprocessor manufacturers. Depending on what you plan to use the PC for, these processors may not have the processing features and speed you need. However, if your intended use for the PC is word processing or surfing the Web, these systems can be very budget-friendly.

Many of the discontinued processors, especially high-end processors, can provide more power for the dollar than the current budget processors at about the same price. So consider what the PC is to be used for and whether your applications can perform as needed with an older processor.

Examples of older-generation processors (at the time this was written) are the American Micro Devices (AMD) Athlon, Duron, Phenom, and Sempron; the Intel Celeron the Pentium 4, many of the early Core 2 Duo processors; and all VIA processors. The processors in this category are typically no longer in production. If you wish to check the currency of a processor, visit the manufacturer's Web site.

Budget Processors   A number of the processors still in production or approaching the end of their production life cycle can be very good bargains when their overall specifications are considered. The processors in this group typically cost more than the older-generation processors, but not that much more, while providing higher performance. Examples of the processors in this group are the AMD Phenom II, the Intel Core 2 Quad, and the Core i7.

High-End Processors   The processors in this category represent the highest performance and cost and generally have much higher speeds and processing power than the current group of budget processors. While the performance of these high-end processors can be as much as 50 percent better than the lower-end processors, their cost can be almost double. This cost differential translates directly into the overall cost of a PC system. The processors in this category are typically better suited for server applications or high-powered specialized workstations. The Intel Core 2 Extreme and the Core i7 Extreme processors fall into this category.

Memory

When it comes to memory on a new PC system, the memory technology is not nearly as important as the amount of memory installed in the PC. Today's operating systems and software applications require much more RAM. A PC with less than 2 gigabytes (GB) of memory may not be able to properly run the newest software releases; and more is always better.

Hard Disk Drives

Like memory, the purchasing consideration for the hard disk drive in a PC system is size. Speed can also be an issue, but most PCs available include the latest drive technologies (primarily SATA), so for most PC buyers, the amount of disk space is much more important. While it depends on what you plan to do with the PC, the hard disk drive on a new PC should have at least 500GB of storage space. And like memory, more is better, but you should pay for more only if you really need it.

CD/DVD Drives

CD drives have essentially gone the way of the floppy disk, having been replaced by DVD burners. However, when looking to purchase a PC system, you should verify that the DVD drive supports the full range of read and read/write format capabilities. Some DVD drives also provide support for dual-layer media.

Some high-end home theater and media center PC systems offer Blu-ray drives (read-only), which allows the PC to serve as the centerpiece of a high definition (HD) home theater setup.

Video Systems

For the most part, standard integrated video graphics are embedded into the chipset on the motherboard. However, if you wish to use the PC for games or high-end video that requires 3-D graphics, then you must request that a higher-end video graphics card be installed in the system or purchase it separately and install it yourself. Nearly all new PCs support video cards using the PCI-Express graphics standard, but some are also available that require an AGP interface.

Peripheral Interface Ports

The number and type of external connection ports on a PC can increase its flexibility for supporting new external devices you may wish to add at a later time. The PC should provide USB 2.0 ports and IEEE 1394 (FireWire) ports, along with a media card reader that has interface slots for a variety of compact flash and memory cards.

Video Displays

When purchasing a new PC system, be sure that the PC package includes a monitor. Many packaged systems are sold without a monitor as a price-point tactic to make the price of the system lower.

Although they are becoming scarce, there are still systems that offer CRT monitors at a much lower price than the flat-panel LCD monitors. Consider the amount of desktop space you have available, the video quality you need, and your budget when deciding on whether or not to purchase a CRT or LCD monitor, its size, and its quality.

Purchasing a Portable Computer

In addition to the considerations discussed in the preceding sections, when looking to purchase a laptop or notebook computer, there are a few additional considerations. The features and issues you should consider when shopping for a portable computer are

- **Cost** A portable computer of comparable features can cost nearly twice as much as a similar desktop PC. What you are purchasing is portability, convenience, and flexibility, so be sure it's worth it.

- **Portability** The key issues with the portability of a portable PC are its overall size and weight. A lighter portable PC can allow you more size, which translates to more display and a slightly bigger keyboard, but depending on the technology used for the PC's batteries, which translates directly to cost, you may want to trade off weight and size to cost.

- **Battery technology** The newest technology in laptop and notebook computer batteries is the Lithium-Ion (Li-On) battery, which provides a lighter, longer-lasting power source than its predecessors. However, there are still older batter technology systems on the market, such as nickel cadmium (NiCad), that are heavier, shorter-lived batteries. Try to avoid these systems if you can afford it.

- **Speed** If you require a certain level of processing power and speed from a portable PC, you may need to move to higher-end models to achieve it. Generally, a portable PC operates from 30 to 70 percent slower than a comparable desktop PC.

■ **Upgradeability** For the most part, portable computers cannot be upgraded as well as a desktop PC. Most of the core features of the system—video, sound, graphics, and the like—are embedded into the motherboard and chipset and cannot be upgraded. Some portable PCs do allow for memory and disk space upgrades, but these can be quite expensive. However, because virtually all portable PCs provide a good array for external interface ports, the system can be upgraded through external devices.

Disposing of Discarded Components

When you purchase a new PC or replace one of its components or peripherals, you shouldn't just toss the old equipment into the trash. PCs contain heavy metals, such as lead, gold, zinc, mercury, and more, which can contaminate the environment if merely tossed into a landfill. Guidelines and, in some cases, laws have been issued that recommend or require certain ways to dispose of computer equipment.

Most PC manufacturers support a recycling program for their equipment. In addition, many states now have designated computer recycling stations where old equipments can be taken to be safely disposed of or recycled. PC monitors are a particular problem because they contain a significant amount of lead. Check with your local waste management company or government agency for the proper way of disposing of unwanted computers, components, and peripherals.

on the
job *For more information on how to dispose of or recycle old computer equipment, visit the Computer Hope Web site at www.computerhope.com/disposal.htm.*

Choosing a Repair Professional

While it's not necessarily as serious of a choice, when choosing a computer professional to perform maintenance or repair activities on your PC, you should approach your decision in much the same way you'd choose an auto mechanic or a medical professional. As with those choices, it's not best to wait until there is a problem before considering who you'll call.

Like doctors and auto mechanics, not all computer technicians have the same abilities, knowledge, and skills. There are large companies and franchise operations, such as the Geek Squad and Fast-Teks, and there are local one-person services, all of which can likely repair your PC. There are a variety of ways you can identify a reliable and capable repair service, including certifications, references, warranties, and years of experience.

The computer industry provides a number of certifications, such as the IC[3] and the CompTIA A+, that establish a standard level of knowledge for computer technicians. When considering a repair service, ask for references and check them. Customer service can be a deciding factor when all other considerations are equal. You may have heard about the service from a friend or relative and, if their experience is positive, consider that a good reference. Ask if the repair service offers a warranty on their work and any parts they install. It shouldn't eliminate a capable repair technician, but one with more experience is likely to be more efficient at troubleshooting and repair of serious problems. Remember that with computer technology emerging almost monthly, it's difficult for technicians to be too savvy on the latest technology.

CERTIFICATION SUMMARY

Expect to see two or more questions on the IC[3] exams relating to computer hardware and software problems and troubleshooting. Know what maintenance and repair is safe for a computer user to perform and those that a professional computer technician should do.

This chapter covered the following areas, each of which you should understand:

- Common computer hardware problems
- Problems that can occur if a computer isn't properly maintained
- Maintenance routines and who should perform them
- The steps used in troubleshooting a computer problem
- What to look for when buying, upgrading, or repairing a computer

Be sure you are familiar with the troubleshooting steps used to identify and isolate a computer issue.

✓ TWO-MINUTE DRILL

Common Hardware-Related PC Problems

❑ The more common hardware-related problems of a PC are: electrical power source, on/off switch, device connections, device configuration, and device drivers.

Hardware Issues Caused by Poor Maintenance

❑ Cleanliness when included with a regular preventive maintenance program is the best prevention for hardware problems.

❑ The more common hardware issues that can develop as a result of poor maintenance procedures are: poor system case cooling and ventilation, slow hard disk performance, power supply degradation, and keyboard and mouse issues.

Preventive Maintenance by Users

❑ The preventive maintenance processes that can be performed by a PC's user include much of the cleaning, checking, and scanning activities.

❑ Actions that a user can perform to keep the PC operating properly are: virus scanning, cleaning the PC exterior, disk drive scanning, and checking power protection devices.

Maintenance by Experienced Professionals

❑ There are some devices and components on a PC that a user should never attempt to maintain, including the internal components of a monitor, the power supply, the microprocessor, memory, and the electrical connections inside the system case.

❑ Unless a user has the knowledge, training, and experience at the level of a computer technician, it's highly recommended that certain maintenance activities be performed only by a professional.

❑ Only a professional computer technician should perform certain maintenance tasks, including: cleaning inside the system case, checking cables and expansion cards inside the system case, checking or replacing the power supply, installation or major upgrades to components inside the system case, and upgrading the BIOS.

General Troubleshooting Steps

❏ General PC troubleshooting involves a five-step process: identify the symptoms of the problem; replicate the problem; evaluate all possible causes for the problem; diagnose each of the possible causes and isolate the likely cause; and apply a correction, configuration, repair, or replacement to solve the problem.

❏ A maintenance log or written record of a PC's past problems, troubleshooting, installations, upgrades, and repairs is a valuable source of information when beginning work to troubleshoot a PC problem.

❏ Troubleshooting questions that should be answered include: when did the problem first happen; is this the first time this problem has happened; what activity was being performed when the problem first showed up; can the problem be re-created; did you add hardware or software to the PC right before the problem appeared; and is there a weather or environmental issue present?

❏ A good place to start troubleshooting an unidentified PC problem is at the power source and the power supply.

❏ The conditions in the PC's environment can strain its cooling system and eventually affect the power supply. As a part of your troubleshooting processes, check out the PC's environment.

❏ A processor problem is more likely an issue with the cooling of the processor or the entire system, the power supply, or a compatibility issue between the motherboard and chipset. The symptoms that a processor is about to fail include: the PC won't boot, the PC boots but doesn't start the operating system, the PC crashes during startup, the PC suddenly has parity error problems, or the PC locks up after a few minutes of operation.

❏ A hard disk problem can be caused by the hard disk drive, the hard disk controller, a SCSI host adapter, cabling, and in many situations, the power supply.

❏ RAM problems occur on a PC typically after new memory is installed. Memory problems can be caused by electrical problems on the motherboard, the configuration of the RAM, compatibility, and improper installation.

❏ Video performance issues can include power or data connection issues, video configuration, monitor compatibility, and device driver issues.

❏ To troubleshoot a power supply, each of the output power connectors should be checked for proper voltage using a multimeter.

❑ To track down an audio or sound problem, verify that no system resource conflicts exist, that the speakers are plugged into the correct jacks, that the speaker wires are not crimped or broken, and that the proper device drivers are installed.

Buying, Maintaining, and Repairing a Computer

❑ Not all computer technicians have the same abilities, knowledge, and skills. Certifications, references, warranties, and years of experience are guidelines that can be used to verify the abilities of a computer technician.

SELF TEST

The following questions are intended to help you be sure that you understand the material included in this chapter. Read the questions and the answer choices carefully.

Common Hardware-Related PC Problems

1. Which of the following are common hardware-related problems of a PC?
A. Electrical power source
B. Device connections
C. Device configuration
D. Device drivers
E. All of the above
F. None of the above

Hardware Issues Caused by Poor Maintenance

2. What is perhaps the best preventive maintenance activity to avoid PC hardware-related problems?
A. Cleaning the PC regularly
B. Defragmentation
C. Diagnostic software
D. Replacing older components regularly

3. What PC hardware-related problems are commonly caused by poor maintenance?
A. Poor system case cooling and ventilation
B. Slow hard disk performance
C. Power supply degradation
D. Keyboard and mouse problems
E. All of the above
F. None of the above

Preventive Maintenance by Users

4. Which of the following preventive maintenance actions can be performed by a PC's user?
A. Cleaning the PC's exterior
B. Virus scanning

    C. Replacing faulty memory

    D. Checking the cable connections inside the system case

Maintenance by Experienced Professionals

5. What devices or components should only be maintained or replaced by a computer professional?

    A. Power supply

    B. Microprocessor

    C. Memory

    D. Keyboard

    E. Mouse

    F. All of the above

6. A computer user with no technical training on the maintenance or troubleshooting processes of a PC suspects that the microprocessor is failing or has become corrupted. What action should the user take to remedy this situation?

    A. Open the system case and replace the microprocessor.

    B. Use a multimeter to determine if the microprocessor is properly operating.

    C. Call a professional computer technician to troubleshoot the problem.

    D. Upgrade the BIOS.

General Troubleshooting Steps

7. Which of the following is not one of the recommended steps in a troubleshooting procedure?

    A. Identify the symptoms of the problem.

    B. Reproduce the problem.

    C. Replace the component involved in the problem that is located closest to the power supply.

    D. Diagnose each of the possible causes and isolate the likely cause.

8. What valuable source of information should be maintained to assist troubleshooting and diagnostic actions in the future?

    A. Manufacturers' documentation

    B. Manufacturers' Web sites

    C. A written maintenance log

    D. Computer technician's experience

9. What major component of a PC is likely the best place to start troubleshooting an unidentified PC hardware problem
   A. The hard disk drive
   B. RAM
   C. CPU
   D. Power supply

10. Which of the following are symptoms that the CPU may be failing?
    A. The PC boots but displays an error code.
    B. The operating system starts but displays an error code.
    C. The PC locks up after a few minutes of operation.
    D. A high-pitched sound is emanating from inside the system case.

11. When do a majority of RAM problems occur?
    A. After new memory is installed
    B. After an electrical storm
    C. When the memory is more than one year old
    D. When changes are made to the BIOS configuration

12. What device should a computer professional use to check a PC power supply for proper voltage?
    A. Screwdriver
    B. Multimeter
    C. ESD strap
    D. None of the above

Buying, Maintaining, and Repairing a Computer

13. What information is not relevant when verifying the knowledge and experience of a computer technical professional?
    A. Certifications
    B. References
    C. Location
    D. Warranties

SELF TEST ANSWERS

Common Hardware-Related PC Problems

1. ☑ **E.** Each of the areas listed in answers **A** through **D** is a common source for PC hardware problems.
   ☒ **A, B, C,** and **D** are incorrect. While each of these areas is a common source for PC hardware problems, none of them is the best answer to the question on its own.

Hardware Issues Caused by Poor Maintenance

2. ☑ **A.** Arguably, cleaning the PC regularly is perhaps the most important preventive action a user can take.
   ☒ **B, C,** and **D** are incorrect. Defragmentation is a valuable tool, but it's more of a performance enhancer. Diagnostic software is helpful for troubleshooting a problem. A user should never replace internal components, but replacing components arbitrarily is not a good practice.

3. ☑ **E.** Each of the problem areas listed in answers **A** through **D** is commonly the result of poor maintenance of a PC.
   ☒ **A, B, C,** and **D** are incorrect. Although each of the choices given in **A** through **D** can be the result of poor maintenance, none is the best answer on its own.

Preventive Maintenance by Users

4. ☑ **A and B.** Cleaning the PC exterior and running a virus checker are actions a PC user can and should perform on a regular basis.
   ☒ **C and D** are incorrect. Only a computer professional should replace memory or check the cable connections inside the system case.

Maintenance by Experienced Professionals

5. ☑ **A, B,** and **C.** Only a qualified computer professional should install any component inside the system case.
   ☒ **D and E** are incorrect. The keyboard and mouse can be installed and maintained by the PC user.

6. ☑ **C.** A qualified computer professional should be called to troubleshoot and diagnose a problem that may be caused by a failing microprocessor.
☒ **A, B,** and **C** are incorrect. The PC user should not open the system case, let alone replace the microprocessor arbitrarily. A multimeter is a good tool for checking the power supply, but not the microprocessor. Upgrading the BIOS is a task best performed by a computer professional.

General Troubleshooting Steps

7. ☑ **C.** Unless troubleshooting has determined a particular component is the source of a PC problem, it's not a good idea to just start replacing components regardless of their location or proximity to other components.
☒ **A, B,** and **D** are incorrect. Each of these choices is a part of a good troubleshooting process, but they are incorrect answers to this question.

8. ☑ **C.** A written maintenance log or record can be a valuable source of information when beginning to troubleshoot a hardware-related PC problem.
☒ **A, B,** and **D** are incorrect. Each of these choices can be a good source of information once a problem has been isolated to a particular component, but neither **A** nor **B** is the best answer available. Answer **D** is a very subjective information source and shouldn't be the first consideration in a troubleshooting process.

9. ☑ **D.** The power supply is the component that fails the most often, which makes it the first suspect in a hardware-related PC problem.
☒ **A, B,** and **C** are incorrect. Hard disk drive, RAM, or CPU problems can stem from a faulty power supply.

10. ☑ **C.** If a PC is able to start up but fails after a few minutes, it is likely that the CPU is overheating.
☒ **A, B,** and **D** are incorrect. These conditions are unlikely to be CPU issues and need further troubleshooting.

11. ☑ **A.** Most hardware-related problems occur immediately after a hardware change has been made.
☒ **B, C,** and **D** are incorrect. Problems that develop after an electrical storm are less likely to be related to the RAM. RAM doesn't necessarily degrade over a fixed period of time. It's possible that a BIOS configuration error could cause RAM issues, but since only a computer professional should make changes to the BIOS, a change to the BIOS is an unlikely source of a RAM problem.

12. ☑ **B.** A multimeter can verify the voltage being supplied by the power supply on each of its output power connectors.

☒ **A, C,** and **D** are incorrect. A screwdriver may be needed to open the system case, but it is not a measuring tool, nor should it be used to test voltage. Anytime the system case is open, an ESD strap should be in use, but like the screwdriver, it is not a voltage measuring device. Simply because **B** is correct, **D** is not.

Buying, Maintaining, and Repairing a Computer

13. ☑ **A, B,** and **D.** Although **A** and **B** are probably the most informative characteristics of a computer professional, the length and coverage of the warranties offered is also valuable to know.

☒ **C** is incorrect. The location of a computer professional has virtually no value in judging his or her qualifications.

5

Computer Software Operations

S oftware is divided into three primary groups: system software, utility software, and application software. System software is the computer software that creates and manages the foundation structure on which other software operates. System software includes the operating system, device drivers, user interfaces, and firmware, such as the system Basic Input/ Output System (BIOS).

Utility software, which is also referred to as special-purpose software, is computer software that performs one or more tasks that help the operating system and the user to manage, diagnose, protect, and fine-tune the interaction and performance of the operating system, the hardware, and the application software. Most operating systems include a relatively wide range of utility software, but some utility software is installed as standalone programs. Examples of utility software are disk management utilities, disk defragmentation utilities, antivirus software, data compression software, and encryption and security utilities.

Application software is task-oriented software that assists a user in the performance of a work-related or recreational task. Application software, which runs on top of the operating system, includes programs like word processing, electronic spreadsheets, database management systems, presentation software, e-mail clients, games, and Internet browsers.

This chapter focuses on system software and its functions and processes. (For more information on utility software and application software, see Chapters 6 and 7.) We'll also look at the benefit of licensing, upgrading, and updating a PC's system software to ensure its best operation.

CERTIFICATION OBJECTIVE

Hardware and Software Integration and Software Development

2.1   Identify how software and hardware work together to perform computing tasks and how software is developed and upgraded.

Without system software the hardware of a PC is unable to do anything other than power up. In order for the CPU, RAM, and hard disk drives to have anything other than a purpose requires instructions in the form of software. The following sections discuss how system software interacts with the hardware to provide an operating environment for the PC's user.

The Fetch-Decode-Execute Cycle

From the outside view of a PC user, what goes on inside of a computer can seem a bit like magic. You push a button or click the mouse and images appear on the display screen with which you can interact to write a letter, compute a budget, or play a game. While it is magic at some levels, what you see on the display is actually the result of hundreds, if not thousands, of instructions being executed by the CPU. How all of this happens is through a series of carefully designed and engineered steps called the fetch-decode-execute cycle.

Computer programs are made up from literally thousands of instructions, each of which may contain one or more commands in the operation codes (opcodes) recognized and executed by the CPU. When the PC is running an application program, each of these instructions must be fetched by the CPU and decoded into its corresponding opcode(s); then each of the opcodes is executed.

The fetch-decode-execute cycle, also called the instruction cycle, involves the CPU obtaining (fetching) an instruction from the PC's memory, decoding it to one or more CPU opcodes, and then individually performing (executing) each opcode. Most new PC CPUs are able to perform the fetch-decode-execute cycle at least one million times per second.

Fetch Cycle

The fetch portion of the fetch-decode-execute cycle requests an instruction to be provided to the CPU from primary memory (RAM), cache memory, a storage device, or the CPU registers. Without going into too much detail, let's step through the sequence of events that occurs during the fetch process.

1. The CPU's program counter register (PCR) contains the address in memory of the next instruction to be executed.
2. The address in the PCR is passed to the CPU's memory address register (MAR).
3. The CPU's control unit then reads the address in the MAR and requests the contents of that address from memory.
4. The instruction retrieved from memory is received and stored in the memory buffer register (MBR).

5. The instruction in the MBR is then transferred to the instruction register (IR).

6. The address in the PCR is incremented to point to the next instruction to be fetched.

Decode Cycle

After the instruction to be executed is stored in the MBR, it needs to be decoded to the corresponding opcodes from the CPU's instruction set; any data addresses associated with the instruction are analyzed to determine the location of the data.

The CPU's instruction set contains a fixed number of opcode instructions, each of which performs a discrete and unique action that doesn't overlap the action of any of the other opcodes. Table 5-1 lists examples of the instruction set for a Pentium CPU.

After the instruction has been decoded to the CPU's opcodes, the decode part of the fetch-decode-execute cycle is completed and the execute part of the process starts.

TABLE 5-1	Opcode (HexadecimalValue)	Mnemonic	Action/Function
Examples of Opcodes in the Intel Pentium Instruction Set	20	AND	Logical AND
	04	ADD	Add
	3C	CMP	Compare
	F6/6	DIV	Unsigned divide
	F4	HLT	Halt
	E4	IN	Input from port
	EB	JMP	Jump to address
	F6/4	MUL	Unsigned multiply
	90	NOP	No operation
	0C	OR	Logical inclusive OR
	E6	OUT	Output to port
	2C	SUB	Subtract
	9B	WAIT	Wait
	34	XOR	Logical exclusive OR

Execute Cycle

Exactly what happens in the execute part of the fetch-decode-execute cycle depends on the opcode to be executed. There are four primary actions that an opcode can perform:

- **Control operation**   This type of opcode is used to change the sequence of operations and to manage the values stored in the CPU registers.
- **Data processing**   This type of opcode is used to process data, including any operations that involve the CPU's arithmetic and logic unit (ALU).
- **Input/Output**   This type of opcode is used to transfer data between the CPU and an input or output device.
- **Data transfer**   This type of opcode is used to transfer data and instructions between the CPU and memory.

In the execute cycle the CPU performs the action requested by the opcode managing the functional units (CU, ALU, and registers) as needed to complete the action.

Data Buffering

In computing terms, a buffer is memory that is used to hold data in transit. Buffers are used to offset the differences in data transfer rates between devices, especially when a sending device has a faster transfer rate than the receiving device. In a computer, there are several buffers, such as the buffer between the keyboard and memory and the buffer between memory and a printer. Buffering allows devices to work independently of one another at their native speeds without the danger of one device overflowing another.

Inside the CPU, the memory buffer register (MBR) stores data that is being moved to or from primary memory and cache memory. Disk cache serves as a buffer between a hard disk drive and primary memory. Most communications devices, including modems and network interfaces, use a buffer between the PC and the network media. All levels of cache memory are buffers that hold incoming instructions until the control unit (CU) requests them.

Interrupts and System Resources

Software running on a PC must have a way to signal other software that it needs a service or some action performed. When an application program needs to output to a peripheral device, such as the hard disk drive, the display, or a printer, it must be able to communicate with the operating system and device drivers, which control and manage the interactions with these devices. To this end, the architecture of a PC includes what are called system resources that can be assigned to specific devices so that requests for service and the details of the requests can be passed to a particular device. A PC's system resources are embedded in the CPU and motherboard or set aside in memory or storage devices, or both.

Generally, the system resources of a PC are divided into two primary groups: interrupts and input/output addresses (I/O addresses). Interrupts are commonly called IRQs (interrupt requests) because they are the component that receives the request for service from assigned devices. In addition to IRQs and I/O addresses, another system resource common to a PC is direct memory access (DMA) channels.

IRQs

As explained earlier in the chapter, a computer uses a three-step standard instruction cycle: fetch-decode-execute. However, there is a fourth step—check for interrupts— that checks the interrupt register, embedded in the CPU, for interrupt requests.

If you have ever been to one of the national chain coffee shop restaurants, such as Denny's, Shari's, Perkins, or the like, you have probably noticed that the cook (a sort of CPU) may communicate with the server (a sort of peripheral device) through a numbered light bar that indicates to the server when his or her orders are ready. While going about their tasks, servers can check for their numbers to be displayed. When a server's number is displayed, he or she can then interrupt the task at hand to pick up and deliver a customer's order. In general, that's how interrupts work on a computer as well.

Inside the CPU, the interrupt register (IR) works much like the lighted number bar in the restaurant. When a PC component needs a service performed by another component, it can set "on" its assigned bit position (IRQ) in the IR by writing a binary 1 to it. The CU checks the interrupt register after each instruction cycle to see if any new requests have been made, that is, if any of the IR's bits has been changed to a 1 (a 1 indicates a request is active; a zero [0] represents the "off" position of an IRQ). When an IRQ is set on (set to a 1), the CPU interrupts (hence the name) its execution of instructions to handle the service request.

For example, when you press a key on the keyboard, the keyboard handler sends a signal over the system bus that sets the keyboard IRQ to a 1. When the CU completes its current instruction cycle, it examines the IR for interrupt requests and, finding the keyboard IRQ, passes the first instruction of the program associated with the keyboard IRQ (the keyboard interrupt handler) to the CPU for processing. It also resets the keyboard IRQ to zero. When the keyboard interrupt handler completes its task, the CU returns to what it was doing before the interrupt was detected.

TABLE 5-2	IRQ Position	Default Assignment	Assignable
Standard Default IRQ Assignments	0	Reserved by system for system timer	No
	1	Reserved by system for keyboard	No
	2	Link to IRQs 8–15	No
	3	COM 2 and COM4 serial ports	Yes
	4	COM1 and COM3 serial ports	Yes
	5	Open	Yes
	6	Floppy disk controller	Yes
	7	LPT1 parallel port 1 or sound card	Yes
	8	CMOS (real-time clock)	No
	9	Open (linked to IRQ 2)	Yes
	10	Open	Yes
	11	Open	Yes
	12	PS/2 port (mouse)	Yes
	13	Math co-processor	Yes
	14	Primary IDE channel	Yes
	15	Secondary IDE channel	Yes

Table 5-2 lists the common default assignments for the IRQs in a computer. The standard configuration of IRQs consists of two banks of eight IRQs (each assigned to a single bit). The first eight IRQs are considered the master set, and the second eight are the slave set. In actual use, however, the slave IRQ set is really just an extension of the master set. IRQ 2 and IRQ 9 are linked to provide a connection between the two IRQ sets, as illustrated in Figure 5-1.

However, when a new device is installed in a PC, its installation software may override the system assignment and assign itself to an IRQ that already has a device assigned to it, which can cause IRQ conflicts and either or both devices to not function properly.

IRQs are checked in a standard priority sequence that inserts IRQs 8–15 between IRQ 1 and 3. So, the priority sequence of the IRQs is 0, 1, 8, 9, 10, 11, 12, 13, 14, 15, 3, 4, 5, 6, and 7.

FIGURE 5-1

Two sets of eight
IRQs are linked
through IRQs 2
and 9

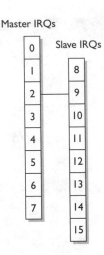

I/O Addresses

In order to communicate with an input/output device connected to a PC, the CPU
lays out an area either in its own address space or in memory that is designed just
for this use. The CPU then assigns an address (actually one or more addresses) to a
specific location in this area. The address assigned to a device becomes the device's
identity to the CPU. The I/O address assigned to a device is a three- or four-digit
hexadecimal (Base 16) number.

When you install a new device, the installation software checks either the device
controller (hardware) or device driver (software), or both, to see if the address the
device is configured for is available. If two devices attempt to share the same I/O
address, one of the devices will probably be logically removed from the system. For
example, if you install a network interface card (NIC) in an expansion port inside
the system unit, through either the installation software or the operating system's
plug and play utilities, the device is assigned the I/O address of 0300–031F, or an 800
bit area starting at address 0300. Communications between the NIC and the CPU
are conducted through this space.

Table 5-3 lists some of the common standard I/O address assignments.

Direct Memory Access

Some I/O devices require a buffer space in memory to temporarily hold the data
read or to be written to a device. In the past, the allocation of this buffer and the
transfer of data into or out of the buffer required the CPU to interrupt whatever

Device	I/O Address
First interrupt controller	0020–0021
Second interrupt controller	0030–0031
Primary IDE interface	01F0–01F7
Video card	03B0–03BB
Sound card	0533–0537

it was doing to service this requirement. However, the development of a direct memory access (DMA) channel allows a device to use a DMA channel to write or read data directly to memory without the need for an intervention from the CPU. A PC typically has eight DMA channels, each of which is assigned or reserved to a specific device. Table 5-4 lists the standard assignments of the DMA channels in a PC's configuration.

When a new DMA-capable device is installed, its installation software or its device driver looks for an open and compatible DMA channel. DMA channels 0–3 are 8-bit transfer channels, and channels 4–7 are 16-bit channels.

System Resource Assignments on a Windows PC
On a PC running Microsoft Windows, the system resource assignments of a given device can be viewed through the Windows Device Manager, which is accessed

DMA Channel	Assignment
0	System board
1	Sound card
2	Floppy disk controller
3	Open/NIC
4	DMA controller
5	Open
6	Open
7	Open

slightly differently in Windows XP and Windows Vista. To display the system resource assignments on a Windows PC, use one of the following two methods:

Displaying Device System Resources on a Windows XP PC   To display the system resource assignments on a Windows XP system, use the following steps:

1. Click (left-click) on the Start button to display the Start menu.
2. Click the Control Panel link to display the Control Panel window.
3. Double-click the System icon to display the System Properties dialog box, shown in Figure 5-2.
4. Select the Hardware tab and click the Device Manager button in the Device Manager section to display the Device Manager dialog box.
5. In the hardware tree displayed in the main pane of the Device Manager dialog box, double-click a device to display the Properties dialog box for the selected device. You may need to expand a particular device class to display the specific devices installed on the PC for a particular hardware type.

FIGURE 5-2

The System Properties dialog box is opened through the Control Panel.

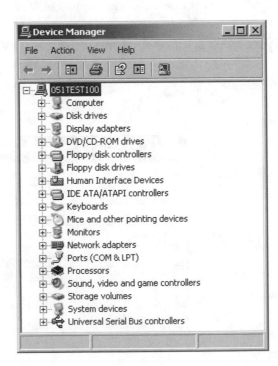

6. Click the Resources tab to display the system resources assigned to the device. Figure 5-3 shows an example of the system resources for a device on a Windows XP system.

Displaying Device System Resources in Windows Vista To display the system resource assignments on a Windows Vista PC, use the following steps:

1. Click the Start button to display the Start menu.
2. Click the Control Panel link to display the Control Panel window.
3. Click the System and Maintenance icon to display the System Properties dialog box.
4. Select the System tab and double-click the Device Manager link, which is located under the Tasks heading in the System menu.
5. In the hardware tree displayed in the main pane of the Device Manager dialog box, double-click a device to display the Properties dialog box for the

FIGURE 5-3

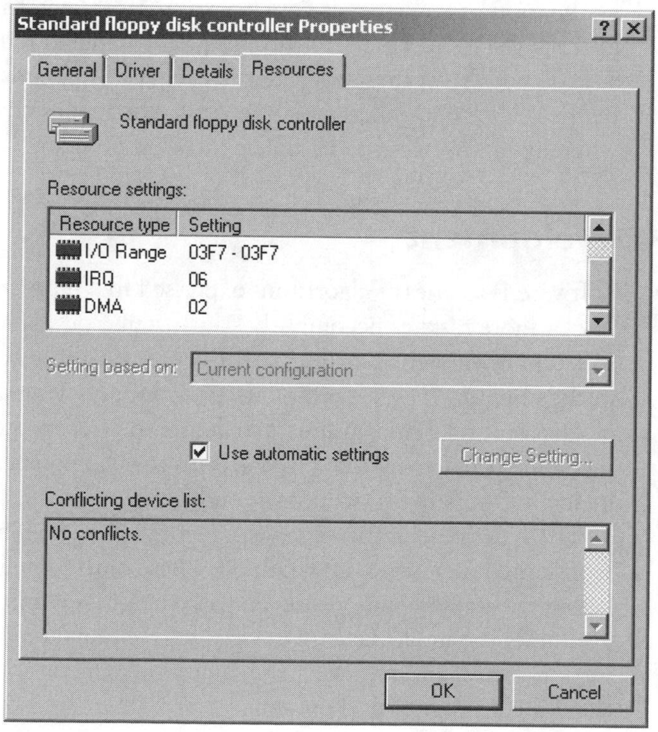

The Properties dialog box for a device, showing its system resource assignments

selected device. You may need to expand a particular device class to display the specific devices installed on the PC for a particular hardware type.

6. Click the Resources tab to display the system resources assigned to the device.

Device Drivers

If I were to go to China, I would definitely need an interpreter to help me speak with anyone who didn't speak English. Similarly, an operating system can't possibly communicate with every device that could be installed on a PC. Windows, Mac OS, and Linux each have a wide range of device interfaces they use to interact with many standard devices. However, as new device technology emerges, operating systems would need to continuously add new device interface software to keep up with the technology. To avoid any interface problems, virtually all peripheral devices and some internal devices come with a custom device driver that is able to speak to both the operating system and the device's controller.

A device driver is system software that provides an interface between a hardware device and operating systems and application software. For example, when an application program needs data from a storage device, it requests the data from the operating system, which, in turn, sends a command request to the device driver. The device driver then translates the requested command into the code understood by the device controller, which retrieves the requested data and writes it to memory where it can be accessed by the application program.

Software Development

Software is a series of algorithms expressed in a programming language that performs one or more tasks or accomplishes a particular outcome. A programming language uses text or numerical codes to represent one or more opcodes (see Table 5-1 earlier in the chapter). For the most part, programming languages were developed as a means for human programmers to define the steps required in an algorithm and to reference the data required by the steps to accomplish a task, calculate a result, or logically compare two values or conditions.

The traditional software development process is a phased activity that is frequently represented in a model in which one phase of the development process is completed before the next begins. However, with the programming languages and tools now available, the model is being revised to one in which the user and the programmer work together (if they aren't the same person anyway) in an iterative way to create the desired program and outputs.

Regardless of whether the software development process is carried out in a phased or iterative manner, the steps that must be performed remain the same. To successfully create software, the steps of planning, designing, specifying, programming, and testing must be performed in the process. The planning step involves the translation of the requesting user's vision into the software's objective and scope. In the designing step, the algorithmic steps that the software must perform are conceptualized and the operating environment of the software is verified to ensure the software will actually run on the users' computers when it's completed and to provide the input data needed to complete the specification step of the project. In the specifying step, the detailed actions that must be performed by the software are specified and approved. The programming step then converts the detail specification of the software into programming code. Finally, the testing step involves the testing, acceptance by the user, and implementation of the software. In many cases, depending on the scope of the software, another step is needed to keep the software running as requested, specified, and hopefully programmed. This step is the maintenance step in which user feedback is used to correct or improve any deficiencies in the software.

If the steps just described in the preceding paragraph are performed one after another with one step being completed before the next step begins, the method being used is commonly referred to as a *waterfall* model. Variations on this legacy model are an iterative process, what's called an agile process, and the extreme programming process.

An *iterative* software development process is commonly used when the vision of the user is not completely worked out or clear. Essentially, the waterfall process is used to create small portions of the software, and as acceptance is gained, more and more of the software is developed and added to the overall software bundle.

The *agile* programming process encompasses the principles of both the waterfall and the iterative development models but is a bit more user-centered. As portions of the software are developed, the user receives a demonstration or performs a test to verify that the completed software portion is what he or she had in mind. If all is well, the next part of the software is developed. Otherwise, the user provides the developer with feedback and suggestions for improvements or perhaps even to start over.

Extreme programming (which is confusingly identified by the abbreviation XP) takes the agile development process to the next level. Essentially, the process is the same as in the agile method, but the scope of each developed piece is much smaller and may even perform only a single step or task.

The iterative, agile, and extreme programming methods of software development are much faster ways to develop software, especially in situations where the user is somewhat unsure of what he or she really wants, which is fairly common. In addition, these development methods are more in sync with the visual (WYSIWYG) nature of online, interactive, or graphics-oriented expectations of users.

Software Licensing, Updates, and Upgrades

Software is rarely purchased outright. When you purchase software at a store or online, you are actually agreeing to abide by certain rules in order to "rent" the software. In addition, as discussed in the preceding section, user feedback and continued testing can cause software to be modified, creating a need for licensed users to update or upgrade the software. Each of these aspects of software "ownership" is discussed in the following sections.

Software Licenses

When you purchase software, regardless of whether it is system software, application software, or utility software, you really are only buying a license to install and use the software. The software itself, which is essentially the programming code used to create it, remains the property of the person or company that created it and holds the copyright.

A software license legally grants to a buyer the right to install and use the software according to the rules and restrictions detailed in its end-user license agreement (EULA). The typical EULA grants a buyer/end user the permission to install one or more copies of the software and to use the software, but restricts the resell, duplication, or other uses that would be an infringement of the software publisher's copyright rights.

There are three basic types of software licenses, with the distinction between them being who controls the ownership of the software:

- **Free license** Also called a freeware or permissive license. The ownership of the software is transferred to the end user, but not the copyright. Free software licenses are optional licenses in that the end user doesn't have to accept the license. However, if the end user takes any action, such as copying or distributing the software, the end user accepts the license by default.

- **Open source license** Also called a copyleft license. Open source software publishers make their original programming available to anyone who agrees to the GNU General Public License (GPL). The GPL grants virtually all of the ownership rights to anyone who agrees to make any improvements made to the software available to anyone under an open source license.

- **Proprietary license** With a few exceptions, all software that is sold is proprietary software. This means that the ownership remains with the software publisher in every case. The end user must accept the license to install or use the software. All Microsoft products carry a proprietary license (EULA) that must be accepted to continue an installation or to start the software.

Software Upgrades and Updates

The difference between a software upgrade and a software update is that a software upgrade replaces an installed version of a software package with a completely new and often renamed version of the software and a software update applies patches and corrections to an installed version of a software package.

Software upgrades often replace an older version of a software package with a newer version or increase the version number of the product. When a user installs Windows Vista on a computer that has been running Windows XP, he or she has performed a software upgrade. The same is true if Microsoft Office 2003 is replaced with Microsoft Office 2007. Users install upgrades hoping to take advantage of improvements and features added to a newer version of a software product.

A software update replaces only the parts of a software package that contain bugs or errors, or that are failing to execute as designed. Most software updates are made available in bundles typically called patches or service packs, which are essentially bandages that are applied to fix specific performance or functional problems in the software. Software updates, like software upgrades, are optional and, if an end user operates on the "If it ain't broke, don't fix it" principle, don't have to be downloaded and applied. However, it is a good practice to download and apply all available patches or service packs from the software publisher, especially those that improve the security of the product.

CERTIFICATION SUMMARY

This chapter covered the three primary types of software: system software, application software, and utility software. You need to know the kinds of software that are included in each type and how they are used on a computer system.

You should also understand how the computer hardware interacts with system software, how application software interacts with system software, and how and when utility software is used.

✓ # TWO-MINUTE DRILL

Hardware and Software Integration and Software Development

❑ Software is divided into three primary groups: system software, utility software, and application software.

❑ System software is the computer software that creates and manages the foundation structure on which other software operates.

❑ Utility software, which is also referred to as special-purpose software, is computer software that performs one or more tasks that help the operating system and the user to manage, diagnose, protect, and fine-tune the interaction and performance of the operating system, hardware, and the application software.

❑ Application software is task-oriented software that assists a user in the performance of a work-related or recreational task.

❑ The CPU uses a fetch-decode-execute cycle to obtain instructions from memory.

❑ The fetch portion of the fetch-decode-execute cycle requests an instruction to be provided to the CPU from primary memory (RAM), cache memory, a storage device, or the CPU registers.

❑ The instructions and any data addresses are decoded to the corresponding CPU opcodes and the location address of the data. A CPU's instruction set contains specific opcode instructions that perform discrete actions.

❑ The execute cycle performs the opcode through the functional units of the CPU as needed to complete the action.

❑ A buffer is memory used to hold data in transit, especially when a sending device has a faster transfer rate than the receiving device.

❑ The architecture of a PC includes system resources that are assigned to specific devices to facilitate requests for service. System resources are divided into three primary groups: interrupts, I/O addresses, and DMA channels.

❑ The CPU checks the interrupt register after each instruction is executed to determine if a request for service has been made.

❑ The CPU assigns an address to a specific memory location that serves as a device's identity to the CPU. The I/O address assigned to a device is a hexadecimal number.

❑ A DMA channel allows a device to write or read data directly to or from memory without the need for intervention from the CPU.

❑ On Windows PC, system resource assignments are viewed through the Windows Device Manager.

❑ A device driver provides an interface between a hardware device and the operating system and application software.

❑ A software license grants an end user the right to install and use software according to the rules and restrictions in its EULA. There are three types of software licenses: free licenses, open source licenses, and proprietary licenses.

❑ The difference between a software upgrade and a software update is that a software upgrade replaces an installed version of a software package with a completely new version of the software and a software update applies patches and corrections to an installed version of a software package.

SELF TEST

The following questions are intended to help you be sure that you understand the material included in this chapter. Read the questions and the answer choices carefully.

Hardware and Software Integration and Software Development

1. Which of the following is not one of the primary groups of software in a PC?
   A. Application software
   B. System software
   C. Simulation software
   D. Utility software

2. What type of software is a PC's operating system typically considered to be?
   A. Application software
   B. System software
   C. BIOS
   D. Utility software

3. Disk defragmentation software is generally considered to be what type of software?
   A. Application software
   B. System software
   C. Antivirus software
   D. Utility software

4. Which of the following is an example of application software?
   A. Office Word 2007
   B. Windows Vista
   C. Registry editor
   D. Windows XP

5. Which of the following is not a step in the CPU's instruction cycle?
   A. Recycle
   B. Fetch
   C. Decode
   D. Execute

6. An opcode is included in what feature of a CPU?
   A. Cache memory
   B. Instruction set
   C. Control unit
   D. Buffers

7. Where are data and instructions held in transit between devices in a PC?
   A. CU
   B. MAR
   C. Buffer
   D. ALU

8. What is the mechanism used by application software to signal the operating system that it needs a service performed?
   A. DMA channel
   B. Interrupt
   C. I/O address
   D. Buffering

9. What designates a peripheral device's identity to the CPU?
   A. DMA channel
   B. IRQ
   C. I/O address
   D. Device driver

10. What is the system resource feature that allows a device to write or read data directly to memory without the need for intervention from the CPU?
    A. DMA channel
    B. IRQ
    C. I/O address
    D. Device driver

11. What utility of a Windows operating system can be used to view the system resource assignments of a device?
    A. Device driver
    B. Device Manager
    C. New Hardware Wizard
    D. System resource assignments are made completely by Windows and cannot be viewed.

12. What system software provides a communication interface between a hardware device and the operating system and application software?

    A. Device driver

    B. Device controller

    C. DMA channel

    D. Interrupt handler

13. Which of the following is not a standard type of software license?

    A. Free license

    B. Open source license

    C. Proprietary license

    D. Shareware license

14. An end user who installs MySoftware, version 2.0 over MySoftware, version 1.5 is performing what type of software maintenance?

    A. Update

    B. Upgrade

    C. Patch

    D. Service pack installation

15. Which of the following is not a software development process that is based on an iterative approach?

    A. Agile

    B. Extreme programming

    C. Iterative

    D. Waterfall

SELF TEST ANSWERS

Hardware and Software Integration and Software Development

1. ☑ **C.** Simulation software, which includes games and analysis software, is a type of application software and not a software category on its own.
   ☒ **A, B,** and **D** are incorrect. Application software, system software, and utility software are the primary three types of software on a PC.

2. ☑ **B.** An operating system is a type of system software.
   ☒ **A, C,** and **D** are incorrect. Application software allows the user to accomplish a task and system software includes the operating system and device drivers. However, BIOS firmware is also categorized as a type of system software.

3. ☑ **D.** Disk defragmentation and other disk management software are types of utility software.
   ☒ **A, B,** and **C** are incorrect. Application software allows the user to accomplish a task and system software includes the operating system and device drivers. However, antivirus software is a type of utility software.

4. ☑ **A.** Each of the components of the Office 2007 suite is application software.
   ☒ **B, C,** and **D** are incorrect. Windows Vista and Windows XP are operating systems and therefore system software. A registry editor is considered utility software.

5. ☑ **A.** The CPU's fetch-decode-execute cycle doesn't include a recycle step.
   ☒ **B, C,** and **D** are incorrect. Each of these answers is a component of the fetch-decode-execute cycle.

6. ☑ **B.** A CPU's instruction set contains discrete opcodes that the CPU is designed to interpret and execute.
   ☒ **A, C,** and **D** are incorrect. Opcodes aren't related to cache memory, but they are handled by the CU and are the result of decoding instructions passed to the CPU from a buffer.

7. ☑ **C.** Data and instructions being passed to the CPU are held temporarily in a buffer.
   ☒ **A, B,** and **D** are incorrect. The CU controls the movement of the data and instructions, the memory address register stores the location in memory of data and instructions, and the arithmetic and logic unit performs logical and arithmetic actions.

8. ☑ **B.** When an application program needs a service performed, such as retrieving data from the hard disk drive, it sets an interrupt to signal the operating system and CPU that a service is requested.
   ☒ **A, C,** and **D** are incorrect. A DMA channel allows a device to write directly to memory, an I/O address provides the identity of a device, and the retrieved data may be temporarily stored in a buffer.

9. ☑ **C.** An I/O address provides the hexadecimal identity of a device.

   ☒ **A, B,** and **D** are incorrect. A DMA channel allows a device to write directly to memory, an IRQ is used to signal a service request, and a device driver serves as the intermediary between hardware and system and application software.

10. ☑ **A.** A DMA channel allows a device to write directly to memory.

    ☒ **B, C,** and **D** are incorrect. An IRQ is used to signal a service request, an I/O address provides the hexadecimal identity of a device, and a device driver serves as the intermediary between hardware and system and application software.

11. ☑ **B.** The Windows Device Manager allows a user to view, modify, and manage the system resources assigned to a device.

    ☒ **A, C,** and **D** are incorrect. A device driver serves as the intermediary between hardware and system and application software device, the New Hardware Wizard assists the user to install new hardware devices, and yes, system resource assignments can be viewed.

12. ☑ **A.** A device driver serves as the intermediary between hardware and system and application software device.

    ☒ **B, C,** and **D** are incorrect. A device controller is a part of a device's hardware or provided from the PC's chipset, a DMA channel allows a device to write directly to memory, and the interrupt handler is a component of the CPU and chipset that checks and clears interrupt requests.

13. ☑ **D.** Shareware is actually a component of proprietary licensing, in that the end user must pay a fee and agree to the terms of a EULA.

    ☒ **A, B,** and **C** are incorrect. Free software and open source software licenses have few restrictions for use and redistribution.

14. ☑ **B.** An upgrade essentially reinstalls a software package with a completely new version of the software.

    ☒ **A, C,** and **D** are incorrect. An update only fixes problems and issues in the current version of a software package. A patch is a type of software update, as is a service pack installation.

15. ☑ **D.** In the waterfall method of software development, each phase is completed and approved before the next phase is started.

    ☒ **A, B,** and **C** are incorrect. These choices are each an iterative or recursive software development method and therefore would be incorrect if chosen.

6

Application Software

Application software is known by a great many names, including some that refer to it by brand (Microsoft Office, OpenOffice, WordPerfect Office, and others), some that refer to it by function (word processing, electronic spreadsheets, role-playing games, information resource management), and still others that refer to it by the name of the individual application (Word, WordPerfect, Quattro Pro, Sphygmic, and others). However you refer to application software, its use is sure to increase your productivity, enjoyment, efficiency, and effectiveness, which is its ultimate purpose.

Application software can be categorized into three general groups: personal productivity software, simulation software, and information management software. Some applications, such as a database system, may actually fit into more than one of these groups based on how it's used, but in general, application developers have one of these groups in mind when a software product is released.

CERTIFICATION OBJECTIVE

Overview of Commonly Used Applications

In this chapter, we discuss the more commonly used applications that fall into the personal productivity, simulation, and information management application software groups. This discussion will identify the general workings of these applications and the benefit each provides to its users.

Personal Productivity Software

As its name implies, personal productivity software is designed to make a user more productive. Just how it goes about doing so depends on you and the productivity improvements you need. If you need to produce documents, reports, brochures, or e-mail, or should you need to find telephone numbers faster, perform accounting more accurately, or make a presentation that truly makes an impact on its audience, software applications are available to accomplish all of this and more.

Office Suites

In its most common usage, personal productivity software is a general term used to describe software packages or suites that include four basic types of personal productivity software: word processing, electronic spreadsheet, presentation graphics editor, and, in most cases, a personal database system. The more popular suites of personal productivity software available on the market include Microsoft Office, Corel WordPerfect Office, OpenOffice, and Sun Microsystems' StarOffice. Each of these suites of application software includes at least a word processor, an electronic spreadsheet, a presentation graphics editor, and a personal database management system. Table 6-1 lists the application software bundled into these personal productivity software suites.

The user interfaces on these application suites are relatively the same, and their functions and features range from full-featured to bare basics. However, don't let the price of the application suite cloud your judgment on which application suite may be best for your personal productivity needs. The prices range from as much as $300 (Microsoft Office 2007 and Corel WordPerfect Office X4) to around $40 (Sun StarOffice) to as little as free (OpenOffice.org).

In addition to the standard office application suites, other personal productivity software is available to help you perform a variety of personal and recordkeeping tasks, including personal planners, calendars, home and office accounting, drawing software, and many others.

Installed and Web-Based Software

For most of the PC's history, dating back to around 1981, application software had to be installed on the PC to be usable. Installing application software (or virtually any software) on a PC required inserting the installation media into the PC and then

TABLE 6-1   Popular Personal Productivity Software Suites and Bundles

Publisher	Suite Name	Word Processing	Spreadsheet	Presentation	Database
Corel	WordPerfect Office	WordPerfect	Quattro Pro	Presentations	None
Microsoft	Office	Word	Excel	PowerPoint	Access
OpenOffice.org	OpenOffice	Write	Calc	Impress	Base
Sun Microsystems	StarOffice	Writer	Calc	Impress	Base

executing the self-installation or setup program. Installed application software can also be downloaded from the Web and installed on a PC. During the installation process, some configuration may be required, but for the most part, once the application is installed, it's ready for use.

Web-based application software doesn't require an installation on a local PC. Whether the application is an online game, a mortgage calculation, or a full-featured suite of personal productivity software, such as Microsoft Office Live (www.officelive .com), Zoho (www.zoho.com), Google Docs (docs.google.com), or Shutterborg (www.shutterb.org), Web-based software can save space on the PC's storage media and, of course, money, since most Web-based applications are free. Application software is provided online by an application service provider (ASP).

Simulation Software

Any software that has the ability to reasonably imitate some real phenomenon, action, or event is simulation software. Simulation software exists to simulate engineering processes, chemical interactions, electronic circuits, and biological processes. Simulation game software allows you to fly an airplane or assume a first-person perspective in a battle or sporting event or just about anything else that can be imagined or witnessed. Simulation software creates a level of virtual reality through a series of mathematical algorithms and formulas.

Information Management Software

Just what information management specifically refers to has not been clearly defined by the information technology industries, but in general, it includes application software that is designed to assist and enable a user to manage content (Web pages and the like), documents, records, library media, geophysical information, digital images, and more.

Information management commonly is used to describe what is also defined as information resources management (IRM). IRM software provides a means to manage and share information assets on an automated network. The three basic functions of IRM are the identification of information assets; a categorization of the content of the information and its value; and a means to store, retrieve, and organize information.

CERTIFICATION OBJECTIVE

Word Processing Applications

2.2.1   Identify fundamental concepts relating to word processing and common uses for word-processing applications (e.g., reviewing, editing, formatting, etc.).

Word processing application software is designed to help a user compose, edit, format, and print professional-looking letters, brochures, documents, and reports. Word processing software, like Office Word, WordPerfect, StarOffice Writer, Google Docs, Zoho Writer, and others, is one of the most popular applications used in homes and offices.

In addition to their most basic functions, many word processing software systems also support the preparation of a variety of specialized documents, including

- Spell checking, grammar checking, and language support (such as a thesaurus)
- Letters and e-mails created from a document template and a data source, such as a spreadsheet or a database table. This feature is commonly known as mail merge
- Tables, references, and indices including tables of content, tables of figures, indices of keywords, endnotes, footnotes, and cross-referencing
- Document version tracking
- Graphics, tables, and page borders, watermarks, and text-to-image alignment

The primary functions of a word processing system are composing, editing, formatting, reviewing, printing, and publishing. Each of these functions is discussed briefly in the sections that follow.

Document Composition

Composing a word processing document involves not much more than just typing in phrases and words and organizing them into paragraphs. When a word processing system is started, a new blank document is also opened. As you type the content of the document, certain features that are enabled by default assist the process of creating the document in a standardized format. Figure 6-1 illustrates a sentence entered into a new blank document in a word processing application's workspace.

FIGURE 6-1

A new document being composed in Word 2007

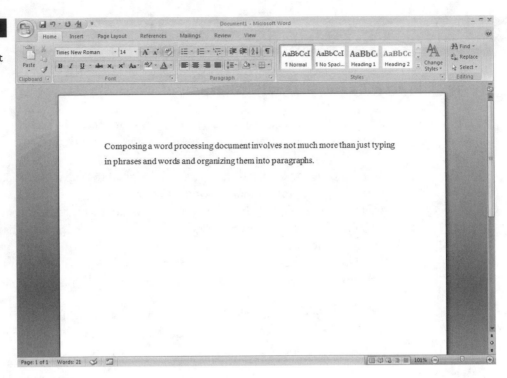

Word processors support the application of document templates. Typically, the default document format is opened when the system starts up. For example, when Microsoft Office Word starts up, a new blank document based on the Normal template is opened. The higher-end word processing systems, such as Word and WordPerfect, offer myriad document templates that provide a preset document layout as well as character and paragraph formatting. Templates for brochures, calendars, contracts, invitations, memos, reports, and stationery, to name only a few template categories, assist the user to quickly create a specialized document type.

A feature called word wrapping eliminates the need for the user to enter a new line character command at the end of each text line. Word wrapping (or as it's commonly known, word wrap) automatically senses the right margin or the bottom margin of the document and moves the cursor (insertion point) to the next line or next page.

As a part of composing a document, images (pictures, clip art, charts, and more) can be inserted into the document to illustrate, emphasize, or decorate the document.

While word processing systems don't support all of the tools available in a graphic image editing application, most do allow you to position, resize, recolor, and adjust the image to suit your needs.

Document Editing

Editing an existing document or one that has just been composed is enhanced by the ability to move the cursor around the document freely. This capability allows the user to place the cursor before the character, word, line, or paragraph to be edited. In addition, the mouse can be used to highlight or select one or more characters, words, paragraphs, and pages so that editing can be applied to all of the selected text.

The actions commonly performed when editing a word processing document are

- **Inserting additional text** To insert text, the cursor is placed at the position in the document where the new text is to be inserted, called the insertion point, and the text is then entered from the keyboard or pasted from another location in the same document or from another document.

- **Replacing existing text** Replacing text involves selecting the text to be replaced using the mouse and then entering the new text or pasting new text to replace the selected text.

- **Removing existing text** Removing or deleting text from a document involves selecting one or more characters, words, lines, sentences, or paragraphs and pressing the DEL key on the keyboard. Text can also be removed, either selected or unselected, using the BACKSPACE key.

- **Copying text within a document** Duplicating text in a document involves copying the text from one part of the document (or another document) to a new location in the document. Depending on the particular word processor in use, the text to be copied is selected and then buttons, icons, menu choices, or shortcut key commands are used to copy the text and paste it into the new location. Figure 6-2 shows text selected in a Zoho Writer document and the Copy command from a pop-up menu being used to copy the text.

- **Moving text within a document** Moving text from one part of a document to another (or even to another document) involves one of two methods: cut and paste or drag and drop. In the cut-and-paste method, selected text is cut from one part of a document and pasted to a new location. In the drag-and-drop method, selected text is dragged using the mouse to its new location.

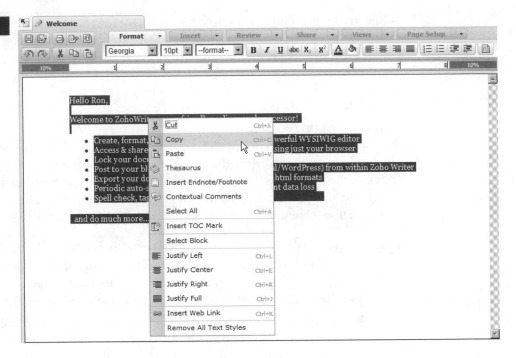

FIGURE 6-2

Text selected in
a Zoho Writer
document as
a part of a copy
action

Formatting a Document

There are two levels of formatting that can be applied to the text in a word processing
document: character and paragraph. Character formatting is applied to change the
appearance of one or more text characters. Paragraph formatting is used to change
the text alignment, line spacing, and the spacing before and after a paragraph break.

Character Formatting

The formatting of text characters can be used to emphasize or mark text. The most
commonly used character formatting features that are available in a word processing
application are

■ **Font** Text fonts are used to set the appearance of text to a particular artistic
style. Examples of commonly used fonts are shown in Table 6-2.

■ **Font size** The size of a font is measured in points. There are 72 points to an
inch. In a font that is 12 points in height (fonts are relatively proportional,
which means that as the height increases, the width increases as well), each
character is approximately one-sixth of an inch in height. A 72-point font
has characters about 1 inch tall. Figure 6-3 illustrates different font sizes in the
Arial font.

Font Name	Font Example
Arial	This is an example of Arial font.
Comic Sans	This is an example of Comic Sans font.
Courier New	This is an example of Courier New font.
Gill Sans	This is an example of Gill Sans font.
Lucida Handwriting	*This is an example of Lucida Handwriting font.*
Times New Roman	This is an example of Times New Roman font.
Verdana	This is an example of Verdana font.

TABLE 6-2

Examples of Commonly Used Word Processing Fonts

- **Font color**   Black is the most commonly used default color for text in a word processing document, which is placed on a white document workspace. However, one of a full range of colors can be applied to both the text itself and its background.
- **Bold**   Also called boldface, this character formatting feature changes the appearance of a text to a thicker and much darker face. See Figure 6-4 for an example text to which the bold feature is applied.

FIGURE 6-3

A comparison of font sizes from small (8 points) to large (72 points)

This is an 8-point font size

This is a 10-point font size

This is a 12-point font size

This is an 18-point font size

This is a 28-point font size

This is a 36-point font size

This is a 48-point font size

This is a 72-point fo

■ **Italics**   Italic text is slanted to the right and converted to a slight calligraphic appearance. See Figure 6-4 for an example of italicized text.

■ **Underline**   The underline feature places a 1-point horizontal line under selected text. In some document standards, italics and underlining are accepted substitutes for each other. Figure 6-4 includes an example of underlined text.

■ **Strikethrough**   Strikethrough character formatting is used primarily in legal documents to indicate a word or block of text that has been replaced, has been revised, or is to be removed before the document is finalized. Figure 6-4 includes an example of text to which strikethrough formatting is applied.

■ **Subscripts and superscripts**   Subscripts and superscripts are used mostly to indicate footnotes, endnotes, and other reference notations. Both are also used in mathematical formulations.

FIGURE 6-4

The most commonly used character formatting features

Regular

Bold

Italics

~~Strikethrough~~

Sub$_{script}$

Super^{script}

UPPER CASE

lower case

Paragraph Formatting

Paragraph formatting is used to change the spacing and alignment of one or more text paragraphs. The most commonly used paragraph formatting features are

- **Paragraph alignment** Text alignment is relative to the margins of a page. Some word processors allow you to align text vertically as well as horizontally, but commonly the text alignment features are (see Figure 6-5):
  - **Left** This alignment feature aligns the text to the left margin of a page. Left alignment is typically the default text alignment of a new, blank document.
  - **Right** This alignment feature aligns the text to the right margin of a page.
  - **Center** This alignment feature aligns the text to the relative center point between the left and right margins of a page.
  - **Justified** This alignment feature inserts additional spaces, if needed, in a line of text to align it to both margins of a page. If a line of text is not long enough to fill between the two margins of a page, the text defaults to left alignment.

- **Line spacing** The default in many word processing applications is to place one and one-half empty lines between the lines of text to open up the text for reading, editing, or to conform to a document standard. The standard line spacing settings available in most work processing applications are single-space (no empty lines between text lines), 1.5 lines (one-half empty line between text lines), and double-space (one empty line between text lines). Line spacing can also be set to an exact point size or set to leave not less than a certain point size of space between lines. See Figure 6-6 for examples of the standard line spacing options.

FIGURE 6-5

Examples of the alignment features of a word processing application

This is an example of **left** alignment

This is an example of **right** alignment

This is an example of **center** alignment

This is an example of **justified** alignment. This is an example of justified alignment. This is an example of justified alignment

FIGURE 6-6

Examples of the standard line spacing options in a word processing application

This is an example of single-space line spacing. This is an example of single-space line spacing. This is an example of single-space line spacing. This is an example of single-space line spacing. This is an example of single-space line spacing. This is an example of single-space line spacing.

This is an example of 1.5 line spacing. This is an example of 1.5 lines spacing. This is an example of 1.5 line spacing. This is an example of 1.5 line spacing. This is an example of 1.5 line spacing. This is an example of 1.5 line spacing.

This is an example of double-space line spacing. This is an example of double-space lines spacing. This is an example of double-space line spacing. This is an example of double-space line spacing. This is an example of double-space line spacing. This is an example of double-space line spacing.

- **Lines before or after paragraphs** Additional white space (empty lines) can be added between paragraphs by setting the space before and space after paragraph options in a word processing application. Depending on which word processing system you use, the default setting may be to insert a 6-point line (in addition to the line spacing in use) either before a new paragraph or after a paragraph. The additional space is added when the ENTER key is pressed, causing a new paragraph to be created.

- **Numbered or bulleted lists** Numbered or bulleted lists can be used to indicate a set sequence of events or items or a list in which all entries are relatively equal, respectively.

- **Borders** A border around the outside edge of a page or one or more paragraphs can add visual appeal to a document page or set apart a section of the document. The standard border for word processing applications is a line border, like the ones shown in Figures 6-5 and 6-6, but several symbols, characters, and preset border designs are available to create custom borders.

- **Shading** Placing a color background behind a block of text can help to emphasize or set apart the text. Applying a combination of font color and a text shade (background) can create a unique effect in a text document.

Reviewing and Proofing a Document

After you or a co-worker or family member has completed a first draft of a document, the next step in finalizing the document is to review and proof the document. The actions of reviewing and proofing a document are linked activities that most word processing software packages allow you to perform simultaneously. These actions can be accomplished in two general steps: checking for spelling and grammar errors, and reviewing and proofing a document.

Checking for Spelling and Grammatical Errors

Full-featured word processing systems include a spell checker, and some also include a grammar checker. A spell checker can be used to automatically scan the document, checking the spelling of the words against a standard dictionary file and suggesting one or more correct spellings for words that are phonetically or structurally similar to what is detected to be a misspelled word. A grammar checker checks phrases and sentences against a standard set of grammar rules and flags the text that it determines may contain a grammatical error.

One of the downsides to spell checkers is that a correctly spelled word may be used incorrectly, but because it is spelled correctly the word or its usage is not flagged. For example, the words whole and hole are each valid words with totally opposite definitions. If either of these words is used inappropriately, a spell checker is unable to determine your real meaning and therefore allows the word.

Grammar checkers are good tools for finding improper verb tense, split infinitives, number conflicts, and passive voice issues in a document, as well as many other common grammatical errors. Some word processing software packages, such as Microsoft Office Word, combine the spelling and grammar checkers into a single review. Figure 6-7 illustrates the application of a spelling and grammar checker on a sentence that obviously has issues.

FIGURE 6-7

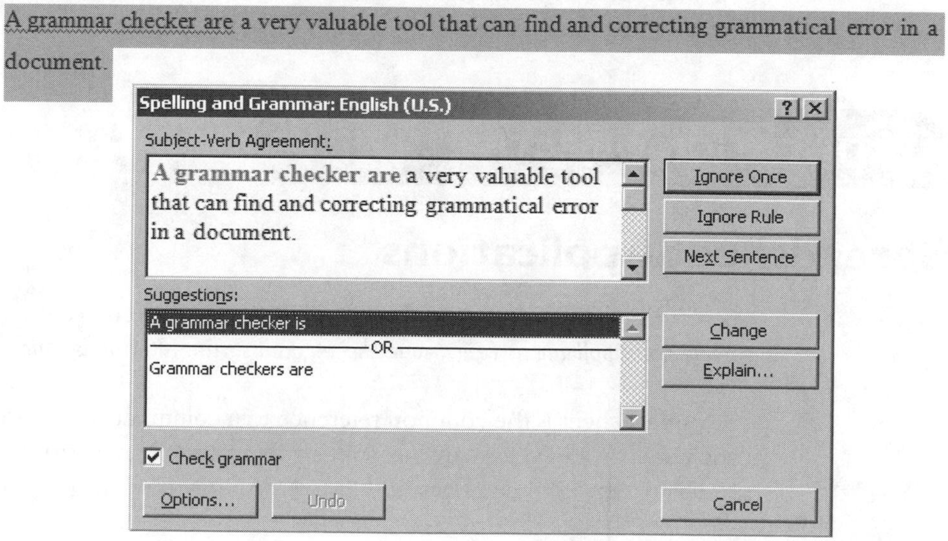

Microsoft Office Word 2007 combines the spelling and grammar checker into a single tool.

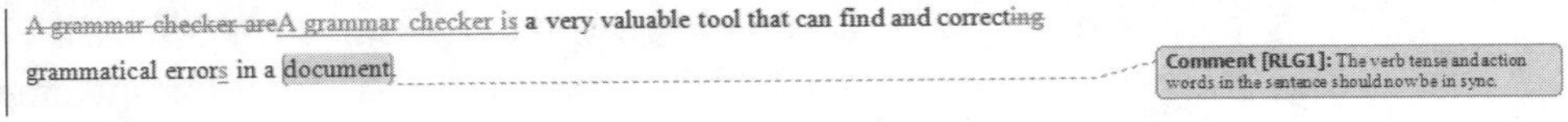

FIGURE 6-8

~~A grammar checker are~~A grammar checker is a very valuable tool that can find and ~~correcting~~ grammatical errors in a document.

Comment [RLG1]: The verb tense and action words in the sentence should now be in sync.

A comment inserted into a Word 2007 document

Reviewing a Document

When you review a document, you are essentially performing a proofing, also called proofreading, action. Proofing involves reading the document for its message, content, and flow. When you review/proof your own document, you can make any necessary changes directly into the document without the need to include any evidence of the change. However, when you proof a document prepared by another user, any changes, suggested changes, or comments should be made so that the impact of the change is apparent and the original text remains visible to the document's author and other reviewers.

When reviewing another user's document (or perhaps even your own), a feature available from full-featured word processing software is the ability to track changes made to a document. The track changes feature shows the complete action being suggested (as illustrated in Figure 6-8). The author of the document then can accept or reject the suggested change.

Another tool that can be valuable to document reviewers, as well as the document author, is the capability to insert comments into a document. When you wish to ask a question, make a suggestion, or simply convey a critique of all or parts of a document, inserting a comment into the document can be an effective way to communicate your message.

CERTIFICATION OBJECTIVE

Spreadsheet Applications

2.2.2   Identify fundamental concepts relating to spreadsheets and common uses for spreadsheet applications (e.g., worksheets, data sorting, formulas, and function, etc.).

A spreadsheet is the common reference to a columnar pad arranged in rows (one per entry) used in many accounting functions. An electronic spreadsheet is similar to a paper spreadsheet in that it is also organized into columns and rows.

However, that's where the similarities end. Electronic spreadsheets, which I'll call spreadsheets from this point on for the sake of simplicity, provide a wide array of data organization, calculation, and charting capabilities.

Spreadsheet Organization

The workspace of a spreadsheet application is organized into crossing rows and columns that form a matrix structure. The rows of a spreadsheet are numbered sequentially top to bottom, starting at the top of the workspace (which is also called a worksheet) with row 1 and continuing to the last row (which can vary from row 256 to row 1,048,576, depending on the particular spreadsheet software). A spreadsheet's columns are assigned alphabetic identities left to right, with column A in the upper-left corner of the workspace and continuing to as high as column XFD (again, depending on the software in use). Each intersection of a row and a column creates an individual cell, into which data, text, or a formulaic calculation can be entered.

The cells of a spreadsheet are identified individually using the combined references of the row and column intersection that creates the cell. For example, a cell that lies at the intersection of column D and row 72 is identified and referenced as cell D72. The first cell (upper-left corner) of a spreadsheet is cell A1, and the last cell in a spreadsheet may be cell XFD1048576, not that you would ever use that many cells in a single worksheet.

Spreadsheet Calculations

One of the strongest features of a spreadsheet application is its ability to perform calculations, which can range from simple arithmetic to complex formulas. Creating a calculation into a spreadsheet cell requires only a few rules, but these rules are essential to obtaining a valid result.

The first rule is that all calculation entries are called formulas, and to create a formula, you must indicate to the spreadsheet software that a formula is being entered. To begin entering a formula into a cell, the first character entered must be an equal sign (=). A formula entered without an equal sign in its first position is considered to be a text entry.

The second rule is that there is a set hierarchy to the arithmetic operations that can be used in a formula that governs which operation is performed first, which second, and so on. Table 6-3 lists the basic arithmetic operators common to virtually all spreadsheet applications. In a formula, multiplication or division is performed

TABLE 6-3	Basic Spreadsheet Arithmetic Operators		
Operation	**Operator**	**Example**	**Explanation**
Divide	/	=A1/D4	Divide the contents of cell A1 by the contents of cell D4.
Multiply	*	=A2*C4	Multiply the contents of cell A2 by the contents of cell C4.
Add	+	=A1+B1	Add the contents of cell A1 to the contents of B1.
Subtract	-	=B5-T6	Subtract the contents of cell T6 from the contents of cell B5.
Exponentiate	^	=A5^3	Raise the contents of cell A5 to the third power.

first on a whichever-comes-first (left-to-right) basis. Addition or subtraction is then performed on the same whichever-comes-first basis. This hierarchy of operations, also referred to as precedence, can yield a different result than expected if the operations are entered in the wrong order.

For example, the formula =8+2*6/3-1 results in 11. The following steps show how this is calculated:

1. Because the first multiply or divide encountered in the formula is 2*6, this operation is performed first, yielding 12.

2. The product of step 1 is then divided by 3, which is the next multiply or divide encountered in the formula, yielding 4.

3. The value 8 is then added to the result of step 2 because it is the first addition or subtraction encountered, resulting in 12.

4. The value 1 is then subtracted from the result of step 3, yielding the value 11.

If you calculated the value 19 from this formula, then you forgot to apply the precedence order of operations. But, what if you wanted to get the result of 19? To force a calculation to be performed out of sequence to the standard precedence, you can enclose elements of the formula in parentheses. Any element inside parentheses is evaluated first, with the normal order of operations applying to the contents of the enclosed element. For example, what if we place parentheses inside the formula =8+2*6/3-1 so that the first addition operation is performed first? The formula would now appear as =(8+2)*6/3-1. This changes the result of the formula to 19. What would be the result of the formula in the variation =(8+2)*6/(3-1)? Did you get 30?

This same rule applies to the contents of cells. The formula =A8+B2*C6/D3-E1 performs the same calculation as before, but including the contents of the cells in the formula. As before, the contents of cells B2 and C6 are multiplied; this product is divided by the contents of cell D3; the quotient is added to contents of cell A8; and the contents of cell E1 are subtracted from the subtotal.

The final rule is that the result of a formula is displayed in the cell occupied by the formula. So, if this formula was entered into cell F1, the result of the formula, whether 11, 19, 30, or whatever, is displayed in cell F1.

Spreadsheet Functions

While virtually all spreadsheet application software supports arithmetic formulas, like those discussed in the preceding section, many provide a library of functions that can be used to perform a variety of standard financial, statistics, higher mathematics, and logical calculations. Table 6-4 lists a sampling of the functions available in Microsoft Office Excel 2007.

TABLE 6-4

Examples of the Functions in Microsoft Office Excel 2007

Function	Category	Calculates/Results
AVERAGE	Statistical	Average for a range of cells
COS	Math and Trig	Cosine of a number
COUNT	Statistical	Tally of numerical values in a range of cells
DATE	Date and Time	Serial number for a specific date
EFFECT	Financial	Effective annual interest rate
FV	Financial	Future value of an investment
IF	Logical	True or false result to a logical test
IRR	Financial	Internal rate of return for cash flows
LOG	Math and Trig	Logarithm of a number to a specified base
NPV	Financial	Net present value of a series of cash flows
ROUND	Math and Trig	Number rounded to a specific number of decimal digits
SLOPE	Statistical	Slope of a linear regression
SUM	Math and Trig	Summation of a cell range
TRIM	Text	Eliminates leading and trailing spaces from a text string

The functions available in a spreadsheet application can be placed into a cell along with the values and references the function needs to complete its calculation. For example, the syntax for the AVERAGE function is =AVERAGE(number1,number2,number3, . . .). Each of the arguments (number1,number2,number3, . . .) in the AVERAGE function can be a single cell or a range of cells. The result displayed in the cell in which the function is entered is the average of the cells indicated in the arguments to the function.

A range of cells is indicated by the reference of the first cell in the range, a colon (:) that indicates a range is being specified, and the reference of the last cell in the range. For example, the entry A1:B12 indicates a range of cells starting with cell A1 and ending with cell B12, inclusive. Figure 6-9 illustrates a cell range specified in a function.

What-If Projections

Among the most frequent uses for a spreadsheet application are forecasts, projections, or using current data to model what the result might be if a key factor were to change. This type of modeling is called a "what-if." If a set of values represents the results from an activity, such as sales results, projected profits, or the volume of space required to contain specific items, entering a new projected or trial value for a key factor, such as units sold, cost of production, or the number of items in inventory, should have the effect of changing the overall results. What-if analysis can be performed on an existing spreadsheet that is opened from disk, modeled, and then not saved back to the disk, thereby discarding the model.

FIGURE 6-9

A function that calculates the average for a range of cells

	A	B	C
1	147852	369524	
2	369524	591196	
3	591196	812868	
4	812868	1034540	
5	1034540	1256212	
6	1256212	1477884	
7	1477884	1699556	
8	1699556	1921228	
9	1921228	2142900	
10	2142900	2364572	
11	2364572	2586244	
12	2586244	2807916	
13			=AVERAGE(A1:B12)
14			1477884

Charts

Another of the more valuable features of a spreadsheet application is its ability to produce charts from a range of data. A chart is a graphical depiction of the data presented in a form that can be used for comparative, relationship, and trend analysis. Most of the spreadsheet applications available support four basic chart types:

- **Bar charts**   A bar chart (see Figure 6-10) compares two or data series by depicting each as a separate bar or a proportion of a horizontal bar with the total bar length representative of the total of the values in each series.

- **Column charts**   A column chart (see Figure 6-11) compares two or data series by depicting each as a separate bar or a proportion of a vertical bar with the total bar length representative of the total of the values in each series.

FIGURE 6-10

An example of a bar chart created from a range of data cells

	A	B	C	D
1	Product	Region 1	Region 2	Region 3
2	123-85	147852	369524	591196
3	123-98	369524	591196	812868
4	123-23	591196	812868	1034540
5	345-78	812868	1034540	1256212
6	345-22	1034540	1256212	1477884
7	658-21	1256212	1477884	1699556
8	753-65	1477884	1699556	1921228
9	123-88	1699556	1921228	2142900
10	456-92	1921228	2142900	2364572
11	745-35	2142900	2364572	2586244
12	258-64	2364572	2586244	2807916
13	951-75	2586244	2807916	3029588
14				
15				

FIGURE 6-11

An example of a column chart

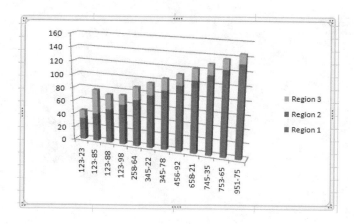

FIGURE 6-12

An example of a line chart

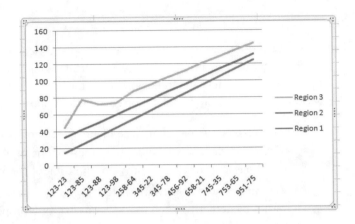

- **Line charts** A line chart (see Figure 6-12) shows the trend in a data series across a group of similar items or over one or more periods of time.
- **Pie charts** A pie chart (see Figure 6-13) depicts two or more data series as a proportion of the total value of all of the data series included in the chart data range. Each proportional segment is shown as a "slice" of the pie. Pie charts can also be shown with the proportional pieces separated or exploded.

Other types of charts that are supported by different spreadsheet applications, although only a few offer all of the charts listed, are scatter charts, area charts, surface charts, donut charts, radar charts, bubble charts, and stock range charts.

Spreadsheet charts can be saved as an object on a worksheet, as a separate chart page, or as a separate chart file to be inserted into other types of documents.

FIGURE 6-13

An example of a pie chart

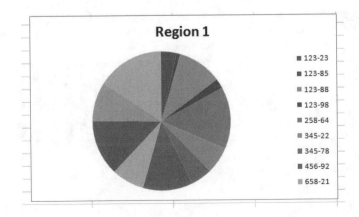

CERTIFICATION OBJECTIVE

Presentation Applications

2.2.3   Identify fundamental concepts relating to presentation software and common uses for presentation applications (e.g., slides, speaker notes, graphics, etc.).

Personal productivity software has essentially replaced manually operated pieces of legacy equipment, with each application linked to at least one of these pieces of equipment. Word processing has replaced the typewriter; spreadsheets have replaced the paper columnar pad and the tabulating machine; and presentation software has replaced the 35 mm slide projector.

In the past, to present a slide show, one had to either photograph the slides or use an overhead projector and transparencies. Don't worry if you aren't sure what all these items are; just know that presentation software provides you with much more capability and certainly a lot more flexibility when it comes to preparing a slide show.

Presentation application software is used to prepare and present a slide show to an audience. Each slide can be individually designed, or a presentation template can be used to quickly prepare a slide show from a written outline of the message you wish to deliver.

Presentation slides can be formatted by their purpose. A title slide layout can be used for the first slide to display the title, the subject matter, the date, and the presenter's name and company or organization, if desired. There are no specific rules governing exactly what must be on a slide and which format is used for what slide. Presentation software provides you with the maximum in flexibility and control for any slide show you wish to prepare.

Slide Format and Layout

Slides can contain text, pictures, digital images, clip art, links to animations or movies, links to Web pages and their content, and even links to other slides in the same slide show. Most of the presentation templates and slide designs available to a presentation application provide for formatted layouts for a variety of slides. Figure 6-14 shows the default slide themes available in Corel Presentations X4. There are some differences in what one presentation software package refers to as a theme and what another may call a template. In Microsoft Office PowerPoint 2007 and Corel Presentations X4,

FIGURE 6-14

The slide
presentation
themes available
in Corel
Presentations X4

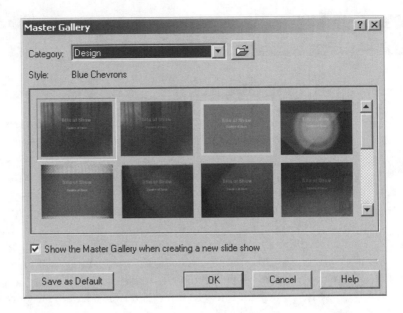

a template is a formatted structure that contains a variety of different slide layouts with a preset color scheme, and a theme is a color scheme only. In many of the online presentation applications, a theme is essentially the same as a template, and this difference exists with other packages as well.

In the more full-featured presentation applications, like PowerPoint and Corel Presentations X4, a variety of slide layouts are available and can be used whenever a particular slide layout is more appropriate to your needs. Figure 6-15 illustrates the slide layouts available in PowerPoint 2007.

Slide Animations and Transitions

Two of the better features of a presentation application are the features that allow you to animate the appearance, emphasis, and disappearance of text onto, on, and from a presented slide and add an attention-grabbing animated transition from one slide to the next.

FIGURE 6-15

The Slide
Layout Gallery of
PowerPoint 2007

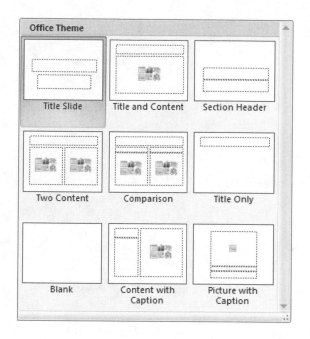

Slide animations allow you to customize how one or more text lines show up, are emphasized, or exit from a slide while it's being projected. Entrance effects include fly in, checkerboard, dissolve, descend, and pinwheel, among many others. Exit effects mirror the entrance effects, but a completely different exit effect can be applied regardless of the entrance effect used. Emphasis effects allow you to blink, flash, change the font, grow the font, and shrink the font, among many more. All three of these effects can be applied to a line of text, an image, or an entire object box.

Slide transitions control the way slides advance during the slide presentation. The default slide transition in virtually all presentation applications is no transition. However, if you would like one slide to fade into another slide, one slide to fly off the screen to the left and the next slide to fly in from the right, or a set of vertical or horizontal bars to reveal the next slide, all of these transitions and more are available for use. Figure 6-16 shows the Slide Transition Gallery for PowerPoint 2007.

FIGURE 6-16

The Slide
Transition
Gallery of
PowerPoint 2007

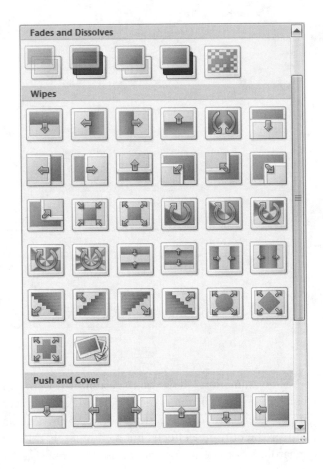

Presenter Aids

Presentation applications also provide support to the presenter in the form of printed notes, handouts, or, if desired, a copy of the slides. As a slide presentation is being prepared, speaker's notes can be added to each of the slides and then printed out with a reduced image of the slide and the notes, one page to a slide. Handouts for the audience can also be printed that show a reduced image of each slide with an area for note-taking adjacent to the slide image. Printed copies of the slides, with one slide per page, can also be printed for use as notes or to share with others.

CERTIFICATION OBJECTIVE

Database Applications

2.2.4 Identify fundamental concepts relating to databases and common uses for database applications (e.g., fields, tables, queries, reports, etc.).

By definition, any software that organizes data into a structure of related records is a database. This can include filing cabinets, Rolodexes, telephone books, and computer-based database application software. A database system can be used to organize data for structured storage and retrieval.

Database applications come in all sizes and capabilities. Some are designed for very large network applications, such as Oracle and IBM's DB2, and others are designed more for personal use, such as Microsoft Office Access 2007, Sun Microsystems' StarOffice Base, MKF Solutions' Database Oasis, FileMaker Pro, and the online database software from Intuit, QuickBase.

The organization of personal productivity database systems is generally that of a relational database. A relational database is organized around relationships that exist between the data in one database table and another. The ability to create logical links (relationships) between database entities reduces the amount of redundant data that is stored in a database. Figure 6-17 shows the relationship created between two tables in an Access 2007 database.

FIGURE 6-17

The relational links created between tables in an Access 2007 database

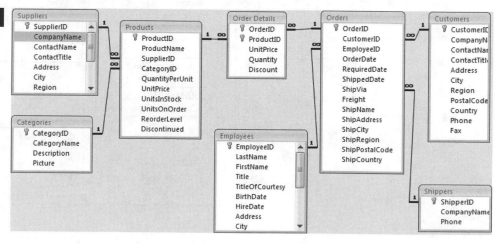

Database Structure

A database system uses a structured organization that is built around a hierarchy of data groups. Fields or individual pieces of data (name, address, account number, etc.) make up records. Each unique and related group of fields (one student, one customer, one product, etc.) is contained in a record. Records with the same set of fields and essentially the same information are grouped into tables (Students, Customers, Products, etc.), and the tables are contained in a database.

The organization of a relational database system is designed to support related "flat" data groupings. In most database applications, a field is limited to a single value. This means that if a field, such as the classes in which a student is enrolled at a school, contains more than one value, the data should be placed into a new table with each class included as a separate record. Figure 6-18 illustrates this principle.

On a paper record, it's easy to list all of a student's information for a particular term. However, to automate the paper system, which must be completely recreated

FIGURE 6-18

The structure and organization of a sample database

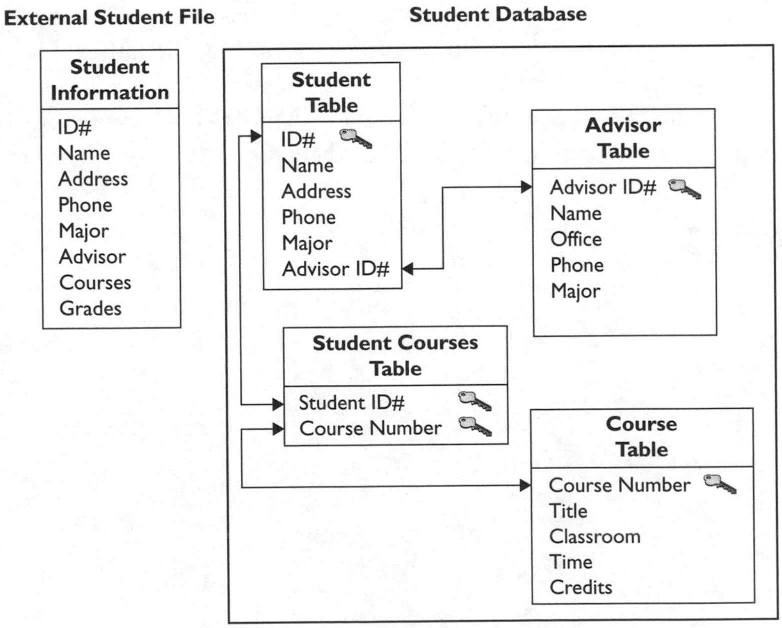

by hand each term, a database structure must be created. The following steps describe the process used to create the student database shown in Figure 6-18.

1. Identify each piece of data in the paper record that is unique to the student (with no duplicates) or typically has more than a single value. For example, the Student ID# is completely unique to one student, the Advisor ID# is unique to one advisor, and students take one or more classes and commonly have more than one set of grades.

2. Identify nonrepeating data that relates to a single entity (student). Address, phone, and for the sake of this example, major are nonrepeating data (fields) that are directly related to the Student ID#.

3. With the information gained in the preceding two steps, we can identify a Student table, a Course table, a Grades table (not shown), and an Advisor table. Notice that separate tables are used to eliminate any repeating data fields in all of the tables.

4. A primary key is assigned to each table (discussed in the next section, "Primary and Foreign Keys").

These steps have defined a student database that identifies any data that may change from term to term or as changes occur in only one instance, which eliminates redundancy in the data. Using the paper system, if a student's phone number changes, all records on which the phone number is written must be updated to ensure that the correct information is available regardless of the record in use. A database system, because it stores a data field only once, ensures that if the phone number is changed, the new phone number is changed on all views of the database information.

However, one additional table is needed. Because we've removed the repeating field Course Number from the Student table, we need to create a bridging table that links the Student table to the Course table. This is the purpose of the Student Course table. In this table, each record is used to link a student to a particular course, requiring both data fields to be assigned together as the primary key.

Primary and Foreign Keys

To ensure uniqueness, a key field is designated for each table and each record in the table must have a unique value for its primary key, as shown in Figure 6-18. The Student ID# field, because it is completely unique to a single student, can be used as the primary key of the Student record. Likewise, the Advisor ID# and the Course Number fields are assigned as the primary keys of the Advisor and Course tables, respectively.

A record can also contain one or more foreign keys, which serve as a link to the primary key of another table. In the Student Courses table, shown earlier in Figure 6-18, the Course Number field, in addition to being a part of the primary key for the Student Courses table, is a foreign key that links a particular student to one of his or her courses.

Reports and Queries

Perhaps the primary value of organizing data into a database application is its capability to produce queries and reports that contain a complete set or the amount of related or linked information needed to answer a specific question.

Database Reports

A report is a structured and formatted listing of data extracted from a database. A report can retrieve data directly from tables or from a particular query. Reports are designed to be printed but can also be viewed on a screen.

On the other hand, a query is frequently used to provide an extraction of data from across a database for use in one or more reports or as a standalone entity for display. It is more efficient to use a query to retrieve data from a database when the selection of the data to be retrieved involves calculations or comparisons, which can be performed in a report, but not nearly as efficiently. In many ways a query is like a bridging function between the database and tables and a report or another visual element.

CERTIFICATION OBJECTIVE

Graphics and Multimedia Applications

2.2.5 Identify fundamental concepts relating to graphic and multimedia programs and common uses for graphic or multimedia software (e.g., drawing, painting, animation tools, etc.).

The primary difference between a graphics application and a multimedia application is the difference between static images and animation. Graphics and photo manipulation software are used to enhance, format, and edit still images, such as line art and photographs.

Both of these application software tools have their place in a personal productivity toolbox. Depending on your needs, one or both of these tools can be used to create graphic images and animations that would otherwise not be available for use.

Graphics application software is also known as illustration software, drawing software, and image and photograph manipulation software. Regardless of what it's called, this type of software application is used to create new drawings, manipulate drawings, or combine two or more drawings.

Drawing Application Software

Graphics software, such as Adobe Illustrator, Corel Draw and Paint Shop Pro, and SmartDraw, contains a variety of drawing and layering tools and features to assist you to create the drawing you want. As shown in Figure 6-19, a number of special-purpose toolkits can be used to create a drawing freehand, using preset shapes and color palettes.

Most of the better graphics software also supports layering. This feature allows you to apply different artistic elements to a drawing one layer at a time. Layering allows

FIGURE 6-19

Adobe Illustrator is one of the more popular graphics applications. (Image courtesy of Kim Harshberger | Design Queue.)

you to add detail, shading, and other drawing styles and effects in a series of overlays. Should you need to change a layered drawing, you'd only need to change the layer containing the detail to be altered and not be faced with redrawing the entire image.

Photographic Manipulation Application Software

Digital cameras have revolutionized the use of digital photographic images on a computer. The need to scan a physical photograph to convert it to a digital format is fast going the way of the floppy disk into computer legacy and legend. However, not all digital photographic images turn out exactly the way you may want to use them in a document or as an image in a presentation, and this fact has given rise to the development of photographic manipulation software.

A variety of photographic manipulation software (also called digital photo editors) is available for both PCs and Macs (it's with this type of software that the battle between PCs and Macs really becomes a religious war). Photo editing software is available on two levels: advanced and beginner (also known as budget). Advanced photo editors, like Adobe Photoshop (see Figure 6-20), Corel Paint Shop Pro Photo, Corel Painter,

FIGURE 6-20

Adobe Photoshop is one of the more popular digital photograph manipulation application packages for both PCs and Macs. (Image courtesy of Kim Harshberger | Design Queue.)

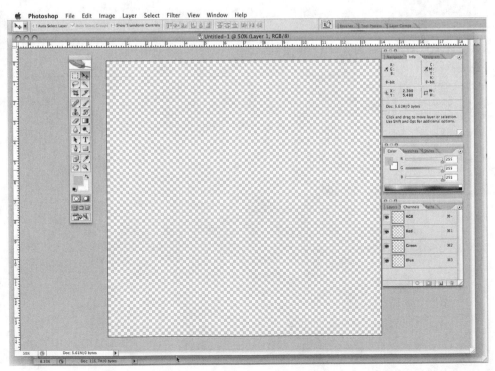

and Serif PhotoPlus, contain many advanced features such as bitmap-based image editing, photographic image enhancement, automated editing tools, and drawing and painting tools.

Beginner-level photo editors, like Adobe Photoshop Elements, Corel Ulead PhotoImpact, Microsoft Digital Image Suite, and Pavel Kanzelsberger's Pixel, generally have a relatively uncluttered user interface with support for image editing, photo correction and enhancement, and basic drawing and painting tools. Beginner-level photo editors include many lower-priced packages (compared to the advanced-level software), and a few are available for free trials or are free altogether.

Animation and Multimedia Software Applications

From the first computer games to the extensive library of video movies available on CDs, on DVDs, and as streaming video from the Internet, viewing animation and multimedia clips and movies has become one of the more popular activities on PCs.

Animation Software

Animation is created from a series of still images that are shown in a rapid sequence to create the illusion of movement. Basic computer animation is created using a process called computer-generated imagery (CGI), which creates this illusion through essentially the same process used to create motion picture or television animations from digital two-dimensional (2-D) or three-dimensional (3-D) still images.

Watching an animation is the simpler side of CGI software for the user. There are a variety of media playback applications that can be used to view an animation, including Microsoft Windows Media Player, RealPlayer, the VLC media player, the Winamp media player, the Adobe media player, and literally dozens of others. Many animation or media players are also multimedia players, which we'll discuss in the next section. Of course, you can always watch a video or animation online through YouTube, Google Video, AOL Video, Veoh, and Metacafe.

Creating an animation requires a different type of software application. There are relatively simple photo and line art (*.gif file) animators, as well as professional-level animation packages that have the ability to create a CGI animation from a variety of media sources. Some of the more popular animation technologies available are

- **Flash**   A Flash animation is based on the technology developed by Adobe in its Flash product. However, there are other animation software packages that can produce a Flash animation, including Mix-FX, CoffeeCup Firestarter, SWiSH Max2, and Selteco Alligator. Creating a Flash animation involves placing still images and effects on a timeline that, when it plays back, creates the illusion of motion or action.

- **GIF animation**   The Graphics Interchange Format (GIF) is a bitmapped image format that supports the creation and playback of still images to create an animation. A GIF animation displays a series of images to create the illusion of motion.

- **CGI animation**   This is the animation technology used to produce video games and many of the recent feature-length animated movies, such as *Shrek* and *Toy Story*. Special, and commonly expensive, software is used to create CGI graphics, such as 3ds Max, Blender, LightWave 3D, Maya, and Softimage.

Multimedia Animation

When animation is created from more than one content format, including text, audio, video, still images, and user interaction, the result is a media-rich multimedia event or object. Multimedia can be used in a staged event, such as a concert or in performance art, or a recorded video that can be viewed on a PC, cellular telephone, MP3 player, or the like.

Multimedia combines visual and audio elements into a single form by linking the elements into a series of timed events, much like a Flash object. The more popular multimedia development software packages are: Adobe Director, Adobe Premier Pro, ColorVision Spyder, Pinnacle Studio, and Ulead VideoStudio Pro.

For multimedia viewing and playback, there are literally dozens of players available, including most of those listed in the preceding section (see "Animation Software"), plus Adobe Media Player, AVS Media Player, and DivX.

Computer-Aided Design Applications

Another type of graphics software is computer-aided design applications that can be used to facilitate the design of mechanical, infrastructure, or structural objects, such as gears, piping systems, electrical systems, or houses and commercial buildings.

The more popular software applications in this general area are AutoCAD, SolidWorks, and CADPro.

CERTIFICATION OBJECTIVE

Software for Specific Applications

2.2.8   Identify other types of software.

In addition to the general-purpose or broad application software discussed earlier in this chapter, a wide variety of software exists that is specifically designed for a single application or a limited range of applications. These software applications are used in a variety of industries, businesses, and, in some cases, even homes.

Project Management Software

Project management software is used in construction, software development, manufacturing, consulting, and other industries to plan, estimate, monitor, and control the tasks, activities, costs, and resource usage of a project. Several very large project management packages are available for large project use, but there are also a few PC-based packages that are regularly used for small to medium-sized projects, such as Microsoft Project, Kidasa Milestones, and MatchWare MindView.

Group Collaboration Software

Group collaboration software, like Microsoft SharePoint, IBM Lotus Notes, and Novell GroupWise, can be either supported on a local or wide area network or accessed on the Web. Collaborative software facilitates the communication, coordination, and collaboration between team or project members. To a certain level, social networking sites, such as LinkedIn, Facebook, and Joined, provide some level of collaborative support as well. Chapter 20 covers collaborative software in more detail.

Specialized Application Software

There is likely a specialized software application for just about any business or personal activity in existence. Software has been developed to facilitate and expedite virtually every business activity performed. Here are just a few examples:

- **Customer relationship management (CRM)** CRM software, such as Siebel CRM, ACT!, and Salesforce CRM, tracks a customer relationship from first contact through and beyond the delivery of the product or service. Many of these packages also provide an interface with call center applications, or include them, so that future contacts with a customer can also be tracked. Sales lead software, while not as robust as a CRM package, performs many of the same tracking features. Products like Goldenseal, Leads360, and GoldMine provide the means to capture sales lead information and track it through to a sale.

- **Process control** For the most part, process control software, which is used to control manufacturing, processing, or facility automation, is highly customized to a particular activity. Generic process control software applications are statistical analysis systems that can help a production or process manager monitor and manage a particular process.

- **Education management** Application software plays a large role in the administration and management of just about every level of education, from preschool to graduate school. Student information systems track the details of a student in his or her classes, activities, and sometimes more. Scheduling software is also used to schedule classes, instructors, and students. Virtually all management and administrative recordkeeping in a school is automated using one or more applications.

- **Travel and tourism** The travel and tourism industry uses a variety of software applications. Special applications used for reservation systems, some of which are now online, track passengers or clients, search out that perfect vacation, and perform several other functions.

CERTIFICATION OBJECTIVE

Application Interactions

2.2.10   Identify how applications interact and share data.

In the past, it was virtually impossible to share data between two different applications because each application package had its own, often proprietary, file formats and data structures. Within today's software suites and even between applications from different software publishers, sharing data between applications is common. However, native file formats and format coding inserted into each particular type of document mean that software of one type can't always directly open a file from another application.

In general, software applications use one of three fundamental approaches to share information:

- **Collaborative environments**   Groupware or workgroup systems like Microsoft Office SharePoint Server (MOSS), Novell GroupWise, Oracle Collaboration Suite, and on a smaller scale Microsoft Groove, provide a central repository for shared documents that can be opened by authorized users for collaboration or coordination. Of these products, all but Groove (and its workalikes) are server-side information management systems that store, catalog, and manage virtually any form of digital document.

- **Database systems**   Most of the word processing, electronic spreadsheet, database, and even, to an extent anyway, presentation software has the ability to write data to and read data from a database system. Software can also save files in a variety of standard, commonly supported file formats, such as rich-text format (*.rtf), comma-separated values (*.csv), plain text (*.txt), and others.

- **Embedded objects**   An embedded object is essentially an object generated by another software application that is included in a document using a feature like Microsoft's Object Linking and Embedding (OLE). For example, a chart generated from data stored in an Excel workbook can be embedded in a Word document. If changes are made in Excel to the data on which the chart is based, the linked chart in the Word document is updated.

- **Remote procedure call (RPC)**   One application, typically under the control of user-created programming, can call or invoke an instance of another software application or routine, passing the called program any data required to complete a task.

CERTIFICATION SUMMARY

This chapter provided a general overview of personal productivity application software, namely word processing, electronic spreadsheets, presentation editors, database management systems, and graphics editors.

You should know the usage of each type of application software and the basic operation of each type.

✓ TWO-MINUTE DRILL

Overview of Commonly Used Applications

❑ Personal productivity software is a software package or suite that includes a word processor, an electronic spreadsheet, a presentation graphics editor, and a personal database system.

❑ Web-based personal productivity software can save storage space, money, and time.

❑ Simulation software has the ability to reasonably imitate a real phenomenon, action, or event through a series of mathematical algorithms and formulas.

❑ Information management software provides a means to manage and share information assets on an automated network to identify, categorize, and manage information assets.

Word Processing Applications

❑ Word processing software helps a user compose, edit, format, and print professional-looking letters, brochures, documents, and reports. Word processing software is one of the most popular applications used in homes and offices.

❑ Word processing software systems support a variety of features and tools, including spell checking, grammar checking, and language support—along with the capability to create merged documents; insert tables, references, hypertext links, and images; and track document versions.

❑ The primary functions of a word processing system are composing, editing, formatting, reviewing, printing, and publishing.

❑ Editing a word processing document is enhanced by the ability to move the cursor around the document freely. Editing a document involves such actions as inserting text, replacing text, removing text, and copying or moving text within a document.

❑ Two levels of formatting can be applied to a word processing document: character formatting and paragraph formatting. Character formatting is applied to one or more text characters. Paragraph formatting changes the text alignment, the line spacing, and the spacing before and after a paragraph break.

❑ Reviewing a document can be accomplished in two general steps: checking for spelling and grammar errors, and reviewing and proofing a document.

Spreadsheet Applications

❑ An electronic spreadsheet is organized into columns and rows. Spreadsheets provide a wide array of data organization, calculation, and charting capabilities.

❑ The rows of a spreadsheet are numbered sequentially top to bottom, starting at the top of a worksheet. A spreadsheet's columns are identified alphabetically left to right with column A in the upper-left corner continuing to the last column of the worksheet.

❑ The intersection of a row and a column creates an individual cell into which data, text, or a formulaic calculation can be entered.

❑ Spreadsheet cells are identified individually with the combined references of the row and column intersection that creates the cell.

❑ A calculation entry is called a formula with the first character an equal sign (=). A formula entered without an equal sign in its first position is considered to be a text entry.

❑ An order of precedence is used for arithmetic operations in a formula. Multiplication or division is performed first, and then addition or subtraction is performed. The result of a formula is displayed in the cell occupied by the formula. Spreadsheets support a wide variety of predefined arithmetic formulas.

❑ A range of cells is indicated by the reference of the first cell in the range, a colon, and the reference of the last cell in the range.

❑ A frequent use for a spreadsheet is what-if modeling. Entering a new projected or trial value for a key factor should have the effect of changing the overall results.

❑ A chart is a graphical depiction of the data presented in a form that can be used for comparative, relationship, and trend analysis. Most of the spreadsheet applications available support four basic chart types: bar charts, column charts, line charts, and pie charts. Spreadsheet charts can be saved as an object on a worksheet, as a separate chart page, or as a separate chart file.

Presentation Applications

❑ Presentation software is used to prepare and present a slide show. Each slide can be individually designed, or a presentation template can be used to prepare a slide show from a written outline.

❑ Slides can contain text, pictures, digital images, clip art, links to animations or movies, links to Web pages and their content, and links to other slides in the same slide show.

❑ Presentation software allows you to animate the appearance, emphasis, and disappearance of text onto, on, and from a presented slide as well as an animated transition from one slide to the next.

Database Applications

❑ Personal database systems are generally relational databases. A relational database contains defined relationships among data elements.

❑ In a database, fields make up records; records are grouped into tables; and the tables are contained in a database.

❑ A key field is designated for each table, and each record in the table must have a unique value for its key. A record may also contain one or more foreign keys, which serve as a link to the primary key of another table.

❑ A database report is a structured and formatted listing of data extracted from a database. A query is used to extract data from a database for use in one or more reports or as a standalone entity for display.

Graphics and Multimedia Applications

❑ Graphics application software is used to create new drawings, manipulate drawings, or combine two or more drawings.

❑ Photographic manipulation software supports bitmap-based image editing, photographic image enhancement, automated editing tools, and drawing and painting tools.

❑ Basic computer animation is created using CGI from 2-D or 3-D still images.

❑ Popular animation technologies available include Flash, GIF animation, and CGI animation.

❑ Multimedia combines visual and audio elements into a single form by linking the elements into a series of timed events.

Software for Specific Applications

❑ Some software applications are tailored to specific applications, such as project management, group collaboration, CRM, process control, education management, and travel and tourism, just to list a few.

Application Interactions

❑ Software suites and applications share data through a collaborative environment, a database system, an embedded object, or an RPC.

SELF TEST

The following questions are intended to help you be sure that you understand the material included in this chapter. Read the questions and the answer choices carefully.

Overview of Commonly Used Applications

1. Which of the following is not one of the applications included in a suite of personal productivity software?
   A. Word processing
   B. Electronic spreadsheet
   C. Web browser
   D. Database

2. What type of software is used to imitate a real phenomenon, action, or event using mathematical algorithms?
   A. Word processing
   B. Simulation
   C. Electronic spreadsheet
   D. Database

Word Processing Applications

3. Which of the personal productivity software applications is primarily used to compose, edit, format, and print professional-looking letters, brochures, documents, and reports?
   A. Word processing
   B. Electronic spreadsheet
   C. Web browser
   D. Database

4. When you insert, replace, and delete text in a business letter, what action are you performing?
   A. Revision
   B. Proofing
   C. Finalizing
   D. Editing

5. What are the two levels of formatting that can be applied to a document?

   A. Character

   B. Page

   C. Paragraph

   D. Document

Spreadsheet Applications

6. What are the organizational elements of an electronic spreadsheet?

   A. Columns

   B. Tables

   C. Rows

   D. Cells

7. Which spreadsheet organizational element is numbered?

   A. Columns

   B. Tables

   C. Rows

   D. Cells

8. Which spreadsheet organizational element is identified by alphabetic characters?

   A. Columns

   B. Tables

   C. Rows

   D. Cells

9. What is the cell reference from a cell in the third row and fourth column?

   A. A1

   B. C4

   C. D3

   D. F4

10. What is the character that must be entered in the first position to indicate a formula?

   A. @ (at sign)

   B. = (equal sign)

   C. $ (dollar sign)

   D. ! (exclamation mark)

11. What is the first operation performed in the following formula?

A1+B2*C3+D4/E5

A. B2*C3

B. D4/E5

C. A1+B2

D. C3+D4

12. When a spreadsheet's content is used to model the effect a key factor might make if it were to change, it is referred to as what?

A. Projection

B. What-if

C. Forecast

D. Pro Forma

13. What feature is used to graphically display the data in a spreadsheet?

A. Picture

B. Model

C. Table

D. Chart

Presentation Applications

14. Which of the personal productivity software applications is used to prepare and present a slide show?

A. Web browser

B. Electronic spreadsheet

C. Presentation editor

D. Database

Database Applications

15. Which of the personal productivity software applications is used to organize data in relational groupings?

A. Web browser

B. Electronic spreadsheet

C. Presentation editor

D. Database

16. Which of the following is not an organizational element in a database system?
    A. Fields
    B. Clusters
    C. Records
    D. Tables

17. What is the value in a database record that uniquely identifies each record?
    A. Primary key
    B. Foreign key
    C. Record identifier
    D. Query

18. What is an extraction of data from one or more tables in a database that can be used as the basis of a report or as a standalone information source?
    A. Reference table
    B. Query
    C. Form
    D. Pivot table

Graphics and Multimedia Applications

19. What type of software application is used to create, modify, or combine drawings?
    A. Web browser
    B. Electronic spreadsheet
    C. Presentation editor
    D. Graphics editor

20. Which of the following is not a type of computer-generated animation?
    A. Flash
    B. Video
    C. GIF animation
    D. CGI

Software for Specific Applications

21. What type of specialized software application can be used to track customer relationships?
    A. CRM
    B. Education management
    C. Graphics and multimedia
    D. Project management

Application Interactions

22. What are the methods used by software suites and applications to share data?

   A. Collaborative environment

   B. Database

   C. Embedded object

   D. RPC

   E. All of the above

   F. None of the above

SELF TEST ANSWERS

Overview of Commonly Used Applications

1. ☑ **C.** Web browsers may be bundled onto distribution media, but they are installed independently of a personal productivity suite.
   ☒ **A, B,** and **D** are incorrect. Word processing, spreadsheet, and database applications are commonly included in personal productivity suites.

2. ☑ **B.** Simulation software imitates a real phenomenon, action, or event using mathematical algorithms.
   ☒ **A, C,** and **D** are incorrect. Only in the widest definition of real phenomena do word processing, spreadsheet, and database software simulate action events.

Word Processing Applications

3. ☑ **A.** A word processing application is used to compose, edit, format, and print a variety of text-based documents.
   ☒ **B, C,** and **D** are incorrect. Spreadsheet, database, and browser applications are used for other types of document production and maintenance.

4. ☑ **D.** Inserting, replacing, moving, and deleting text from a text document is the act of editing.
   ☒ **A, B,** and **C** are incorrect. Revising is a form of editing, and proofing and finalizing are actions taken after editing is completed.

5. ☑ **A and C.** A word processing system typically supports character and paragraph formatting.
   ☒ **B and D** are incorrect. Page and document formatting is carried out through character and paragraph formatting.

Spreadsheet Applications

6. ☑ **A, C,** and **D.** Spreadsheets are organized through rows, columns, and cells.
   ☒ **B** is incorrect. A table can be added to a spreadsheet worksheet to organize cells into a commonly addressed element.

7. ☑ **C.** Rows are identified top to bottom with integer numbers.
   ☒ **A, B,** and **D** are incorrect. Columns are identified left to right with alphabetic characters. Cells are identified by the identifiers of the column and row that intersect to form the cell. Tables are identified with a name assigned to the table when it's created.

8. ☑ **A.** Columns are identified left to right with alphabetic characters.
   ☒ **B, C,** and **D** are incorrect. Rows are identified top to bottom with integer numbers. Cells are identified by the identifiers of the column and row that intersect to form the cell. Tables are identified with a name assigned to the table when it's created.

9. ☑ **C.** The fourth column (from the top-left corner) of a spreadsheet is column D. The third row down on a spreadsheet is row 3. Therefore the cell in the third row and fourth column is D3.
   ☒ **A, B,** and **D** are incorrect. Cell A1 is at the intersection of column A and row 1; cell C4 is at the intersection of column C and row 4; and cell F4 is at the intersection of column F and row 4.

10. ☑ **B.** An equal sign is used to indicate that a cell entry is a formula.
    ☒ **A, C,** and **D** are incorrect. The other characters listed have specific cell reference uses in a spreadsheet.

11. ☑ **A.** Because the order of precedence is multiplication or division first, multiplication (B2*C3) is performed before all other operations.
    ☒ **B, C,** and **D** are incorrect. The second operation performed is D4/E5, followed by A1+(B2*C3), and then the quotient of D4/E5 is added.

12. ☑ **B.** What-if modeling is a common use of a spreadsheet.
    ☒ **A, C,** and **D** are incorrect. Spreadsheets generally are used to produce projections, forecasts, and pro forma financial statements and need not be what-if analyses.

13. ☑ **D.** A chart is used to display spreadsheet data graphically.
    ☒ **A, B,** and **C** are incorrect. A picture can be inserted into a spreadsheet; spreadsheets are used to model data-generated models; and a table can be created on a spreadsheet to narrow an analysis.

Presentation Applications

14. ☑ **C.** Presentation editing software is used to prepare and present a slide show for presentation to an audience.
    ☒ **A, B,** and **D** are incorrect. A Web browser can be used to show a slide presentation on the Internet, but not to create the slides. Database and spreadsheet applications cannot be used for this purpose.

Database Applications

15. ☑ **D.** A database application is used to organize data in relational groupings.
    ☒ **A, B,** and **C** are incorrect. The other applications listed cannot be used to organize data in relational groupings.

16. ☑ **B.** Clusters are a logical disk organizational method and not something used within a database application.

    ☒ **A, C,** and **D** are incorrect. Databases are organized in fields, which make up records that make up tables.

17. ☑ **A.** Each record in a database table must have a unique identifying value, which is the record's primary key.

    ☒ **B, C,** and **D** are incorrect. Foreign keys can be included in a record for use in linking to other tables. A query is a data extraction type. The primary key is the record identifier in a database table.

18. ☑ **B.** A query is a data extraction that can be used as the basis of a report or as a standalone information source.

    ☒ **A, C,** and **D** are incorrect. There is no element officially identified as a reference table. A form is used to display, edit, or enter data into a database. A pivot table can be used to create a link between two database tables.

Graphics and Multimedia Applications

19. ☑ **D.** Graphics software can be used to create, modify, or combine drawings and other image types.

    ☒ **A, B,** and **C** are incorrect. A Web browser can be used to display graphics. Spreadsheets can contain an inserted graphic, as can presentation software.

20. ☑ **B.** Video is not a form of CGI, although CGI objects can contain animation.

    ☒ **A, C,** and **D** are incorrect. Flash, GIF animations, and CGI are all forms of computer-generated animations.

Software for Specific Applications

21. ☑ **A.** CRM (customer relations management) is a specialized application that can be used to track sales leads and customer interactions.

    ☒ **B, C,** and **D** are incorrect. Education management software is used to track and manage student records and institutional operations. Graphics and multimedia designate a general type of software application that can be used for a variety of purposes. Project management software is a specialized application, but it's used for tracking and managing the activities and costs of a project.

Application Interactions

22. ☑ **E.** All of the choices listed in Answers A through D are methods that can be used to share data between applications.

☒ **A, B, C, D,** and **F** are incorrect. While each choice is a valid way to share data between applications, each answer, on its own, is not the best answer available, which certainly makes Answer F incorrect.

7

Special-Purpose Software

I n addition to personal productivity software (see Chapter 6), other types of software can be used to protect, diagnose, secure, educate, entertain, and conduct business. Each of these special-purpose applications can enhance your computing experience.

Unfortunately, because any computer that is connected to a network, whether the Internet or a local network, is vulnerable to threats and the problems that can arise from the overall complexity of its operating system and application software, special-purpose software must be used to protect and secure the computer. Special-purpose software is a general classification for software applications that protect a computer from computer viruses and other threats, facilitate communications with other computers and the network, provide education and training, and support personal and business assistance.

This chapter looks at the following categories of special-purpose software:

- Diagnostics software
- Antivirus and malware protection software
- Training and education software
- Personal communications software
- Personal and business software

Each of these groups of special-purpose software is discussed in the sections that follow.

CERTIFICATION OBJECTIVE

Utility Programs

2.2.7   Identify the types and purposes of different utility programs (e.g., virus, adware and spyware detection programs).

The utility software installed on a PC creates a kind of software toolbox. The software tools can be used when a software or hardware problem occurs or when a PC is threatened by a computer virus, spyware, or intruders. Hardware and software diagnostic applications are used to determine the potential source of a performance issue on a PC. Virus, adware, malware, and spyware detection and protection applications scan a PC's memory and storage looking for malicious software that could damage, disrupt, or destroy data, software, or the PC itself.

Utility software can be divided into two major groups: diagnostics and system protection software. Diagnostics software can be used on a PC for both preventive maintenance and the determination of the source of a hardware or software problem. System protection software includes applications that can detect computer viruses and other forms of malicious programs.

Diagnostics Software

There are several types of special-purpose diagnostics software that can be used to keep a PC performing as it should:

- General diagnostics software
- Optimizing and cleaning software
- Monitoring software

General Diagnostics Software

Typically diagnostics are considered to be something that is done only when a hardware or software problem occurs. However, the regular use of most diagnostics software can also help to prevent problems before they happen. PC diagnostics applications perform a variety of scans, analyses, and cleanup functions. In nearly all of the general diagnostic applications, the three basic functions are scanning, diagnosis, and repair.

The scan function searches the hardware, system files, user files, and temporary files for possible threats, errors, and conflicts that could affect the performance of the system. The diagnosis function then identifies any problems found by the scan function and indicates the severity of each problem found. The repair function then attempts to correct the condition causing each problem.

on the **!** **O** o b   *It's always a good idea to create a backup of the system before running the repair function of a diagnostics software application. In fact, most of the better systems perform this step or at minimum advise you to do so.*

A few of the more popular diagnostic software applications available (some are free and some must be purchased) are Norton Utilities (www.Symantec-Norton.com),

PCDocPro (www.pcdocpro.com), Micro2000 (www.micro2000.com), TuffTEST (www.tufftest.com), Uniblue SpeedUpMyPC (www.uniblue.com), and PCDiag (www.pcdiag.com).

Optimizing and Cleaning Software

Optimizing and cleaning software ranges from single-purpose Windows Registry cleaners, disk defragmenters, and Desktop cleaners to packages that offer all of these plus other utilities.

The Windows Registry stores data needed to find, run, and manage software and users on a PC, along with other current operating environment information. On a PC that is used regularly, especially if software or hardware is frequently installed or removed, the Registry can have information left behind that is no longer valid. This obsolete information can eventually slow down the performance of the operating system and perhaps even cause processing errors and system crashes. Your first clue that the Registry may be clogged up is that the startup sequence takes longer to complete. Using a Registry cleaner, such as RegCure (www.regcure.com), Registry Fox (www.registryfox.com), or Reg Sweep (www.regsweep.com), can identify and allow you to eliminate any invalid or obsolete data from the Registry.

A PC's hard disk drive (as well as removable storage devices) can become fragmented as the operating system, without a single continuous storage block on the disk, fragments a file into several smaller disk locations. This can appear as a performance problem when fragmented files are retrieved. Disk defragmentation software optimizes the layout of the hard disk by physically arranging the data stored on the disk so that a file's fragments are placed closely together or contiguously, if possible. This process creates larger blocks of free space on the disk, which helps to prevent fragmentation in the future. Some of the more popular disk defragmentation software packages available are Diskeeper (www.diskeeper.com), Norton Defragmentation (www.Symantec-Norton.com), PerfectDisk (www.perfectdisk .com), and Smart Defrag (www.iobit.com).

A desktop cleaning utility, such as the Desktop Cleaner (www.pcdesktopcleaner .com), ZigZag Cleaner (www.uniphiz.com), and Cleaner 1.1 (www.softcomplete .com), removes any Windows Desktop icons that have not been used for a period of time and gives you the option to archive or delete icons you no longer use.

Monitoring Software

Monitoring software allows you to keep track of how a PC is used by recording the Web sites that are visited, files that are transferred, documents accessed, and even the keystrokes used. The records of these activities, and more, are available for viewing by the monitor administrator (only) as a log file, as screen captures, or through an e-mail or cellular phone text message. The popular monitoring software packages available include Spector Pro (www.spectorsoft.com), SpyAgent (www.spytech.com), and IAmBigBrother (www.internetsafety.com).

System Protection Software

A PC connected to the Internet or one that is connected to a fairly large local or wide area network is vulnerable to a variety of threats, such as computer viruses, adware, malware, spyware, and intrusion. While most of these threats tend to be self-inflicted, meaning that the malicious software is often innocently downloaded or allowed by the user, a PC must be protected from these threats to avoid serious problems or data loss.

System protection software includes three groups of utilities that can help to protect a PC from outside infection or access: antivirus software, malware detection software, and firewall software. Each of these groups of protection software is discussed in the sections that follow.

Antivirus Software

A *computer virus* is a malicious software program that has the ability to copy or save itself to a PC without the knowledge of the PC's user. Regardless of how a virus gains access to a PC, in order to carry out its intended purpose, it must be able to execute its instructions and have access to memory or secondary storage. To gain this capability, many viruses are either attached to or embedded in what is seemingly a legitimate or well-known program or file.

Computer viruses can be divided into two basic groups: resident and nonresident. A resident computer virus replicates itself by running in the background and attacking programs running on the PC, including application software and the operating system. A nonresident virus must have a host program to attach to; when that host program is started, the nonresident virus infects other programs that help to spread the virus when they are started.

Antivirus software attempts to disable and destroy various types of computer viruses, including all of these:

- ■ **Virus** The term computer virus has come to mean all types of malicious software, including the various types of malware described in this section and the following section (see "Malware Detection Software").

- **Worm**   A computer worm is a software program that is able to replicate itself across a network without the need to attach itself to other programs or files. In terms of the damage caused, a worm is typically less harmful than a virus. The major damage caused by a worm is the consumption of network bandwidth.

- **Rootkit**   A rootkit can consist of one or more software programs that are designed to seize control of an operating system, masking its presence by replacing essential system software and assuming their identities. A rootkit can also provide a back door to a system by compromising the login procedures.

- **Trojan horse**   A Trojan horse is camouflaged as a graphic, file, or program a user wishes to capture, download, or install on a PC, but contains a virus, a rootkit, or some other type of malicious software.

Antivirus software searches for recognizable patterns in files and programs. The methods most commonly used to detect a computer virus or other malware are

- **Signatures**   Antivirus software references a signature database that contains a recognizable binary pattern that is unique to a virus. However, because a virus can embed itself in a file, every file must be searched in its entirety.

- **Malicious activity**   Certain types of software behavior can be attributed to a virus, which, if detected by the antivirus software running in the system's background, causes the source of the suspicious activity to be checked using another detection method.

- **File analysis and emulation**   These detection methods are considered to be heuristic analysis approaches. File analysis scans through programs stored in a PC's disk storage looking for commands and instructions that may be malicious, such as erase the hard disk drive. File emulation uses a protected and isolated sandbox, which is an enclosed logical partition in which a suspicious file can be scanned or executed safely to determine if the file contains a serious threat.

If the antivirus software identifies a threat to the system, depending on the settings configured by the user, the software may remove the suspected file or attempt to restore the file to its original state.

Malware Detection Software

In common usage, the terms computer virus and malware have become interchangeable, but there are certain types of malware, a shortened version of the term malicious software, that can be categorized outside of the virus classification.

In general, *malware* consists of software programs that become resident on a PC to provide information back to their source.

The more common types of malware are

- **Adware**   The term adware is a shortened form of advertising-supported software. Adware is typically downloaded along with a file or Web page and is activated when a specific software program is executed, which is commonly a Web browser. Once activated, adware then displays pop-up ads or Web pages in a continuous sequence or begins a series of Web pages that claim that the user committed to an agreement and owes money.

- **Crimeware**   This type of malware is used by its creators to gather and transmit personal information, especially financial information, for the purposes of identity theft or fraudulent purchases made online.

- **Spyware**   This is perhaps the most insidious type of malware. Spyware can record and report keystrokes used to access a site, including passwords, or log the Web pages visited by a user, any items the user clicked on, and any financial information, such as a credit card, used to purchase an item online.

Firewall Software

A *firewall* can be either hardware or software with the purpose of protecting a computer or a network from unauthorized access from across a network and unsolicited network traffic. Hardware devices are typically installed between the Internet connection and a local area network (LAN). However, a software firewall can be used to protect either a network or an individual PC.

Firewall software, such as Check Point's ZoneAlarm, prevents access by unauthorized network users, as well as hackers, by blocking any incoming messages that are not specifically permitted by the firewall's settings as configured by the user. Many versions of firewall software also incorporate the protection of antivirus and malware systems.

Another protection provided by many software firewalls is a proxy server. A *proxy server* can save bandwidth, speed up information downloads, and prevent access to unauthorized Web sites or file servers by the users on a network or PC. A proxy server is configured with a list of blocked sites and Internet addresses to which requests for information aren't to be forwarded. The proxy server also keeps copies of the Web pages last or most frequently requested by users on the network and provides the information requested from its storage without needing to access the site over the Internet.

Education and Entertainment Software

2.2.6 Identify fundamental concepts relating to education and entertainment programs (e.g., computer-based training (CBT), video, audio).

The variety of educational and entertainment software available in today's market is virtually overwhelming. In the education software realm alone there are literally thousands of software titles to learn mathematics, writing skills, foreign languages, programming, career skills, and much more. Entertainment software includes games, games, and did I mention games? The fields of educational or training software and entertainment software have literally exploded to the point where there are now college degrees specializing in game design and digital entertainment.

Education software includes how-to videos, e-books, and documents that can be downloaded from the Internet along with any proprietary playback software clients. Digital entertainment software actually does boil down to computer video games.

Configuring a PC for CBT and Digital Entertainment

Both computer-based training (CBT) and digital entertainment systems require the right PC configuration. To get the maximum enjoyment and benefit from educational and entertainment software, you must configure your PC with the applicable hardware and software components. This includes the right video and audio controllers and their associated device drivers, audio and video codecs, primary memory, high-resolution monitor, speakers, and, of course, the CBT or entertainment software.

Chapters 1 and 2 cover audio and video controllers and device drives, memory, monitors, and speakers. Refer to those chapters for more information on these components and systems. The one remaining component in the configuration of a PC for digital entertainment consists of the audio and video codecs.

A codec, which is short for compressor/decompressor or coder/decoder, depending on the source, is a software program that decodes a digital video or audio stream into a format that can be used to generate video images or audio sounds on a monitor or through speakers, respectively. A codec is also used to compress or encode analog video or audio signals into a digital format for transmission or storage purposes.

Other Software Types

2.2.8 Identify other types of software (e.g., chat, messaging, web conferencing, accounting software).

While there are dozens of other application software types, most of them can be grouped into two additional general categories: personal communications and business applications. Personal communications software is used to chat, message, conference, and otherwise communicate with one or more other PC users. Business application software, which can also be used for personal accounting and record-keeping, covers the full spectrum of business-related functions and information processing needs.

Personal Communications Software

Personal communications software includes the software applications that you can use to communicate person-to-person across a network. This includes chat software, messaging software, Web-based conferencing software, telephony software, and more.

Chat and Messaging Software

Since ICQ (which is a play on the phrase "I seek you") was introduced almost 15 years ago, the ability to "chat" with one or more other persons in a private session using text messaging has advanced to Flash- and Java-based chat software. *Chat* applications, which typically require a software client to be installed on your local PC, support online-hosted chat rooms and private sessions provided by a messaging service server on the Internet.

The more popular chat services available include Microsoft Live Messenger (www.live.com), Yahoo! Messenger (www.yahoo.com), Skype (www.skype.com), and cross-service platforms like Meebo (www.meebo.com) and Zoho Chat. Many of these chat services also provide support for video chat as well.

Web Conferencing Software

Web conferencing applications that allow multiple people in multiple locations to join into either an audio conference, video conference, or even an audio-video conference have been around almost since the days of early messaging systems.

Web conferencing, which can be as simple as a video chat session or as complex as an international two-way video conference with dozens of participants, requires very little in the way of specialized equipment. By definition, a user must have a Web camera, a sound capture device (typically, a microphone), speakers, and perhaps a locally installed client for the conferencing service.

Web conferencing can be divided into four categories: audio conferencing, video conferencing, webinars, and real-time conferencing.

Audio Conferencing   Audio conferencing over the Internet works essentially the same as a landline telephone conference, with the exception that instead of dialing into a conferencing service over the telephone, you navigate to a particular Web site and enter a pass code to join the discussion. Some services have limits on the number of participants, although the limits are usually high enough that they pose no real limitations.

Although called audio conferences, most of the Web-based services also allow a one-way shared image stream that is typically used for presentation slides or the like. The more popular audio conferencing services include most regional telephone companies and Web providers like Genesys (www.genesys.com), Intercall (www.intercall.com), and Premiere Global (www.premiereglobal.com).

Video Conferencing   Web-based *video conferencing*, which is also called video teleconferencing, allows two or more locations to connect visually (and typically audibly as well) over the Internet. For the most part, the video streams and audio streams are two-way (full-duplex), meaning that they are transmitted to each location simultaneously. The primary difference between Web-based audio conferencing and video conferencing is the live video stream that provides the major benefit of video conferencing.

Video conferencing can be hosted on virtually any PC or network server. Web-based video conferencing is a service also provided by audio conferencing services. In addition, there are web-only conferencing services and video conferencing software providers like Cisco Systems' Webex (www.webex.com), Nefsis (www.nefsis.com), inSORS (www.iocom.com), Internet MegaMeeting (www.megameeting.com), LifeSize Communications (www.lifesize.com), and Citrix Online (www.gotomeeting.com).

Telephony Software   Voice communications over the Internet is supported by a group of protocols that is referred to collectively as the Voice over Internet Protocol (VoIP). There are occasions where an audio conference is just between two individuals who wish to have a conversation. There are definite advantages and disadvantages to using the Internet as a telephone system, but you just can't beat the price.

One of the most popular software applications available to support personal telephone communications is Skype (www.skype.com). This software application is able to complete and support free voice connections between PCs that each have the Skype software installed.

Business Application Software

Whether for a small or large business or personal or home use, business application software is generally one of the more prominent types of software available. Business applications such as accounting, inventory, asset management, retail sales, customer relations management (CRM), and more are available for installation on a network or a single PC system.

Business application software (BAS) is generally designed and configured for the size of an organization. Enterprise-level software is designed to operate on multiple autonomous operating locations with a central controlling point that is connected over the Internet or a proprietary wide area network (WAN). General business software, such as Intuit's QuickBooks, can be adapted to a small business or a sole proprietorship.

Successfully installing, configuring, and using a BAS is based primarily in the ability of a company or an individual to match the needs of the organization to the appropriate application. This is the topic discussed in the following section.

CERTIFICATION OBJECTIVE

Choosing the Right Application

2.2.9 Identify how to select the appropriate application(s) for a particular purpose, and problems that can arise if the wrong software product is used for a particular purpose.

Choosing the wrong software application can negate any benefit the application may have promised to deliver. Unless a company or individual creates their own application software, the choice to be made is which of the available applications best fits the needs of the organization.

Choosing the application that best addresses the needs of an organization doesn't have to be a gamble. Using a structured approach in the selection process can help to guarantee that the software application chosen will meet the operational needs of the organization and provide the best tools to its employees with a minimal amount of disruption.

A structured approach to choosing a software application involves four major phases:

- Identify and prioritize requirements.
- Research and identify the software application systems available.
- Select the software application(s) that best satisfy the requirements of the organization.
- Install and test the selected software application.

Identifying Requirements

There can be a huge difference between what you and the employees, management, and suppliers may want and what the organization really needs. The requirements of an organization must be carefully considered and narrowed down to those that meet the current and future operational needs. However, the requirements should also address any improvements the organization wishes to make in its functional systems. In general, any requirements identified by the organization should be categorized into those that are must-haves, those that would provide an operational advantage or improved efficiencies, and those that would be nice to have, but are not truly essential.

Research and Identify Software Available

Before the general availability of the Internet and its information resources, this phase of the selection process was far more difficult. However, the Internet and Web provide a ready source of information about the software applications available and their features. It is safe to assume that if any software application doesn't have the information you need available online, it is probably not worth your consideration. Trade publications or the knowledge of the success of an application in another organization in the same general industry or activity are also good sources of information.

Once you have identified the short list of software applications to be considered, you can contact the vendors for more information or a demonstration.

Compare Requirements to Features

After you have obtained all of the information available about a software application, you should begin a detailed comparison of the application's features and your requirements list. This comparison should proceed from the must-have requirements identified first and then on to the advantageous and nice-to-have features and requirements.

Must-have requirements are those on which a software application is qualified. An application that cannot provide the must-have requirements would be disqualified from consideration. A software application that can provide the requirements identified as advantageous, provided that the application met the must-have requirements, may provide additional benefit to the organization. If, after meeting all other requirements, a software application is able to provide some or all of the nice-to-have requirements, the application may be the best choice.

Installing and Testing Software

Your final decision on a software application cannot be made until after the software is installed and tested in your environment (or a reasonable representation of your environment). An application that appears to satisfy your requirements on paper may not in fact be able to deliver on its promises. However, if after a successful test, the selected software functions as expected, you should begin training the end users and completing the full installation.

CERTIFICATION SUMMARY

Utility software is used for a variety of maintenance, troubleshooting, protection, and other as-required purposes. You should be familiar with the different types of utility software and how and when each is used.

You should also be aware of other types of software, including education, entertainment, and other types of software commonly used. You should also understand the problems that could arise if the wrong (or at least inappropriate) software is used for a purpose other than that for which it was designed.

✓ TWO-MINUTE DRILL

Utility Programs

❑ Utility software is used when a software or hardware problem occurs or when a PC is threatened by a computer virus, spyware, or intruders.

❑ Utility software can be divided into two major groups: diagnostics and system protection software. Diagnostics software is used for both preventive maintenance and finding the source of a hardware or software problem. System protection software detects computer viruses and other forms of malicious programs.

❑ Special-purpose diagnostics software includes general diagnostics software, optimizing and cleaning software, and monitoring software.

❑ Diagnostics software helps to prevent PC problems through scans, analyses, and cleanup functions.

❑ Optimizing and cleaning software includes Registry cleaners, disk defragmenters, and Desktop cleaners.

❑ Monitoring software tracks how a PC is used by recording Web sites visited, files transferred, documents accessed, and keystrokes.

❑ System protection software includes antivirus software, malware detection software, and firewall software.

❑ A computer virus is malicious software that copies itself to a PC without the knowledge of the PC's user.

❑ Computer viruses fall into two basic groups: resident and nonresident. A resident computer virus replicates itself by attacking programs running on the PC, including application software and the operating system. A nonresident virus attaches to a host program and is started when the other program is started.

❑ Antivirus software attempts to disable and destroy computer viruses, worms, rootkits, and Trojan horses.

❑ The methods used to detect a computer virus or other malware are signatures, malicious activity, and file analysis and emulation.

❑ The common malware types include adware, crimeware, and spyware.

❑ A firewall protects a computer or a network from unauthorized access from across a network and unsolicited network traffic.

Education and Entertainment Software

❏ Education software includes how-to videos, e-books, and documents that can be downloaded from the Internet, along with any proprietary playback software clients.

❏ Entertainment software is primarily games.

❏ A codec compresses or encodes analog video or audio signals into a digital format for transmission or storage purposes.

Other Software Types

❏ Personal communications software is an application used to communicate person-to-person across a network, including chat software, messaging software, Web-based conferencing software, and telephony software.

❏ Chat applications support online-hosted chat rooms and private sessions using a messaging service server on the Internet.

❏ Web conferencing applications allow multiple people in multiple locations to participate in audio conferences, video conferences, and audio-video conferences. Web conferencing can be divided into four categories: audio conferencing, video conferencing, webinars, and real-time conferencing.

❏ Web-based video conferencing allows two or more locations to connect over the Internet.

❏ VoIP emulates a telephone conversation using the Internet as a telephone system.

❏ Business application software includes accounting, inventory, asset management, retail sales, and CRM.

Choosing the Right Application

❏ Choosing the wrong software application can negate any benefit the application may have promised to deliver.

❏ A structured approach to choosing a software application involves four major phases: identify and prioritize requirements, research and identify the software application systems available, select the software application(s) that best satisfy the requirements of the organization, and install and test the selected software application.

SELF TEST

The following questions are intended to help you be sure that you understand the material included in this chapter. Read the questions and the answer choices carefully.

Utility Programs

1. What type of software application is designed to help identify or remedy problems on a PC?
   A. Diagnostics software
   B. Business application software
   C. Personal communications software
   D. System protection software

2. Which of the following is not an example of an optimizing and cleaning software application?
   A. Registry cleaner
   B. Disk defragmentation
   C. Antivirus
   D. Desktop cleaners

3. If you wish to track the activities being performed on a PC, what type of utility software would you use?
   A. Monitoring software
   B. Personal productivity software
   C. Firewall software
   D. Malware detection software

4. What are the two basic types of computer viruses?
   A. Resident
   B. Malicious
   C. Nonresident
   D. Benign

5. Which of the following are types of malware that an antivirus application attempts to disable and destroy?
   A. Computer virus
   B. Worm
   C. Rootkit
   D. Trojan horses
   E. All of the above
   F. None of the above

6. What are the methods used to detect a computer virus or other malware on a PC?

    A. Signature

    B. Malicious activity

    C. File analysis

    D. File emulation

    E. All of the above

    F. None of the above

7. Which of the following is not a common type of malware?

    A. Adware

    B. Cookies

    C. Crimeware

    D. Spyware

8. What software application attempts to protect a computer or a network from unauthorized access from across a network and unsolicited network traffic?

    A. Proxy server

    B. Malware detection software

    C. Firewall

    D. Monitoring software

Education and Entertainment Software

9. What type of software application includes how-to videos and e-books?

    A. Education software

    B. Entertainment software

    C. Codec

    D. Personal communications software

10. A computer game is what type of software application?

    A. Education software

    B. Entertainment software

    C. Codec

    D. Personal communications software

11. What software compresses or encodes analog video or audio signals into a digital format for transmission or storage purposes?
    A. Personal communication software
    B. Codec
    C. Proxy server
    D. All of the above

Other Software Types

12. What software application is used to communicate person-to-person across a network?
    A. Personal communications software
    B. Education software
    C. Entertainment software
    D. Personal productivity software

13. Which of the following is not a type of personal communications software?
    A. Chat
    B. Messaging
    C. Conferencing software
    D. Network operating system

14. What is the technology that emulates a telephone conversation over the Internet?
    A. Text chat
    B. VoIP
    C. VPN
    D. Proxy server

Choosing the Right Application

15. What is a major disadvantage to choosing the wrong software product for an application?
    A. Slow reporting
    B. Misplaced data
    C. Loss of expected benefits
    D. Improper training

16. Which of the following is not a phase in a structured approach to choosing a software application?
    A. Identify and prioritize requirements
    B. Research and identify the software application systems available
    C. Qualify the software vendor's representatives
    D. Install and test the selected software application

SELF TEST ANSWERS

Utility Programs

1. ☑ **A.** Diagnostics software helps to identify or remedy problems on a PC.
    ☒ **B, C,** and **D** are incorrect. Business application software is a form of special-purpose application software designed to track and record business activity. Personal communications software is used to communicate over the Internet with one or more users. System protection software includes antivirus and malware detection software.

2. ☑ **C.** While an antivirus application can be seen as a cleaning application in some ways, it is classified as a system protection application.
    ☒ **A, B,** and **D** are incorrect. Registry cleaners, disk defragmentation, and Desktop cleaners are utility software designed to help you keep a computer clear of clutter and unused software and coding.

3. ☑ **A.** Monitoring software tracks Web sites visited, files opened, applications started, and even keystrokes entered.
    ☒ **B, C,** and **D** are incorrect. Personal productivity software includes applications like word processing spreadsheets and the like and is more likely to be tracked than to be a tracker. A firewall application protects a network or a PC from outside intrusion. Malware detection software scans a PC for malicious software.

4. ☑ **A** and **C.** Computer viruses are either resident or nonresident.
    ☒ **B** and **D** are incorrect. Computer viruses are certainly malicious and rarely benign, but these aren't official categories for computer viruses.

5. ☑ **E.** Viruses, worms, rootkits, and Trojan horses are all malware that antivirus software seeks out to destroy.
    ☒ **A, B, C, D,** and **F** are incorrect. Each of the first four choices is an example of malware that an antivirus program scans for and seeks to destroy. However, none of these choices provides the best and most complete answer to this question on its own, which certainly makes Answer F wrong.

6. ☑ **E.** Signatures, malicious activity, file analysis and emulation are all methods used by antivirus software to identify malware.
    ☒ **A, B, C, D,** and **F** are incorrect. Each of the first four choices is an example of malware that an antivirus program scans for and seeks to destroy. However, none of these choices provides the best and most complete answer to this question on its own, which certainly makes Answer F wrong.

7. ☑ **B.** Just like in real life, not all cookies are bad.
    ☒ **A, C,** and **D** are incorrect. Adware, crimeware, and spyware are types of malware.

8. ☑ **C.** A firewall attempts to block unauthorized access to a network or PC.
   ☒ **A, B,** and **D** are incorrect. A proxy server can block outbound requests, but rarely deals with inbound traffic. Malware detection and monitoring software are applications that run on a PC to protect it against threats and misuse.

Education and Entertainment Software

9. ☑ **A.** Education software is used to gain new knowledge and skills.
   ☒ **B, C,** and **D** are incorrect. Entertainment software is a close relative to education software, but it's primarily designed to entertain. A codec is used to encode and decode audio and video streams. Personal communications software facilitates communications across a network.

10. ☑ **B.** A computer game is classified as entertainment software.
    ☒ **A, C,** and **D** are incorrect. While there is education software that is also entertaining, it is generally classified separately. A codec is used to encode and decode audio and video streams. Personal communications software facilitates communications across a network.

11. ☑ **B.** A codec is used to encode and decode audio and video streams.
    ☒ **A, C,** and **D** are incorrect. Personal communications software facilitates communications across a network. A proxy server is used to provide faster access times and to block outbound Web file requests. Answer D is incorrect because only Answer B is correct.

Other Software Types

12. ☑ **A.** Personal communications software facilitates person-to-person communications across a network.
    ☒ **B, C,** and **D** are incorrect. Education software is used to gain new knowledge and skills. Entertainment software is a close relative to education software, but it's primarily designed to entertain. Personal productivity software can include e-mail, but generally doesn't support text or voice messaging.

13. ☑ **D.** A network operating system (NOS) is often used with personal communications software, but it is considered to be system software.
    ☒ **A, B,** and **C** are incorrect. While each of these choices is a type of personal communications software, none of these choices is the best answer on its own.

14. ☑ **B.** VoIP technology uses the protocols of a network to emulate telephone conversations over the network.
    ☒ **A, C,** and **D** are incorrect. Text chat is a personal communications application that can be used to "talk" with another person across a network. A virtual private network (VPN) is a technology that allows a user to access a network through a secure and private connection. A proxy server is used to provide faster access times and to block outbound Web file requests.

Choosing the Right Application

15. ☑ **C.** This is the best choice of those given.

☒ **A, B,** and **D** are incorrect. There are many disadvantages associated with the use of the wrong application for any purpose, including disruption, confusion, and frustration. These choices are symptoms that the wrong application may be in use.

16. ☑ **C.** Applications are analyzed primarily using information gained from the Web and a vendor's printed material (which typically may also be downloaded from the Web), so the qualifications of the vendor's representatives may have very little to do with how well the application meets an organization's requirements.

☒ **A, B,** and **D** are incorrect. These choices are phases in a structured approach to choosing the right software application.

8

Operating System Fundamentals

E ssentially, a computer operating system provides the interface between the human user and the computer hardware. Without an operating system, the user would have to write or acquire a specific interface for each of the devices and components of the computer and interact with each device separately and only one at a time. A computer's operating system (OS) not only provides the capability for the human to use and interact with the computer, but to do so seamlessly and really without a thought to how it all works.

For the IC[3] exams, you need to understand the role of the operating system and how it functions. You also need to know a bit about the different popular operating systems currently in use on PCs and how two or more operating systems can be installed on a single PC. In newer operating systems, security is an important feature and you need to know how rights and privileges, which control what a user is allowed to do, are assigned and managed. This chapter focuses on these areas, plus a bit on the process of troubleshooting an operating system problem.

CERTIFICATION OBJECTIVE

Operating Systems

3.1 Identify what an operating system is and how it works, and solve common problems related to operating systems

In the sections that follow, we look at the basic structure and components of popular PC operating systems, how they work, how they can be made to coexist on a single PC, how they manage the rights and privileges of the PC's users, and how to troubleshoot a suspected problem with an operating system.

Let's begin by first looking at a more in-depth definition of what a computer operating system is. An *operating system* (an OS or an O/S) is a collection of system software components that manage, carry out, and safeguard a computer by performing the following actions:

■ Acts as the logical interface between the user and the computer hardware

■ Manages, coordinates, and services the requests for hardware interaction issued by application software executing on the PC

- Provides a logical environment in which application software can execute on the PC
- Provides a user interface through which the PC's user can interact with application software, with the operating system, and, in some cases, directly with the hardware.

As illustrated in Figure 8-1, an operating system is logically placed between the user and the hardware. Requests issued by the user directly or indirectly from a software application with which the user is interfacing are passed to the operating system, which, in turn, interacts with the device driver of the hardware device to service and complete the request made.

In the days before computer operating systems, the system programmer had to program specialized routines to read from, control, or write to each of the peripheral devices of the computer. As new and different devices were attached to the computer, new input/output routines had to be created. Finally, someone got the brilliant idea to standardize all of these routines into a single central program that application programs could then interface with for input/output operations. From this relatively small start, the PC operating systems we know and use today have grown.

Operating System Components

An operating system is composed of three major component groups: kernel, user interface, and file system, among other supporting components.

Kernel   The *kernel* is the part of an operating system that is loaded to memory when the computer is started up. The kernel contains the basic functions of the operating systems, including memory management, input/output handling, file management, and communications. As shown in Figure 8-2, the kernel resides

FIGURE 8-1

A computer operating system serves as a go-between for hardware, application software, and the user.

FIGURE 8-2

The kernel of an operating system resides in memory and provides services to application software and the user interface.

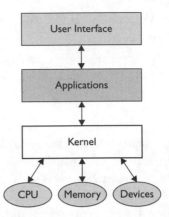

in memory and provides services to application software and the user interface (command interpreter) as needed. The services that aren't included in the kernel are called into memory temporarily and executed, as needed.

User Interface   The *user interface (UI)* of an operating system accepts commands from the user and interprets them to facilitate communications between the operating system and the user. The UI in nongraphical operating systems is called a command interpreter and is also known as a command-line interpreter (CLI) or shell. Regardless of whether an operating system uses a graphical user interface (GUI), like the Windows Desktop, or a command-line prompt (see Figure 8-3), a control language that is made up of a collection of commands that are typically unique to the operating system is used by the user or the UI to request specific actions and functions

FIGURE 8-3

The Windows command prompt is a command interpreter.

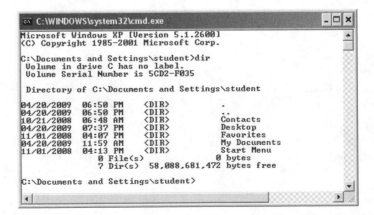

of the operating system. All of the major operating systems (Linux, Mac OS, and Windows) available for PCs provide both a GUI and a CLI interface.

File Systems   On any computer that includes one or more storage devices, including installed and removable drives, the operating system running on that computer must include a *file system* service. A file system provides the methods used to organize files on the storage media, to store files (data) on the media, and to provide access control and other types of file protection.

To an operating system, a file is a fixed-length set of binary data that may represent a software program, a document, or a string of values. Operating systems consider all files to be containers, much like a sealed box. What's in the file is of no concern to the operating systems' file system, only the container itself—something like how a shipping container service only loads the containers in ships and planes and moves them point-to-point.

A file system also manages a hierarchy of files using a structured arrangement that is commonly called a *file tree*. As shown in Figure 8-4, a file system sets up a hierarchical arrangement of files that all stem from a root folder or directory (\ ). As the figure shows, a folder can contain files and other folders. The complete name of each file or folder includes the names of the storage device (C:) and the names of the folders that lie on the path to a particular file or folder (\APPS\WP). The path that is taken to reach a file or folder constitutes the pathname of that item (C:\APPS\WP).

Each of the major operating systems has at least one file system it supports. Table 8-1 lists the file systems supported by each of the more popular operating systems.

FIGURE 8-4

A file system supports a hierarchy of files and folders.

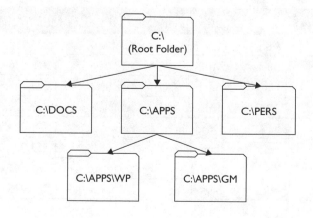

TABLE 8-1	File Systems Supported by Popular Operating Systems

File System	Operating System(s)
Extended FAT (exFAT)	Windows CE and Windows Vista
Extended file system (extn, where n represents a generation number, such as ext4 is the Fourth Extended file system)	Linux
Extended Hierarchical File System (HFS+)	Mac OS X
File Allocation Table (FATn, where n represents the number of bits used to express storage cluster addresses, such as FAT16 or FAT32)	Windows XP
New Technology File System (NTFS)	Windows Vista and Windows XP
Transactional NTFS (TxF)	Windows Vista

Data Storage Measurements   At one time, believe it or not, storage space—memory and disk space—was measured in thousands of bits or bytes. In those simpler times, the metric representation for thousand (kilo) was used to express the amount of space available or in total, such as 64 kilobytes (KB). Advancements in storage technology have fostered increases in the amount of storage space available on a PC, which has increased our vocabulary with new capacity terminology. Table 8-2 lists the various capacity (volume) measurements commonly in use today for both bits and bytes.

A file system also provides a means to protect files and folders. A password can be assigned to each item that must be entered to access a protected item. File attributes,

TABLE 8-2	Data Measurements Used for File Systems

Abbreviation	Prefix	Decimal	Example	Unit Value
K	Kilo	Thousand	Kilobyte	1,024
M	Mega	Million	Megabyte	1,048,576
G	Giga	Billion	Gigabyte	1,073,741,824
T	Tera	Trillion	Terabyte	1,099,511,627,776
P	Peta	Quadrillion	Petabyte	1,125,899,906,842,624
E	Exa	Quintillion	Exabyte	1,152,921,504,606,846,976
Z	Zetta	Sextillion	Zettabyte	1,180,591,620,717,411,303,424
Y	Yotta	Septillion	Yottabyte	1,208,925,819,614,629,174,706,176

which establish how a file or folder can be used, can be assigned to a file or folder. The file systems of the leading operating systems allow system administrators to restrict what actions individual users or groups of users can perform on a single file or a folder (for more information on users and groups, see "User Rights and Privileges" later in the chapter).

In Windows operating systems, the file attributes that can be assigned to a file or folder are

- **Archive**   This file attribute indicates a file or folder should be included in the next system backup. The archive attribute is set on when a file or folder contains a stored change.
- **Hidden**   This file attribute indicates that a file or folder is not to be included in folder listings.
- **Read-only**   This file attributes indicates that a file or the files within a folder can only be opened for viewing. A file that doesn't have this attribute set can be opened for reading and writing, which means it can be modified, stored, or deleted.
- **System**   OS programs and data files are typically set with the system attribute, which by default excludes them from folder listings.

On Windows systems, only the Hidden and Read-only attributes are generally available for a user to set, as shown in Figure 8-5. The Archive attribute is set using an advanced function.

Linux systems also support a variety of file attributes. However, most of the file attributes assigned to directories and files in Linux are assigned by the OS and utility programs. A few of the file attributes used in a Linux system are

- **Append only**   A file with this attribute can only have data added to it.
- **Compressed**   A file with this attribute is compressed each time it is written to the hard disk.
- **Immutable**   A file with this attribute set cannot be modified, renamed, or deleted.
- **Indexed**   A directory with this attribute set is indexed.
- **Undelete**   The contents of a file with this attribute set are saved, which allows for the file to be undeleted, should it be deleted in error.

The Properties
dialog box for a
Windows folder

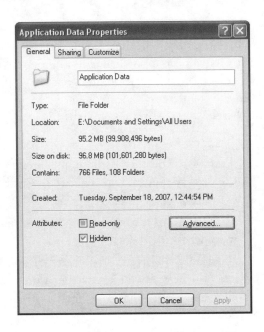

Operating System Services

Operating systems provide a number of services that are vital to the operation of a
computer. These services include

- **Program execution**   This OS service loads requested programming into main
  memory from permanent storage (like the hard disk drive). It also provides
  support for the execution of instructions by the CPU.

- **Input/output services**   This OS service provides the mechanisms to perform
  input/output operations for the user and application software.

- **Memory management**   Common operating systems, such as Windows and
  Mac OS, are multitasking systems (see "Operating System Environments"
  later in this section), which means that memory must be allocated to more
  than one process continuously. This means that in order to support the
  memory needs of the programs running on the PC, blocks of memory may
  need to be swapped in and out of active memory to virtual memory so that
  they can be used for different processes.

- **File-system management**   This OS service provides the mechanisms that
  read, write, create, and delete files from permanent storage devices.

- **Inter-computer communications**   This OS service manages the transmission and receipt of messages and data between devices within a computer or between a computer and a network.

- **Error detection and correction**   This OS service monitors the computer's operations for errors committed by the CPU, memory, bus controllers, input/output devices, and application software.

Hardware Interface

Chapter 2 provides an overview of how an operating system interacts with the system bus structure, memory, caching, and the CPU using interrupts and other system resources.

Operating System Environments

An OS environment is primarily defined by the processing capabilities of the OS and whether or not the OS can coexist on a computer with other operating systems.

Processing Capabilities   An operating system can be one of several operating types that define the capabilities and operating levels of the operating system. An operating system is classified to one or more of the following types:

- **Multiprocessing**   Often confused with multitasking or parallel processing. A multiprocessing OS is able to utilize the processing capabilities of a computer that has more than one microprocessor or CPU core. A multiprocessing OS allocates instructions to its processors. UNIX is a multiprocessing OS.

- **Multitasking**   A multitasking OS is able to support multiple programs running concurrently, but not simultaneously (see Chapter 2 for more information on how a CPU executes instructions). Linux, Mac OS, and Windows systems are multitasking operating systems.

- **Multithreading**   A multithreading OS supports multiple parts of a single program to run concurrently, sharing the resources of a single CPU. The Sun Microsystems UltraSPARC T1 OS is perhaps the most popular of the multi-threading operating systems.

- **Multiuser**   A multiuser OS has the capability to support multiple logged-in users concurrently, with each provided a separate operating space (shell). UNIX is a multiuser OS that uses a time-sharing process to support the shells of multiple users.

Multiple OS Environments Virtually all PCs can host a multiple OS environment that stores two or more operating systems on its system storage. In a multiple OS environment, the user must make a choice as to which OS is to be started when the computer is booted up. This type of PC environment is commonly referred to as a multiboot system.

On a multiboot system, each OS is stored in its own dedicated space on the hard disk (preferably a separate disk partition) and an entry is added to the boot manager that links to the OS's system loader. When the computer is booted up, a multiboot manager, such as the Linux GRUB (www.gnu.org/software/grub), OSL2000 from OSLoader.com (www.osloader.com/), or EasyBCD from NeoSmart Technologies (http://neosmart.net), opens and displays a list of the operating systems on the PC. The user then selects the OS to be started from the list and continues to boot the system.

User Rights and Privileges

In conjunction with the file permissions (see "File Systems" earlier in this section) assigned to the folders or directories and their files and subfolders and subdirectories, rights and privileges can also be assigned to specific users or groups of users. Rights refer to the logon rights of a user that control which users are allowed to log on to a PC. Privileges assigned to a user determine which folders and files a user can access and what the user is able to do with the folder or file. User privileges often override the file permissions settings of specific folders or files.

User Logon Rights Users are grouped into two categories that determine whether or not a user or group is allowed to log on to a computer or network or is denied logon rights using specific access methods. User rights are assigned by the system or network administrators to protect the resources of the PC or the network to which it is connected. Users are restricted to a specific method of logging in, such as from the keyboard or from the network.

User Privileges Windows operating systems create a link between users and groups and folders and files. User privileges are established at the file or folder level and assigned to a user or group to indicate which groups or users can access the file or folder and what each is able to do with the file or folder after accessing it.

Table 8-3 lists the user privileges that can be assigned to a user or group for a specific file or folder.

Linux file and folder permissions are simpler and more complex than the Windows settings at the same time. A directory (the Linux equivalent of a folder) can be

TABLE 8-3	Windows Operating Systems File Permissions	
Permission Setting	**Effect on Folders**	**Effect on Files**
Full Control	View, create, modify, and delete files and subfolders	Open, view, create, modify, and delete files
List Folder Contents	View and list files and subfolders and execute files	None
Modify	Read and write subfolders and files and delete the folder	Read, write, and delete a file
Read	View and list files and subfolders	View and access file contents
Read & Execute	View and list files and subfolders and execute files	View and access file contents and execute files
Write	Add new files and subfolders	Write to an existing file

assigned three levels of access permissions: read, write, and execute. These permissions can be assigned to three ownership levels: the owner of the file (the user that created it or assumed ownership), the group to which the owner belongs, and other nonowner users. Each of the ownership groups can be assigned permissions to read, write, or execute the file.

The read permission allows an ownership level to open the file to view its contents only. The write permission allows an ownership level to open, view, modify, write, copy, move, and delete a file. The execute permission allows the file to be executed. These same permissions can be assigned to a directory, although the execute permission is essentially meaningless on a directory.

Common Operating System Actions

Before you can actually interact with an operating system and use any of the applications or functions on a computer, you must establish an authorized access to the computer through the OS. Once you have "logged in" with the operating system, you are able to perform any task or access any data for which you have permissions.

In virtually all cases, the login action is accomplished through a login box in which your username and password are entered. The OS then verifies these credentials and either allows or denies the access.

On the other hand, once access is allowed by the OS, other types of direct interactions with the operating system may be needed, depending on the situation.

You may need to restart the operating system or place it into a standby (also known as hibernation or sleep) mode. You may also need to cancel a process that is no longer responding to user commands. At the end of your session, you may want to shut down the operating system, which effectively shuts down the computer. In the sections that follow, the general processes used in each of these actions are explained.

Login and Logout

The login screens used for a Linux, Mac OS, or Windows PC are quite similar. Essentially, each presents a window that contains separate boxes for a username and a password. It is possible to configure a particular user account so that a password is not required, but under reasonable security guidelines, this is not recommended. Each of these operating systems allows a certain number of login attempts (typically three), after which it is assumed that an unauthorized login attempt is being made and the login function is suspended for a period of time or until an administrator clears the account.

The logout process is also very similar on these operating systems. From a system menu, such as the Apple menu of the Mac OS, the Start menu of a Windows OS, or the Main menu of a Linux GUI, the logout command is selected. The logout request is then verified through an "Are you sure?" type of prompt; if it is verified, the user account access is terminated.

Restarting the OS

The process (and terminology) used to restart a particular operating system varies with the operating system in use. Linux is shut down and rebooted using the Reboot command on the main menu of a Linux GUI. A MAC OS is restarted using the Restart command on the Apple menu. On a Windows PC, the OS is restarted by choosing the Turn Off Computer option on the Start menu and then clicking the Restart option on the Turn Off Computer dialog box that appears. As discussed later (see "Canceling an Application"), the need to restart a PC's operating system can also vary with the OS and the type of problem you are trying to correct.

Putting the System to Sleep

The major operating systems for PCs, Linux, Mac OS, and Windows, each allow you to place the OS and typically some or all of the PC's hardware into a standby, sleep, or hibernation mode. This action, which is Sleep on Mac OS and Windows systems beginning with Windows XP (before that it was Stand By), and Suspend on a Linux system, means that the operating system cuts power from all unnecessary components and devices of the computer, with the exception of primary memory. Many notebook computers enter this mode automatically whenever their cover is closed. Hibernation, which is a deeper level of Sleep, copies the contents of memory to the hard disk so that all power can be lowered.

Canceling an Application

On occasion an application may not respond to keyboard or mouse commands. A variety of factors may be the cause of this problem, but most likely one of the three conditions exists: the application is waiting for unavailable resources, the application has ceased operation and the OS is attempting to recover or cancel it, or the OS has failed completely.

The first condition typically resolves itself, and the application recommences when the needed resources become available. The second condition is another situation where the first action is to wait it out. In the third situation, the PC typically must be powered off and rebooted. However, conditions arise where an application should be killed. Linux, Mac OS, and Windows operating systems provide a method to cancel a running application, with the application command available on their system administration menus.

Shutting Down the System

Either as a means to protect a computer during bad weather or as a part of a security plan, on occasion you may want to power off or shut down a PC. It is normally not a good idea to just power the computer off while the OS is active and running normally. There are registers and OS operating environment data that should be saved before the system is shut down. Using the OS' shutdown process allows the OS to save any data it needs for proper future operation.

On a Windows Vista or Windows 7 system, the Shutdown command is located on the same menu (accessed through the Windows button) as the Sleep function. On a Mac OS system, pressing the power button displays the Shutdown dialog box from which the system can be powered off. On a Linux system, you must exit the X Window or KDE (K Desktop Environment) GUI and enter the shutdown command at the command-line interface.

Other Operating Systems

In addition to the operating systems in a desktop or laptop computer, there are specialized operating systems designed specifically for other types of computers, including

- **Embedded computer operating systems** Because embedded computers are built into other devices, such as in automobile ignitions and microwave ovens, their operating systems are made up of specialized circuits and firmware (software saved on read-only memory).
- **Handheld operating systems** The operating systems in handheld devices, such as personal digital assistants and smart phones, are smaller than the typical desktop computer operating system and as a result have fewer capabilities.
- **Real-time operating systems (RTOS)** This type of operating system is used in devices that are designed to react or detect real-time events, such as medical, factory control, and air traffic control systems.

On any type of computing device, its operating system commonly interacts with other operating systems in the course of completing a task. This interaction between operating systems is more commonplace that many users realize. Here are a few examples of when multiple operating systems interact:

- **Network connections** When a Linux, Mac OS, or Windows computer connects to a network, the local operating system establishes a dialog with the network operating system (NOS) on a network server.
- **Handheld device functions** The personal assistance functions of a handheld device interact with the cell phone call services operating system in a smart phone.
- **Embedded computer devices** The timing operating system of a microwave oven interacts with the "cooking" system operating system within the device.

Managing Files

The ability to locate, manipulate, and manage files and folders on a computer is a foundation service of virtually every operating system. Without this capability, the user would not have the flexibility to categorize, group, or classify data files as the user best needs them organized. In the sections that follow, the processes involved with file management on a PC are explained.

File Management Systems

GUI-based operating systems provide an easy-to-use file management system through which the user is able to manage the folders and programs on the computer. On a Windows system, the Windows Explorer is used to perform file management and can be accessed through any of the file type links on the Start menu or through a device icon on the My Computer window. On a Mac OS, the Finder provides access to the files and folders of the system and is accessed through the Finder icon on the Dock. On Linux systems, such as Red Hat with KDE, the Disk Navigator provides a view of the file systems and directories on the system.

Another level of file management is performed by accessing a specific device directly and viewing its folder and file contents. Using the Windows My Computer link, the Mac OS Finder, or the Disk Navigator in Linux, the data storage devices installed on the local PC or any virtual or physical devices mapped to the PC that are located on remote servers and perhaps even the Internet are displayed. Each is identified with a specific icon to indicate its device type or is classified under a device type heading in the display.

Displaying Files and Folders

The file manager function of any operating system presents the file and folders of a system in a hierarchical structure, with the highest-level folders listed first. Generally, when first displayed, the folders are displayed in a collapsed form, meaning that the contents of the folder are hidden. Expanding the folder, typically by clicking a plus-sign symbol, displays the second-level contents of the folder, which can include other folders.

Depending on the file manager in use, certain files may not be included in the file list displayed. System files (files reserved to the operating system), which are also called hidden files, aren't generally displayed by default, unless overridden by the user. The application files, meaning program and configuration files specific to a particular application, and data files created by the user through an application, are included in the default file list.

The standard file manager displays files in a two-pane window. The left pane shows the file hierarchy, and the right pane displays the files contained within a selected folder or directory. The file list in the file manager's right pane can be sorted by its properties fields, which generally are the filename, its size in kilobytes (KB), its file type, and the date it was created or last modified. To sort the file list by one of these properties, simply click the label of the field column on the title bar above the file list.

File manager utilities also allow the user to change the view type used for the folder and file display. Commonly, the file list can be changed to represent each file with a thumbnail object (a good choice for graphic files or presentation slides); a tile or large icon; a small icon; a multicolumn list; or a single list that displays the filename and the file's size, type, and modification date.

Naming Files

As mentioned in the preceding section, system files aren't included in file lists by default. Users can change the view configuration of the file manager to display hidden files at any folder level. Another reason a file may not be displayed where the user expects to see it can be that the file was inadvertently saved to a different folder or that some form of a standard naming convention wasn't used, making the file hard to find.

Filenames should follow some form of a standard format that assigns a predictable and self-explanatory name to each file saved to a storage medium. Each of the standard operating systems has different rules for what can be used to name a file; for instance, Linux doesn't allow spaces or punctuation in a filename, but Windows provides for a very flexible scheme for naming files that allows a maximum of 255 characters for a filename. Windows filenames can include spaces and some special characters, but Windows excludes the use of device names, reserved system elements, and certain special characters: asterisk (*), colon (:), less-than sign (<), greater-than sign (>), question mark (?), backward slash (\ ), forward slash (/), and vertical bar (|).

File Properties

Windows files and folders carry identifying properties and characteristics with them that can be displayed and modified, if desired. Right-clicking a filename and choosing Properties from the pop-up menu displays the Properties dialog box, on which three groupings of properties, accessed through the General, Summary, and Custom tabs of the dialog box, can be viewed.

The Properties dialog box for a particular file includes information about the file author; its creation and modification dates; its attributes (read only, hidden, and if the file should be archived); its location; and additional properties that control its archiving, indexing, compression, and encryption. These same properties are available for a folder as well and can be applied to all files and folders within the folder, if desired.

Manipulating Files

The file manager utilities of the major operating systems facilitate the management of files and folders by supporting a variety of file actions, including

- **Find files**   Using the operating system's search utility, a file or folder can be located and displayed by the file manager.
- **Managing files**   File manager utilities allow users to create, move, copy, rename, or delete a file in or from a folder/directory.
- **Managing folders**   File manager utilities allow users to create, move, copy, rename, or delete a folder/directory.
- **Retrieve deleted files**   Operating system file managers include a function that can be used to reactive a file or folder that was previously deleted.

on the job

The undelete function on each of the primary operating systems can only retrieve a deleted file or folder if the undelete action occurs before defragmentation is performed on the storage medium.

- **Select and manage multiple files**   File management actions can be applied to multiple files at one time by selecting two or more nonadjacent files or a range of contiguous files or folders. To select noncontiguous files, hold down the CTRL key while clicking the files you wish to select. To select a range of contiguous files, hold down the SHIFT key and use the mouse to select the range of files you wish to include.
- **Trash/recycle bin**   The trash or recycle bin is generally located on the operating system's desktop or primary GUI and not typically thought of as a part of the file management system. This receptacle for deleted files serves as a safety net against those "oops" moments when you really didn't want to remove a file. Files placed into the trash/recycle bin can be restored. However, once you empty the trash/recycle bin, the files are removed from the system.

There are some precautions that should be considered when you manipulate files, including

- **File/folder names**   Folders/directories and files should be named using a standardized, easy-to-remember convention.

- **Logical file and folder organization** Files and folder/directories should be organized so that related or like files are stored together so that they are easily found and can be managed together.
- **Unneeded or obsolete files** To preserve storage space and to unclutter folders/directories, any unneeded or obsolete files should be archived and then removed.
- **Shared or restricted files** Files that are shared by multiple applications or with other users may prevent certain management or maintenance actions. A local copy of these files may be necessary to accomplish a management action, especially read-only files.

Before any major file management actions, any critical or important files should be backed up. In fact, it's a best practice to back up these files on a regular basis.

File Management Issues

There are two primary causes for a particular file or folder to become unavailable:

- **Storage medium capacity** If a storage medium is nearing its maximum storage capacity, you may not be able to open or perform maintenance on a file or folder. You may be denied access to a file by the hard disk controller or in a worst case scenario the file may become corrupted. Disk drives should be regularly backed up and preventive maintenance performed, including defragmentation and the removal of unneeded files or folders.
- **File associations** Specific file types, as indicated by the filename extensions or file type properties of files, can be linked or associated with a particular application. For example, files with the .DOCX extension are automatically linked with Microsoft Word 2007 and files with the .TXT extension are linked to a general text editor, such as Microsoft Notepad. Table 8-4 lists a sampling of Windows filename extensions and the application to which each is commonly associated. One benefit of a file association is that an application can be launched by opening an associated file.

System Printers

The operating system manages a list of the printers installed on the computer. Regardless of which operating system is running on the computer, a list of the printers installed on the computer can be viewed or managed using a built-in printer utility.

TABLE 8-4	Common Windows Filename Extensions and Associations	
Extension	**File Type**	**Common Associations**
.BMP	Bit-map graphic file	Paintbrush and other graphics editors
.COM	MS-DOS command file	Windows operating system
.DLL	Dynamic link library file	Windows operating system and applications
.DOCX	Office 2007 word processing file	Word 2007
.XLSX	Office 2007 spreadsheet file	Excel 2007
.GIF	Graphical interchange format file	Graphic editor application
.HLP	Help information file	Windows help system
.ICO	Icon files	Windows desktop manager
.SYS	System files	Windows operating system
.TMP	Temporary files	Windows operating system, download managers, Web browsers
.TXT	Text files	Windows Notepad
.ZIP	Compressed files	PKZIP, WinZip, and other file compression applications

On a Windows Vista or Windows 7 system, the printer list is viewed through the Windows button and the Printers and Fax link; on a Windows XP system, the same link is on the Start menu; on a Mac OS computer, the printer list can be displayed through the System Preferences link on the Apple menu; and on a Linux system, the printer list is displayed from the Main Menu and System link.

Adding or removing a printer from a system is performed through a utility that is accessed from the printer list. However, most new printer systems come with an installation or setup utility that can be used to install a new printer, including the device drivers needed for the printer to operate efficiently.

Common OS Problems

Like virtually all software, regardless of its type, system software, including an operating system, can have issues or problems from time to time. Most OS problems aren't really an issue with the operating system but are commonly caused by an application issue instead. However, there can be issues with an operating system, especially when a newer version or type of operating system is installed on a PC.

Software Incompatibility

There are situations where an operating system may not be totally compatible with a certain version of an application, a file type, or even a particular type of media. For example, a legacy MS-DOS application is unlikely to run on a Windows Vista system without the addition of a special software utility called an emulator. Software created for a specific version of an operating system may not be compatible with newer (or older) versions of that operating system without an update made to the application by its creator.

File Corruption

All operating systems have a collection of files that are essential to its startup, operation, and shutdown. Should one or more of these files become corrupt, the operating system is likely to not start up or to perform improperly. On a Windows system, if the message "windows\system\config\system file corrupt or missing" is displayed when the system is starting up, the OS may need to be reinstalled either in a recovery mode or through a totally clean installation.

File corruption on a computer can occur from a variety of causes, including

- **Degradation of hard disk or other storage media** Hard disk drives are primarily mechanical devices that can degrade or fail completely from heavy use over a relatively long period of time.
- **File system corruption** A file system can become corrupt because of device degradation or because the system power is interrupted during a write operation.
- **Inadvertent media initialization or formatting** A user may accidentally reinitialize or reformat a medium, which erases all of the data saved on the medium.
- **Malicious damage** Hackers, viruses, and other malicious attacks on a system can corrupt a storage device, rendering all of the data on the device corrupt or unreadable.
- **User error** Users can remove, overwrite, or rename key files of the operating system, although typically such changes are unintentional, or they can remove shared files without performing an uninstall operation, which can cause critical files to be missing or unusable for the operating system.

The Mac OS includes a file recovery utility, and Linux and Windows both support file recovery utilities that can be downloaded from open source libraries or purchased. File recovery software can correct many file corruption problems, but not all.

Startup Problems

There are a variety of reasons for an operating system to fail to start up properly. However, the more common reasons are corrupted system files (see "File Corruption") and bad or incompatible device drivers.

The best way to isolate the source of a startup problem is to start up the system in what is called Safe mode on Linux, Mac OS, and Windows systems. A Safe mode startup loads only essential operating system components, none, or just a few, of the device drivers for the system's peripheral devices, and only those user interface components required to troubleshoot the startup issues. If a system is able to start up in Safe mode, the cause of the problem is in a system element not included in Safe mode.

OS Maintenance Precautions

When changing the settings of an operating system, you should know and understand the purpose of each setting and any possible ramifications each may have or cause. Many of the system settings can impact more than just their primary area. For example, something as simple as changing the color settings for the desktop could make the text or icons less visible, making it difficult to locate a particular icon.

A best practice to use when changing system settings, especially when changing more than just one or two settings, is to keep a written record of each setting's original configuration and to create a system backup before making any changes. This way, should the setting change not produce the desired results, you can troubleshoot which change caused the undesired effect.

The permissions to access the operating system's settings and configuration should be limited to a single person where possible. On a Windows system, for example, only the user or users who have been designated as system administrators can make changes to the most important operating system settings.

Troubleshoot Common OS Problems

The process used to troubleshoot an operating system really depends on the operating system in use. The troubleshooting steps used with each operating system tend to be as unique as each OS; troubleshooting a Windows OS requires a different process that those used with a Mac OS or a Linux system.

As discussed earlier in this section (see "Software Incompatibility"), many system problems occur at startup and are caused by recent changes made to the configuration, components, or newly installed hardware or software. As in any troubleshooting effort, a structured, step-by-step process must be used to isolate the root cause of an operating system problem.

The first place to start should always be with any changes, hardware or software, that have been made since the system last worked as it should. Sometimes problems don't appear when the change is first made, because until you restart Windows, some changes, especially configuration changes, don't take effect until then. Identifying the changes made to a system is likely to also identify the cause of the failure. However, if the problem occurs after the system starts up and the user has logged in, the focus of the problem shifts to other types of configuration settings, such as the user's profile, and an application, service, or device driver that is started at login. Typically, these types of errors produce a message box or an error message (or perhaps the proverbial "blue screen of death") with an error number or message that can be researched in the OS creator's knowledge base or a technical Web site. If all else fails, the system may need to be restored from a backup source or reinstalled.

CERTIFICATION SUMMARY

Expect to encounter at least two questions that relate to operating systems and how their configuration can contribute to computer problems. You should also be familiar with the components of an operating system and the differences between a GUI and a command-line interface. In addition, study file systems and how they can be configured to allow or deny other users to have access to stored data.

TWO-MINUTE DRILL

Operating Systems

❑ An operating system is a collection of system software components that manage, carry out, and safeguard a computer.

❑ The actions of an OS include acting as the logical interface between the user and the computer hardware; managing, coordinating, and servicing requests for hardware interaction from software; and providing a logical environment in which application software executes. An OS also provides a user interface through which users interact with software, the OS, and hardware.

❑ An OS consists of a kernel, a user interface, and a file system. The kernel is loaded to memory when the computer starts up and contains the basic functions of the OS: memory management, I/O handling, file management, and communications. The user interface accepts commands and facilitates communications between the OS and the user.

❑ A nongraphical user interface is a command interpreter or shell. Windows, Linux, and Mac OS also feature a GUI.

❑ A file system manages the disk storage and hierarchy of files and folders (directories) and provides a means to protect files and folders.

❑ An OS provides services vital to the operation of a computer, including program execution, I/O services, memory management, file-system management, inter-computer communications, and error detection and correction.

❑ An OS is classified as one or more of the following types: multiprocessing, multitasking, multithreading, or multiuser.

❑ Most PCs have the capability to host multiple operating systems as a multiboot system. In a multiple OS environment, the user chooses which OS is to be started. This type of PC installation is commonly referred to as a multi-boot environment.

❑ Using user privileges, an OS creates a security link between users and groups and folders and files.

❑ Most of the problems with an OS system occur during system startup. Startup issues on a Windows system can be caused by malware, bad device drivers, newly installed and incompatible hardware, missing or corrupt files, and incorrect or incompatible configuration settings.

❏ In addition to the operating systems of desktop and laptop computers, there are specialized operating systems for embedded, handheld, and real-time devices. These operating systems, as well as those of the desktop or laptop computer, interact with other operating systems to complete a task.

❏ The major operating systems for PCs can be placed into a standby, sleep, or hibernation mode. This action cuts power from all unnecessary components and devices of the computer, with the exception of primary memory. Many notebook computers enter this mode automatically whenever their cover is closed.

❏ Specialized operating systems are designed specifically for other types of computers, including: embedded computers, handheld computers, and real-time computing or control devices.

❏ Operating systems commonly interact with other operating systems, especially when performing network connections and working with handheld and embedded devices.

❏ The file manager function of an operating system displays files and folders in a hierarchical structure or as individual folders or directories. The file manager facilitates the management of files and folders by supporting a variety of file actions, including: finding files, managing files and folders, recovering deleted files, selecting and managing multiple files, and removing files or folders to a trash or recycle bin.

❏ Operating systems maintain a list of the printers installed on a computer. The printer's list can be viewed or managed using a built-in printer utility, which also supports adding or removing a printer.

❏ An operating system can develop problems, such as incompatibility with certain applications, file types, or media. Files can become corrupted for a variety of reasons, including degradation of hard disk or other storage media, file system corruption, inadvertent media initialization or formatting, malicious damage, and user error.

❏ To isolate the possible source of an OS startup problem, start the system in Safe mode, which loads only essential OS components.

SELF TEST

The following questions are intended to help you be sure that you understand the material included in this chapter. Read the questions and the answer choices carefully.

Operating Systems

1. Which of the following is not typically considered to be a basic OS function?
   A. Providing a user interface
   B. Communications through a modem
   C. Servicing requests for hardware interaction
   D. Executing and managing application software

2. What system software provides a logical interface between the user and the computer hardware; manages, coordinates, and services requests for hardware interaction from software; and maintains a logical environment in which application software executes?
   A. BIOS
   B. Boot loader
   C. Device drivers
   D. Operating system

3. What is the name of the component of the OS that is loaded to memory when a computer starts up?
   A. I/O management
   B. File-system management
   C. Kernel
   D. Core

4. Which of the following is the term typically used for a nongraphical user interface on a computer?
   A. GUI
   B. TUI
   C. CLI
   D. DUI

5. What is the component of an OS that manages the disk storage and hierarchy of files and folders and provides a means to protect files and folders?
   A. File system
   B. Disk controller

C. Cache memory

D. Disk partition

6. Which of the following is not a service provided by an OS?

A. I/O services

B. Memory management

C. Device drivers

D. Inter-computer communications

7. What is the term used for an OS that is able to execute multiple parts of an application program concurrently?

A. Multiprocessing

B. Multitasking

C. Multithreading

D. Multiuser

8. What is the term used for an OS that has the capability to store and host multiple operating systems?

A. Multithreading

B. Multiboot

C. Multiprocessing

D. Multitasking

9. Which of the following is not included in the Windows user privileges for a file or folder?

A. Read

B. Write-only

C. Read & Execute

D. Full Control

10. What is the primary cause of problems that occur with an OS?

A. Memory errors

B. Malware

C. Device drivers

D. Changes made to hardware or software

11. Which of the following is not a suspended power mode for a Mac OS or Windows system?

    A. Hibernate

    B. Sleep

    C. Standby

    D. Suspend

12. Should a file stored on a permanent storage medium become corrupted, which of the following could be the source of the problem?

    A. Storage media degradation

    B. File system corruption

    C. Inadvertent formatting of the media

    D. Malicious damage

    E. All of the above

    F. None of the above

SELF TEST ANSWERS

Operating Systems

1. ☑ **B.** Communications through a modem involves the support of the OS typically, but this action is not a basic function of an OS.
   ☒ **A, C, and D** are incorrect. These are all basic functions of an OS.

2. ☑ **D.** In addition to the duties listed in the question, an operating system also provides a user interface through which users interact with software, the OS, and hardware.
   ☒ **A, B, and C** are incorrect. Each of these choices performs very specific tasks, none of which are listed in this question.

3. ☑ **C.** The kernel of the OS is loaded to memory when a PC starts up and remains resident during all times.
   ☒ **A, B, and D** are incorrect. I/O management and file system management are functions supported by the kernel. Core is a legacy name for main memory, so it is incorrect.

4. ☑ **C.** A command-line interpreter (CLI) provides a nongraphical command-line interface.
   ☒ **A, B, and D** are incorrect. A GUI is a graphical user interface; Windows and Mac OS both feature one. I made up the TUI choice, so it's obviously incorrect, and I hope you haven't had any interface at all with a DUI.

5. ☑ **A.** A file system provides the basic support and organizational functions for the disk drive.
   ☒ **B, C, and D** are incorrect. The disk controller interacts with the CPU and bus structure to transfer data; cache memory is used to temporarily store data and instructions for the CPU; and a disk partition is a logical structure used to define portions of the hard disk.

6. ☑ **C.** Device drivers are separate entities from an OS.
   ☒ **A, B, and D** are incorrect. These are all basic functions of an OS.

7. ☑ **B.** A multitasking OS is able to execute different parts of an application program, such as the Microsoft Office Word main program and the dictionary or thesaurus applications, concurrently.
   ☒ **A, C, and D** are incorrect. Multiprocessing requires more than one CPU or core processor; multithreading is able to execute separate threads of the same program. A multiuser OS is able to log in and support multiple users on a single computer.

8. ☑ **B.** A multiboot PC has two or more operating systems installed in separate partitions of its hard disk.
   ☒ **A, C, and D** are incorrect. See the answer to Question 7 for information on why these choices are incorrect.

9. ☑ **B.** Write-only is not a file privilege that can be assigned to a Windows file or folder.
    ☒ **A, C,** and **D** are incorrect. The file privileges that can be assigned to a Windows file or folder include Read, Read & Execute, and Full Control.

10. ☑ **D.** Most problems with an OS occur when the system is started and typically are the result of changes made to the hardware, software, or configuration of the OS.
    ☒ **A, B,** and **C** are incorrect. Memory errors, malware, and bad device drivers can cause operational problems, but these typically don't involve the OS.

11. ☑ **D.** Suspend mode is used on Linux systems and is used to suspend the operations of the OS.
    ☒ **A, B,** and **C** are incorrect. Sleep is the suspension function for both Windows Vista and Mac OS. Standby is the previous name for the Sleep on older Windows systems. Hibernate is available on some OS versions and is a deeper level of the Sleep function.

12. ☑ **E.** Each of the problems in A through D can be a cause for a file failure on any operating system.
    ☒ **A, B, C, D,** and **F** are incorrect. None of the answers listed in A through D is the best answer available, although each is individually a possible cause for a file failure. Answer F is just wrong.

9

User Interfaces

- Manipulate the Desktop,
  Files, and Disks

- Change System Settings

✓ Two-Minute Drill

Q&A Self Test

A s described in Chapter 8, a user interface is one of the basic functions of an operating system. Users gain access to a computer system through the user interface by following a login process and then can either enter the command they wish to execute on a command line or choose it from a graphical user interface (GUI) or a menu. The user interface of an operating system (OS) provides access to the application software installed on a computer, the configuration settings of the OS, the interface itself, as well as access to the installed system components of the OS, and stored data.

This chapter provides an overview of the user interfaces of popular operating systems and how a computer system is configured through the user interface. Most of the discussion focuses on GUI systems, but we'll also look at command-line interfaces as well.

CERTIFICATION OBJECTIVE

Manipulate the Desktop, Files, and Disks

3.2   Use an operating system to manipulate a computer's desktop, files, and disks.

Without an operating system, using a computer the way we currently do would be virtually impossible. The earliest computers provided a very limited operating environment in which programs to be executed had to be either programmed on the command prompt or loaded from a storage device and then executed. The operating systems of today's computer systems have, for the most part, advanced to the point where a single mouse click can launch a major interactive application.

When a computer starts up, the first interaction with its operating system is a login process. The purpose of the login is to make sure that the person attempting to gain access to the computer is a known user who can be authenticated logically to be whom he or she claims to be and authorized to access the system components and application software for which he or she has been granted permission. As indicated in the preceding statement, the three steps involved in granting a user access to a computer (and possibly the network to which the computer is attached) are identification, authentication, and authorization.

User Identification

The key part of the login process is user identification. If a user's identification code (user ID) cannot be verified by the operating system, there's no need to continue with the login process. When a Windows, Mac OS, or Linux system (with a GUI) starts up, at least one text box or icon is displayed. If a text box appears, the user is to enter his or her user ID and click the OK or Continue button. If only icons are displayed, such as on the Mac OS X login screen shown in Figure 9-1, the user clicks the icon that identifies the user account he or she wishes to log on to the computer. If a password is enabled for the user account selected or entered, a password dialog box displays into which the password associated with the user account being logged in is entered.

If the user ID represents a valid user account, the OS is able to verify the ID in a list of users who have an authorized account on the PC or network. However, should the user ID not be included as a valid account, an error message is displayed and the login screen is refreshed. Unless the user ID is an exact match (character case is

FIGURE 9-1

The Mac OS X login screen (Image courtesy of Marcin Wichary, guidebookgallery .org.)

typically not optional), the user ID is rejected, even if the ID is merely misspelled or mistyped. When the user ID is verified as a valid user account, a password dialog box displays, unless no password is associated with the account (not a good situation).

User Authentication

After a user account ID has been verified as valid, the next step in a user login is to authenticate the user as actually being the person associated with the user ID. This requires that the user know the password associated with the user account, under the assumption that the password is secret and not shared with other users. It is the combination of the user ID and the password that allows the OS to authenticate logically that the person logging on to the computer is an authorized user.

 on the job

A password is meant to be known only by the person for whom a user account is established. Passwords should always be robust, meaning that they are not easily guessed or hacked. The standard rules for developing a strong password are: the password should be at least 8 characters in length, with 14 characters better; the password should contain a combination of letters, numbers, and symbols selected from different areas of the keyboard with few repeating patterns; the password should not represent a common word, such as the word password or the user ID; and the password should not be stored on the computer in plain text or written down in a location that is easily accessed physically.

Authorization

After a user ID has been verified and the combination of the user ID and password are authenticated, the OS can apply the user rights and permissions assigned to the user to authorize access to certain programs, folders, and files. If a user account is not authorized access to a particular program, the program will not start when selected and a message is displayed to inform the user that he or she doesn't have sufficient permissions to start the program. The same type of message is displayed for folders and files to which the user is not authorized access.

User Interface Components and Features

PC operating systems offer both a GUI and a nongraphical interface to users. For the most part, nongraphical user interfaces are used primarily by system administrators for maintenance and troubleshooting.

Nongraphical User Interfaces

A nongraphical user interface consists of only a few components: the active disk drive, perhaps the active folder, and, definitely the most important component, the command line. Figure 9-2 shows the command line of a Windows OS. Notice that the active drive (C:) and the active folder (\Program Files\) are included in the prompt. This is essentially the same format used by Linux and Mac OS for their command lines, as well. The first position of the command line immediately follows the command-line prompt. The command line is where the command to be executed is entered along with any parameters and arguments required for the command.

Graphical User Interfaces

A GUI combines multiple technologies to facilitate an intuitive, easy-to-navigate interface for users. The most popular operating systems all incorporate a GUI as their primary user interface. Figure 9-3 shows an example of a PC operating system's GUI.

The combination of technologies that is most common in PC operating systems is the window, icon, menu, and pointing device (WIMP) interaction method. A windowing system is used to construct and arrange icons and selections on windows and menus displayed on the desktop of the GUI. The windowing system also manages the interaction between the pointing device (mouse) to reflect its movement and selection of an object for viewing or execution. The desktop itself is arranged, displayed, and controlled by a windowing manager.

FIGURE 9-2

A Windows command-line prompt

FIGURE 9-3

A view of the
Microsoft Vista
GUI (Image
courtesy of
Microsoft
Corporation.)

The most common components and elements of a GUI are the visual devices
used to initiate, control, and interact with the OS or an application program, which
includes

- **Controls** On any GUI, a variety of buttons, text boxes, list boxes, radio buttons, check boxes, and other controls provide a means of interface to the user.
- **Cursor** As the mouse is moved, its motion coordinates are translated by the windowing manager to a position on the screen that overlays the GUI desktop. Moving the mouse pointer (cursor) over a selectable item on the display is the first step in opening or executing the item.
- **Dialog boxes** Communications from the user to the OS are accomplished through mouse clicks, but the OS must communicate (at least for the time being) through a variety of dialog boxes, including message boxes, properties boxes, warning boxes, and confirmation boxes.

■ **Icons** The graphic representations of a file, folder, or program are represented on the GUI desktop using an icon. Functionally an icon is a form of a button; clicking the icon starts the viewing or execution process for the software or data to which the icon is linked.

■ **Menus** Lists of related actions and commands are gathered into a menu. To activate a command from a menu, the mouse pointer is placed over the item and the mouse button is clicked to make the selection. Figure 9-4 shows an example of a GUI menu.

■ **Toolbars** A toolbar is a collection of smaller icons, each of which is associated with a command or program. A toolbar presents commonly used tools that can be activated much like an icon on the GUI desktop. Figure 9-5 illustrates the toolbars in a browser application.

FIGURE 9-4

The Windows
Start menu is an
example of a GUI
menu.

- Set Program Access and Defaults
- Windows Catalog
- Windows Update
- Microsoft Update
- Search Online
- Microsoft Default Manager

- Accessories ▶
- Dell Accessories ▶
- Microsoft Office ▶
- Startup ▶
- Internet Explorer
- Remote Assistance
- Windows Media Player
- Windows Movie Maker
- Games ▶

FIGURE 9-5

The toolbars of the Opera Web browser application are examples of GUI toolbars.

- **Windows** Windows, not the OS, are the containing elements used to hold icons, lists, and command sets in a GUI. For example the Windows Control Panel is a window that contains a set of icons (see Figure 9-6).

- **Wizards** Wizards, which are available in virtually all GUI operating systems, in one form or another, are a series of instructional or guiding dialog boxes that step you through a configuration, creation, or other operating system process one step at a time. Figure 9-7 illustrates a Windows wizard.

FIGURE 9-6

The Windows Control Panel is an example of a GUI window.

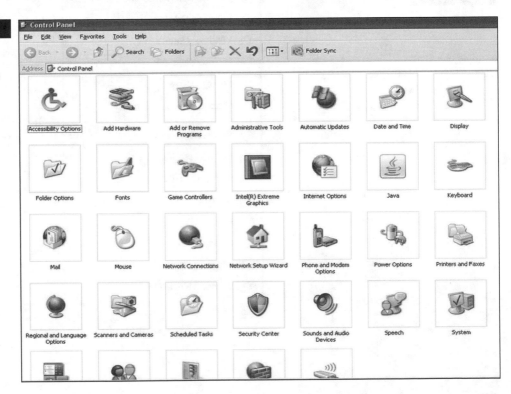

FIGURE 9-7

The Windows Add
Hardware Wizard
is an example of
the GUI wizard
element.

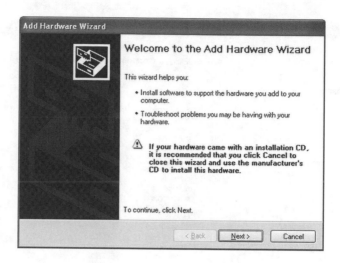

OS Component Access and Management

As discussed in Chapter 8, the primary components of an operating system include
process management, main memory management, and the command-line interpreter.
The user or administrator of an OS has some access to and control over these functions,
but only for configuration, typically. The following sections discuss how each of these
components can be viewed, configured, and monitored.

Process Management

Each of the major PC operating systems, Windows, Mac OS, and Linux, provides a
utility that can be used to view the processes running on the computer at any one
time. In the Windows environment, the utility is the Task Manager (see Figure 9-8).
The latest Mac OS versions provide the Activity Monitor utility, and from the Linux
command line, you can view the list of active processes using the *ps* command. Using
the applicable utility for an OS, an active process can be stopped (or killed), be
paused, or have its priority increased.

Memory Management

Although the management of main and cache memory on a PC is primary done
through the CPU, the chipset, and the operating system kernel, users can monitor
memory usage and determine if a process is occupying too much memory or is not

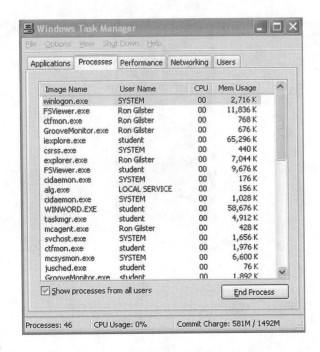

FIGURE 9-8

The Processes tab of the Windows Task Manager lists the processes running on a PC.

receiving enough memory. The long-term remedies to either condition are complex, but if either condition persists, it may be time for more memory on the PC (along with a faster CPU, bus, and so on).

In a Windows OS environment, the Task Manager is also the memory usage monitor. The Performance tab on the Task Manager (see Figure 9-9) not only provides numerical metrics on the allocation and usage of memory but also includes real-time graphs that depict the current CPU utilization and the memory page file usage and status.

In the Mac OS environment, the System Memory page of the Activity Monitor (see Figure 9-10) displays much the same information on the current usage of memory as the Windows Task Manager.

File Management

File management is something that a PC user must perform on a continuous basis to avoid storage device performance problems and to ensure that enough free disk space is available for the OS to use for its myriad functions, such as temporary files, virtual memory, and other such processes.

FIGURE 9-9

The Performance
tab of the
Windows Task
Manager displays
system memory
information.

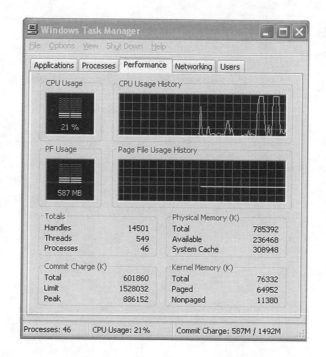

On a Windows system, file management is performed primarily in the Windows Explorer (see Figure 9-11), which is in use anytime devices and their folder and file contents are displayed. The Windows Explorer allows the user to perform a full range of file management activities, including: creating a new folder, deleting an existing folder or file, renaming a folder or file, sharing a folder or file with other users, managing the attributes of a folder or file, creating a shortcut for a folder or file, and even changing the icon used to represent a folder on the Explorer display. The Explorer also provides capabilities to copy or move a folder or file to a new location or to send a folder or file to a variety of devices, compressed folders, and more.

In a Mac OS the tool used for file management is the Finder. The Finder, which is officially named the Macintosh Desktop Experience, provides for the management of files, disks, and the execution of application software.

Networking Management

All of the popular operating systems include tools and functions that allow a PC user to manage the PC's connection to a network, and although the process is slightly different on a Windows, Mac OS, or Linux system, the results are very much the same.

FIGURE 9-10

The System
Memory page
of the Mac OS
Activity Monitor
displays the
status of main
memory. (Image
courtesy of Lloyd
Chambers of
Diglloyd.com.)

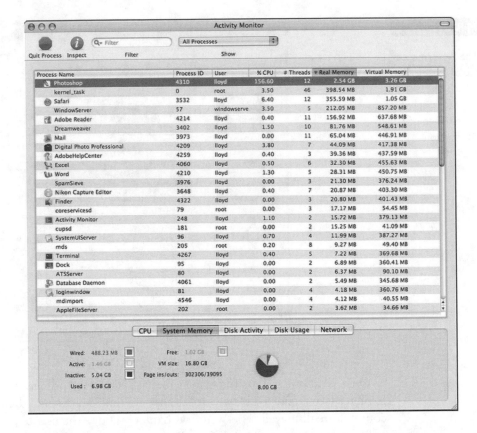

On a Windows system, a connection to a local network is accomplished through the Network Connections icon located on the Windows Control Panel. On this window, a new connection can be created using a wizard or the properties of an existing connection can be managed. Figure 9-12 shows an example of the Network Connection Properties dialog box on which management and maintenance of a network connection are performed.

On the Network Connection Properties dialog box, the protocols (software) associated with the connection can be added and activated. As shown in Figure 9-12, the configuration of the connection is made to the network device, in this case a wireless network interface card (NIC). It is actually the NIC that is connected to the network, and the PC interacts with the NIC, which serves as a middleman between the PC and the network media.

On a Mac OS, a connection to a network is accomplished through the Network tab on the Mac OS Preferences page (see Figure 9-13). Like on its Windows

FIGURE 9-11

Examples of
the Windows
Explorer window
identifying files
with thumbnails
(back screen) and
in a detailed list
(front screen)

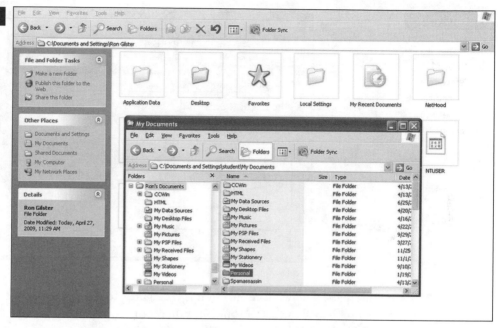

FIGURE 9-12

The network
connection
properties
of a wireless
connection on a
Windows PC

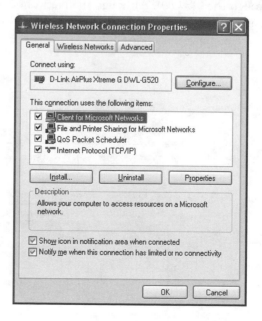

FIGURE 9-13

The Network tab on the Mac OS Preferences page is used to manage network connections.

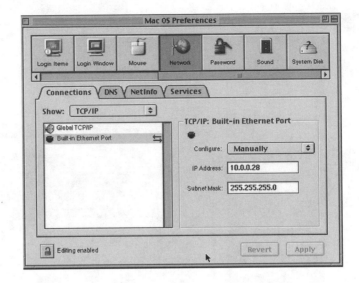

counterpart, a network connection is configured to the network connection, which as Figure 9-13 shows, is the built-in Ethernet port.

By far the simplest way to configure a network connection on a Linux system is through the OS GUI. Although the Network dialog box (see Figure 9-14) is located on a variety of menus in the different Linux flavors, typically you'd find it on either a System or a Connections link.

FIGURE 9-14

The Network dialog box on a Linux system is used to manage a network connection.

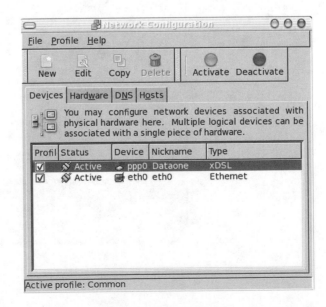

Manipulate Windows and Desktop Items

One of the benefits of a GUI is that application windows and desktop items can be manipulated. This includes resizing, repositioning, renaming, copying, moving, and more. Many of the capabilities available to the user are dependent on the version of the operating system in use.

Knowing the version or release number of the operating system can be valuable information when looking for help on the Web. The version or release number of the installed OS is accessed in a variety of ways, depending on the OS type. On a Mac OS, it is displayed by the About This Mac link; on a Windows system, entering the command **winver** in the Run box displays the system information; and on a Linux system, it is accessed through the System menu.

Working on the Desktop

The standard operation elements of a GUI, including those provided by a Linux, Mac OS, or Windows operating system, are windows, icons, menus, and pointing devices (WIMP). Using these four elements, the user is able to manipulate the items on the Windows or Linux Desktop or the Mac OS Finder to start applications, open files, and perform other actions.

Modifying Windows   When an application is started, it is opened in its own window, which can be manipulated to suit the needs of the user.

The standard actions that can be performed on a GUI window are

- **Close**   When the actions or information contained in a window are no longer needed, the user can close the window by clicking the "X" button in the upper-right corner of the window (on Linux and Windows systems) or the red button in the upper-left corner of a Mac OS window.

- **Maximize**   To enlarge a window to its largest size (typically full view) on a Linux or Windows window, click the Maximize button located in the upper-right corner of the window. The Mac OS maximize (zoom) function, which is the green button in the upper-left corner of the window, enlarges the window to fit the data only.

- **Minimize**   The minimize function of Linux and Windows, which is located in the upper-right corner of a window (with a minus sign on the button), is used to reduce the window to the system tray. On a Mac OS, the yellow button in the upper-left corner reduces the window and adds it to the Dock.

- **Move** To move a window in any of the GUI operating systems, you click down on its title bar and move it to its new location before releasing the mouse button.
- **Resize** Changing the size or shape of a GUI window is done by clicking down on the corner "grip" area, marked with either dots or ribs, and then dragging the window's outline to the desired size and shape.

Another action you may wish to use is to display all open windows at once, arranging the windows horizontally, or vertically, or in a cascading fashion. On a Mac OS, only the windows contained in a single folder can be arranged using the View Options selections. However, in Linux and Windows, all of the windows open on the Desktop can be viewed in one of the three arrangements mentioned earlier. A variety of commands available in Linux, such as *skippy*, can be used to arrange the windows on the desktop. On a Windows system, right-clicking an empty space of the Taskbar provides options to cascade all open windows or arrange them horizontally or vertically on the Desktop.

Starting and Running Programs

Programs can be started from the Desktop using a link on the Start menu, through an icon or shortcut on the Desktop, or from a command-line interface (CLI) prompt. When a program starts up, it opens in its own window.

If multiple programs are running on the system, each in its own window, you are able to switch between programs, without affecting the current actions of either program, simply by clicking into the window of another program or by clicking on its Taskbar entry.

Help is available for the Desktop and the operating system through a Help link on the Start menu (Windows), on the Main menu (Linux), or on the menu bar at the top of the Mac OS desktop. In every case, you have both local help files and online help resources available from the publisher of the operating system. Of course, you can also use a search engine to locate technical Web sites for help from other users.

Manipulating Desktop Folders and Icons

In addition to the folders and icons placed on the operating system's desktop, users can also add, remove, copy, rename, and display the properties of folders and icons (shortcuts) on the desktop.

Creating Desktop Folders and Icons If a particular application, folder, utility, or Web site is accessed frequently, an icon or shortcut can be added to the desktop of the GUI interface to facilitate its access more readily than navigating through other folders or menus. Creating an icon on a Windows XP, Windows Vista, or Windows 7 Desktop is accomplished by navigating, using the Explorer, to the item to be added to the desktop; you then right-click it and choose Send to and Desktop; alternatively, you can right-click an open space of the desktop and choose the New and then Shortcut functions from the pop-up menus. Essentially the same process is used to create a folder on the desktop into which files and other shortcuts can be added. The only difference in the process is choosing Folder instead of Shortcut from the pop-up menu. In either case, the full pathname and filename of the program or Web site URL is entered as the location of the shortcut target and a name that is to appear on the desktop is assigned.

Creating an icon on a Windows Vista or Windows 7 desktop is a bit different, in that all you do is drag the menu or file manager link onto the desktop.

Removing Desktop Folders and Icons   Removing an icon or folder from the desktop is accomplished using one of two primary methods. The first method is to right-click the icon or folder to be removed and then choose Delete from the pop-up window. The second method is to click the icon or folder and, while holding down the mouse button, drag the icon to the Trash Can or Recycle Bin icon on the Desktop.

Moving or Copying Desktop Folder and Icons
Shortcuts for applications added to a system are typically added to the Start menu of a Windows Desktop. However, you may want to move or copy the shortcut to the Desktop to create an icon the process is relatively simple: click the application or folder link on the Start menu and then drag it to the Desktop. A shortcut that is on the desktop can also be moved or copied into a Desktop folder either by using drag-and-drop or by right-clicking the shortcut, choosing Copy, and pasting it into the folder.

Renaming Folders and Shortcuts   To change the name of a Desktop folder (or any folder for that matter) or shortcut icon, right-click the item, choose Rename from the pop-up menu, and enter the new name. If the name you wish to assign to the item already exists in the Desktop folder, the change action is canceled by the operating system.

Displaying Folder and Shortcut Properties   To change the target folder, program, or URL of a Desktop folder or shortcut, you need to access its properties. Right-click the item and choose Properties from the pop-up menu to display the properties dialog box.

CERTIFICATION OBJECTIVE

Change System Settings

3.3 Identify how to change system settings, install and remove software

Once an operating system is installed and running as it should on a PC, there are certain configuration settings that can be used to change its appearance and some of its functions. The following sections discuss the settings that can be configured by a user to make the system his or her own.

GUI Appearance

Most users like to customize the appearance of the GUI desktop to their own liking, which fortunately PC operating systems all support. In fact, the methods and tools that can be used to customize the GUI for any of the popular operating systems are essentially the same.

On a Windows system, most of the tools used to change the appearance of the desktop, windows, message boxes, and the overall appearance of the entire system are located on the Windows Control Panel. On the Control Panel (see Figure 9-6 earlier in the chapter), the Display and the Toolbar and Start Menu icons each display a dialog box through which most of the display elements of the GUI can be changed.

The Display icon displays the Display Properties dialog box, shown in Figure 9-15. On this dialog box, the theme, the desktop wallpaper, the screensaver, and the overall color scheme can be changed as you wish. The Display Properties dialog box also provides tools to manage the video display device.

On a Mac OS system, the appearance of the GUI is customized using the Color Sync, Displays, and Dock icons to open their pages on which the settings for each of these areas can be modified as desired. The same types of controls are also available on the System pages of a Linux system.

System Preferences

Accessing the system preference settings in the major operating systems is accomplished through essentially the same process. In a Windows OS, the major system preferences, those that affect the performance and characteristics of the user interface and the primary utilities, are accessed through the Control Panel (shown earlier in Figure 9-6). On a Mac OS, the system preferences are accessed through

FIGURE 9-15

The Display
Properties dialog
box can be used
to change the
appearance of the
Windows GUI.

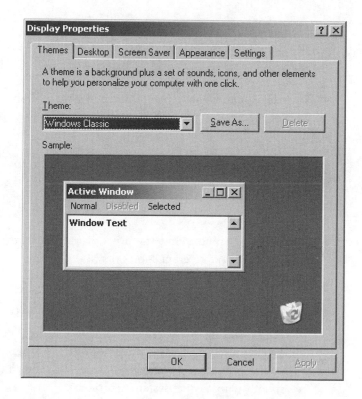

the Apple menu and the System Preferences panel. On a Linux system, the system
preferences are accessed on the main menu through the Control Center.

Although each OS includes a slightly different set of preference setting icons, for
the most part the system preferences that can be accessed for management include

- Accessibility settings
- Add or remove software or hardware
- Administrative tools
- Date and time settings
- Language settings
- Media capture device settings
- Mouse, keyboard, and pad settings
- Network settings
- Power management settings

- Security settings
- Sounds and speaker settings
- User account settings

To access a particular system preference setting, simply click the setting you wish to view or modify. For example, here are the procedures used for system preferences common to all operating systems:

- **Date and time settings**   Use the link or icon to display the date and time preferences or properties dialog box and adjust the time or date for the operating system (and the one displayed on the GUI and used to time/date stamp file actions).
- **Display settings**   Use the link or icon to display the general display properties or preferences or, on a Mac OS, the properties of the installed display. On the Display properties dialog box, you can change the resolution and color depth of the monitor, activate/deactivate a screensaver, set the desktop wallpaper, and manage the settings for two or more displays.
- **Audio settings**   Use the link or icon for sound or audio devices to display a dialog box on which you can adjust the settings for audio volume, audio device preferences, and recording devices; you can also associate specific sounds with specific system functions.
- **Mouse, keyboard, and pad settings**   Use the link or icon for the keyboard, touchpad, and mouse, which could be separate icons on some OS versions, to display a dialog box on which you can adjust the settings for each of these input devices.
- **Accessibility settings**   Use the link or icon for Accessibility or Universal Access to display a dialog box on which you can turn on or adjust the performance of keyboard, mouse, display, and sound utilities and other assistive technologies to enable the system for a person with disabilities.
- **Security settings**   Use the Security link or icon to display a system security manager on which you can enable/disable virus protection, configure a firewall, and control which user accounts have access to system preferences and other resources.

Install or Remove Software

The process used to install a software application on a computer is one of two general types: the process used on a Mac OS or Linux system and the process used on a Windows system. In either case, before you begin the installation process, you should create a backup copy of the installation media, assuming you are installing from distribution media. If the software is downloaded from the Web and then installed, retain the receipt or licensing agreement and back up the downloaded package prior to installation.

The process used to remove an application, like those used to install the application, also varies by OS. In the sections that follow, a general overview is given on the processes used to install and remove software on the different operating systems.

Installing and Removing Applications on a Mac or Linux System   When you install an application on a Mac or Linux system, all of the files associated with the application are placed into a single folder or directory, except, of course, the operating system files used by the application (as well as other applications). The installation is managed by an installer utility in the operating system or one packaged with the new application.

To remove an application from a Mac or Linux system, you only need to delete the folder containing the application's files and clean up any folders, files, and desktop icons related to the application.

Installing and Removing Applications on a Windows System   Because of its internal structure and registration processes, installing an application on a Windows system can be a bit more complicated than this action on a Mac or a Linux system. Most Windows applications include a setup utility that guides the installation and, using information entered by the user, controls the placement and distribution of the application's files and programs into the appropriate locations.

Once the software is installed, provided that it interacts directly with the operating system when it's running, it will appear in the Windows Add or Remove Programs dialog box that is accessed through the Control Panel. To remove an application, locate it in the Currently Installed Programs list on the Add or Remove Programs dialog box and click Remove. On older Windows versions, the system may need to be restarted to complete the installation or removal, something no longer required by Windows Vista or Windows 7.

After installing an application, it is a good practice, especially on systems where multiple users have access, to access the primary folder of the application and set user permissions levels to control which users have or don't have access to the application and its associated folders and files.

Update or Upgrade Applications   Software publishers frequently provide Web sites that can be either manually or automatically accessed to download updates or upgrades to software installed on a PC, including the operating system. Because users don't often know or investigate the content of publisher-supplied upgrades and updates, it's a best practice to back up the system prior to installing an upgrade, even automatically applied upgrades.

When an application is installed, perhaps not all of its features were chosen for installation. In cases like this, additional features or upgrades can be added to the system from the installation media or from an online source. Once again, it's a very good idea to back up the system before making software changes.

One way to avoid the potential pitfalls of installing and upgrading application software is to subscribe to an online application service, such as Google Docs, Windows Live, Zoho, and even industry- or hobby-specific applications. Many of these services also provide document storage space, but typically, your files can be saved on your local PC as well.

Common Problems with Installing or Running an Application

There are a variety of issues or problems that can come up when you are installing or attempting to start application software, including the following:

- **User is not authorized to install or remove an application** The primary or administrator user of a local computer may not be authorized to install or remove an application. This can be especially true on networked computers. The system or network administrators may wish to control the installation of applications to networked computers to maintain standardization and to minimize system conflicts and troubleshooting tasks.

- **Defective installation media** Should the CD-ROM or DVD, or any other media, containing the installation files for an application become corrupted, damaged, or incomplete (lost media units), the application is not likely to install completely or correctly. This is one very good reason to create a backup copy of installation media before the installation is started.

- **Installation failure** When installing a new application on a PC, there are many potential outcomes: one that is good and several that are bad (or at least not good). The good result is that the installation proceeds flawlessly and the application runs properly, which is the most common outcome, thankfully. However, several not-so-good results can occur after the installation completes, including these:
    - The new application doesn't appear on the desktop, in the Start menu, or in a folder.

■ Thenew application shows on the desktop or system menu but will not start running, or it does start up but displays a fatal error message and closes.

■ Other existing applications will no longer start or run properly.

■ Existing files that are associated with the new application (perhaps created with an earlier version of the software) cannot be opened or viewed in the new application.

These problems, along with a few others, are sure indications that one or more parts of the installation failed. You should reattempt the installation and, should the problems persist, contact technical support for the application.

■ **Online applications** When running an online application, if access is denied or the application is not available, it's likely that the username and password is incorrect or there is a problem with the profile either the user or the application service provider (ASP) created. If a second login produces the same result, the user profile should be edited by the user or technical support for the Web site should be contacted. Another, although somewhat less likely, problem is that the ASP site is down and not available.

Privacy and Security Settings

Securing a PC involves more than just locking the room in which it sits. There are a number of privacy and security settings that can be configured to protect the data and software stored on the PC. The settings that can be configured and the practices that can help to protect the system include the following:

■ **Administrator login** Use the administrator login only when necessary and create a limited user login for normal computer use.

■ **Automatic updates** Any automatic update services should be configured to prompt the user when an update is available and not to automatically install the update.

■ **BIOS password** Setting a BIOS password prevents unauthorized changes to the hardware configuration of a computer. If you set this password, be sure to use a password you can remember!

■ **Guest login accounts** Disable the default Guest account on the PC.

■ **Local security policy** This is actually a group of security settings that can be used to configure how often login passwords must be changed; if multiple failed login attempts lock out additional attempts and for how long; and if the virtual memory and primary memory are cleared when the computer is shut down.

■ **Screensaver password** If you use a screensaver, a password can be assigned that must be entered before the system can be accessed after the screensaver is activated.

■ **System services** Many services that are started when a PC is booted up can be disabled to free up memory and to reduce the security threats to the computer. The services that you may want to consider for disabling include indexing services, any instant messaging services, remote procedure call (RPC) services, routing and remote access services (if the computer isn't a network server), the Telnet service, and unnecessary Universal Plug and Play (UPnP) services.

CERTIFICATION SUMMARY

This chapter covered how you work with an operating system to manage and maintain the GUI and its desktop, as well as stored data, files, and storage devices. For the IC³ exam, you need to be familiar with the processes used to set or change the settings of the operating system and to install or remove software from a computer.

TWO-MINUTE DRILL

Manipulate the Desktop, Files, and Disks

❑ The purpose of a login is to identify, authenticate, and authorize the user account and password combination.

❑ After a user ID is identified as valid, the user account is authenticated with a password, which, if valid, accesses the system information on what the user account is authorized to access or perform.

❑ PC operating systems offer both a GUI and a nongraphical interface to users. Nongraphical user interfaces are used primarily by system administrators for maintenance and troubleshooting. A GUI combines multiple technologies to facilitate an intuitive, easy-to-navigate interface for users.

Change System Settings

❑ The components and elements of a GUI include controls, cursor, dialog boxes, icons, menus, toolbars, windows, and wizards.

❑ The major PC operating systems provide a process management utility that is used to view the processes running on the computer. The Windows Task Manager, the Mac OS Activity Monitor, and the Linux *ps* command are process management utilities. The Task Manager and Activity Monitor can also be used to monitor memory usage.

❑ File management should be performed continuously to avoid storage device performance problems and to ensure free disk space is available. The Windows Explorer and the Mac OS Finder are file management tools.

❑ Popular operating systems include tools for the management of a PC's connection to a network.

❑ A user has access to and can modify certain settings that configure the hardware and software of a PC, especially in the areas of GUI appearance and privacy and security.

❑ The standard operational elements of a GUI interface are windows, icons, menus, and pointing devices. When an application is started, it is opened in its own window, which can be manipulated to suit the needs of the user.

❑ The standard actions that can be performed on a GUI window are: close, maximize, minimize, move, and resize. All open windows can be displayed on the desktop in a cascading fashion, arranged horizontally, or arranged vertically.

❑ GUI-based operating systems include a file management system that facilitates the management of folders, files, and programs. The file manager displays files and folders in a hierarchical structure in a collapsed form, by default. Folders can be expanded to view the contents of the folder.

❑ Filenames should follow a standard convention that assigns a predictable and self-explanatory name to each file or folder. Windows allows a maximum of 255 characters for a filename. Windows files and folders carry identifying properties and characteristics with them that can be displayed and modified if desired. The properties include the file author; its creation and modification dates; its attributes and location; and its archiving, indexing, compression, and encryption settings.

❑ A storage medium nearing maximum storage capacity may deny access to a file or cause a file to become corrupted. Disk drives should be regularly backed up, and preventive maintenance performed, including defragmentation and the removal of unneeded files or folders.

SELF TEST

The following questions are intended to help you be sure that you understand the material included in this chapter. Read the questions and the answer choices carefully.

Manipulate the Desktop, Files, and Disks

1. Which of the following is not an action associated with the login process of a PC?

  A. Accounting

  B. Authenticating

  C. Authorizing

  D. Identifying

2. What login action is the password most associated with?

  A. Accounting

  B. Authenticating

  C. Authorizing

  D. Identifying

3. What are the two most common forms of PC user interfaces?

  A. Text

  B. GUI

  C. CLI

  D. Symbol

4. Which of the following is not a component or element of a GUI?

  A. Command strings

  B. Cursor

  C. Dialog box

  D. Icon

5. What is the GUI element that provides a step-by-step guide through the completion of a setup or configuration process?

  A. Dialog box

  B. Menu

  C. Window

  D. Wizard

6. On a Windows PC, what is the system tool that is used to manage the processes running on the PC?

   A. Activity Monitor

   B. Task Manager

   C. The *ps* command

   D. No such tool is available on a Windows system

7. What is the Windows feature on which file management can be performed by a PC user?

   A. Activity Monitor

   B. Finder

   C. Task Manager

   D. Windows Explorer

8. What characteristics of a GUI does the acronym WIMP represent?

   A. Wallpaper, icons, memory, pointing devices

   B. Windows, icons, menus, and pointing devices

   C. Windows, icons, menus, and programs

   D. Wizards, icons, menus, and programs

9. What menu link on a Windows system is used to view the characteristics, properties, and attributes of a file?

   A. About

   B. Attributes

   C. Details

   D. Properties

10. What could be the possible cause of a file becoming unavailable or corrupted?

    A. Improper maintenance on the internal physical components of a hard disk drive

    B. Hard disk drive nearing capacity

    C. The file's name being too long

    D. Power failure while the file is in use

11. Which of the following is not a commonly available arrangement for open windows on an OS GUI desktop?

    A. Cascading

    B. Horizontal

    C. Inverse

    D. Vertical

Change System Settings

12. Which of the following actions should be considered and possibly applied to enhance the security of a PC?

 A. Disabling guest accounts

 B. Setting local security policies

 C. Disabling unneeded services

 D. Setting a BIOS password

 E. All of the above

 F. None of the above

13. What feature can be used in conjunction with a screensaver on a Windows PC to prevent unauthorized access to the PC?

 A. BIOS password

 B. Local security policy

 C. Screensaver password

 D. Screensaver lockout

14. What component is affected when a PC's network configuration is set?

 A. CPU

 B. Disk drive

 C. Network interface

 D. OS

SELF TEST ANSWERS

Manipulate the Desktop, Files, and Disks

1. ☑ **A.** When you log in to a remote access server, such as the ones at your Internet service provider (ISP), accounting is enabled to track the time you are connected for billing or service tracking. However, a PC in an office or home typically doesn't require this service.
   ☒ **B, C,** and **D** are incorrect. Identifying, authenticating, and authorizing are steps performed by the login process during the login process.

2. ☑ **B.** A login password is associated with the authentication step of the login process.
   ☒ **A, C,** and **D** are incorrect. Accounting is not typically used on local PCs; authorizing takes place after authentication; and identifying the user account ID is the first step performed in the login process, usually before the password is used.

3. ☑ **B** and **C.** In effect, a text interface is a CLI, but a CLI goes a bit further than just text entries, which are an older legacy interface type.
   ☒ **A** and **D** are incorrect. I'm not aware of any user interface that uses symbols, which would amount to changing a PC's identity to the PC formerly known as . . . .

4. ☑ **A.** Command strings are the primary interface mode of a CLI.
   ☒ **B, C,** and **D** are incorrect. These are all elements or components of a GUI.

5. ☑ **D.** A wizard guides a user through a configuration process one step at a time.
   ☒ **A, B,** and **C** are incorrect. A dialog box is used to accept formatted and screened user input; a menu is a list of commands or links; and a window contains a group of related actions.

6. ☑ **B.** The Task Manager has several functions available, including a tab that is focused on the processes currently running on a PC.
   ☒ **A, C,** and **D** are incorrect. The Activity Monitor and the *ps* command are essentially the Mac OS and Linux equivalents of the Windows Task Manager, respectively.

7. ☑ **D.** The Windows Explorer displays drives, folders, and files and supports file management and maintenance.
   ☒ **A, B,** and **C** are incorrect. The Activity Monitor is very much like the Windows Task Manager, which is used to manage processes and applications, and the Finder is essentially the equivalent of the Windows Explorer.

8. ☑ **B.** The operating elements of a GUI are windows, icons, menus, and pointing devices.
   ☒ **A, C,** and **D** are incorrect. WIMP is an acronym for windows, icons, menus, and pointing devices, which are the operating elements of a GUI.

9. ☑ **D.** The characteristics, properties, and attributes of a file are displayed on a Windows system through the Properties link on a pop-up menu.

☒ **A, B,** and **C** are incorrect. The About link is used to display information about the operating system. There is no Attributes or Detail link available, but the attributes and all of the details of a file can be viewed on the Properties display.

10. ☑ **B.** A hard disk drive, and any other type of storage device, can cause file read and write problems or corrupt one or more files when it nears its capacity.

☒ **A, C,** and **D** are incorrect. The internal physical components of a hard disk are not available for maintenance. A filename that exceeds 256 characters could cause a filename not to be opened, but it doesn't necessarily damage the file. A power failure that occurs exactly at the millisecond a disk write is occurring (an extremely remote change of this) could possibly cause a file to become corrupt, but otherwise only the file's data in memory would be lost, without damage to the file.

11. ☑ **C.** There is no inverse order arrangement available on OS GUIs.

☒ **A, B,** and **D** are incorrect. Open windows on a GUI display can be viewed in a cascading, horizontal, or vertical arrangement.

Change System Settings

12. ☑ **E.** All of these actions listed in answers A through D can be used to enhance the security of a PC.

☒ **A, B, C, D,** and **F** are incorrect. Each of the choices in answers A through D can be used to enhance the security of a PC. However, none of these choices is the best answer alone. Answer F is just wrong.

13. ☑ **C.** Setting up a password that is required to gain access to a system after the screensaver is activated secures the PC while the user is away from the system for a relatively extended time.

☒ **A, B,** and **D** are incorrect. A BIOS password and configuring local security policy settings can also enhance the security of a PC but aren't associated directly to a screensaver, although the lockout policy can be invoked if multiple attempts are made to access the PC.

14. ☑ **C.** When the network configuration settings are set on a networked PC, the settings selected are applied to the network interface.

☒ **A, B,** and **D** are incorrect. Network configuration settings made to the network interface are used and supported by the components listed in these answers.

Part II

Key Applications Exam

Objectives Map: Key Applications Exam

Official Objective	Study Guide Coverage	Chapter Number
Be able to start and exit an application, identify and modify interface elements, and utilize sources of online help	Start, Work with, and Exit an Application	10
Perform common file-management functions	Common File-Management Functions	11
Perform common editing and formatting functions	Common Editing and Formatting Functions	11
Perform common printing/outputting functions	Common Printing and Outputting Functions	11
Be able to format text and documents including the ability to use automatic formatting tools	Formatting Documents	12
Identify common uses for word processing (such as creating short documents like letters and memos, long documents like reports and books, and specialized documents such as Web pages and blog entries) and identify elements of a well-organized document	Common Uses of Word Processing	12
Be able to use word-processing tools to automate processes such as document review, security, and collaboration	Reviewing, Securing, and Collaborating on Word Processing Documents	13
Be able to modify worksheet data and structure and format data in a worksheet	Working with the Data, Format, and Structure of a Worksheet	14
Be able to sort data, manipulate data using formulas and functions and create simple charts	Manipulate Data Using Formulas and Functions	15
Be able to create and format simple presentations	Creating and Formatting Simple Presentations	16

10

Working with Common Application Workspace Features

CERTIFICATION OBJECTIVE

- Start, Work with, and Exit an Application

✓ Two-Minute Drill

Q&A Self Test

T his chapter provides a look at the processes used to start and exit a Windows application, specifically a Microsoft Office 2007 application, and at the elements and features available in the Office 2007 workspace. The Office 2007 applications share many common workspace features. The general layout and functions of the common workspace layout is essentially the same for each of the Office applications.

To help you prepare for the IC³ exam, this chapter discusses the navigation of folder and file hierarchies to locate and open a specific file, how to change the visual appearance of an application workspace, how to customize an application's configuration and settings, and how to work with an application's help system. With a good working knowledge of these areas, you shouldn't have trouble answering the applications sections of the IC³ exams.

CERTIFICATION OBJECTIVE

Start, Work with, and Exit an Application

1.1   Be able to start and exit an application, identify and modify interface elements, and utilize sources of online help.

The process used to start any Windows application is a relatively simple one, despite the fact that there are several ways to do it. Once an application has started, there are OS-level changes that can be used to change the appearance of all applications that run on the Windows Desktop, as well as application-specific appearance settings that can be used to change the look of a single application or all of the applications in a suite (such as Office 2007). Another common feature of nearly all Windows applications is a local or online help system, which, as we'll discuss later in the chapter, can be essentially one and the same.

Starting a Windows Application

One of two primary methods can be used to start a Windows application:

■ From the Start menu
■ From the Desktop

Starting an Application from the Start Menu

Whether you are using a Windows XP, Windows Vista, or even Windows 7 operating system, each features a Start button and a Start menu. Figure 10-1 shows the Start button (in the lower-left corner) and the Start menu of a Windows XP system, and Figure 10-2 shows the Start button and Start menu of a Windows Vista system. The Windows 7 Start menu is virtually identical to the Windows Vista Start menu (see Figure 10-2).

On any of these Windows versions, clicking the Start button displays the Start menu. While the Windows Vista Start menu includes a few more program groups and links to special-purpose windows (such as the Control Panel), both of these Start menu types have a pane that contains the most recently used (MRU) programs on the left side of the display, with the most frequently used (MFU) programs toward the top of the list. Recommended system utilities and applications are located above the MFU pane. The right side of the Start menu contains links to special-function dialog boxes, windows, applications, and folders (called jump lists) that provide quick and easy access to these functions.

If the application you wish to start is listed in the MRU pane, you only need to click its entry once to start the program. However, if the application isn't included in

FIGURE 10-1

The Windows XP
Start menu

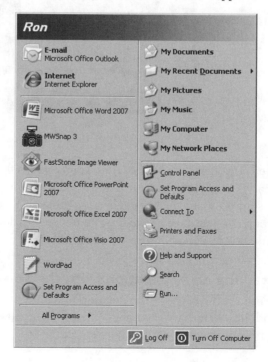

FIGURE 10-2

The Windows
Vista Start menu
(Image courtesy
of Microsoft
Corporation.)

the list, you can click the All Programs option to display its menu, which contains
nearly every application and utility installed on the PC. If the application you want
to start is included in an application group, hold the cursor over the name of the
group to open its submenu. Locate the application you want to start and click its
link. Figure 10-3 shows an example of the All Programs menu.

Starting an Application from the Desktop

Windows XP supports the creation of icons on its Desktop for applications, folders,
and files. Windows Vista and Windows 7 support the creation of thumbnails of the
application workspace or a sample graphic on their desktops and the Desktop Sidebar

FIGURE 10-3

The All Programs
menu of a
Windows XP
system

(see Figure 10-4). If the application you want to start has an icon or thumbnail on the
Windows Desktop, click its icon or thumbnail to start the application.

Identify and Manipulate Application Workspace Elements

When you start a Windows application, a new window is opened that contains the
application's workspace. All user interaction with the application takes place in
or on its workspace. Standalone and single-purpose applications have a workspace

design unique to the particular application. Application suites, such as Microsoft
Office and Corel WordPerfect X4, use a workspace design that is common to each
of the applications in its bundle. To help you visualize the concept of an application
workspace, let's look at the common workspace of the Office 2007 suite of applications.

Common Workspace Elements

An application workspace must have certain elements in order for the workspace
to provide control to the user. As illustrated in Figure 10-5, a workspace must have
one or more menus that list the commands and features available to create, edit, and

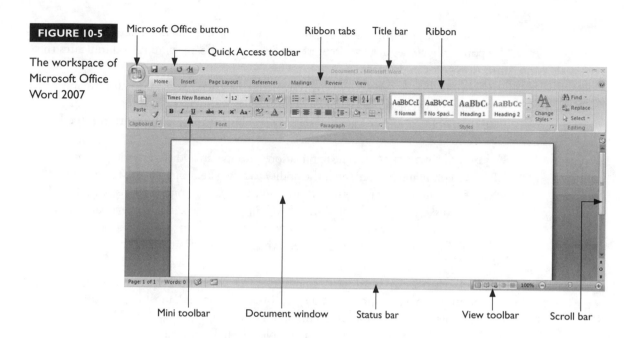

The workspace of
Microsoft Office
Word 2007

Microsoft Office button   Ribbon tabs   Title bar   Ribbon

Quick Access toolbar

Mini toolbar   Document window   Status bar   View toolbar   Scroll bar

format a document or control the functions of the application. In some workspaces, some or all of the menus are replaced by toolbars. The Office 2007 workspace uses a form of a toolbar that is called a Ribbon (see Figure 10-5). Of course the workspace must have a document or activity window, pane, or work area in which a document is prepared or an action (think computer games) takes place. A title bar, a status bar, and workspace navigation aids (such as a scroll bar) provide information and further control over the document or activity window.

Navigating Around an Application Window

There are several ways to navigate around an open application window and its workspace. Perhaps the most commonly used method is using the mouse pointer, but shortcut keys and, in some applications, a Go To command can be used as well.

Mouse Pointers and Cursors   Another very important element of an application window and workspace is the *cursor* or *mouse pointer*. When you move the mouse and its pointer over a menu, the Mac OS Dock, the Office 2007 Ribbon, or selected text or data in an application workspace, the pointer is actually a pointer, indicated by an arrow or pointing finger graphic. In a word processing document workspace, the pointer becomes a cursor, represented with an I-Beam symbol, and indicates the insertion point in the document.

Cursors can be customized using downloadable cursor sets. A desktop theme also applies a thematic set of cursor characters as well. However, typically within a particular application, the general cursor set relevant to that application is used.

Keyboard Shortcuts   Some applications provide, in addition to their menus, Ribbons, command buttons, etc., the ability to navigate around a document, select document content, and perform certain commands using combinations of keyboard keys, called *shortcuts*. Microsoft Office 2007 supports over 210 such keyboard shortcuts that can be used to perform a wide variety of actions within an application window. Table 10-1 lists a small sampling of the keyboard shortcuts supported by Office 2007.

Go To Command   If you wish to navigate to a particular page in a word processing document or to a specific cell of a spreadsheet document, most application suites provide some form of a Go To command. For example, in a Word 2007 document workspace, the Go To function is available through either the Find or Replace command on the Home tab of the Word 2007 Ribbon or by pressing the F5 key.

TABLE 10-1		
A Sampling of the Keyboard Shortcuts Supported by Office 2007	**Function or Command**	**Shortcut Keys**
	Bold	CTRL-B or CTRL-SHIFT-B
	Bulleted list	CTRL-SHIFT-L
	Close or exit	ALT-F4
	Copy	CTRL-C or CTRL-INSERT
	Cut	CTRL-X or SHIFT-DELETE
	Go to	CTRL-G or F5
	Help	F1
	Insert page break	CTRL-ENTER
	New document	CTRL-N
	Paste	CTRL-V or SHIFT-INSERT
	Print	CTRL-P or CTRL-SHIFT-F12
	Save	CTRL-S or SHIFT-F12 or ALT-SHIFT-F2
	Undo	CTRL-Z or ALT-BACKSPACE

The Go To function in Word 2007 allows you to designate the particular document element (section, page, line, reviewer, etc.) you wish to go to, moving either forward or backward in the document.

Manipulating Workspace Elements

Using Microsoft Office Word 2007 as an example, let's quickly look at the usage of the workspace elements identified in Figure 10-5.

Microsoft Office Button   Microsoft has grouped the functions and features that are common to the Office 2007 applications onto a common set of menus and submenus (available in Word 2007, Excel 2007, PowerPoint 2007, and Access 2007). The primary menu containing these common items is displayed by clicking the Microsoft Office button. Figure 10-6 shows the menu displayed by clicking this button.

FIGURE 10-6

The menu displayed by the Microsoft Office button

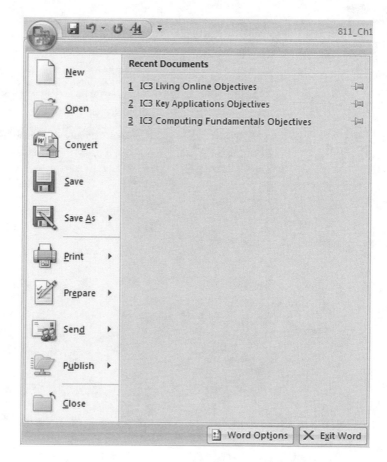

In earlier versions of Office, most of the functions contained on the Office button's menu were repeated on the toolbars and menus of each application. With the exception of a few of the menu options custom to a particular application, such as the Word Options button at the bottom-right corner of the menu, the remainder of the options are standard to the Office applications.

The right pane of the display is used for a list of recently opened or saved documents by default. However, any of the menu options that have a right-facing arrow following the option name display what amounts to a submenu specific to that option in the right pane. You don't have to click an option to see its submenu; merely hold the mouse pointer over an option to display its submenu. Figure 10-7 shows an example of a menu option's submenu.

FIGURE 10-7

The submenu for the Print option on the Microsoft Office button's menu

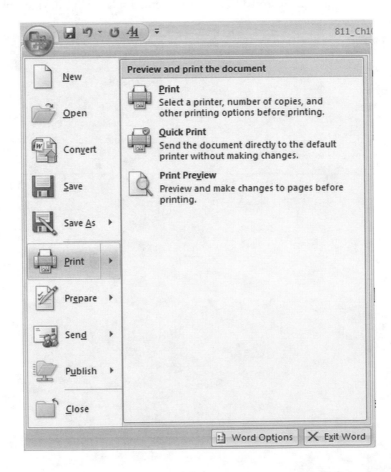

FIGURE 10-8

The Office Word
2007 Ribbon

Clicking an option on the submenu typically opens a dialog box on which you can specify or control the action you've selected.

The Ribbon Office 2007 has shifted what in previous versions were included on menu bars and toolbars into contextually organized tabs of a single toolbar element, which is called the Ribbon. The Office 2007 Ribbon contains the features, functions, commands, and tools unique to each of the Office applications. For example, the tabs of the Office Word 2007 Ribbon (see Figure 10-8) are as follows:

- **Home** This tab contains the standard character and paragraph formatting commands, features, styles, and Clipboard functions that are the most commonly used actions in a Word document.

- **Insert** This tab contains icons and commands that are used to insert a wide variety of objects and effects into a document, including page breaks, pictures, tables, hypertext links, headers, page numbers, symbols, and special character features like Drop Cap and text boxes.

- **Page Layout** This tab contains the commands and functions that can be used to set or modify the layout of a document by changing the document theme (color scheme), the margins, the page borders, the paragraph indention and spacing, and the arrangement of overlapping elements.

- **References** This tab contains the features and commands used to add references, such as a table of contents, endnotes and footnotes, reference citations, a bibliography, an index, and a table of authorities to a document.

- **Mailings** This tab contains all of the features, functions, and commands used to create envelopes, labels, and merged documents. In previous versions of Word, the items included on the Mailings tab were distributed over several menus.

- **Review** This tab consolidates the functions and commands used by a document reviewer to proof a document, insert and manage comments, and track changes made to the document, as well as the commands used to accept or reject any changes made to the document, compare the document to another version of the same document, and protect the document against further changes.

■ **View** This tab contains the icons that allow the user to change the view of the workspace and to show or hide editing elements, such as a ruler, an alignment grid or guidelines, or a document map, as well as to scale the workspace display by zooming in or out or viewing multiple pages. The workspace window can be made to view multiple documents horizontally or vertically cascading or side-by-side. The macros feature is accessed from the View tab as well.

■ **Add-Ins** This optional tab is not a default tab but is activated only when a Microsoft or third-party add-in or a macro is installed or activated.

The tabs on the Ribbon of the Office 2007 applications are arranged so that users can find related functions intuitively. If you want to change the view of the workspace, it's logical that you'd select the View tab; if you want to add a reference citation in a term paper or report, you'd select the References tab; if you want to insert an object or document element, it's a good bet that the commands used to do so are located on the Insert tab; and so on.

Quick Access Toolbar Another new feature to Microsoft Office with the 2007 version is the Quick Access toolbar (see Figure 10-9). This feature adds a convenience to the workspace that is very similar to the Quick Launch (Tray) on the Windows Desktop. This customizable toolbar, which is located just to the right of the Microsoft Office button on the title bar, contains, by default, icons for Save, Undo, Redo, and Styles (display the Styles pane). Just about any of the standard document features can be added to the Quick Access toolbar, but the convenience of this feature begins to diminish as more and more icons are added to it.

Mini Toolbar The ability to display a pop-up menu has been a feature of several of the more popular application suites for some time. However, Office 2007 has taken this one step further by adding a Mini toolbar that contains the most frequently used

FIGURE 10-9

The default contents of the Office 2007 Quick Access toolbar are Save, Undo, Redo, and Styles.

FIGURE 10-10

The Office 2007
Mini toolbar and
its associated
pop-up menu

character formatting features and that is displayed whenever you right-click the text in a document, a worksheet cell, or a part of a presentation slide. The Mini toolbar, shown in Figure 10-10 along with the pop-up menu, displays automatically whenever you hold the mouse pointer over a block of selected text.

View Toolbar   Located at the lower-right corner of the workspace at the right end of the status bar, the View toolbar can be used in lieu of the selections in the Views and Zoom groups on the View tab. The five icons on the View toolbar (see Figure 10-11) can be used to change the document window view to (left to right) Print Layout (the default view that is essentially a print preview), Full Screen Reading, Web Layout, Outline, or Draft.

To the right of the View icons is the Zoom slider, which can be used to zoom in or out on the document window. Moving the slider to the left (or clicking the Minus button) zooms the view of the document out, and moving the slider to the right (or clicking the Plus button) zooms the document view in (enlarges the size of the text).

FIGURE 10-11

The View toolbar
can be used to
quickly change
the view layout
of the document
window.

Navigate Files and Folders

The ability to navigate to a specific folder or file on a storage device is an essential feature of any document preparation or editing application. Without this capability, all of the documents saved to a storage device would all be in the same location, which could be confusing or cause documents to be overwritten.

Application suites in general use a common utility object for functions that open documents, save documents, print documents, and possibly more. Office 2007 also places the menu selections to activate these functions on its common Microsoft Office button menu (see Figure 10-6 earlier in the chapter).

When you select the Open option on the Microsoft Office button menu, the Open dialog box is displayed. The Open dialog box (see Figure 10-12) is the same dialog box displayed by any of the Office 2007 applications. By expanding the drives and folders, you can navigate down to a specific file, select it, and open it to an application workspace.

Change the Appearance of a Workspace

In addition to the capability to change the visual appearance of the OS desktop, you can also change the appearance of the workspaces of the Office 2007 applications. Using the application options button on the Microsoft Office button menu,

FIGURE 10-12

The Office 2007 Open dialog box

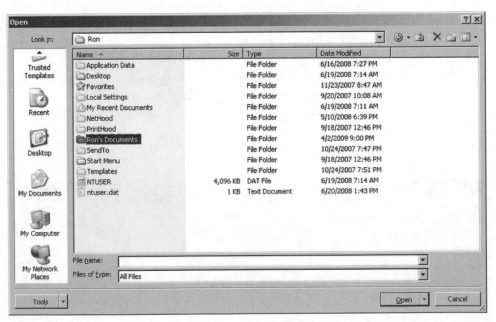

such as the Word Options button, shown earlier in Figure 10-6, the color scheme of the workspace can be changed from the Blue default to either silver or black. In some applications, such as Office Excel 2007 and Access 2007, the elements included on the workspace can be selected, as well as the workspace view.

Customize Application Configuration and Settings

The application options button on the Microsoft Office button menu can also be used to customize the configuration and settings for the application and, for many of the settings, all of the applications in the Office 2007 suite. Figure 10-13 shows the Advanced submenu that displays when the Word Options button is clicked.

In addition to the configuration settings shown in Figure 10-13, the Advanced settings menu, along with the other settings options listed in the left pane, can be used to change the look, actions, and support functions of an Office application.

FIGURE 10-13

The Advanced options menu associated with the Word Options button

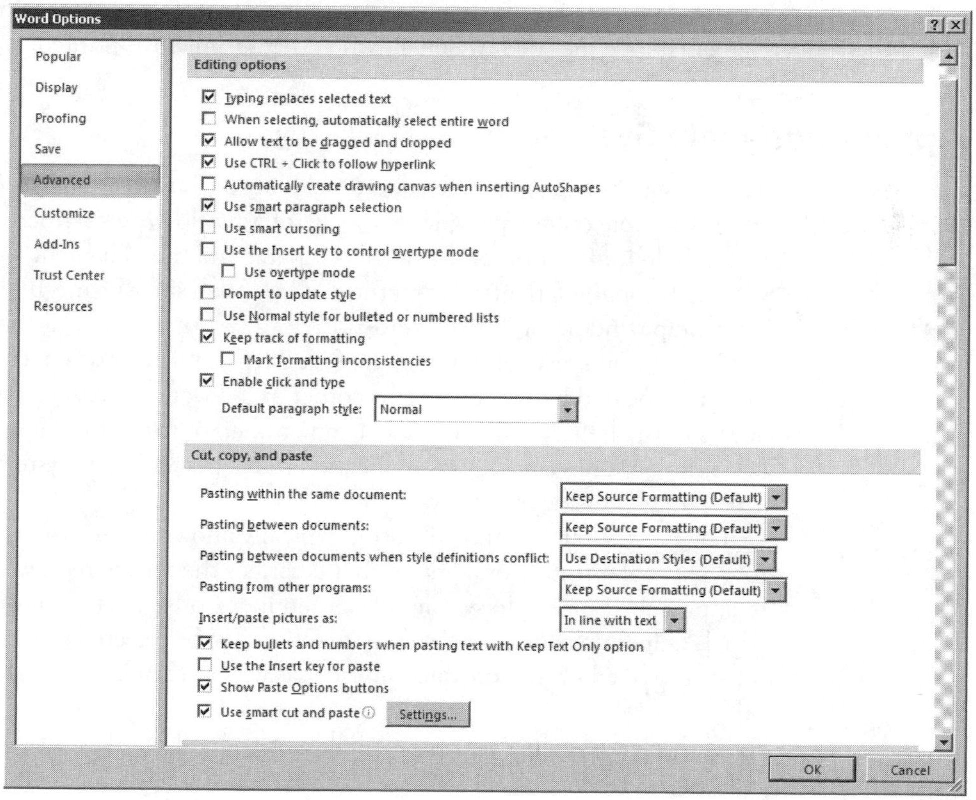

Change Application Defaults

Application software, especially personal productivity applications, allow users to change the default settings for such things as where files are stored, printing preferences, and when and how often the document is saved automatically, if at all. In most applications, these settings are accessed through a master settings function or from an Options or Preferences link on an application menu.

For example, in Microsoft Office Word 2007, the default settings mentioned in the preceding paragraph can be configured through the Office button's menu using the Word Options button. Clicking this button displays the settings and options that can be configured to the user's preferences in variety of areas, including display, proofing, and save options, plus many more detailed function settings through the Advanced link.

In the Save settings, the user can set the default file format, the location to which documents are to be saved by default, how often an automatic save is to be performed, and the location in which the document is to be saved. In the Advanced settings, print settings can be configured that control the content and document elements to be included by default when the document is printed.

Application Help Systems

The more popular application suites, including both the installed software suites and those available online, provide relatively robust help systems. Microsoft and Corel install help information on the local computer and then augment this information with additional information from their online Web sites. Figure 10-14 shows the main help window for Office Word 2007.

On the workspace for any of the Office 2007 applications, a question mark button is located in the upper-right corner of the workspace that provides direct access to the help system, both local and online, for the current application. A de facto standard has emerged in application suites that the help system also can be accessed by pressing the F1 key.

The help system for an application typically allows you to search the help system for a particular feature or a phrase that describes the function on which you are seeking help. Some help systems display an index or subject matter menu from which help for a particular action or function can be selected from a list of help topics provided by the software publisher as well as related information or help from other parties.

With myriad help resources available, you should rank or prioritize the help sources by how likely they are to provide you with the help you need.

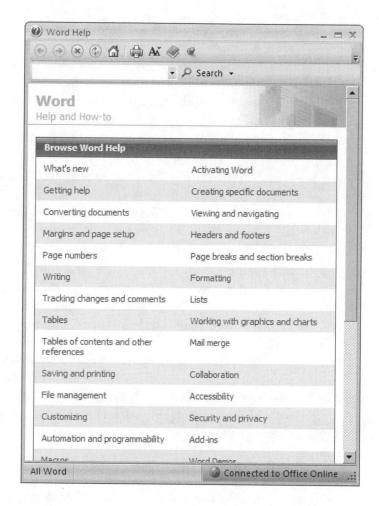

FIGURE 10-14

The main window
of the Microsoft
Office Word 2007
application

Another consideration is the quality of the information you'll receive. The help
resources typically available and the type of information each can provide are
discussed in the following list.

- **Printed documentation**   Not every application provides printed documentation
  with the installation media beyond the information you need to successfully
  install the application. With the Internet so widely adopted, software publishers
  find that they can reduce their costs by providing application help through
  the Web.

■ **Online help websites**   Another source for application help is the Internet. There are myriad blogs (supported by an application publisher's user group or certified users), frequently asked questions (FAQs), tutorials, and how-to sites available on the Web that can be located easily using an Internet search. For the most part, these sites can be very helpful when you are trying to find how to do something in an application, but if what you want is an opinion or advice, consider that no one is required to get a truth-and-honesty license before posting anything to the Web.

■ **Friends, classmates, coworkers, or teachers**   Often the best help comes from others who are working with the same applications to perform the same tasks as you. What your friends, classmates, coworkers, or teachers know that an online site or even an application's help system does not is the context in which a certain solution is applicable.

■ **Help desks**   Some application publishers provide or support a help desk activity that provides a person with whom you can communicate on the phone, through an online chat, or by e-mail to discuss the situation with which you need help. The help desk organizers could be a users' organization, the application publisher, an experts group, or perhaps even the vendor or value-added reseller (VAR) from whom you purchased the application. It's possible that your company or school has help desk support available that may be able to help you with a particular application problem because they have better knowledge of their environment and the types of tasks you are attempting to accomplish.

Access to an automated help system, such as the help system available for most applications, typically is through an icon, a menu link, or a function key on the keyboard (just about universally the F1 key). The help system in most applications opens in a new window and displays some form of a menu or a list of the help topics available. In addition, the help system typically provides an index of help topics and how-to tutorials, as well as a search function that can be used to search for specific topics.

The search function in most applications, like Office 2007, returns a list of links for any topic that relates to your search criteria. It's typically better to start a search in a help system at the highest level and then drill down to the specific help you need. For example, if you need help with printing handouts in PowerPoint 2007, you should search for handouts or printing handouts and then select the link that may best answer your specific question.

Exiting an Application

The best way to exit an application window and stop the application is accomplished by clicking the Exit button, which is accomplished by clicking the "X" button in the extreme upper-right corner of a Windows window (or clicking the red light button at the top of the Mac OS file). If any changes had been made to the document in the application window, you are asked whether you wish to save these changes. There are occasions when you may not wish to save the changes, such as when running a what-if projection on a spreadsheet, but typically you do want to save any changes made to the document. Click the Yes button and save the document. When this action is completed, the application window closes.

CERTIFICATION SUMMARY

There are several ways to start an application in any Windows-based operating system: from the Start menu, from the All Programs menu, from a Desktop icon, or by opening a document created with a particular application. The user interface or workspace of each application can be personalized to suit your particular wishes or needs, including the layout of the workspace and the menus, toolbars, or Ribbons of the application.

Virtually all Windows-based applications provide either a local or an online help system, or both in many instances. Local help covers the basic functions of the application and the online help, typically from the vendor's Web site, deals with more advanced topics.

✓ TWO-MINUTE DRILL

Start, Work with, and Exit an Application

- ❏ Two primary methods are used to start a Windows application: from the Start menu or from the Desktop.

- ❏ Clicking the Start button displays the Start menu and the MRU list of applications, recommended system utilities and applications, and special-function dialog boxes, windows, applications, and folders. The All Programs menu contains the applications and utilities installed on a PC.

- ❏ To start an application from an OS desktop, click the application's icon or thumbnail.

- ❏ When you start an application, a new window is opened that contains the application's workspace. All user interaction with the application takes place in or on its workspace.

- ❏ An application workspace has elements that provide control to the user, including menus, commands, and features to create, edit, and format a document and to control the functions of the application.

- ❏ Microsoft Office 2007 applications, for example, include such elements as a title bar, a status bar, the Microsoft Office button, the Ribbon, the Quick Access toolbar, the Mini toolbar, the View toolbar, and the document workspace.

- ❏ Application suites typically use common utility objects for functions that open documents, save documents, print documents, and more.

- ❏ Most applications also allow the appearance and configuration settings of the application's workspace to be customized.

- ❏ Popular application suites, both installed and available online, provide help systems that are augmented with additional information from the publisher's Web sites.

- ❏ Some applications provide the ability to navigate a document, select document content, and perform certain commands using keyboard shortcuts. The Go To command can be used to navigate to a particular document page.

❑ Applications allow users to change the default settings for the default file format, the location to which documents are to be saved by default, how often an automatic save is to be performed, and the location in which the document is to be saved.

❑ Applications provide help systems that use both locally installed and Web-based content to provide help, how-to, and general question answers. Other forms of help are: printed documentation, online help Web sites, friends, classmates, coworkers, teachers, and help desks.

SELF TEST

The following questions are intended to help you be sure that you understand the material included in this chapter. Read the questions and the answer choices carefully.

Start, Work with, and Exit an Application

1. What are the two primary methods that can be used to start a Windows application?
   A. From a command line
   B. From the Start menu
   C. From the Run command box
   D. From the Desktop

2. On what Windows feature can a list of the most recently used applications be found?
   A. Start menu
   B. Desktop
   C. Help system
   D. Microsoft Office button

3. Where are icons or thumbnails that can be used to start an application placed in Windows XP?
   A. All Programs menu
   B. Microsoft Office button
   C. Start menu
   D. Desktop

4. What is another term used for the application window that opens when an application is started?
   A. Desktop
   B. Workspace
   C. Dialog box
   D. Message box

5. What is the application window that provides for user control and interaction with an application called?
   A. Desktop
   B. Workspace
   C. Dialog box
   D. Message box

6. Which of the following is not a common feature of an application workspace?

    A. Title bar

    B. Menu bar or Ribbon

    C. Most Frequently Used Features list

    D. Status bar

7. Which of the following tabs on the Office Word 2007 Ribbon is optional?

    A. Home

    B. Add-ins

    C. Insert

    D. Review

8. What is the general usage of the features, functions, and commands on the Home tab of the Office Word 2007 Ribbon?

    A. Standard character and paragraph formatting commands, features, styles, and Clipboard functions

    B. Insert objects and apply effects, including page breaks, pictures, tables, hypertext links, and headers and footers

    C. Features and functions to create envelopes, labels, and merged documents

    D. To change the view of the workspace and to show or hide editing elements

9. True or False: Microsoft Office 2007 applications generally use common utility objects to open, save, or print documents.

    A. True

    B. False

10. True or False: The latest versions of most application suites don't install local help information but provide help information only from online Web sites.

    A. True

    B. False

SELF TEST ANSWERS

Start, Work with, and Exit an Application

1. ☑ **B and D.** Applications are started by clicking a link on the Start menu or its All Programs menu or by an icon or thumbnail on the Desktop.
   ☒ **A and C** are incorrect. An application can possibly be started from a command line, but GUI-based applications typically have problems starting this way. The Run command box can be used to start an application, but this is far from a typical way to do so.

2. ☑ **A.** A list of the MRU applications is found in the right pane of a Windows Start menu.
   ☒ **B, C,** and **D** are incorrect. The desktop entries can be organized in several ways, but frequency of use is not one of them. The Help system and the Microsoft Office button don't list any applications, except that the Microsoft Office button lists common features and commands.

3. ☑ **D.** Icons and thumbnails that can be used to start an application can be added to the desktop of a GUI OS.
   ☒ **A, B,** and **C** are incorrect. In a Windows XP, they are placed on the Desktop. Windows Vista and Windows 7 generally place icons and thumbnails on other features.

4. ☑ **B.** When an application starts up, it displays its workspace.
   ☒ **A, C,** and **D** are incorrect. The Desktop is a GUI OS feature. Dialog and message boxes do display in applications, as well as just about anywhere they are needed, but are not necessarily displayed when an application starts, that is, unless there is a problem.

5. ☑ **B.** The workspace provides the features that allow the user to actually use the application to accomplish a task.
   ☒ **A, C,** and **D** are incorrect. I realize this almost repeats the preceding question, but you need to understand the purpose of the workspace and its functions and features—hint, hint.

6. ☑ **C.** While an application may list frequently or recently used files, it most likely doesn't list other applications that are frequently or recently used.
   ☒ **A, B,** and **D** are incorrect. The title bar, menu bar or Ribbon, and status bar are common to virtually all GUI-based application workspaces.

7. ☑ **B.** The Add-ins tab only appears when add-ins have been installed on an Office 2007 application, including Office Word.
   ☒ **A, C,** and **D** are incorrect. The Home, Insert, and Review tabs are standard to the Office Word 2007 Ribbon.

8. ☑ **A.** The Home tab is kind of like the normal tab in that it includes most of the formatting functions commonly used when a document is created or edited.

    ☒ **B, C,** and **D** are incorrect. They describe the features of the Insert tab, those of the Mailings tab, and those of the View tab, respectively.

9. ☑ **A.** Microsoft Office has used common objects for standard features (such as Open, Print, Save, and others) in its last few versions.

    ☒ **B** is incorrect. The statement in Question 9 is true.

10. ☑ **B.** Most of the popular application suites install local help files for the more commonly requested areas and supplement the local help information with additional help topics online.

    ☒ **A** is incorrect. The statement in Question 10 is false.

11

Using Common Application Program Features and Functions

As discussed in Chapter 10, many applications suites, like Microsoft Office 2007, use standard utility functions to facilitate a variety of actions that are common to all of their applications. These standard utilities are used to perform such actions as file management, printing, saving files, publishing files to a network, and to a certain extent, editing and formatting. This chapter discusses these common functions and how they are applied.

Common File-Management Functions

1.2   Perform common file-management functions.

When you are working with an application that is one of a suite of applications, such as Office Word 2007, Office Excel 2007, or Office PowerPoint 2007, file management is generally performed using a common utility. File management tasks involve creating, saving, opening, preparing a document for distribution, and publishing a document to a network.

Creating a New Application Document

When you start up just about any personal productivity application, a new, blank document is automatically opened in the document workspace based on the default document template. The document template on which this document is based typically formats the new document using a default standard formatting and style set by the application's publisher.

For example, when Office Word 2007 opens, a new, blank document is opened in the document workspace using what is called the Normal template. The Normal template sets the margins at one inch on all sides and sets the Normal font style to regular Times New Roman 12-point font. With these settings, the Normal template serves the general formatting needs of most letters or reports.

In addition to the Normal template, Office Word 2007 also provides myriad other templates (as do most of the popular word processing applications) for the preparation of a wide variety of document types. Figure 11-1 shows the template library of Word 2007. To create a new document using a template from the template library,

FIGURE 11-1

The template library of the active Office 2007 application is displayed on the New Document dialog box.

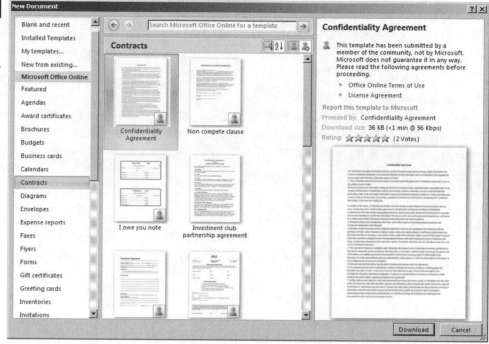

which includes templates installed with the application, user-created templates, and templates available from the publisher's Web site, use the new document option on the application's main menu and select the template on which you wish to base the document.

In Office Word 2007, a new document is created using the following steps:

1. Click the Microsoft Office button to display its menu and click the New option to display the New Document dialog box. The New Document dialog box is a common feature used with each of the Office 2007 applications, but it is customized to the particular Office 2007 application you are using. The New Document dialog box is shown in Figure 11-1.

2. Click the thumbnail of the document template on which you want to create a new document in the center pane and then click Create or Download, depending on the source of the template. The "create" button is labeled Create or Download according to whether the template is locally installed or available from the Web.

INSIDE THE EXAM

For the IC3 Module 2 exam, you not only need to know the sequence of the steps used to accomplish a task (typically with the mouse), but you also need to know the most efficient choices to make from the Ribbon or menus to complete any given outcome. My advice is to practice the standard file management actions described in this book until you are very familiar with the steps and commands used in each.

3. A new document is opened in the document workspace that has the working title of Document*n*, where *n* is the next sequential number in the sequence of documents that have been opened in the current application session. For example, if three new documents have been opened in the current session, the new document will have the name of Document4.

These steps "create" the document in the document workspace, but not on the user's computer. The steps used to complete the creation of a document are discussed in the next section.

Saving a New Document

Saving a document to a permanent storage device is considered by many as the step that completes the creation of the document. The process of saving a document involves assigning a unique identifying name and navigating to the location on the storage device where the document is to be stored.

Saving an Office 2007 Document

In the Microsoft Office 2007 applications, the steps used to save a new document are as follows:

1. Click the Microsoft Office button to display its menu and click either the Save or the Save As option. When you're saving a new document for the first time, either of these options displays the Save As dialog box, shown in Figure 11-2. This happens under the assumption that you don't really want to save the document with the name Document4 or the like.

2. On the Save As dialog box, use the device/folder/file tree in the main pane to navigate to the location in which you want to save the file. Then enter an identifying name in the File Name text box and use the Save As Type pull-down list to select the file format type you wish to use for the saved document (the file types available change with the application in use; see the next section, "Document File Types," for more information). Click Save to save the document in the file type selected to the storage location chosen.

A definite best practice is to save a document multiple times while it's being "created." However, the more popular application suites include an automatic document save function that saves a copy of the document-in-process "as-is" for possible recovery purposes.

Document File Types

At one time, a document created by an application could only be saved to the format of that application. However, most of today's popular application software suites include the capability of saving a document to a variety of file format types. This capability provides a basic means of sharing files between applications, especially applications

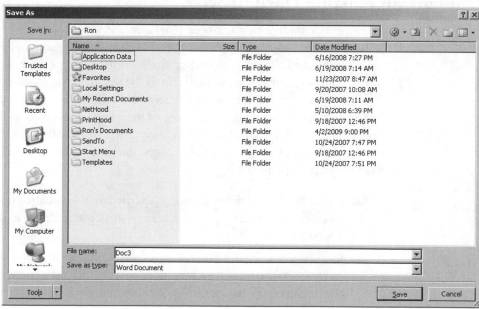

FIGURE 11-2

The Save As dialog box is used in the Office 2007 applications to save a document with a different name or file location.

Application	File Type	Default Filename Extension
Word 2007	Document	.docx
Excel 2007	Workbook	.xlsx
PowerPoint 2007	Presentation	.pptx
Access 2007	Database file	.accdb

from different publishers, and for creating backward-compatible files that can be opened by earlier editions of a particular application.

Office 2007 uses a new set of file formats that is based on the Extensible Markup Language (XML). These file formats are indicated by the addition of a four-digit filename extension (see Table 11-1). Because of the switch to XML-based formats, Office 2007 file formats aren't backward-compatible with earlier versions of its applications. However, the Office applications each include the capability to save a document into a format that can be opened and edited by earlier application versions. In Word 2007, a document can be saved as a Word 97-2003 document (.doc), and Excel 2007 and PowerPoint 2007 have a similar capability.

Opening an Existing Document

Opening a document that has been placed on a storage device also uses a common utility in the Office 2007 application suite. Understand that the phrase "opening a document" actually refers to finding the document on a storage device, copying it into memory, and making it available to the application. When you open a document, all of these steps and a few more are executed by the Open utility.

Depending on the application in use or its version, the Open utility is found on the application suite's common menu, such as the Microsoft Office button's menu, or on the File menu bar option. To open a document in Office Excel 2007, for example, the following steps are used:

1. From the document workspace, click the Microsoft Office button to display its menu and click the Open option to display the Open dialog box, shown in Figure 11-3.

2. Use the device/folder/file tree in the main pane of the Open dialog box to navigate to the location where the document to be opened is located. Select the document to be opened by clicking it and then click Open.

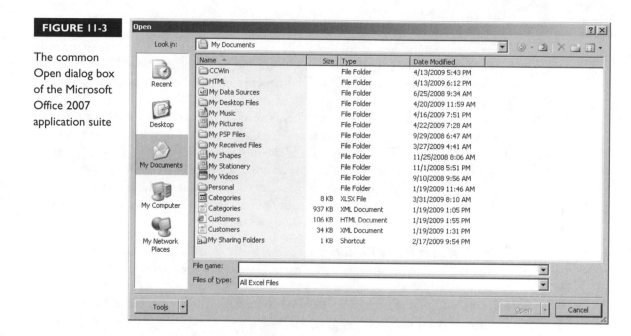

FIGURE 11-3

The common Open dialog box of the Microsoft Office 2007 application suite

---

Common Editing and Formatting Functions

1.3   Perform common editing and formatting functions.

Perhaps the most significant benefit of electronic applications is the capability that allows you to modify a document regardless of how long ago the document was created. The most common actions performed on any document are editing and formatting.

Editing and Formatting a Document

Virtually all personal productivity software applications include capabilities to edit, modify, reformat, reorganize, and review their documents. All of these actions can be grouped under the editing action, but let's look at them briefly, one at a time.

Editing a Document

The most dramatic demonstration of editing we can look at is the editing that can be performed on a word processing document. So, let's look at Office Word 2007 to show the editing features and capabilities common to the more popular word processing applications.

When a document is edited, text blocks (words, phrases, sentences, paragraphs, and even pages) can be added, removed, replaced, and reformatted with any text in the document affected. The combination of the mouse and the cursor (mouse pointer) provides the user with the capability to position the cursor at an insertion point, which can be in front or behind a specific character, word, or line in the document, or to select a block of text. Either of these actions is the first step performed in the process of editing. Let's look at some specific editing actions.

Inserting Text into a Document   To insert text into a document, the mouse is used to locate the cursor (which is normally an I-beam character) at the exact location to which the next text is to be inserted. When the cursor is inserted into a document, it creates what is called an insertion point, which is represented by a flashing vertical line (see Figure 11-4). Notice that when you are typing, even in

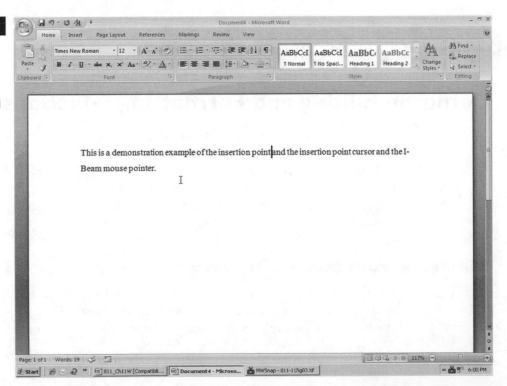

FIGURE 11-4

The I-beam cursor and the insertion point shown in a Word 2007 document a new document, the insertion point is always in the position at which the next character typed is placed. After the insertion point is placed, inserting text requires only that you begin typing.

Removing Text from a Document   There are two primary methods that can be used to remove text from a document: using the BACKSPACE key on the keyboard and using the DEL key on the keyboard. To use the BACKSPACE key to remove text, place the insertion point behind (to the right) of the text to be removed and press the BACKSPACE key once for each character to be removed.

To use the DEL key to remove text from a document, you can use one of two methods: deleting one character at a time or selecting a block of text and removing it all at once. To remove one character at a time, place the insertion point in front of (to the left) of the text to be removed and press the DEL key once for each character to be removed. To remove a selected block of text, use the mouse to select the text to be removed and then press the DEL key once.

Replacing Text in a Document   To replace text in a document, the method used depends on whether the replacement text is to be entered or moved or copied from a different location in the document (or perhaps even another document). Either method replaces existing text with new text.

To replace text, whether it's a single character or more, use the mouse to select the text to be replaced and begin typing the replacement text. In effect, this method deletes the text being replaced and inserts the new text in its place.

To replace text with text cut or copied from another location, cut or copy the text to be used as the replacement, then use the mouse to select the text to be replaced, and paste the replacement text. This method can also be used to insert text cut or copied from another location at the insertion point.

Apply Common Formatting to a Document

There are two levels of formatting that can be applied to the text in a document: character formatting and paragraph formatting. Character formatting includes the effects that can be applied to a single character without impacting the formatting of the text around it. Paragraph formatting affects all of the characters and lines of text included in one or more paragraphs.

Character Formatting   As discussed in Chapter 10, nearly all of the character formatting tools are placed on the standard or main toolbar, the Format selection on the menu bar, or the default tab of an application's ribbon for convenience purposes.

The character
formatting
features on the
Home tab of
the Word 2007
Ribbon

For example, the character formatting tools and commands are located on the Home (default) tab of the Word 2007 Ribbon, as shown in Figure 11-5. Character formatting tools and commands are commonly grouped as font features.

These are the common character formatting features supported by nearly all applications (see Figure 11-6 for examples of most of the formatting features in this list):

- **Bold** Applying Bold (also called boldface) increases the width of the font and darkens the appearance of the text.

- **Italics** Applying Italics tilts the font to the right and applies a script look to the text.

- **Underline** Underline places a 1-point line under the text.

- **Strikethrough** Strikethrough formatting is primarily used in documents to indicate replaced or removed text.

- **Font** The font of a character string provides the overall look and style of the text. A wide range of text font choices are available, ranging from block text to script and to symbols.

Samples of the
most commonly
used character
formatting effects

Bold This rule applies to **you** and all of your co-workers.

Italics Henry is currently reading *Gone with the Wind*.

<u>Underline</u> The new rules go into effect on <u>Monday, August 17th</u>.

~~Strikethrough~~: This procedure controls the processes used for ~~some~~ <u>all</u> existing products.

Subscript: In a recent article, Mr. Gilster stated that he really enjoys writing$_4$.

Superscript: The problem requires that X be raised to the 7th power (X^7).

Case: This Is An example of a TEXT LINE with different CASES applied.

- **Font size**   The character size of a font is measured in points. The standard measure is that there are 72 points in a vertical inch and the size of a character is stated in points, such as 12-point font, which is one-sixth of an inch in height. The smallest font typically supported is either 4-point or 6-point font.

- **Font color**   The font color (or text color) can be assigned from the standard or custom palettes of the application. The Office 2007 applications, like most application suites, use a standard palette function that includes both standard and customizable text colors.

- **Case**   The case of a character or text string can be either upper (capital letters) or lower (small letters).

- **Subscript**   Subscripting reduces the font size of one or more characters to about two-thirds of the active font size and lowers the character to extend below the active font baseline.

- **Superscript**   Superscripting reduces the font size of the affected characters to about two-thirds of the active font size and raises the character to text above the active font ascender line (top edge of the font size).

- **Highlighting**   Just as you would use a highlighter pen to emphasize a string of text in a book or document, you can highlight text using a standard palette of highlighting colors.

Paragraph Formatting   Character formatting can be applied to an entire paragraph, but it is technically applied to each individual character in the paragraph. On the other hand, *paragraph* formatting is used to alter the format, alignment, and spacing of one or more paragraphs in a document.

Document templates apply a standard combination of paragraph formatting styles to an entire document, in addition to setting margins, page size, and the fonts of the document. However, you may want to use a custom set of paragraph formats in a particular document. The paragraph formatting tools and commands, like the character formatting options, are typically located on the standard or main toolbar, the Format selection on the menu bar, or the default tab on an application's ribbon for convenience purposes. For example, the paragraph formatting tools and commands are located in the Paragraph group of the Home tab of the Office Word 2007 Ribbon, just to the right of the character formatting (Font group) options.

FIGURE 11-7

The alignment
choices of
the paragraph
formatting
options

Paragraph

The common paragraph formatting tools available in most personal productivity software include (see Figure 11-9 for examples of the paragraph formatting options):

■ **Paragraph alignment**   A paragraph can be aligned relative to the left and right margins of a document using four alignment choices (Figure 11-7 illustrates the different alignment options and Figure 11-8 illustrates their effect):

   ■ **Left alignment**   This is the default alignment used by virtually all word processing software. The text is aligned to the left margin. The effect is that the paragraph typically has an uneven right edge.

   ■ **Center alignment**   This effect aligns the midpoint of each line of the text to a center point that is equidistant from the right and left margins. The effect is that both the right and left edges of a paragraph can be uneven.

FIGURE 11-8

The effect of each
of the paragraph
alignment options

Left Align

This rule applies to you and all of your co-workers. The new rules go into effect on Monday, August 17th. This procedure controls the processes used for some all existing products. In a recent article, Mr. Gilster stated that he really enjoys writing.

Center Align

This rule applies to all workers. This procedure controls the processes used for existing products. Henry is currently reading Gone with the Wind. Mr. Gilster stated that he really enjoys writing.

Right Align

This rule applies to all new and existing workers. The rules go into effect on Monday, August 17th for one year. This procedure controls existing products. The new rules go into effect on Monday, August 17th. Mr. Gilster stated that he really enjoys writing.

Justified Align

This rule applies to you and all of your co-workers. Henry is reading Gone with the Wind. The new rules go into effect on Monday, August 17th. This procedure controls the processes used for existing products. In a recent article, Mr. Gilster stated that he really enjoys writing.

FIGURE 11-9

Examples of
the commonly
used paragraph
formatting
options

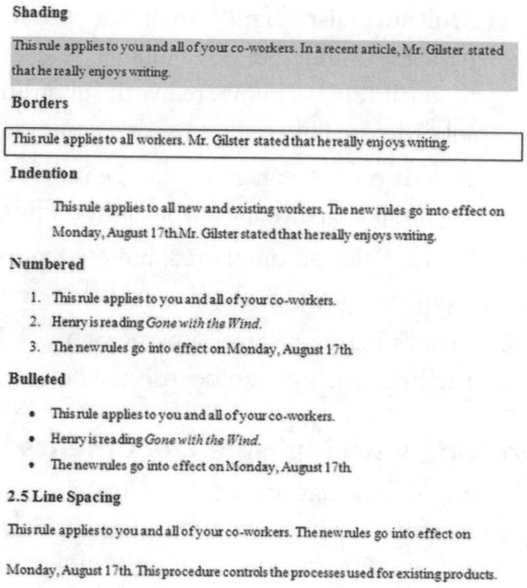

Shading

This rule applies to you and all of your co-workers. In a recent article, Mr. Gilster stated that he really enjoys writing.

Borders

This rule applies to all workers. Mr. Gilster stated that he really enjoys writing.

Indention

This rule applies to all new and existing workers. The new rules go into effect on Monday, August 17th.Mr. Gilster stated that he really enjoys writing.

Numbered

1. This rule applies to you and all of your co-workers.
2. Henry is reading *Gone with the Wind.*
3. The new rules go into effect on Monday, August 17th.

Bulleted

- This rule applies to you and all of your co-workers.
- Henry is reading *Gone with the Wind.*
- The new rules go into effect on Monday, August 17th.

2.5 Line Spacing

This rule applies to you and all of your co-workers. The new rules go into effect on

Monday, August 17th. This procedure controls the processes used for existing products.

- **Right alignment** This effect aligns the text to the right margin with the effect that the paragraph's left edge is uneven.
- **Justified alignment** The alignment effect aligns a paragraph to both the left and right margins and inserts whitespace into each text line to affect the alignment.
- **Line Spacing** The default line spacing is typically 1.5 spaces, which means that one and one-half blank lines separate each line of text. The line spacing can be set from 1 line (single-spaced) to 3 lines (triple-spaced) or to an exact number of points.
- **Shading** The background of a selected paragraph can be set to one of the colors on the color palette.
- **Borders** A paragraph can have a border placed on one or all four sides for emphasis.
- **Numbering** A paragraph can be automatically indented and numbered relative to the paragraph preceding it or as the first in a numbered list.
- **Bullets** A paragraph can be indented with a variety of bullet symbols as a part of a bulleted list.

- **Multilevel list** This formatting option, when available, sets up a series of paragraphs that can be numbered and have subordinate items (such as in an outline) also numbered with subordinate numbering, bulleted and have subordinate bulleted items, or a combination of both.

- **Indention** A paragraph can be indented from or toward the left margin to set the paragraph apart from surrounding text.

- **Sort** Selected numbered, bulleted, or normal text can be sorted on the first words in each paragraph or on other designated sort criteria.

- **Spaces before or after a paragraph** Additional blank lines (in addition to the line spacing) can be inserted before or after a paragraph.

Working with Multiple Documents in the Workspace

On occasion, you may want to view two or more documents in the workspace at the same time for comparison purposes or for quick reference. Multiple documents can be viewed in the workspace in a horizontal or vertical arrangement (as illustrated in Figures 11-10 and 11-11, respectively). Each document is opened in its own workspace pane and can be edited independently. To activate the workspace for a particular document in a multiple document view, click into the workspace pane.

FIGURE 11-10

Multiple documents opened in a horizontal arrangement in the workspace of a word processing application

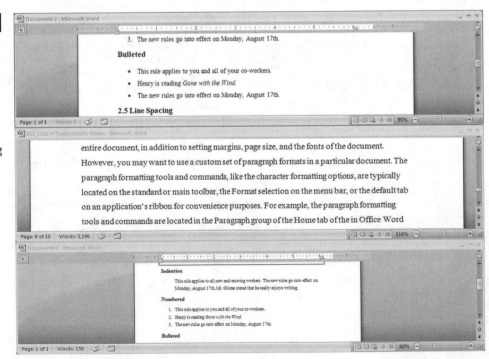

FIGURE 11-11

Multiple documents opened in a vertical arrangement in the workspace of a word processing application

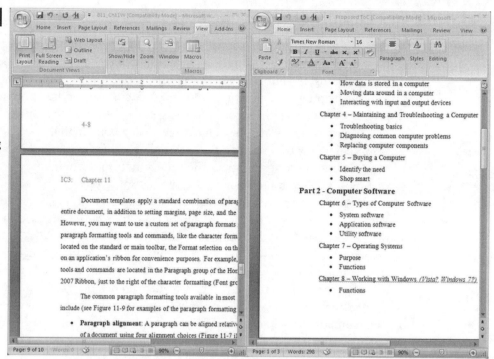

Another similar feature that can be used with a single document is the Split option. This option allows you to designate a horizontal position at which the document is divided into two workspace panes at that position. This can be tricky when you go to save the document if editing or formatting has been performed in both panes, unless, of course, you want to create two versions of the same document.

CERTIFICATION OBJECTIVE

Common Printing and Outputting Functions

1.4   Perform common printing/outputting functions.

At the risk of being obvious, all personal productivity software provides a print function. However, printing isn't the only way to output a document. You may want to share a document on a network for collaboration, reviewing, or just viewing.

Printing and Document Output Functions

Printing a document is a standard feature in all application software packages. However, many applications provide multiple printing options. These options range from printing an entire document to printing only one or more pages of a document, to printing only a selected block of data. A document can be printed on the default printer or another printer connected to a computer or on the network. The printing options are typically included on a single dialog box, as illustrated by the common Print dialog box used in the Office 2007 applications shown in Figure 11-12.

Different applications adapt the print function to their specific needs. For instance, an electronic spreadsheet application typically includes the option of printing only the active worksheet, an entire workbook, or just a selected range of data. Presentation applications commonly provide options to print full-sized copies of the presentation slides, handouts, or notes pages.

Some applications provide the capability of a quick print, which prints directly to the default printer designated in the operating system, and the option of printing the document to a file so that it can be e-mailed, archived, or used in some other way.

Printing a document isn't the only output option available in most applications. A document can be saved to a public folder on a network server, published to

FIGURE 11-12

The Print dialog box common to the Office 2007 applications

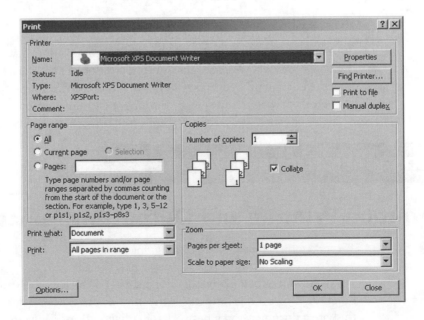

an information sharing environment, such as Microsoft Office 2007 SharePoint Server (MOSS) or a document or information resource management (IRM) system, or converted to a PDF (Portable Document Format) or an XPS (XML Paper Specification) document.

In those applications that support publishing a document to a shared medium or management system, measures are available to ensure the document doesn't contain private information or comments, that security is appropriately applied, that a digital signature is attached, or that the document is compatible with the application versions that potential viewers may use to open the document. The Prepare submenu of the Microsoft Office button lists the preparation options available to ensure a document is properly prepared for distribution as shown in Figure 11-13.

FIGURE 11-13

The Prepare options on the Microsoft Office button's menu

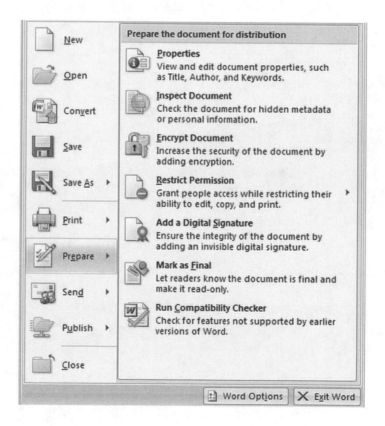

CERTIFICATION SUMMARY

The file-management functions of an application include creating, saving, deleting, and other file-management actions documents created using a particular application. Many applications support a variety of file types that can be created and managed to allow for backward compatibility as well as portability.

Editing and formatting are the primary actions performed by document-oriented applications. Editing includes such actions as inserting, replacing, moving, copying, or removing content from a document. Formatting involves making visual changes to the document's background, character and paragraph styles, colors, borders, and graphics-based effects.

Documents are typically created for sharing information with others. Documents can be printed to hard copy or saved as a shared file on a network for others to review, edit, format, or distribute.

✓ TWO-MINUTE DRILL

Common File-Management Functions

❑ Document file management tasks involve creating, saving, opening, preparing a document for distribution, and publishing a document to a network.

❑ A new document is automatically created when an application starts or a new document can be created using the new document option and choosing a document template for the new document.

❑ Saving a new document to a storage device completes its creation by assigning an identifying name and navigating to the location on the storage device where the document is to be stored.

❑ Today's application software suites provide the capability to save a document in a variety of file format types to provide a means of sharing files between applications and creating backward-compatible files for use with earlier application editions.

❑ Office 2007 uses file formats based on XML. These file formats use a four-digit filename extension. These file formats aren't backward-compatible with earlier versions.

❑ The common causes of the File Not Found error are wrong storage media, wrong folder, and filename spelling. A common cause of not being able to open a file with an application is that the file format is not associated with an application. Another reason may be that the file format is not a standard format recognized by the OS or an application.

Common Editing and Formatting Functions

❑ Personal productivity software applications include capabilities to edit, modify, reformat, reorganize, and review their documents.

❑ When a document is edited, text blocks (words, phrases, sentences, paragraphs, and even pages) can be added, removed, replaced, and reformatted with any text in the document affected.

❑ To insert text into a document, the mouse is used to place the cursor at the location the next text is to be inserted.

❑ The two primary methods used to remove text are the BACKSPACE key and the DEL key.

❑ To replace text, the mouse is used to select the text to be replaced and then type the replacement text. To replace text with text cut or copied from another location, cut or copy the replacement text; select the text to be replaced; and paste the replacement text.

❑ The two levels of formatting are character formatting and paragraph formatting. Character formatting is applied to a single character without impacting the formatting of the text around it. Paragraph formatting affects all of the characters and lines of text included in one or more paragraphs.

❑ Character formatting includes Bold, Italics, Underline, Strikethrough, Font, Font size, Font color, Case, Subscript, Superscript, and Highlighting.

❑ Paragraph formatting alters the format, alignment, and spacing of one or more paragraphs. Common paragraph formatting options include paragraph alignment (Left, Center, Right, and Justified), line spacing, shading, borders, numbering, bullets, multilevel lists, indention, sort, and spaces before or after a paragraph.

❑ Multiple documents can be viewed in the workspace in a horizontal or vertical arrangement. Each document is opened in its own workspace pane and can be edited independently.

❑ Verify that the Insert/Overtype toggle button is in the correct state before starting to insert new content into a document. The Copy command places a copy of the selected text on the Windows Clipboard and leaves the copied text in its original location. The Cut command places a copy of the selected text on the Clipboard and removes the cut text from its original location. The Paste command then inserts or replaces the copied or cut text at the insertion point.

❑ Formatting can be applied using the Format Painter, which is used to copy and apply the formatting of one text block to another.

❑ The Find tool allows you to look for a selected word or phrase in a document, including instances where the sought-after text is contained in other words or phrases. The Replace tool incorporates the Find function but replaces text with the replacement text.

Common Printing and Outputting Functions

❑ Printing a document is a standard feature in all application software packages. Different applications adapt the print function to their specific needs. For example, an electronic spreadsheet application typically includes the option

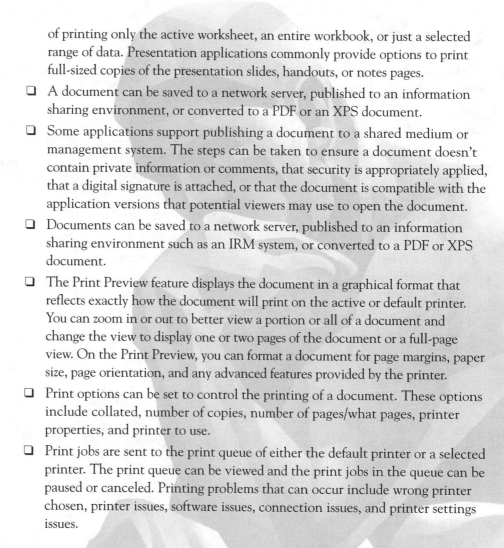

of printing only the active worksheet, an entire workbook, or just a selected range of data. Presentation applications commonly provide options to print full-sized copies of the presentation slides, handouts, or notes pages.

❑ A document can be saved to a network server, published to an information sharing environment, or converted to a PDF or an XPS document.

❑ Some applications support publishing a document to a shared medium or management system. The steps can be taken to ensure a document doesn't contain private information or comments, that security is appropriately applied, that a digital signature is attached, or that the document is compatible with the application versions that potential viewers may use to open the document.

❑ Documents can be saved to a network server, published to an information sharing environment such as an IRM system, or converted to a PDF or XPS document.

❑ The Print Preview feature displays the document in a graphical format that reflects exactly how the document will print on the active or default printer. You can zoom in or out to better view a portion or all of a document and change the view to display one or two pages of the document or a full-page view. On the Print Preview, you can format a document for page margins, paper size, page orientation, and any advanced features provided by the printer.

❑ Print options can be set to control the printing of a document. These options include collated, number of copies, number of pages/what pages, printer properties, and printer to use.

❑ Print jobs are sent to the print queue of either the default printer or a selected printer. The print queue can be viewed and the print jobs in the queue can be paused or canceled. Printing problems that can occur include wrong printer chosen, printer issues, software issues, connection issues, and printer settings issues.

SELF TEST

The following questions are intended to help you be sure that you understand the material included in this chapter. Read the questions and the answer choices carefully.

Common File-Management Functions

1. Which of the following is not a document file-management task?
    - A. Creating a document
    - B. Editing a document
    - C. Saving a document
    - D. Publishing a document

2. True or False: When a personal productivity application starts up, a new, blank document must be opened by the user.
    - A. True
    - B. False

3. What can be used as the basis of a new, blank document with a predefined document style?
    - A. Document outlines
    - B. Document layouts
    - C. Document templates
    - D. Previously saved documents

4. When a document is saved, what document characteristics must be specified?
    - A. File format type
    - B. File name
    - C. Document size
    - D. Language

5. What is the basis of the Office 2007 file formats?
    - A. XPS
    - B. RTF
    - C. XML
    - D. Backward compatibility

Common Editing and Formatting Functions

6. What is the general term used to describe the action of inserting, removing, replacing, or reformatting text in a document?

  A. Editing

  B. Formatting

  C. Modifying

  D. Publishing

7. What is the location in a document where text is inserted?

  A. Paragraph

  B. Character

  C. Page

  D. Insertion point

8. What are the two keys on the keyboard that can be used to remove text from a document?

  A. BACKSPACE

  B. INSERT

  C. ESC

  D. DEL

9. In an action to replace a block of text in a document, the text block being replaced is selected. What are the alternative next steps that could be used to complete the replacement action?

  A. Delete existing text

  B. Type new text

  C. Paste new text

  D. Insert new text

10. What are the two primary levels of formatting in a word processing application?

  A. Page

  B. Character

  C. Document

  D. Paragraph

11. Which of the following are formatting options typically applied to characters in a document?

  A. Bold

  B. Alignment

  C. Italics

  D. Case

12. In what type of formatting are alignment, line spacing, shading, numbering, and indention formatting options generally included?
    A. Page
    B. Character
    C. Document
    D. Paragraph

13. True or False: When it's necessary to view more than one document at a time, each document must be viewed in its own discrete workspace.
    A. True
    B. False

Common Printing and Outputting Functions

14. True or False: Printing is typically not the only output method available in application software.
    A. True
    B. False

15. In lieu of printing, what other actions can be taken to share a document?
    A. Saved to a shared network folder
    B. Published to an IRM
    C. Converted to a PDF or XPS document
    D. All of the above
    E. None of the above

SELF TEST ANSWERS

Common File-Management Functions

1. ☑ **B.** Editing a document is considered to be a completely optional step that doesn't impact the management of a document file.

☒ **A, C,** and **D** are incorrect. File management tasks involve creating, saving, storing, and sharing documents.

2. ☑ **B.** Virtually all personal productivity applications open a new, blank document based on a default template when the application starts up.

☒ **A** is incorrect. The statement in Question 2 is false.

3. ☑ **C.** Document templates provide a set of formatting, style, and layout, designed to produce a document of a specific type or purpose.

☒ **A, B,** and **D** are incorrect. There may be document outlines defined in a template, but there are no specific document outlines. Document layouts are typically included in a document template but aren't available on their own. Okay, so a previously saved document could be used as the basis of a new document, but it most likely is not a template.

4. ☑ **A** and **B.** Application documents are generally assigned a default name and file format, but these elements should be assigned when a document is saved.

☒ **C** and **D** are incorrect. The document size is calculated by the application, and the language is a consideration that must be made before the document is saved.

5. ☑ **C.** The Office 2007 default file formats are based on XML and add an "X" at the end of the filename extension to indicate this format.

☒ **A, B,** and **D** are incorrect. XPS is a Microsoft XML-based portable document format, but it's not a default application file format. RTF is an optional file format choice that is used to create files that can be shared with applications on different platforms. The Office 2007 file formats are not backward compatible, but a format can be used to save a file so that earlier versions of Office can open the file.

Common Editing and Formatting Functions

6. ☑ **A.** When content in a document is inserted, removed, replaced, or reformatted, the action taking place is editing.

☒ **B, C,** and **D** are incorrect. Formatting is generally included in editing, as is modifying. However, publishing is an output function.

7. ☑ **D.** While a case can be built for any of the answer choices, the exact spot where new text is inserted into a document is the insertion point, which likely falls inside of a page or paragraph.
☒ **A, B,** and **C** are incorrect. It's also true that the next thing to be inserted at the insertion point is a character, but in this usage, it is more of a result than an action.

8. ☑ **A** and **D.** The BACKSPACE key can be used to back out text you wish to delete, and the DEL (DELETE) key can be used to remove characters beyond the insertion point.
☒ **B** and **C** are incorrect. The ESC (ESCAPE) key has no related function to remove text. The INSERT key can be used to toggle the entry action of the keyboard from insert to typeover, which I agree is a way to remove text, but the use of the INSERT key is not considered a deletion action.

9. ☑ **B** and **C.** Remember we are talking about a replacement operation, which would by definition eliminate deleting text or inserting text.
☒ **A** and **D** are incorrect. After the text to be replaced is selected, the replacement text can be entered or pasted.

10. ☑ **B** and **D.** The primary formatting levels in word processing applications are character and paragraph.
☒ **A** and **C** are incorrect. Page formatting is more of a layout activity, and document formatting is an extended form of paragraph formatting.

11. ☑ **A** and **C.** Bold and italics are character formatting options that are applied to one or more characters at a time.
☒ **B** and **D** are incorrect. Case and alignment are paragraph formatting options.

12. ☑ **D.** Any formatting that affects an entire paragraph at one time is considered a paragraph formatting option.
☒ **A, B,** and **C** are incorrect. Page formatting is more of a layout activity, and document formatting is an extended form of paragraph formatting.

13. ☑ **B.** Most personal productivity applications support the capability to view multiple documents in the active workspace.
☒ **A** is incorrect. The statement in Question 13 is false.

Common Printing and Outputting Functions

14. ☑ **A.** In addition to printing, application software typically allows for the distribution, sharing, and publishing of documents.
☒ **B** is incorrect. The statement in Question 14 is true.

15. ☑ **D.** All the preceding choices are document actions that can be used in place of printing to share a document.
☒ **A, B, C,** and **E** are incorrect. The choices given in Answers A through C are separate document actions that can be used as alternatives to printing a document in order to share it. However, none of these choices is the best answer to the question alone, which makes Answer F wrong.

12

Using Word Processing Workspace Features

Formatting a word processing document can involve much more than the formatting steps introduced in Chapter 11. The format of a document can also include controlling pagination, bulleted and numbered lists, headers and footers, columns, tables, and many other document elements. These and other formatting elements can be created manually, but the better word processing systems also provide automatic functions to create, format, and lay out the overall appearance and structure of a document.

This chapter provides an explanation of the tools, functions, and features of a word processing system to create or modify the formatting of a document and its major elements. For the IC³ exams, you should know and understand how each of these formatting options is applied, as well as when and why.

CERTIFICATION OBJECTIVE

Formatting Documents

2.1 Be able to format text and documents including the ability to use automatic formatting tools.

Formatting text and formatting a document may sound like essentially the same action, but some text formatting actions affect an entire document in that they change the organization and structure of the document. The topics included under this certification objective can be divided into these two categories. The actions of creating and modifying a bulleted or numbered list, inserting symbols, applying a style, and creating and modifying a table are text formatting actions. The actions of inserting or removing page and other breaks, displaying editing and formatting symbols, inserting page numbers, headers and footers, and dividing a document into columns are all document formatting actions.

In the sections that follow these two levels of formatting, text formatting and document formatting, are discussed as separate topics with each of the formatting actions of each formatting level explained. A good way to differentiate text formatting from document formatting is:

- Text formatting doesn't change the layout of the document; it only affects the content of the document.
- Document formatting doesn't change the content and characteristics of the document content; it does affect the layout of the document and its content.

The format of the text in a document can provide much more than visual appeal, although a visually appealing document is much more inviting and often easier to read. Text formatting can be applied to specific blocks of text to organize it, to separate it, and to provide an implicit order to the information. The text in a document can be formatted as individual characters, paragraphs, and even larger blocks. Chapter 11 discusses the application of character and paragraph formatting tools and the use of what is called direct formatting, or individually applying formatting options one at a time. In this section, we look at some of the more automated methods to apply formatting to the text of a document.

Text Styles

The primary text formatting tools and features of a word processor are generally grouped as a variety of styles. A style is a formatting set that defines a specific combination of formatting options, which can include a font (including size, color, and effects), text alignment, borders, and shading, and perhaps other formatting options as a single text treatment. A style is a kind of formatting superset that can combine character, paragraph, list (numbered or bulleted), and table formatting options.

Quick Styles

Microsoft Office Word 2007, for example, includes a wide variety of predefined Quick Styles OTB (out of the box). Figure 12-1 shows the Quick Styles Gallery on the Home tab of the Word 2007 Ribbon that contains the styles that are installed with Word 2007. To apply a Quick Style from the gallery, click into the paragraph or select the text block to which the Quick Style is to be applied and then click the style choice.

FIGURE 12-1

The Word 2007 Quick Styles Gallery

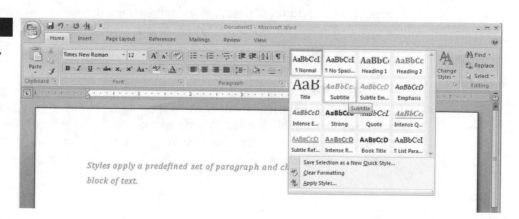

on the **Job** *The Microsoft Office 2007 applications provide a sampling feature for many of its formatting options. To sample the effect of a formatting choice, such as a Quick Style, click into the paragraph to which you want to apply a style and then hold the mouse pointer over different style choices.*

Custom Styles

In addition to the Quick Styles included in the Quick Styles Gallery, Word 2007 also supports the creation of new and customized styles. If one of the Quick Styles doesn't suit your needs, you can create a custom style. Modifying an existing style and saving it as a new style is perhaps the easiest way to create a custom style, but you can also define a completely new style.

To modify an existing style, click into the paragraph you want to format, right-click that location, and click the Paragraph link on the pop-up menu that appears to display the Paragraph dialog box (see Figure 12-2). Change the paragraph settings as you wish and click OK to apply the paragraph formatting you've defined. Right-click the paragraph again and move the mouse pointer over the Styles selection. Click the Save Selection As A New Quick Style option; enter a name for the new style in the dialog box that displays; and click OK.

To modify an existing Quick Style, right-click the style thumbnail in the Quick Styles Gallery and then choose Modify from the pop-up menu. On the Modify Style dialog box, change the settings of the style as you wish, and click OK to apply the changes. Any text formatted with the modified style is updated to reflect the changes made.

Text Formatting

When formatting a document, you may also wish to set the options for line spacing, spacing before and after paragraphs, and tab settings, in addition to a few other formatting features and options. These formatting options are explained in the following sections.

Line Spacing

Line spacing controls the amount of white space between the lines of text in a document. Virtually all word processing applications provide for a variety of preset line spacing settings as well as the capability to create custom line spacing within some or all of a document.

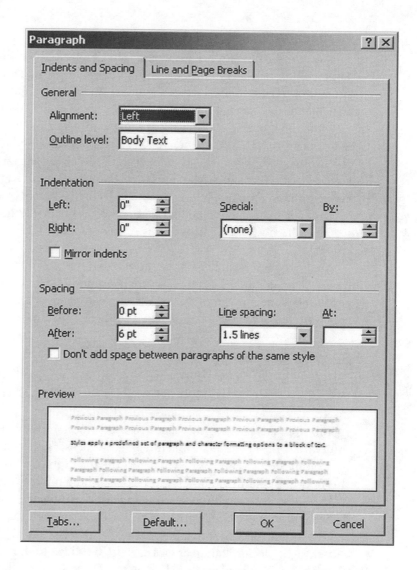

FIGURE 12-2

The Word 2007
Paragraph dialog
box

In a Word 2007 document, the line spacing options available are: 1, 1.15, 1.5, 2, 2.5, 3, and 3.5. A line spacing of 1 reduces the space between lines to one line set to the point size of the font in use; 1.15 adds an additional 15 percent of white space; 1.5 has 50 percent more white space between lines than the 1-line spacing option; and so on.

Paragraph Spacing and Indent Settings

The formatting functions of word processing applications include a variety of paragraph formatting options, including spacing before and after a paragraph and the amount of indention, if any, that should be applied to a paragraph. These options are available in the Paragraph group on the Home tab of the Word 2007 Ribbon.

While line spacing controls the spacing within a paragraph, additional lines of spacing can be added before or after a paragraph break (hard return). On most word processing applications, the available before and after paragraph spacing options include: Auto (defaults to the line spacing in use), 0 or no additional spacing before or after a paragraph, or spacing sized in a fixed number of points in 6-point increments, up to and including 1,584 points (or about 132 inches of 12-point line spacing). In most cases, the default is Auto or 6 points for both the before and after spacing.

A paragraph format can also be set to indent only its first line or to create a hanging paragraph. When the first line indention is set, the first line of text in a new paragraph is indented from the left margin by the amount of indention set by the user (one-half inch is the typical default value for first line indenting).

Setting Tab Stops

Tab stops can be very useful when you are creating a nonbulleted list or an informal table. Tabs give you the ability to format text into columns without the trouble of inserting section breaks or columns into the document.

Tab stops are added to the ruler in a word processing document at evenly spaced intervals by default or at custom intervals of the user's choosing. The ruler is a horizontal rule typically displayed across the top of the document workspace when this option is selected to be shown. By default, the ruler is typically hidden.

Individual tabs can be added to the ruler by clicking the mouse on the ruler at the distance from the left edge of the page at which you wish to place a tab. The default tab is a left tab, meaning that any text after the tab is left-aligned to it. However, center, right, decimal, and bar tabs can also be added to the ruler through the Tabs dialog box that is displayed by clicking the Tabs button on the Paragraph formatting dialog box. The tab settings available are

- **Center tab**   A center tab aligns text much the same way that the Center alignment function does, with the exception that the center tab can be placed anywhere across a document.
- **Right tab**   A right tab aligns text to the left of itself relative to the right edge of the page.

- **Decimal tab**   A decimal tab aligns numbers on either side of a decimal point (period).
- **Bar tab**   A bar tab inserts a vertical bar at the tab position and isn't used to align text.

Once a tab has been added to the ruler, it can be changed by double-clicking the tab mark on the ruler and changing its properties in the Tabs dialog box that displays. A tab's position on the ruler can be changed by simply clicking it and dragging it to its new position. A tab can also be removed from the ruler by clicking it and dragging it off of the ruler, or else it can be removed in the Tabs dialog box.

Page and Section Breaks

In a typical multipage document, different parts (sections) of the document may require a different format or even a different page orientation. Unless a document is divided into two or more sections (as needed for number of formatting changes), inserting page numbers is a one-time deal, with the page numbering applying to the entire document. However, if the document is sectioned into separate parts, page numbers must be managed in each section, that is, if the page numbering is not to be continuous throughout the document but unique to each section.

Breaks can be inserted into a document for a variety of reasons or special purposes. The two most commonly used document breaks are the page break and the section break. A *page* break is exactly what it sounds like: it forces a page end and new page at the point it is inserted into a document. A *section* break is used to segregate a document into two or more sections, each of which can have its own page and document formatting. All documents contain at least one section, but when a continuous break is inserted into a document, the document is divided at the breakpoint into essentially two separate documents.

Word 2007 provides four types of section breaks:

- **Continuous break**   Creates a new section and starts it on the same page as the break.
- **Next page**   Creates a new section that starts on the page following the break.
- **Even page**   Creates a new section that starts on the next even-numbered page after the break.
- **Odd page**   Creates a new section that starts on the next odd-numbered page after the break.

A section break is often inserted into a document to restart the page numbering, to change the document headers or footers, to change the page orientation from portrait to landscape or vice versa, or to apply a new formatting style in each section of the document.

The easiest type of document break to create is a page break (or what is sometimes called a hard break). Virtually all word processing system automatically create soft page breaks at the end of a page in a continuous document (a document without hard page breaks). This is a valuable feature because it allows text to flow forward and backward as the document is edited. However, there may be occasions in a document when a topic or header must be moved to the top of a new page, so a hard page break must be inserted to force the document to a new page. To enter a hard page break, you press the CTRL and ENTER keys of the keyboard together. In most word processing systems, including Word 2007, unless you have configured the workspace to display all formatting characters, page breaks only show in the Draft view of a document.

Page and section breaks can be deleted from a document. To view the breaks inserted into a document, view the document in Draft mode and delete the break as you would a character or object.

Displaying Formatting Characters

Each of the formatting elements, including spaces, tabs, indention markers, hard returns, page breaks, section breaks, object anchors, and more, can be displayed in a word processing document. The ability to see these characters can help you to determine why a certain formatting is seemingly in error. To display the formatting characters in a Word 2007 document, click the Word Options button on the Office button's menu and choose the Display link.

Numbered and Bulleted Lists

A true time-saving feature of the better word processing systems is the capability to create numbered or bulleted lists using a partially automated process. Numbered and bulleted lists provide you with the capability to create an itemized list that implies a sequence (numbered list) or equally weighted points (bulleted list) using either a single-level format or a multilevel format (in which some or all items have subitems).

Numbered Lists

A single-level numbered list, like the one shown in the top part of Figure 12-3, separates a list of items into discrete entries with an implied hierarchy or sequence. To create a numbered list in Word 2007, you can use one of two methods: from the pop-up menu or using the Numbering icon in the Paragraph group on the Home tab of the Word 2007 Ribbon.

To create a numbered list from the pop-up menu, right-click the line on which you want to start the numbered list and hold the mouse pointer over the Numbering selection. Choose the numbering style you want to apply from the Numbering submenu (which includes a gallery of numbering styles). You can also define a new numbering style if you'd like.

To create a numbered list from the Ribbon, select the Home tab and either click the Numbering icon in the Paragraph group of the Home tab to apply the last used numbering style or click the down arrow on the right of the icon to display the Numbering submenu from which you can select the numbering style you want to apply.

Regardless of how you applied numbering in a document, when numbering is applied, the Numbering icon turns gold (or another color, depending on the

FIGURE 12-3

Examples of
a single-level
numbered list
and a single-level
bulleted list

Numbered List

1. Eagles
2. Michael Jackson
3. Led Zeppelin
4. Pink Floyd
5. AC/DC
6. Garth Brooks
7. Billy Joel
8. Shania Twain

Bulleted List

- AC/DC
- Billy Joel
- Eagles
- Garth Brooks
- Led Zeppelin
- Michael Jackson
- Pink Floyd
- Shania Twain

workspace color scheme) to show that it's engaged. When you have completed the numbered list, you can cancel the numbering feature by either clicking the Numbering icon to disengage it or pressing the ENTER key twice to cancel the numbering feature.

Bulleted Lists

A single-level bulleted list, like the one shown in the lower part of Figure 12-3, separates a list of items into discrete entries without an implied hierarchy or sequence. The process used to create a bulleted list is very much like that used in the preceding section to create a numbered list using one of two methods: from the Quick Access menu or using the Bullets icon in the Paragraph group on the Home tab of the Word 2007 Ribbon.

To create a bulleted list from the Quick Access menu, right-click the line on which you want to start the bulleted list and click the Bullets icon on the Quick Access menu (as shown in Figure 12-4). Alternatively, you can click the Bullets icon in the Paragraph group on the Home tab or the Word 2007 Ribbon. In either case, clicking the Bullets icon applies the last bullet style used in the document. If you would like to use a different bullet style, click the down arrow on the right of the icon to display the Bullets menu from which you can choose the bullet style you wish to use. If you wish, you can also define a new bullet style.

Regardless of how you applied bullets in a document, the Bullets icon turns gold, indicating that the Bullets feature is active. When you have completed the bulleted list, you can cancel the Bullets feature by either clicking the Bullets icon or pressing the ENTER key twice.

Multilevel Lists

Some lists, either numbered or bulleted, need to include subitems (which in turn have subitems). The better word processing systems provide either direct support for this type of list or provide paragraph formatting to facilitate its construction. Microsoft Office Word 2007 includes a preset feature that sets up the formatting for

FIGURE 12-4

The Quick Access menu includes the Bullets icon

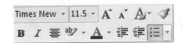

Examples of
multilevel lists

Multilevel Numbered List

1. Eagles
   a. Their Greatest Hits (1971-1975)
   b. Hotel California
2. Michael Jackson
   a. Thriller
3. Led Zeppelin
   a. Led Zeppelin IV
   b. Physical Graffiti
4. Pink Floyd
   a. The Wall
   b. The Dark Side of the Moon
5. AC/DC
   a. Back in Black

Multilevel Bulleted List

- Eagles
  o Their Greatest Hits (1971-1975)
  o Hotel California
- Michael Jackson
  o Thriller
- Led Zeppelin
  o Led Zeppelin IV
  o Physical Graffiti
- Pink Floyd
  o The Wall
  o The Dark Side of the Moon
- AC/DC

a multilevel list. You may be familiar with multilevel lists in the form of a document outline. Figure 12-5 illustrates two-level numbered and bulleted lists.

To create a multilevel list in Word 2007, click the line on which you want to start the list and then click the Multilevel list icon in the Paragraph group on the Home tab of the Word 2007 Ribbon to apply the last-used multilevel list format. If you want to choose the multilevel list format to be applied, click the down arrow to the right of the Multilevel list icon to display the Multilevel list menu, from which you can choose a list style or create a new style.

Modifying a List

When you are entering the items in a list, pressing the ENTER key at the end of each item automatically drops to the next line and applies the next number, bullet, or number pattern. If you delete or cut an item from a list, any items after the removed item are automatically renumbered. This is also true when you insert a new item into a list; the numbering is automatically adjusted for the new item.

The formatting of a list can be modified like any other paragraph formatting style. The line spacing; the amount of indention; and even the number, symbol, or level of an item can be modified.

Tables

A table can have a variety of uses in a word processing document. It can be used to show characteristics, measurements, results, and any manner of other facts about one or more related entities. A table is constructed of a specific number of rows and columns. Where a row and a column intersect, a cell is created. Cells serve as the containers to hold data.

Artist	Album	U.S. Sales (millions)	Worldwide Sales (millions)
Michael Jackson	*Thriller*	28	109
Eagles	*Their Greatest Hits (1971–1975)*	29	42
Led Zeppelin	*Led Zeppelin IV*	23	37
AC/DC	*Back in Black*	22	45
Pink Floyd	*Dark Side of the Moon*	15	40

Look at Table 12-1; this table has five rows, and each row contains the information for one recording artist. The table also has four columns that set the data fields for each row. With the data arranged this way, it is easy to compare one entity to another and one piece of data to another.

To create a table in a word processing document, you must first collect and organize the data that will populate the table so that you can gauge how many rows and columns the table requires. With this information, you are ready to begin creating the table. In Microsoft Word 2007, there are several methods that can be used to insert a table into a document: using the Table grid, the Insert Table option, and the Draw Table option. In the sections that follow, each of these methods is explained.

Table Grid

To insert a table using the Table grid, click the Table icon in the Tables group on the Insert tab of the Word 2007 Ribbon to display the Table menu (see Figure 12-6). At the top of the Table menu is a grid of small squares, with each square indicating

Insert Table

- Insert Table...
- Draw Table
- Convert Text to Table...
- Excel Spreadsheet
- Quick Tables ▶

a table cell. Click the square that represents the lower-right corner cell of the table you want to create. The selected square indicates the number of rows and columns defined in the table inserted into your document.

Insert Table

The second choice on the Tables menu (see Figure 12-6), beneath the Table Grid, is Insert Table. Clicking this option displays the Insert Table dialog box, on which you can specify the number of rows and columns you want the new table to include.

Draw Table

This option is the least used of the options available to create a new table, but its action is actually relatively simple, especially if you want to create a table with uneven row heights and column widths. To create a table using this method, click the Draw Table option on the Tables menu to change the cursor to a pencil symbol. Using the pencil, draw the outline shape of the table and then draw the rows and columns as you wish them to be sized vertically and horizontally. When you have completed creating the table, click into the document outside the new table to cancel the Draw Table function.

Change the Properties of a Table

Editing the content of a table is done essentially the same as editing text in any other part of a word processing document. However, you may want to change the properties, row heights, column widths, table and cell alignment, or the overall format or style of a table. The settings are made on the Table Properties dialog box (see Figure 12-7), which can be displayed by right-clicking inside the table you want to modify and selecting Table Properties from the Quick menu that displays.

The tabs on the Table Properties dialog box are used to change the settings and some formatting of a table. The following describes the use of each tab:

- **Table** The properties of a table include such things as the alignment of the table relative to the page margins, a specified overall width for the table, and if you wish to allow text to wrap around the table. In addition, you can add or change the table's borders or shading, as well as the properties of the rows, columns, and cells.

- **Row** The options on this tab are used to set a fixed, minimum, or maximum row height and whether rows can break across page breaks, and if a certain row is to be used as a heading at the top of pages.

FIGURE 12-7

The Table
Properties dialog
box of Word 2007

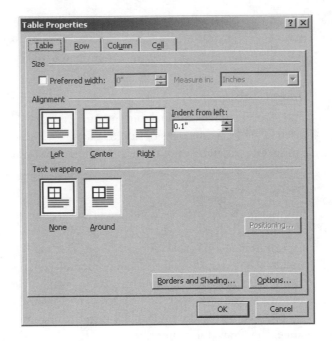

- **Column** The one option on this tab is used to set a fixed, minimum, or maximum column width.
- **Cell** The options on this tab are used to set a preferred width (which overrides the AutoFit feature) if used and the vertical alignment of the contents of a cell.

Spreadsheet Tables

Another method to add a table to a word processing document is to insert a spreadsheet object (table). Word processing applications that are a part of a personal productivity suite of applications are typically at least partially linked to an electronic spreadsheet application, like the way Word 2007 and Excel 2007 are. As shown in Figure 12-6 earlier in the chapter, one of the options that can be used to insert a table into a Word 2007 document is the Excel Spreadsheet choice on the Insert Table menu. Clicking this menu choice starts an instance of Excel 2007 as an object inserted into the Word document (see Figure 12-8). The Excel worksheet object can be edited and formatted just like any other Excel worksheet to create the table layout and format you want. Chapter 14 provides the details of formatting an Excel worksheet.

FIGURE 12-8

An Excel spreadsheet object can be inserted into a Word document as a table.

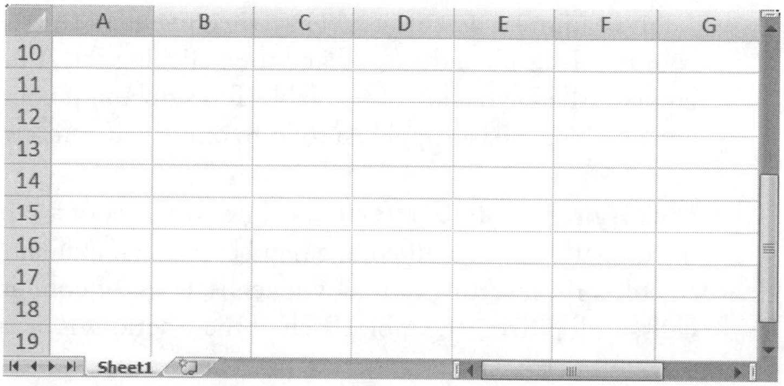

	A	B	C	D	E	F	G	
10								
11								
12								
13								
14								
15								
16								
17								
18								
19								

Sheet1

Modify a Table

Regardless of the method used to insert a table into a word processing document, the processes used to format, change the table structure, sort, and change the text formatting and alignment of the table are the same. In fact, a table, with a few exceptions, is formatted essentially the same as any block of text.

Modifying Columns and Rows One of the first changes typically made to a table after its data content has been entered is to change the structure of the table so that each column, row, and cell is sized appropriately to its data. A table and its rows and columns can be resized through the Table Properties dialog box (see "Change the Properties of a Table" earlier in this section), using the V-Split or H-Split cursor, or using the AutoFit feature.

The V-Split cursor (see Figure 12-9) is displayed whenever the cursor is moved over the side border of a column. When the cursor changes to the V-Split cursor, click down and hold to drag the column wider or narrower. You can also double-click the column border to AutoFit the column to its contents. If you wish to only resize a single cell, click into the cell and use the cursor to resize only the borders of that cell. A horizontal version of this cursor (H-Split cursor) appears when the cursor is held over a row's borders and is applied in the same manner as the V-Split cursor.

FIGURE 12-9

The V-Split cursor (resizing tool) is used to resize a table's columns.

You can resize an entire table by selecting all of the rows or columns (which, of course, selects all of the cells) and then clicking the AutoFit selection in the Cells group of the Layout tab of the Table Tools ribbon. If you don't want to AutoFit the entire table, you can apply AutoFit to only one (or more) cell, row, or column.

Modifying Table Structure   The structure of a table in a word processing document can be modified in a number of ways, including inserting additional rows or columns, inserting or removing cells, rows, or columns, splitting cells, merging cells, and splitting the table. Each of these actions is discussed in the following list:

- **Inserting cells, rows, or columns**   The first step to insert a row or column into a table is to select the cell, row, or column beside which you wish to insert an element above or below or to the left or right. To select a cell, click into the cell. To select a row or column, use the mouse to highlight the cells in the row or column you wish to insert a row or column beside. To insert a row, you have two options: inserting a cell and shifting the other cells down or inserting a row above or below a selected row. If you insert a cell and choose the option to shift cells to the right, a cell is inserted and any cells to the right of the new cell are shifted to the right. To insert a column, select a cell or all of the cells in a column and then choose Insert Column and choose between inserting the column on the right or left of the selected cells.

- **Splitting cells**   To split one or more cells into two or more new cells, select the cell(s) to be split, right-click the cell(s), and choose the Split Cells option. You are prompted for the number of columns (cell splits) and rows you wish to divide the cell(s) into; set these values and click the OK button to split the cell(s).

- **Merging cells**   To merge two or more cells into a single cell, highlight the cells to be merged, right-click the selected cells, and choose the Merge Cells option.

- **Deleting cells, rows, or columns**   To delete one or more cells or an entire row or column, select the cell(s), row, or column and right-click the selected area, and choose the Delete Cells, Delete Rows, or Delete Columns option from the pop-up menu as appropriate to complete the delete action.

- **Splitting a table**   To split a table into two tables separated by a blank line, click the row you wish to be the top row of the bottom table and click the Split Tables option on the Table Tools Layout tab.

■ **Converting a table to text** The contents of a table can be converted into text without a table structure, or a block of text that is separated with tabs can be converted into a table. To convert a table to text, click into the table and click the Convert Table To Text command on the Table Tools Layout tab. To convert text to a table, select the text to be included in the table, click the Tables icon on the Insert tab, and click the Convert Text To Table option.

Format a Table

There are a variety of ways a table and its contents can be formatted to both stand out on a page and to achieve the look and purpose you want for the table. The contents of a table can be sorted, a table style can be applied, the content inside each cell can be aligned, and as with all text in a word processing document, character formatting can be applied to the contents in a cell (or a range of cells).

To sort the contents of a table, click into the table and click the Sort icon in the Paragraph group of the Home tab to display the Sort dialog box, shown in Figure 12-10. You can choose up to three sort fields and set the criteria for each. Clicking OK sorts the data as specified.

You can format the table one cell, row, or column at a time if you'd like, but word processing systems that support tables typically also provide some table styles (AutoFormats) that can be used to set the format, color scheme, and style of the table all at once. Figure 12-11 illustrates Table 12-1 shown earlier in the chapter after it has had a table style applied to it.

FIGURE 12-10

The Word 2007 Sort dialog box

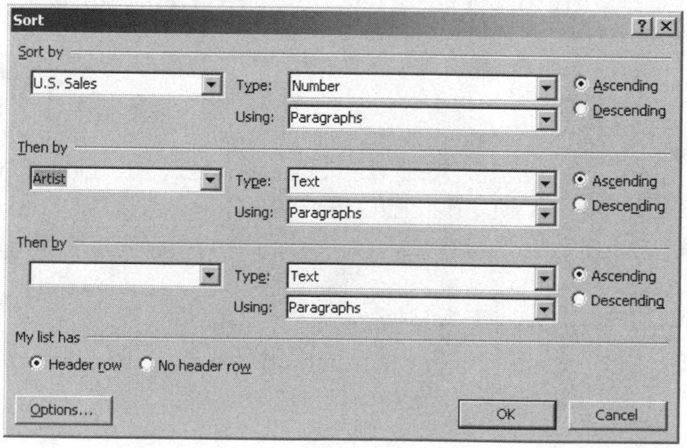

Artist	Album	U.S. Sales (millions)	Worldwide Sales (millions)
Michael Jackson	*Thriller*	28	109
Eagles	*Their Greatest Hits (1971-1975)*	29	42
Led Zeppelin	*Led Zeppelin IV*	23	37
AC/DC	*Back in Black*	22	45
Pink Floyd	*Dark Side of the Moon*	15	40

To apply a table style to a Word 2007 table, click into the table and select the Design tab of the Table Tools ribbon. Then scroll through the Table Style Gallery, holding the mouse pointer over a style thumbnail to sample it on the table, and click the style you want to apply.

To align the content of the cells in a column, a row, or one or more individual cells, select the row or column or the cell or range of cells you wish to align (you can hold down the CTRL key on the keyboard to select cells that aren't adjacent), and click the icon of the alignment you wish to apply in the Paragraph group of the Home tab. The content is aligned relative to the side borders of the cell, plus any additional buffering (cell padding) applied to the cell. To adjust the amount of cell padding defined for a table or cell, display the Table Properties dialog box (see "Change the Properties of a Table" earlier in the chapter) and choose the Advanced button on the Cell tab.

To add, modify, or remove table borders or to apply or remove shading from the table, use the following steps:

- **Table borders** To add, modify, or remove table borders, which include the gridlines inside the table as well, select the table and click the Borders icon on the Home tab of the Word 2007 Ribbon. On the menu that displays, any border that is in effect is highlighted. The border options can be toggled on and off to add, change, or remove the table borders.

- **Table shading** To apply shading to one or more cells, rows, or columns, including as much as an entire table, select the elements to be shaded, click the Shading button on the Home tab, and then choose the color you wish to apply to the table.

Inserting and Formatting Images

Although an inserted picture or other object isn't necessarily a part of a word processing document's format, its inclusion in a document certainly impacts the format. A graphic file or object can clarify parts of a document's content or illustrate a point of the discussion. Perhaps the graphic inserted into a document may be the letterhead banner in the header or footer, or it can be the focus of the document's content. In any case, graphic objects should be used sparingly, where possible, and relate to the document directly.

Inserting Graphic Objects into a Document

The process used to insert a graphic object into a word processing document varies slightly with the type of object to be inserted. The procedures used to insert objects into a Word 2007 document are as follows:

- **Clip art**   Clip art includes a variety of image file that are contained in a library of images typically installed with the application that have a common standard image file format. To insert clip art into a Word 2007 document, open the Insert tab and click the Clip Art icon to display the Clip Art task pane, in which you can search for a particular image of a particular media type or image topic within a specific image collection. The images meeting the search criteria are displayed and can be inserted into the document at the current insertion point.

- **Pictures**   A picture is considered to be any image saved with a supported graphic file format (such as gif, jpg, or tif), which could be a drawing, a scanned image, or a digitized photograph. To insert a picture into a Word 2007 document, open the Insert tab and click the Picture icon to display the Insert Picture dialog box, on which you can navigate to the folder containing the picture to be inserted. Either click the thumbnail of the picture to be inserted and then the Insert button or double-click the thumbnail to insert the picture at the current insertion point. Art created in another application, such as a freehand graphics or illustration application, is inserted into a document using the same process used for a picture.

- **Shapes and drawn objects**   A shape is a predrawn outline in a particular shape (such as a square, hexagon, or circle) that can be inserted into a document. To insert a shape into a Word 2007 document, open the Insert tab and click the Shapes icon to display the Shapes gallery. Click the shape you wish to insert at the current insertion point. If you wish to create a custom shape, you can open a new drawing canvas and create the object to be inserted.

■ **Text art** Text art is stylized text to which graphical effects are applied. In Word 2007, the text art tool is WordArt. To insert a WordArt graphic into a Word 2007 document, highlight the text you wish to convert into a WordArt object and then open the Insert tab and click the WordArt icon to display the WordArt gallery. Choose the WordArt style you wish to apply to convert the selected text.

Formatting Inserted Images

After an image has been inserted into a word processing document, the image object can be manipulated and formatted to fit the document and its purpose. To change the dimensions, size, rotation, and alignment of the image object, click the image to select it and use one of the following actions as needed:

■ **Align an image** An image can be aligned (left, center, or right) using the same tools used for aligning text. However, if you wish to align the image to a Word 2007 document's text, right-click the image and choose the Format Picture link to display the Format Picture dialog box. Choose the Layout tab and select the text-to-image alignment you desire.

■ **Crop an image** To reduce the amount of an image displayed in a Word 2007 document, right-click the image and choose the Format Picture link to display the Format Picture dialog box. Choose the Picture tab and adjust the Crop From parameters to the amount of the image to be displayed. It is often easier to edit and crop an image file in a drawing application and then insert the image into a Word 2007 document.

■ **Format an image** To format an image object in a Word 2007 document, including its borders, size, and alternative text tags, right-click the image and choose the Format Picture link to display the Format Picture dialog box. Choose the tab of the formatting you wish to apply and adjust its format as desired.

■ **Resize an image** Click and hold one of the resizing handles located on the sides and corners of the image and drag the image to the size (bigger or smaller) to the size desired. To retain the proportional size of the image, use one of the corner handles.

Inserting Symbols and Special Characters

Symbols are small bits of art that can be used to mark a word or sentence, to add humor or emphasis, or to separate blocks of text, plus a lot more uses. Special characters are like symbols, and there are symbols for many special characters, but they typically have a definite and specific purpose, such as a dollar sign ($), at sign (@), pound or number sign (#), asterisk (*), and so on. The most frequently used special characters are located on the keyboard and may or may not require the SHIFT key to be pressed to enter their images.

To enter a symbol, place the insertion point where the symbol is to go and click the Symbol option in the Symbols group of the Insert tab on the Word 2007 Ribbon to display the most frequently used symbol gallery. To see the full gallery of available symbols, click the More Symbols link to display the Symbol dialog box. Symbols are organized by their font set, so you may need to look through a few sets to find the symbol you want to use. When you locate it, click it, and then click Insert to insert the symbol into the document at the insertion point. If you want to insert only one symbol, you can then click Cancel to close the Symbol dialog box. Other word processors may have a menu selection on their Insert or Format menus or use a function key to display their symbol gallery.

Some special characters can be entered into a document using a serial combination of characters or a combination of keystrokes entered as a single entry. For example, if you wish to enter the symbol for "registered" (the ® symbol), you can enter the characters left parenthesis [(], "r," and right parenthesis [)] in a series. This combination of keys is automatically recognized and converted to the registered symbol. In Word 2007, this action is called AutoCorrect and the default key sequences (and the ability to add more) are accessed through the Microsoft Office button, the Word Options button, the Proofing selection, and the AutoCorrect button, which displays the AutoCorrect dialog box (see Figure 12-12).

Formatting a Document

When you use a document template for a new document, for the most part the formatting of the document, its layout, is defined, including its margins. However, in cases where you want to define a new template or customize a new document, it's very important to know how to set up the document margins, insert or remove page and section breaks, view and hide embedded formatting characters, add page numbers to a document, insert and modify page headers and footers, and, when needed, format all or a portion of a document into multiple columns on the same page. The sections

The AutoCorrect
dialog box defines
the key sequences
used to produce
special characters
and symbols
automatically.

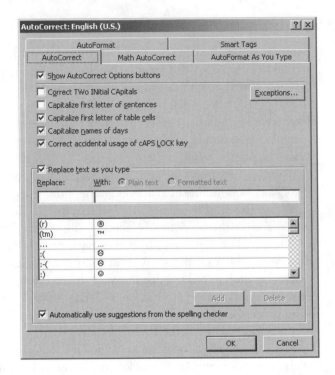

that follow discuss these topics and provide a brief step-by-step process on how each
of these actions is performed.

Modifying Document Margins

Although you can manually adjust the margin sizes of a document, the better word
processing systems have a number of preset margin formats that can be easily applied to
a document. In the Word 2007 application, the default margin sets (see Figure 12-13)
are included on a gallery that is accessed through the Margins icon in the Page Setup
group of the Page Layout tab of the Word 2007 Ribbon. To apply one of the margin sets
included in the gallery, click it to automatically adjust the margins to the settings of the
format selected.

On some word processors, the margins of a document or section can only be
adjusted manually using a dialog box or display similar to the Page Setup dialog
box displayed by the Custom Margins option on the Margins gallery in Word 2007,
shown at the bottom of Figure 12-13.

FIGURE 12-13

The Word 2007
Margins gallery

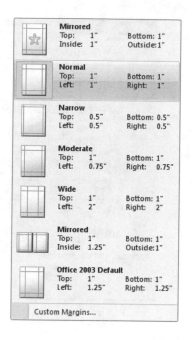

Columns

A section break (see the preceding section) is often used to set apart a page containing columnar information. Without inserting a section break before and after a page containing columns, the entire document would be reformatted to a specific number of columns. All documents start out formatting to one column, but word processing documents or sections can be formatted into up to three columns, as well as some special columnar formatting.

Figure 12-14 shows the Word 2007 Columns dialog box on which up to three columns can be specified along with their width and the size of the gap between the columns. A vertical line can also be inserted into each of the gaps for visual separation purposes.

Headers and Footers

Other document features that are often used with section breaks are document headers and footers. In a document that includes front matter (such as an introduction, table of contents, preface, and the like), you may want to use small roman numerals for the page numbers (like i, ii, iii, iv, etc.) and then switch to Arabic numerals for the main

FIGURE 12-14

The Word 2007
Columns dialog
box

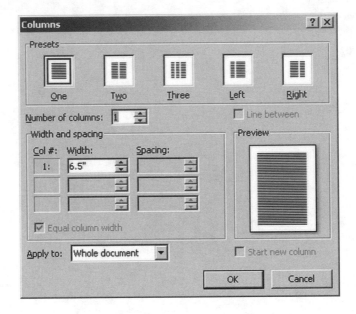

body of the document (like 1, 2, 3, etc.). Document page numbers (discussed more
in the following section) are typically included in the page header or footer. To use a
different page numbering scheme in separate parts of the document requires that each
scheme be in a different section of the document.

In fact, as illustrated in Figure 12-15, different sections can even have different
header and footer formats. Word 2007, as well as many other word processing
systems, provides a gallery of header, footer, and page number formats that can be

FIGURE 12-15

The footer of
one section and
the header of
the next section
can be formatted
differently.

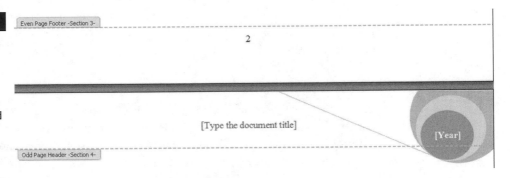

applied to an entire document, multiple sections of a document, or just a single document section. Figure 12-15 shows the footer for one section and the header of another section. To access the header, footer, and page number format galleries in Word 2007, click the applicable icon in the Header & Footer group of the Insert tab on the Word 2007 Ribbon.

Page Numbers

As described briefly in the preceding section, page numbers are typically inserted into the header or footer of a document. Word 2007 provides a gallery of page number (header or footer) formats that can be used to locate the page number at the top or bottom of the page of a document or section. When you select a location for the page number from the Page Number menu (displayed by clicking the Page Number icon in the Header & Footer group on the Insert tab), such as Bottom of Page (as shown in Figure 12-16), a gallery of footer styles is displayed. You can choose one of the preset page number formats or customize your own using the Format Page Numbers option.

FIGURE 12-16

The Page Number menu and the gallery of page number styles for the bottom of a page

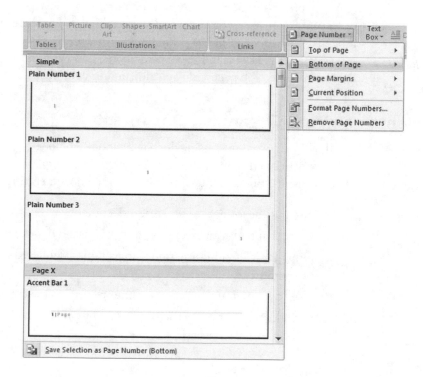

Nonprinting Characters and Formatting Symbols

Should you wish to display any nonprinting characters or the formatting symbols inserted into the document (and typically not displayed), you can choose to do so for an individual document using either the configuration options of the document workspace or a toggle button control. Most of the better word processing systems provide a toggle button or function key control that displays or hides these characters. Word 2007 includes the Show/Hide Formatting Characters button, which has a paragraph symbol on it, on the Home tab.

CERTIFICATION OBJECTIVE

Common Uses of Word Processing

2.2.1 Identify common uses for word processing

Word processing applications are commonly used in virtually all types of industrial, business, medical, and educational fields. For the most part, word processing is used to create and format short documents like letters and memos; long documents like legal documents, reports, and even this book; and specialized documents like Web pages, blog entries, and in certain cases, e-mail messages.

Elements of a Well-Organized Document

In all usages, a word processing document should include or apply certain characteristics and elements to be considered a well-organized document. The characteristics and elements of a well-organized document include the following:

- Use outline formats to organize a document.
- Use consistent formatting for similar text and data elements.
- Organize related information using a table, a bulleted list, or a numbered list, as appropriate.
- Use consistent and appropriate line spacing and paragraph spacing.
- Include information in the headers and footers that clearly identifies parts of a document as appropriate.

■ Avoid using design and formatting that make a document difficult to read, such as using all uppercase letters or hard-to-read colors.

■ Use formatting and design elements that support the purpose of the document and the needs of the reader.

CERTIFICATION SUMMARY

The overall format of a document can directly impact its readability or usability. Document-based applications generally include a wide array of formatting features and tools that can be used to change the look-and-feel of an entire document or just one or more sections of the document.

Arranging information into a list, either bulleted or numbered, or a table can help to improve the reader's understanding of related, yet independent data. In the same way, changing the margin size, arranging information into columns, and inserting simple page-related data, such as page numbers and strategically placed page breaks, can also help the user to understand the message or information in a document.

✓ TWO-MINUTE DRILL

Formatting Documents

❑ A style is a formatting set that defines a specific combination of formatting options, including font, text alignment, borders, and shading that combines character, paragraph, list, and table formatting options.

❑ Numbered and bulleted lists provide the capability to create an itemized list that may imply a sequence or a set of equally weighted points in either a single-level format or a multilevel format.

❑ A single-level numbered list itemizes discrete entries with an explicit hierarchy or sequence.

❑ A single-level bulleted list separates a list of items into discrete entries with no implicit hierarchy or sequence.

❑ Some list items, whether numbered or bulleted, may include subitems, which create a multilevel list.

❑ The formatting of a list can be modified like any other paragraph formatting style. The line spacing, the amount of indention, and even the number, symbol, or level of an item can be modified.

❑ A table can be used to show characteristics, measurements, results, and any manner of other facts about one or more related entities.

❑ A table is constructed of a specific number of rows and columns. Where a row and a column intersect, a cell is created. Cells serve as the containers to hold data.

❑ In Word 2007, a table can be inserted into a document using the Table grid, the Insert Table option, or the Draw Table option. A table can also be added to a word processing document by inserting a spreadsheet object.

❑ The contents of a table can be sorted, a table style can be applied, the content inside each cell can be aligned, and as with all text in a word processing document, character formatting can be applied to the contents in a cell or a range of cells.

❑ Symbols are small bits of art used to mark a word or sentence, to add humor or emphasis, or to separate blocks of text, among other uses.

❑ Special characters have a definite and specific purpose, such as a dollar sign ($), at sign (@), pound or number sign (#), asterisk (*), and so on. The most frequently used special characters are located on the keyboard.

❑ Separate parts of a document may require different formats or page orientations, which require the document to be divided into two or more sections by inserting continuous (section) breaks.

❑ A forced page break (hard page break) can be inserted into a document. By default, word processing systems automatically create soft page breaks at the end of a page, which allows text to flow forward and backward as the document is edited.

❑ A document can be formatted with up to three columns.

❑ Header, footer, and page number formats can be applied to an entire document, multiple sections of a document, or just a single document section.

❑ Page numbers are typically inserted into the header or footer of a document.

❑ The workspace of a word processing system can be configured to display non-printing characters or formatting symbols in a document. Most word processing applications provide a toggle button to display or hide these characters.

❑ Line spacing controls the amount of white space between the lines of text in a document. Line spacing ranges from 1 to 3.5 lines of spacing between lines of text. Spacing can be added before or after a paragraph break. A paragraph can be set to indent its first line or to create a hanging paragraph. First-line indention indents the first line of a paragraph from the left margin.

❑ Tab stops are added to the ruler in a word processing document at evenly spaced intervals by default or at custom intervals of the user's choosing. The ruler is a horizontal rule typically displayed across the top of the document workspace. Individual tabs can be added to the ruler. However, center, right, decimal, and bar tabs can also be added to the ruler.

❑ The two most common document breaks are page breaks and section breaks. A page break forces a page end and a new page. A section break divides a document into sections, each of which can have its own page and document formatting.

❑ Each of the formatting elements, including spaces, tabs, indention markers, hard returns, page breaks, section breaks, object anchors, and more, can be displayed in a word processing document.

❑ The structure of a table in a word processing document can be modified in a number of ways, including inserting additional rows or columns, inserting or removing cells, rows, or columns, splitting cells, merging cells, and splitting the table.

❑ Graphic objects, including clip art, pictures, shapes and drawn objects, and text art, can be inserted into a document. Image objects can be manipulated and formatted to fit the document and its purpose.

Common Uses of Word Processing

❑ A word processing document should include or apply certain characteristics and elements to be considered a well-organized document. The characteristics and elements of a well-organized document include the following: use of outline formats to organize a document; consistent formatting for similar text and data elements; information organized into a table, a bulleted list, or a numbered list, as appropriate; consistent and appropriate line spacing and paragraph spacing; information in headers and footers to identify parts of a document; avoidance of design and formatting that make a document difficult to read; and use of formatting and design elements that support the purpose of the document and the needs of reader.

SELF TEST

The following questions are intended to help you be sure that you understand the material included in this chapter. Read the questions and the answer choices carefully.

Formatting Documents

1. What term is used for a formatting set that defines a unique combination of formatting options, such as font, text alignment, and may include character and paragraph formatting?
   A. Preset
   B. Style
   C. Template
   D. Thumbnail

2. What formatting element would you apply to create a list of steps that must be completed in a prescribed sequence?
   A. Bulleted list
   B. Numbered list
   C. Section
   D. Table

3. What formatting element would you apply to create a list of items that make equally important points?
   A. Bulleted list
   B. Numbered list
   C. Section
   D. Table

4. What formatting element is applied to compare the characteristics and measurements of a list of related items?
   A. Bulleted list
   B. Numbered list
   C. Section
   D. Table

5. What is the term used for the editable entity created by the intersection of a row and column in a table?

    A. Cell

    B. Data

    C. Field

    D. Item

6. Which of the following cannot be used to insert a table into a Word 2007 document?

    A. Table grid

    B. Insert table

    C. Draw table

    D. Excel spreadsheet

    E. All of the above methods can be used to insert a table into a Word 2007 document.

7. True or False. The contents of a table can be sorted, formatted, and aligned in the same manner as any text in a word processing document.

    A. True

    B. False

8. Which of the following statements are true?

    A. Symbols are small bits of art that can be used to mark a word or sentence, add humor or emphasis, or separate blocks of text, among other uses.

    B. Special characters typically have a definite and specific purpose, with many special characters located on the keyboard.

    C. Symbols and special characters are different names for the same exact characters.

    D. Word 2007 doesn't include support for symbols.

9. What formatting element must be applied to facilitate a different document format in separate parts of a document?

    A. Hard page break

    B. Columns

    C. Section break

    D. Soft page break

10. What is typically the maximum number of columns a word processing document can implement?
- **A.** Two
- **B.** Three
- **C.** Four
- **D.** No limit

11. True or False: Word 2007 allows only one header and footer style to be used in a document.
- **A.** True
- **B.** False

12. True or False: Displaying nonprinting characters or formatting symbols in a document requires the configuration of the document workspace to be permanently changed.
- **A.** True
- **B.** False

Common Uses of Word Processing

13. What formatting element is used to add more white space between lines of text?
- **A.** Kerning
- **B.** Line spacing
- **C.** Paragraph spacing
- **D.** Tab stops

14. Which of the following is not a type of tab stop available in Word 2007?
- **A.** Center
- **B.** Horizontal bar
- **C.** Left
- **D.** Right

15. Which of the following can be inserted into a document to change the formatting for a portion of the document?
- **A.** Character breaks
- **B.** Page breaks
- **C.** Paragraph breaks
- **D.** Section breaks

16. Which of the following are graphic object types that can be inserted into a word processing document?

    A. Clip art

    B. Picture

    C. Plain text

    D. Table

17. Which of the following are elements of a well-organized document?

    A. Consistent formatting for similar text and data elements

    B. Information organized into a table, a bulleted list, or a numbered list

    C. Consistent and appropriate line and paragraph spacing

    D. All of the above

    E. None of the above

SELF TEST ANSWERS

Formatting Documents

1. ☑ **B.** A style defines a unique set of document, paragraph, and character formatting options.
   ☒ **A, C,** and **D** are incorrect. There are preset elements, but none of them are called a preset. A template may include a style, but it can also include illustrations, text, and more. A thumbnail is used to represent the effects of a gallery item.

2. ☑ **B.** A list of sequenced items is best formatted into a numbered list.
   ☒ **A, C,** and **D** are incorrect. A bulleted list implies that no sequence exists. A section is a document separation that can be uniquely formatted. A table can imply a sequence, but it is usually used to compare information.

3. ☑ **A.** A bulleted list has no implicit sequence and is used to list equally weighted items.
   ☒ **B, C,** and **D** are incorrect. A numbered list explicitly states a sequence. A section is a document separation that can be uniquely formatted. A table can imply a sequence, but it is usually used to compare information.

4. ☑ **D.** A table arranges items in rows and columns so that the data of each item can be compared or contrasted.
   ☒ **A, B,** and **C** are incorrect. A list of sequenced items is best formatted into a numbered list. A bulleted list implies that no sequence exists. A section is a document separation that can be uniquely formatted.

5. ☑ **A.** A cell is created by the intersection of a row and column in a table and can be edited to hold data and be formatted.
   ☒ **B, C,** and **D** are incorrect. Data is the entry made to a cell. A field is similar to a cell, but is part of an unbounded layout. An item is just about anything.

6. ☑ **E.** Depending on the word processing system in use, you can find all or at least most of these methods to insert a table into a document, especially in Word 2007.
   ☒ **A, B, C,** and **D** are incorrect. Each of these choices is a valid method that can be used to insert a table into a Word 2007 document. However, none of these choices is the best answer to the question on its own.

7. ☑ **A.** Text inside a table can be formatted just like text in the body of a document. The general rule is text is text.
   ☒ **B** is incorrect. The statement in Question 7 is true.

8. ☑ **A and B.** Symbols and special characters are distinctively different, although the symbol sets available in most word processors include most of the special characters in a font set.

☒ C and D are incorrect. Symbols are small pictures, icons, and the like (and a few characters as well), and special characters are typically included in a font set and generally have a definite usage.

9. ☑ **C.** Also called a continuous break; this element must be used to separate the parts of a document.
☒ **A, B,** and **D** are incorrect. A hard page break or a soft page break only moves the insertion point to the top of a new page. Unless a whole document is formatted into columns, to use column formatting requires a new section.

10. ☑ **C.** A Word 2007 document allows up to four columns.
☒ **A, B,** and **D** are incorrect. A document can have only one (sort of the default) or two columns, but four columns is the maximum. Obviously Answer D is incorrect.

11. ☑ **B.** Each section of a document can have a unique header or footer.
☒ **A** is incorrect. The statement in Question 11 is false.

12. ☑ **B.** Most word processing applications have a toggle button that can be used to display formatting and nonprinting characters.
☒ **A** is incorrect. The statement in Question 12 is false.

Common Uses of Word Processing

13. ☑ **B.** Line spacing can add from 1 to 3.5 lines of white space between text lines.
☒ **A, C,** and **D** are incorrect. Kerning is a character spacing function; paragraph spacing adds extra lines before or after a paragraph; and tab stops are used to align text across a line.

14. ☑ **B.** There is a bar tab available, but it inserts vertical bars at the tab stop position.
☒ **A, C,** and **D** are incorrect. Tab stops can be added to a document for center tab, left tab, and right tab alignments.

15. ☑ **D.** Section breaks divide a document into separate sections that can be formatted individually.
☒ **A, B,** and **C** are incorrect. There is no character break available in a word processing application; page breaks are used to advance text to the top of a new page; and a paragraph break is not an inserted element, in the sense of section or page breaks.

16. ☑ **A and B.** Both clip art and picture files are graphic objects that can be inserted into a word processing document.
☒ **C and D** are incorrect. Neither plain text nor a table structure is a graphic object.

17. ☑ **D.** All of the elements or characteristics listed in A through C are common to well-organized documents.
☒ **A, B, C,** and **E** are incorrect. While A, B, and C are each characteristics or elements of a well-organized word processing document, none of them is the best answer available. E is incorrect because D is correct.

13

Formatting and Reviewing Documents

T he capability to share documents across a network has opened the door to cooperation, collaboration, and coordination (the 3-Cs) in the preparation of documents. Using the same application software or even different applications or platforms, users are able to work together in pairs, teams, or groups to create, share, edit, and publish documents on a network.

While the objective for this chapter centers on the capabilities of word processing systems to facilitate sharing, reviewing, and collaboration on a document, we also need to cover some of the features and tools that may be used to complete a formal document. To that end, this chapter also discusses the use of language tools, such as spelling and grammar checkers, and the processes used to insert references, such as a table of contents or endnotes, into a document.

CERTIFICATION OBJECTIVE

Reviewing, Securing, and Collaborating on Word Processing Documents

2.1 Be able to use word-processing tools to automate processes such as document review, security and collaboration.

Some of the major benefit areas of word processing applications are in the tools and features that can be used to review a document, secure a shared document, and collaborate on a document with other users over a network. Reviewing documents includes actions like spelling and grammar checking, language support, and tracking changes and comments inserted into a document by reviewers. Sharing a document with others, for review or for collaboration, may require that the document is secured to prevent unauthorized readers from accessing and opening the document. These features and the processes used to apply them are discussed in the sections that follow.

Using Language Tools to Check a Document

The language tools provided by the better word processing systems typically include spelling checkers, grammar checkers, thesaurus lookup tools, research tools, and perhaps even language translation. These tools can assist the user to identify and correct any language errors contained in a document. They aren't infallible and are limited to the abilities of the users to a certain extent, but these tools are very valuable to avoiding small inadvertent errors commonly made when a document is first created.

Spelling and Grammar Checkers

Spelling checking utilities have become a de facto standard in word processing systems and are frequently available in other applications as well, even spreadsheet, presentation, and web page development software, among others. However, the best demonstration of the capabilities and benefits of a spelling checker is in a word processing application, where typically a grammar checker is coupled with the spelling checker.

Essentially what a spelling checker does is compare a string of characters to the words in a word list (dictionary) looking for a match. If the character string isn't found in the dictionary, it's flagged as possibly misspelled and the words in the dictionary that are the closest match, if any, are suggested to the user. This all works well, provided the dictionary doesn't contain misspelled words and the language being checked matches that of the dictionary. Most spelling checkers allow the user to add words to the dictionary, which can be the source of misspelled words in the word list.

A *grammar checker* scans text looking for violations of its established rules. These rules can include such things as the number of spaces after a period, passive sentences, sentences missing a verb or a subject (which are flagged as sentence fragments), comma usage, and more. Any text string that appears to violate one of the grammar checker's rules is flagged for possible correction. Word 2007 includes the capability to check for and flag errors in spelling and grammar automatically as text is entered. Figure 13-1 illustrates how Word 2007 flags spelling and grammar errors.

As the spelling and grammar checking proceeds through a document, each suspected error detected stops the checking process and displays a message or dialog box that provides suggested corrections, or controls that allow the user to ignore the suspected error and accept it as is.

In Figure 13-1, the text contains a variety of misspellings and grammar and sentence errors that were flagged by the automatic checking feature of Microsoft

FIGURE 13-1

Spelling, grammar, and language errors flagged by the spelling and grammar checking utilities of Word 2007

Now is the tyme for all good men to come to the aide of their country. The lazy brown dog jumpted over the green log. Let a seeping dog lay. I can not believe he eight the hole thing.

Office Word 2007. Notice that words spelled correctly but used incorrectly are not flagged (like "seeping" in Figure 13-1). There are some words that are commonly interchanged in error, such as effect and affect, it's and its, whole and hole, and there and their, which most grammar checkers do find. However, commonly used words (at least with the current state of the spelling and grammar checking art) are difficult to detect as erroneous. For this reason, you shouldn't rely on spelling and grammar checkers to proofread a document for you. Proofreading is still a human process.

Language Tools

Word processing systems typically have other language tools in addition to the spelling and grammar checkers, including the following tools:

- **Thesaurus**   This language tool can be used to look up synonyms and antonyms for a word.
- **Translation**   This tool is used to translate the language in a document from one language to another.
- **Research**   This tool is used to locate a word or phrase in a reference source.
- **Word count**   This tool is used to count the number of characters, words, sentences, paragraphs, and lines in a document.

Inserting and Formatting Document Elements

The better word processing systems include features, utilities, and tools to generate, format, and insert a variety of document elements into different types of documents, such as formal documents, white papers, research articles, and academic papers. These documents may require specific reference elements like a table of contents, footnotes, reference citations in the format of commonly used reference standards, figure and table captions, and indexing.

Insert Date and Time

Word processing applications provide the capability of inserting a date/time element into a document that can be automatically updated each time the document is modified or not, depending on the options chosen. Word 2007 offers seventeen date only, date and time, or time-only options that can be inserted into a document. If the automatically update option is selected, each time the document is opened, the inserted date or time is updated to the current date or time.

Insert and Modify a Table of Contents

The *table of contents* function in a word processing application searches a document for specified heading styles and creates a cross-reference table that lists the logical page number on which each heading is located. The logical page number of a document page is generated by the word processing system's page number control function. In contrast, a physical page number is the actual page position of a page in the entire document file. For example, in a document that has a cover page and a table of contents, logical page number 1 might actually be the eighth physical page of the document.

In Office Word 2007, a table of contents is inserted into a document using the Table Of Contents icon on the References tab of the Word 2007 Ribbon (see Figure 13-2). Clicking the Table Of Contents icon displays the Table Of Contents menu, which includes a gallery of the Built-In (predefined) table of contents styles, shown in Figure 13-3.

To insert a table of contents into a document using the default settings, you only need to click the table of contents style you wish to insert. The default settings search the active document for instances of the standard Office styles Heading 1, Heading 2, and Heading 3. For each instance of one of these headings, an entry is inserted into the table of contents along with the logical page number of the instance. Figure 13-4 illustrates a table of contents inserted into a document based on the default settings.

A table of contents can be reformatted or modified to include additional items, completely refreshed or updated, or reconfigured to include additional or fewer text styles. To change the settings of a table of contents or to refresh its contents (for example, after additional text is added to a document and the page numbers have changed), the same process used to create the table of contents, even if the table of contents was inserted automatically, is used to modify it as well.

To access the settings that define the structure and contents of a table of contents, you open a create, insert, or add table of contents dialog box on which you can specify the text styles to search for and how you wish the table of contents

The Table Of Contents option on the Word 2007 Ribbon's References tab

FIGURE 13-3

The Table Of
Contents menu
includes a gallery
of table of
contents styles.

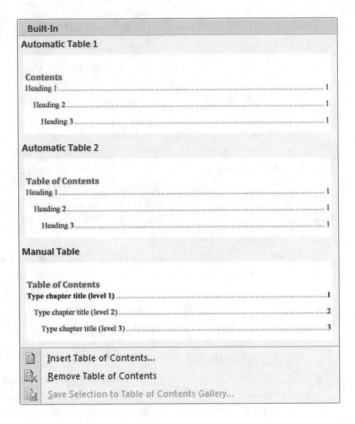

Built-In

Automatic Table 1

Contents
Heading 1 1
   Heading 2 1
      Heading 3 1

Automatic Table 2

Table of Contents
Heading 1 1
   Heading 2 1
      Heading 3 1

Manual Table

Table of Contents
Type chapter title (level 1) 1
   Type chapter title (level 2) 2
      Type chapter title (level 3) 3

   Insert Table of Contents...
   Remove Table of Contents
   Save Selection to Table of Contents Gallery...

FIGURE 13-4

A sample table
of contents
inserted into a
word processing
document

Table of Contents

FIGURE 13-5

The Table Of Contents dialog box in Word 2007

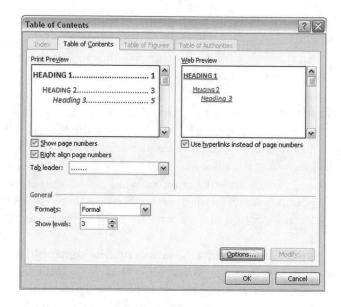

to display the corresponding logical page numbers. In Word 2007, these settings are accessed on the Table Of Contents dialog box, shown in Figure 13-5, which is accessed through the Insert Table Of Contents option on the Table Of Contents menu (shown in Figure 13-3 earlier).

Insert References into a Document

When it's necessary or desired to insert footnotes, endnotes, or a reference citation using a specific formatting style, the better word processing systems provide the features and tools to insert these references into a document and track them. In the three sections that follow, we look at how these tools are applied in Word 2007.

Insert a Footnote A *footnote* is a numbered text reference that is inserted at the bottom of a page with the associated reference number inserted after the document text to which the reference is tied. Figure 13-6 illustrates the formatting used for a

FIGURE 13-6

An example of a footnote added to a document page

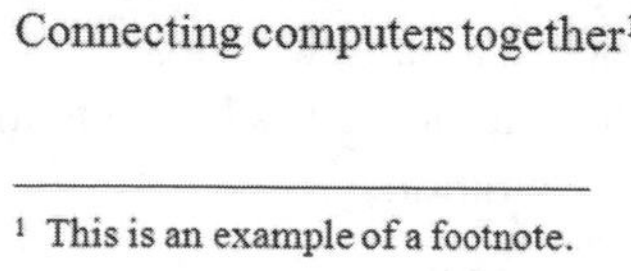

Connecting computers together[1]

---

[1] This is an example of a footnote.

footnote. In Word 2007, the Insert Footnote icon on the References tab of the Word 2007 Ribbon is used to add the next sequential footnote at the bottom of the page (in the page footer). The corresponding reference is inserted in the text at the active insertion point.

Insert an Endnote   An *endnote* is something like a footnote, but instead of the reference being placed at the bottom of the page, it is inserted on the next line available of the last page of the document. As with the footnote, the reference number is inserted at the insertion point.

To insert an endnote into a Word 2007 document, click down the insertion point where you want the reference number to be inserted and then click the Insert Endnote option in the Footnotes group of the References tab.

Insert a Reference Citation or Bibliographic Item   If you've ever had to write a research or project paper that required the use of reference citations and a bibliography page, then you know how difficult the citations can be. Using a word processing application, citations and bibliographic items can be formated and inserted into a document relatively easily.

Many of the better word processing system have similar features in this area to those of Office Word 2007, which includes support for indexing, inserting, and listing references in a document or a bibliography. In addition, Word 2007 has the capability to format citations in accordance with a specific citation style standard, such as the style standards of the American Psychological Association (APA), the Modern Language Association (MLA), or *The Chicago Manual of Style*, among others.

Often the citations used in a document refer to one primary source or perhaps even several sources. A feature of reference citation tools is the capability to create a list of reference sources. In Word 2007, this tool is called the Source Manager, which can be used to organize the information relating to a reference source that can then be used for creating reference citations or bibliographic entries. To insert a footnote, endnote, or other reference citation in a Word 2007 document, the reference's information must be first entered into the Source Manager.

To insert a reference citation, select the reference style you wish to use in the Citations & Bibliography group of the References tab from the Style pull-down list (choosing from ten different style standards) and then click the Insert Citation icon. If the reference is for a new source, you can insert it into the Source Manager and then insert the citation or use an existing reference source from a list of available sources for the citation.

To insert a bibliographic citation in a Word 2007, click the Bibliography button, and click the format you wish to use or the Insert Bibliography option, if only one format is available.

Insert Hyperlinks

Another way to link a document to its sources or perhaps to additional information or related documents is to insert a hyperlink into the document. A hyperlink (a shortened form of hypertext link) is an embedded link to an external document, Web site, or file located on either a local or networked source. Hyperlinks are obviously more effective in documents that are to be viewed electronically, either as an attachment to an e-mail message or as an online document.

A hyperlink is made up of two primary parts: a displayed title and a URL. The display title could be the URL itself, or a reference name can be assigned as the displayed title.

Reviewing Documents and Tracking Document Changes

When more than one person is responsible for the content of a document, it is likely that each of the collaborators may have a different idea of what the content should be or perhaps a different way to word specific passages of the document. In any case, a base document is typically prepared and then forwarded or shared with the other team members for their corrections, additions, omissions, and comments. However, it can be difficult for the primary author to know exactly what changes are made, if there isn't some method used to indicate and track any modifications made to the original document and who made them.

Tracking Changes

Word 2007 includes a Track Changes function that, when enabled, tracks any and all changes made to the document and by whom. Figure 13-7 illustrates the markup made to a document that has the Track Changes function enabled. In addition,

FIGURE 13-7

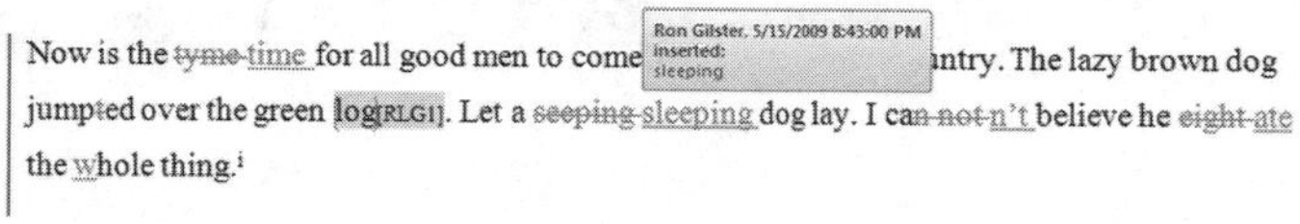

A Word 2007 document showing Track Changes markups

Now is the tyme time for all good men to come [Ron Gilster, 5/15/2009 8:43:00 PM inserted: sleeping] ntry. The lazy brown dog jumped over the green log[RLG1]. Let a seeping sleeping dog lay. I can not n't believe he eight ate the whole thing.[i]

as shown by the pop-up box, the date, time, and person making the change are recorded as well as the change itself. The changes reflected by the Track Changes markup can be either accepted or rejected by the document owner.

Reviewer Comments

In addition, reviewers can insert comments into a document, whether the Track Changes function is enabled or not. The comments can be any text entry and are associated with the work immediately preceding the insertion point of the document. The inclusion of a comment is marked by the initials of the person inserting the comment and the next sequential number of that person's comments. Holding the cursor over the top of a comment tag (the [RLG1] entry in Figure 13-8) displays a pop-up box containing the information and text of the comment, as shown in Figure 13-8.

Protecting a Document

Even though you are collaborating with other users on a particular document, there may be parts of a document you wish to protect against certain types of changes or even certain people. Most word processing applications include a capability to restrict formatting and editing changes to a specific set of formatting choices or editing types.

For example, Word 2007 allows the author of a document to restrict both access to and changes in a document using the settings in the Restrict Formatting and Editing pane (see Figure 13-9). Within the Formatting Restrictions of the Restriction Formatting and Editing pane, you can limit the styles that may be applied, define the types of editing, if any, you wish to allow, and designate which specific users or groups can access and perform editing on the document.

FIGURE 13-8

An example of a comment tag and the pop-up box of a comment inserted into a Word 2007 document

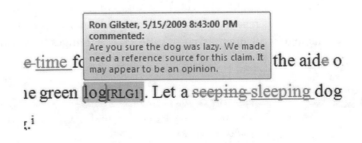

FIGURE 13-9

The Restrict
Formatting and
Editing pane of
Word 2007

CERTIFICATION SUMMARY

In spite of our best efforts to produce error-free documents, errors do occur. Word processing applications, and a few others, include such error-checking tools as a spelling checker, a grammar checker, language tools, and automatic correction features. The ability to track any changes made to a document by its creator or other reviewers allows any suggested changes to the document to be reviewed, accepted, or rejected.

When appropriate, reference elements can be added to a document for both convenience and citation. A table of contents, a table of figures, and the like can be inserted in a document to help the reader find information. Other references, including endnotes, footnotes, and bibliographic references, can be included in a document when appropriate.

TWO-MINUTE DRILL

Reviewing, Securing, and Collaborating on Word Processing Documents

❑ The language tools included in word processing systems include spelling checkers, grammar checkers, thesaurus lookup tools, research tools, and perhaps even language translation.

❑ A spelling checker compares a word to a list of words in a dictionary. If the word isn't found, it's flagged as misspelled (or unknown) and the words that are the closest match are suggested.

❑ A grammar checker scans text looking for violations of its rules, which can include the number of spaces after a period, passive sentences, sentence fragments, and comma usage.

❑ Word processing systems provide other language tools, including a thesaurus, translation, research, and word count.

❑ The Table of Contents function searches a document for specified heading styles and creates a cross-reference that lists the logical page number on which each heading is located.

❑ A footnote is a numbered text reference inserted at the bottom of a page that corresponds to a reference number inserted after the text to which it is associated.

❑ An endnote is inserted on the next line available of the last page of the document. Like the footnote, the reference number is inserted at the insertion point.

❑ If you've ever had to write a research or project paper that required the use of reference citations and a bibliography page, then you know how difficult the citations can be. Using a word processing application, citations and bibliographic items can be formatted and inserted into a document relatively easily.

❑ The citations in a document typically refer to one or two primary sources. One feature of reference citation tools is the capability to create a list of reference sources.

❑ Word 2007 includes a Track Changes function that tracks any and all changes made to the document and by whom.

❑ Reviewers can insert comments into a document, which can be any text entry.

❑ Most word processing applications include a capability to restrict formatting and editing changes to a specific set of formatting choices or editing types.

SELF TEST

The following questions are intended to help you be sure that you understand the material included in this chapter. Read the questions and the answer choices carefully.

Reviewing, Securing, and Collaborating on Word Processing Documents

I. Which of the following is not a language tool included in a word processing application?
- A. Appropriateness checker
- B. Grammar checker
- C. Spelling checker
- D. Thesaurus

2. True or False: A spelling checker can find and flag any word that is spelled correctly but used incorrectly.
- A. True
- B. False

3. What word processing application utility scans the text of a document looking for language rule violations, including such things as the number of spaces after a period, passive sentence voice, sentence fragments, and comma usage?
- A. Document checker
- B. Grammar checker
- C. Spelling checker
- D. Thesaurus

4. Which of the following are common document elements supported by word processing applications?
- A. Table of contents
- B. Footnotes
- C. Endnotes
- D. Reviewer comments
- E. All of the above
- F. None of the above

5. What is the text reference element that is inserted at the bottom of a page and corresponds to a reference number inserted into the same page?
   A. Endnotes
   B. Footnotes
   C. Reviewer comments
   D. Table of contents

6. What is the text reference element that is inserted on the last page of a document and corresponds to a reference number inserted at the insertion point?
   A. Table of contents
   B. Reviewer comments
   C. Footnotes
   D. Endnotes

7. Which of the following are document element types that can be inserted into a word processing document to indicate a reference source?
   A. Reference citation
   B. Bibliographic citation
   C. Off-page note
   D. Reference endnote

8. What document element can a reviewer use to communicate with a document's author or other reviewers using only the document itself?
   A. Table of contents
   B. Footnotes
   C. Endnotes
   D. Reviewer comments

9. What Word 2007 feature can be used to identify and capture any changes made to a document?
   A. Protect Document
   B. Endnotes
   C. Footnotes
   D. Track Changes

10. True or False: Word 2007 has no provision or feature that allows a document's author to restrict who can access a document and what they can do to or with the document.
    A. True
    B. False

SELF TEST ANSWERS

Reviewing, Securing, and Collaborating on Word Processing Documents

1. ☑ **A.** At least none of the major word processing applications have included an appropriateness checker as yet.
   ☒ **B, C,** and **D** are incorrect. Word processing systems generally have grammar and spelling checkers and a thesaurus tool.

2. ☑ **B.** Spell checkers only test words to see if they are spelled correctly. Some grammar checkers can check usage, but there's nothing better than human proofreading, at least not yet.
   ☒ **A** is incorrect. Not all word processing systems include usage checking.

3. ☑ **B.** Grammar checkers scan phrases and sentences using a set of rules, either built-in or user defined, for errors in grammar.
   ☒ **A, C,** and **D** are incorrect. Document checkers scan a document for private or personal information. Spelling checkers check for misspelled words, and a thesaurus is used to look up words that mean the same (synonyms) or words that mean the opposite (antonyms).

4. ☑ **E.** All of the choices in answers A through D are features common to word processing systems.
   ☒ **A, B, C, D,** and **F** are incorrect. Each of the document element features listed in answers A through D are typically included in a word processing application, but none of these choices is the best answer by itself. Answer F is therefore wrong.

5. ☑ **B.** A footnote is inserted at the bottom of a page and is linked with a number inserted at the insertion point.
   ☒ **A, C,** and **D** are incorrect. Endnotes are inserted at the end of a document. A reviewer comment has some of the characteristics of a footnote, with the exception that the comment is not added to the document; it is only attached to it for reference purposes. A table of contents is inserted as an entire entity, and documents typically don't have more than one table of contents.

6. ☑ **D.** An endnote is inserted at the end of a document and is linked with a number inserted at the insertion point.
   ☒ **A, B,** and **C** are incorrect. A footnote is inserted at the bottom of a page. A reviewer comment has some of the characteristics of an endnote, with the exception that the comment is not added to the document; it is only attached to it for references purposes. A table of contents is inserted as an entire entity, and documents typically don't have more than one table of contents.

7. ☑ **A** and **B.** A reference or bibliographic citation is included either in the document itself, as a part of an endnote or footnote, or in a bibliographic entry, which has the same information.
☒ **C** and **D** are incorrect. Off-page notes are not a commonly supported feature by word processing systems, and endnotes are just endnotes.

8. ☑ **D.** A reviewer comment tag is inserted into a document at the insertion point and references the text of the comment.
☒ **A, B,** and **C** are incorrect. See the answer for Question 5 or 6 for more information on the other choices.

9. ☑ **D.** The Track Changes feature does what its title implies: it tracks changes made by any reviewer, contributor, or author to the document. The author of the document can then view the suggested changes and either accept or reject them.
☒ **A, B,** and **C** are incorrect. The Protect Document feature of Word 2007 restricts who can access the document and what they can do with it. Endnotes and footnotes have absolutely nothing to do with tracking changes.

10. ☑ **B.** The Protect Document feature allows a document's author to restrict who can access a document and what they can do to or with the document.
☒ **A** is incorrect. The statement in Question 10 is false.

14

Basic Spreadsheet Functions

I've long contended that if you could learn only one personal productivity software application, it should be an electronic spreadsheet application. A spreadsheet application may not be the best tool for writing a letter, but it seems that one uses a computer more for organizing data than for just about any other activity. This chapter looks at the basics of electronic spreadsheet application software and its organization, formatting, and usage.

CERTIFICATION OBJECTIVE

Working with the Data, Format, and Structure of a Worksheet

3.1 Be able to modify worksheet data and structure and format data in a worksheet.

You must know and understand some fundamental actions and functions of electronic spreadsheet software in general, and Microsoft Office Excel 2007 in particular, to be prepared for the section of the IC³ exam that covers basic spreadsheet functions. The following sections focus on one or more of these basic functions, including data organization, entering and editing data, modifying the workspace structure, formatting data, printing, and identifying common uses for a spreadsheet.

Spreadsheet applications are organized into a set of independent worksheets that together constitute a workbook. When you save a spreadsheet document, you are saving a workbook. For most electronic spreadsheet applications, the only limit on the number of worksheets that can be in a workbook is bound by the amount of memory on the PC. However, a more practical limit is around 248 worksheets in a workbook.

A worksheet is organized in rows and columns, with each column creating a separate field within each row. The organization of a worksheet is based on the columnar pad (see Figure 14-1). Columnar pads have a variety of formats and uses, such as accounting ledgers, checkbook registers, receipts, invoices, and the like. All columnar pads use columns and rows to organize data.

As shown in Figure 14-2, a worksheet in an electronic spreadsheet application, like the columnar pad, is arranged in *rows* (horizontal) and *columns* (vertical).

FIGURE 14-1

A paper columnar pad was the source of the basic idea used to organize data in an electronic spreadsheet application.

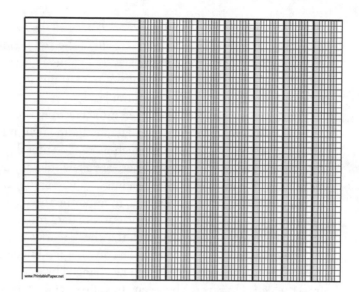

The rows are numbered top to bottom, and the columns are lettered left to right. The intersection of a row and a column creates a *cell*, which is the data unit of a spreadsheet. Everything entered into a worksheet—data, formulas, and formatting—is contained in a cell.

Structuring a Well-Organized Worksheet

When setting up a worksheet, which is generally done with a particular purpose in mind, you should consider several points, including these:

- Organize data logically to support readability.
- Label rows, columns, and the worksheet clearly and effectively.
- Input accurate data into worksheet cells.

FIGURE 14-2

A spreadsheet organizes data into rows and columns.

	A	B	C	D	E	F
1		Column 1	Column 2	Quarter	Year-to-Date	
2	Row 1	123	4566	4588	9277	
3	Row 2	234	6512	6655	13401	
4	Salesperson	546	7531	7722	15799	
5	Representative	842	9542	9859	20243	
6	Subtotal	1745	28151	28824	58720	
7						

Inserting and Modifying Data into Cells

The value displayed by a cell is the result of the cell's content. If text or a data value is entered into a cell, the cell displays that value. However, if a calculation is entered into the cell as a formula, the results of the formula are displayed (see Chapter 15 for more information on worksheet formulas).

For the most part, data is entered into cells from the keyboard, one cell at a time. A cell can hold a variety of data, including text, numbers, dates, percentages, monetary values, formulas, and much more. To enter data into a cell, simply click into the cell and begin typing. There are a few rules for data entry, especially when working with formulas, but for headings, values, and other general data, just type in the data or text needed, keeping in mind the three considerations listed in the preceding section. To complete the entry of data into a cell, press the ENTER key or one of the arrow keys, or else click the check mark to the left of the formula bar.

The existing data in a cell can be edited or modified as needed. Data entered into a cell, or even a range of cells, can be changed by re-entering the data or formula into the cell. However, when you click into a cell, its contents are displayed on the Formula bar, which is located just above the cell area (see Figure 14-3). The Formula bar is a better place to edit or modify the contents of a cell. After a cell's contents have been modified, you have two choices for saving the new data: either click the check mark icon to the left of the formula bar or press the ENTER key on the keyboard. Should you wish to cancel the modification and revert back to the cell's previous entry, click the "X" icon adjacent to the check mark icon.

Another method that can be used to enter values or text into a cell is using the fill cells function of the spreadsheet application. The Fill function in Excel 2007 can be used to fill cells in any direction from one or more cells containing the first few entries of a series. For example, if "January" is entered into cell A1 and "February" is entered into cell B1, selecting cells A1 and B1 and using the fill handle (the small box in the lower-right corner [the cursor changes to a plus sign]) of cell B1, you can fill in the remainder of the months of the year in cells C1 through L1. This same function will fill in the days of the week, the hours in a day, a series of numeric values, and more.

FIGURE 14-3

The Formula bar on the Excel 2007 workspace

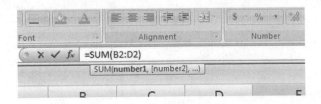

Manipulating the Structure of a Worksheet

In some situations, you may need to widen a column, increase the height of a row (or decrease the size of either), or combine or merge two or more cells to create a heading row or column. Spreadsheet application software includes the tools to facilitate these changes.

Change Column or Row Size

In addition to entering text, data, or a formula into a worksheet cell, you can also change the structure of a worksheet by making its rows taller or shorter or making its columns wider or narrower. Changing the height of a worksheet row or the width of a worksheet column directly changes the cells in the row or column, or both, that is modified. Figure 14-4 shows the worksheet shown earlier in Figure 14-2 with row 3 adjusted to an increased row height and column D adjusted to a narrower column width. Notice that the results of the data and formulas in the cells of column D are no longer able to display because the cells are too narrow. This is indicated by the "###" displayed in each cell.

To change the width of a column or the height of a row, you have three primary methods to choose from:

- **AutoFit options** The width of a column or the height of a row can be set to automatically adjust to the width or height of the longest or tallest data string entered or to be displayed in any cell in the column or row.

- **Format Cells menu** If the width or height of a single cell is adjusted, the corresponding row and column sizes are automatically adjusted as well. Figure 14-5 shows the Format Cells menu of Excel 2007.

- **Manual resizing** Rows and columns (and all of their cells) can be automatically resized to fit their contents by moving the cursor over the top or bottom border of a row label or the right border of a column label to

---

FIGURE 14-4

A worksheet showing the height of row 3 and the width of column D modified

	A	B	C	D	E	F
1		Column 1	Column 2	uarte	Year-to-Date	
2	Row 1	123	4566	###	9277	
3	Row 2	234	6512	###	13401	
4	Salesperson	546	7531	###	15799	
5	Representative	842	9542	###	20243	
6	Subtotal	1745	28151	###	58720	
7						

FIGURE 14-5

The Format Cells
menu displayed
by Excel 2007

display the Horizontal Split (H-Split) or the Vertical Split (V-Split) cursor
(see Figure 14-6). Click and hold the cursor and drag the row or column to
the size you want or double-click the cursor to automatically adjust the row or
column using the AutoFit function.

The process used to change the width of a column is essentially the same one
used to increase or decrease the height of a row, except that the cursor changes into
the H-Split.

exam
watch
You may be asked to set the width of a worksheet column to a specific size. If you do encounter this question on the exam, use the column resizing options of the Format button in the Cell group and not the V-split icon.

FIGURE 14-6

The V-Split cursor
can be used to
change the width
of a worksheet
column.

Merging Cells

To combine or merge two or more cells of a row or column, different processes are used, depending on the direction of the merge. To merge cells of a single row and center-align the content in the leftmost of the cells across the merged cells, highlight the cells to be merged, either horizontally, vertically, or both, and then click the Merge & Center button in the Alignment group of the Home tab.

Inserting and Deleting Cells, Rows, and Columns

Although a spreadsheet worksheet has ample cells, rows, and columns for just about any use, occasionally you may wish to insert one of these elements in a particular area of a worksheet to add additional data or calculations. The processes used for inserting a cell, row, or column, and perhaps even a worksheet are roughly the same, but each has its own particular steps. The processes used to insert these elements into a worksheet are as follows:

- ■ **Insert cells** To insert a cell into a worksheet, click into the cell that you wish to insert a new cell either to the left or above, right-click the cell, choose Insert, and then choose either Shift Cells Right or Shift Cells Down to add the new cell, moving the adjacent cells either to the right or down.

- ■ **Insert rows or columns** To insert a row or column into a worksheet, click the row or column designator (either a number or a letter) on the left side or the top of the worksheet to select an entire row or column, right-click the selected row or column, and then click Insert to add the element. You can also insert a row or column by right-clicking a cell, clicking Insert, and then choosing either Entire Row or Entire Column, depending on which you wish to insert.

- ■ **Insert worksheet** Should you need more than the default number of worksheets in a workbook, you can click the Insert Worksheet tab on the Tab row at the bottom of the workspace to add a new worksheet at the end of the existing worksheet. You can also use the shortcut keys SHIFT-F11 to insert a new worksheet before the active worksheet.

If you insert a worksheet into a workbook, you may want to name the worksheet by entering a unique name on its tab. To name, or rename, a worksheet, double-click its tab and enter the name you wish to assign to it.

Should you wish to delete a cell, row, column, or worksheet, use the following steps:

■ **Delete cell**   To delete a cell (and its contents, if any), right-click the cell to be deleted, choose Delete from the pop-up menu, and choose between Shift Cells Up or Shift Cells Left to delete the cell and shift the adjacent cells accordingly.

■ **Delete row or column**   Click the row or column designator to select the row or column to be deleted, right-click the selected row or column, and click Delete. Remember that if you delete a row or column with content in its cells, the content is removed as well.

■ **Delete worksheet**   To delete a worksheet from a workbook, first check that the worksheet to be deleted isn't linked to any other worksheets in the workbook or any external workbooks. If the worksheet can be deleted without causing problems elsewhere, right-click the tab of the worksheet you wish to delete and choose Delete. If the worksheet contains any data, you are prompted to verify that this is what you intended to do. If so, click Yes to complete the deletion.

Another way you can insert or move rows and columns is through the copy or cut and paste process. To copy or cut a row or column, click the row (number) or column (letter) designator to select the row or column, right-click the selected area, and choose either Cut or Copy as you need to copy or move the selected cells to the Clipboard. You can then click into the first cell in a column (Row 1) or the first cell in a row (Column A), right-click the cell, and choose Paste to place the row or column, replacing its contents. If you wish to insert the row or column above or to the right of the selected cell, choose Insert Copied Cells from the pop-up menu.

Formatting Worksheet Content

In the same way that text can be formatted in a word processing document, data in a worksheet can be formatted for emphasis, readability, and style. There are two levels of formatting that can be applied to data in a spreadsheet: cell and worksheet. Cell formatting changes the appearance characteristics of data in one or more cells, and as you might guess, worksheet formatting changes the appearance of the worksheet on the whole.

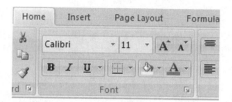

The standard character formatting styles, including bold, italics, underline, font and font size and color, can be applied to the data in any cell or range of cells. In Excel 2007, the character formatting features are located in two groups on the Home tab of the Excel 2007 Ribbon.

The Excel 2007 Font group, shown in Figure 14-7, contains the text formatting most commonly used including Bold, Italics, Underline, Borders, Fill color, Font color, Font, and Font size, along with tools to increase or decrease the font size of the data. To apply these character formatting effects, click into a cell or select a range of cells and then click the button of the formatting effect you wish to apply.

You can also apply formatting to one or more cells using a preset formatting style generally available with a spreadsheet application. For example, Excel 2007 has a variety of predefined cell styles that can be applied to a single cell or a range of selected cells. These styles are available on the Cell Styles Gallery (see Figure 14-8) that is accessed from the Cell Styles button in the Styles group of the Excel 2007 Ribbon.

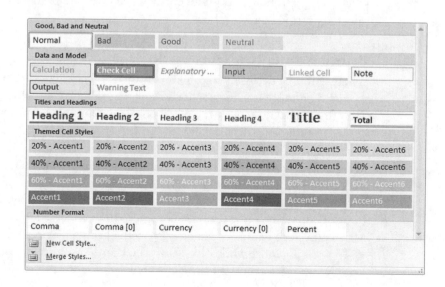

To apply a cell style to one or more cells, either click into a single cell or select a range of cells and then click the cell style you wish to use. You can sample the effect of a cell style in Excel 2007 by hovering the mouse pointer over the thumbnail sample of a particular cell style.

To set the style of an entire worksheet, you can apply a particular cell style to the whole worksheet, or you can open a new workbook based on a particular workbook template that predefines the style and formatting of its worksheets and cells.

Although it's not technically a cell formatting function, the Word Wrap feature can alter the height or width of a cell that contains text. This feature, which is located on the Home tab of the Excel 2007 Ribbon, uses the width of a cell (actually the column width) to insert soft line returns in the text to force it to fit into the cell, even if on multiple lines within the cell. Because the text wraps around to new lines within a cell, the height of the cell (actually the row height) can change with the amount of text entered into the cell.

Printing Spreadsheet Data

After all of the calculations are completed, all or part of a worksheet needs to be printed for reference and sharing purposes. While a worksheet can be shared electronically, there are times and situations where a printed copy of a worksheet's information works better than an electronic copy, such as when you want to share only the results and not the detail data used to produce the results. The following sections explain how to print an entire workbook, one or more worksheets, or a selected portion of a worksheet.

Printing an Entire Workbook

Rarely will it be necessary to print an entire workbook, but there are situations where a printed or hard-copy document showing a workbook's contents can be useful, such as a printed backup copy of the workbook's data, formulas, or calculated results.

To print the displayed data and results of an entire Excel 2007 workbook (all of the worksheets in a workbook), the process used is fairly straightforward. The print functions in Excel 2007 are located on the Microsoft Office button's menu (see Figure 14-9), which is displayed by clicking the Microsoft Office button. The option to print an entire workbook is located on the Print dialog box that is displayed by selecting the Print option of the Print option's submenu, which is located in the left pane of the Microsoft Office button's menu, to display the Print dialog box, shown in Figure 14-10.

To print an entire workbook, select the Print An Entire Workbook option in the Print What section of the Print dialog box (see Figure 14-10) and then click OK.

FIGURE 14-9

The Print options
of the Microsoft
Office button in
Excel 2007

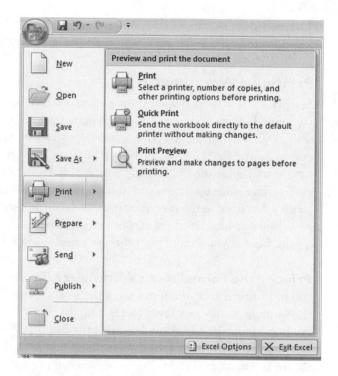

FIGURE 14-10

The Microsoft
Office 2007 Print
dialog box

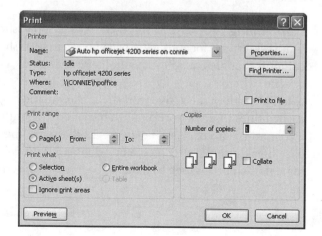

The worksheets of the workbook are printed in the order of their physical sequence (as indicated on the Tab bar) using the page break settings of each worksheet.

Printing a Worksheet

Essentially, this is the default print setting of nearly all spreadsheet applications. In fact, you don't really have to do much more than select Print to print the content of the active spreadsheet. To print an entire worksheet, you can select the Quick Print option on the Print menu (see Figure 14-9) or you can enter the shortcut command CTRL-P to display the Print dialog box and click OK.

You have some options as to just what is printed when you print a worksheet. The process described in the preceding paragraph can be used to print the displayed data of a worksheet. However, there may be occasions when you want to print the formulas in a worksheet or you wish to print the worksheet using a certain page break pattern.

Printing the Formulas of a Worksheet   To print the formulas in a worksheet, you must first display the formulas of the worksheet in the workspace. In Excel 2007, the formulas can be displayed by clicking the Show Formulas option in the Formula Auditing group on the Formulas tab of the Excel 2007 Ribbon. Selecting the Show Formulas option changes the display of the active worksheet to something like that shown in Figure 14-11. At this point, you can print the worksheet using the standard printing process.

Controlling Worksheet Page Breaks   Spreadsheet applications all define standard settings for automatic page breaks in worksheets. The number of rows or columns that are bound by an automatic page break varies by application, but in general, where an automatic page break occurs is controlled by the row height and column width of the active worksheet. Automatic page breaks are indicated by dashed lines inserted horizontally after a row (height of page) and vertically after a column (width of page). Figure 14-12 illustrates the dashed line of an automatic page break inserted after a column where a page break occurs. However, typically the same dashed line is used to indicate page breaks inserted by the user as well.

FIGURE 14-11

The Show Formulas option applied to an Excel 2007 worksheet

	Jan	Feb	March	Quarter Total
Ron	123	4566	4588	=SUM(B2:D2)
Connie	234	6512	6655	=SUM(B3:D3)
Lindsey	546	7531	7722	=SUM(B4:D4)
Camryn	842	9542	9859	=SUM(B5:D5)
Subtotal	=SUM(B2:B5)	=SUM(C2:C5)	=SUM(D2:D5)	=SUM(B6:D6)

FIGURE 14-12

Automatic
page breaks are
indicated by
dashed lines in
Excel 2007.

G	H
ment 6	Mid-Ter
0	9
0	8
8	7
1	5
0	7
5	8

To get a sense of where the spreadsheet application has inserted page breaks or where any page breaks you have inserted are occurring, you can use the standard Print Preview function. However, in Excel 2007, you can change the workspace to the Page Break Preview (shown in Figure 14-13), on which you can drag the page breaks to where you wish them to occur in the worksheet.

The page break indicator lines are typically not displayed until you have used the print preview to view a worksheet or have actually printed the worksheet.

Printing a Portion of a Worksheet   In situations where you want to print only a selected range of cells from a worksheet, the process involves selecting the range of cells to be printed and choosing the Selection option in the Print What section of the Print dialog box (refer back to Figure 14-10 earlier in this section).

Scale to Fit   On worksheets that may be too wide (too many columns) or too long (too many rows) to fit onto a printed page easily, you can use the Scale to Fit option in Excel 2007 to reduce the height or width of the worksheet data so that it does fit the page. Scale to Fit allows you to reduce the scale of the worksheet print area's width so that it fits horizontally on a printed page with the length printed on multiple pages; or you can reduce the print area's height to a single page and let the

FIGURE 14-13

The Excel 2007
Page Break
Preview

	A	B	C	D	E	F	G	H	I	J
1	Student Name	Assignment 1	Assignment 2	Assignment 3	Assignment 4	Assignment 5	Assignment 6	Mid-Term Exam	Final Exam	Average Score
2	Ron	81	84	90	75	50	80	90	50	75
3	Carly	50	80	88	81	84	90	88	84	81
4	Connie	84	90	75	50	80	88	75	80	78
5	Jeana	90	75	50	80	88	81	50	88	75
6	Jessica	88	81	84	80	75	50	75	75	76
7	Markus	80	88	81	84	90	75	81	90	84
8	Rob	75	50	80	88	81	84	80	81	77
9										
10										
11			Page 1						Page 2	
12										
13										
14										
15										

width print on additional pages; or you can reduce both the height and the width
to print the worksheet on a single page (although the font may end up so small that
you may not be able to read it).

Repeating Rows or Columns   It is possible to repeat one or more rows or
columns on each page of a printed worksheet. These rows or columns may contain row
or column headings, constant values, or general instructions or information regarding
the data in the worksheet. To designate the rows or columns you wish to repeat on each
printed page, select them using the tools on the Sheet tab of the Page Setup dialog box.

Headers and Footers   Another printing feature available on the Page Setup
dialog box is the ability to add headers and footers when you print a worksheet. On
the Headers/Footers tab of the Page Setup dialog box, you can choose to have no
headers or footers, choose an existing or previously used header or footer from a pull-
down list, or create a custom header or footer. Controls are also available to create
different headers or footers for the first printed page or for even and odd pages.

Common Uses of Spreadsheets

Spreadsheet applications are very useful for organizing, cross-referencing, and
calculating information. Spreadsheet software was developed initially as an
accounting tool and is still frequently used for that purpose. However, a spreadsheet
can be used for a wide variety of applications. Some of the most common uses follow:

- **Budgeting**   A spreadsheet is commonly used to develop budgets for home
  or office, both simple and complex. In addition, actual expenditures can be
  added to a budget worksheet to monitor or analyze the planned versus actual
  states of the budget.

- **Data collection and organization**   A spreadsheet can be used to collect,
  organize, and sort data collected from virtually any quantifiable measurement,
  such as counts, physical measurements, monetary amounts, and more.

- **Financial statements**   This is perhaps one of the most common uses for
  spreadsheet software. The matrix organization and the embedded functions
  of a spreadsheet allow for easy construction of a balance sheet, income
  statement, or other financial analysis and reporting documents.

- **Forecasts and projections**   Using the built-in functions of a spreadsheet,
  a calculated value can be generated and used as a projection of what may
  happen in the future.

- **Graphics**   Its built-in capability to produce graphics and charts from the data in a worksheet adds to the power and value of a spreadsheet application. Data is often better understood, in terms of past performance, trends, or future projections, in a graphical form.

- **Inventory**   Another common use for a spreadsheet is tracking the inventory or value of items. Regardless of whether the items being tracked are production parts or a personal collection, a spreadsheet provides for a virtually unlimited number of fields or characteristic values for the item on a particular row.

- **Statistical sampling**   Using the built-in mathematical, financial, and logical functions of a spreadsheet, data can be analyzed in a variety of ways to produce a solution, index, or central tendency indicators, such as averages, medians, distributions, future or present value, and more.

- **What-ifs**   A spreadsheet can be used to project the impact of a future value, quantity, or contingency on an existing range of data and its calculated results. After the new value is plugged into a worksheet and the new results are reviewed, the worksheet changes can be discarded or saved as a new workbook.

The types of uses in this list are generic and, in many cases, overlapping. Spreadsheets can be used for virtually anything that involves the organization of data into a list, table, or matrix, including to-do lists, scratch pad calculations, sequencing task lists, organizing events, tracking the progress of a project, or the allocation of resources. As I stated earlier in the chapter, if you had to learn only one application, a spreadsheet is the one to learn.

CERTIFICATION SUMMARY

The worksheet workspace of an electronic spreadsheet application is arranged in a tabular form, dividing into intersecting rows and columns. Much like a paper columnar sheet, data can be organized in a matrix format with each row holding the data of a single entity and each column segregating the entity's data into fields. The intersection of a row and column is a cell.

Like other personal productivity applications, an electronic spreadsheet can be formatted visually and printed or distributed. Spreadsheet applications have a wide range of practical uses in an equally wide range of industries and organizations.

✔ TWO-MINUTE DRILL

Working with the Data, Format, and Structure of a Worksheet

❑ Spreadsheet applications are organized into a set of independent worksheets that together constitute a workbook.

❑ A worksheet is organized in rows and columns, with each column creating a separate field within each row. The intersection of a row and column creates a cell, into which data is entered.

❑ The width of columns and the height of rows can be changed to suit the user's needs. Columns and rows can also be merged as needed. To change the width of a column or the height of a row, three methods can be used: AutoFit, the Format Cells menu, or using manual resizing. To merge two or more cells, use the Merge & Center feature.

❑ There are two levels of formatting that can be applied to data in a spreadsheet: cell and worksheet. Cell formatting changes the appearance characteristics of data in one or more cells, and worksheet formatting changes the appearance of the worksheet as a whole.

❑ To print an entire workbook, the Print An Entire Workbook option is selected on the Print dialog box. The worksheets of the workbook are printed in the order of their physical sequence.

❑ The default print setting of nearly all spreadsheet applications is to print an entire worksheet. The shortcut command CTRL-P can be used to access the Print dialog box.

❑ To print the formulas in a worksheet, you must first display the formulas. Once the formulas are displayed in the workspace, they can be printed.

❑ Spreadsheet applications define standard settings for automatic page breaks in worksheets, which vary by application, row height, and column width. Automatic page breaks are indicated by dashed lines inserted horizontally and vertically. The same dashed line is used to indicate page breaks inserted by the user.

❑ To print a selected range of cells from a worksheet, the range of cells is selected and then the Selection option of the Print function is used.

❑ Spreadsheet applications are very useful for organizing, cross-referencing, and calculating information. Spreadsheet software was developed initially as an accounting tool and is still frequently used for that purpose.

❑ A spreadsheet can be used for a wide variety of applications. Some of the common uses are budgeting, data collection and organization, financial statements, forecasts and projections, graphics, inventory, statistical sampling, and what-ifs.

SELF TEST

The following questions are intended to help you be sure that you understand the material included in this chapter. Read the questions and the answer choices carefully.

Working with the Data, Format, and Structure of a Worksheet

1. What are the major elements that make up a spreadsheet workbook?

    A. Spreadsheets

    B. Worksheets

    C. Workspaces

    D. Cell ranges

2. The intersection of what two spreadsheet organizational elements creates a cell?

    A. Row

    B. Range

    C. Tab

    D. Column

3. Which of the following cannot be used to change the height of an Excel 2007 spreadsheet row?

    A. AutoFit

    B. Format Cells

    C. Resize

    D. H-Split cursor

4. What command feature can be used to merge two or more cells in Excel 2007?

    A. Merge Cells

    B. Combine Cells

    C. Merge & Center

    D. Cells cannot be merged in Excel 2007

5. What are the two levels of formatting that can be applied to a spreadsheet?

    A. Worksheet

    B. Workbook

    C. Cell

    D. Row

6. True or False: In order print all of the contents of a workbook, each individual worksheet must be printed individually.

   A. True

   B. False

7. What spreadsheet element is printed by the default print settings of nearly all spreadsheet applications?

   A. Cell

   B. Row

   C. Column

   D. Worksheet

   E. Workbook

   F. Page

8. In Excel 2007, what shortcut command can be used to display the Print dialog box?

   A. CTRL-A

   B. CTRL-P

   C. ALT-P

   D. CTRL-ALT-DEL

9. What action must first be taken before you can print the formulas in an Excel 2007 worksheet?

   A. Select the Print Formulas command.

   B. Display the macros in a worksheet.

   C. Display the formulas in a worksheet.

   D. Formulas cannot be printed in Excel 2007.

10. What display element is used to indicate a page break (either automatic or manually inserted) on an Excel 2007 worksheet?

   A. Solid line

   B. Dotted line

   C. Double line

   D. Dashed line

11. True or False: It is not possible to print only a selected range of cells in a spreadsheet application.

   A. True

   B. False

12. Which of the following are common uses for a spreadsheet application?

    A. Cross-referencing

    B. Budgeting

    C. Accounting

    D. Inventory

    E. Forecasts and what-ifs

    F. All of the above

    G. None of the above

SELF TEST ANSWERS

Working with the Data, Format, and Structure of a Worksheet

1. ☑ **B.** A spreadsheet workbook is made up of at least one worksheet.
   ☒ **A, C,** and **D** are incorrect. A spreadsheet is not made up of itself; the worksheet is displayed in the workspace, but the workspace is not a part of the workbook; and cell ranges can be selected on an individual worksheet.

2. ☑ **A** and **D.** On a worksheet, the intersection of rows and columns creates cells.
   ☒ **B** and **C** are incorrect. A range of cells consists of cells in one or more rows, in one or more columns, or both; a tab is associated with an individual worksheet.

3. ☑ **C.** Excel 2007 doesn't include a Resize feature that can be used to change the height of a row.
   ☒ **A, B,** and **D** are incorrect. AutoFit, the row height setting on the Format Cells dialog box, and the use of the H-Split cursor can each be used to change the height of a row.

4. ☑ **C.** The Merge & Center command in Excel 2007 can be used to merge two or more selected cells and center the contents of the leftmost cell across the resulting merged cells.
   ☒ **A, B,** and **D** are incorrect. Excel 2007 doesn't include a Merge Cells command, nor does it include a Combine Cells command. Cells can definitely be merged in Excel 2007.

5. ☑ **A** and **C.** The two levels of formatting that can be applied in a spreadsheet are cell and worksheet. Cell formatting affects individual cells, and worksheet formatting changes the look and style of the entire worksheet.
   ☒ **B** and **D** are incorrect. A workbook is a collection of worksheets, and each worksheet can have a different format. A selected row is formatted using cell formatting.

6. ☑ **B.** An entire workbook can be printed.
   ☒ **A** is incorrect. Worksheets can be printed individually, but the entire workbook can be printed, which prints each worksheet in their physical order.

7. ☑ **D.** If no changes are made to the default print settings, an entire worksheet is printed when the Print or Quick Print function is chosen.
   ☒ **A, B, C, E,** and **F** are incorrect. Each of these spreadsheet elements can be printed individually using the settings of the Print function. To print a cell, row, column, or page, the Selection option is selected. The Print An Entire Workbook option can be selected to print all of the worksheets in a workbook.

8. ☑ **B.** The shortcut command CTRL-P is common to all Office 2007 applications as well as any other Windows applications.

☒ **A, C,** and **D** are incorrect. CTRL-A is used to select all of the content in a document; ALT-P is used in Excel 2007 to display the Page Layout tab on the Excel 2007 Ribbon; and CTRL-ALT-DEL can be used to display the Windows Task Manager.

9. ☑ **C.** Before the formulas can be printed from an Excel 2007 worksheet, they must first be displayed.

☒ **A, B,** and **D** are incorrect. Excel 2007 doesn't include a Print Formulas command; displaying the macros in a worksheet doesn't cause the formulas to be visible; and if they are first displayed, formulas can definitely be printed from an Excel 2007 worksheet.

10. ☑ **D.** Page breaks are indicated in an Excel 2007 worksheet by dashed lines inserted horizontally and vertically to show the boundaries of each page.

☒ **A, B,** and **C** are incorrect. Page breaks use a dashed line and none of these line types.

11. ☑ **B.** A range of selected cells can be printed using the Selection option of the Print function in Excel 2007.

☒ **A** is incorrect. A selected range of cells can be printed.

12. ☑ **F.** A spreadsheet can be used for almost any application, except perhaps producing a professional-looking letter, which should be prepared by a word processing application for best results.

☒ **A, B, C, D, E,** and **G** are incorrect. Answers A through E are all valid uses for a spreadsheet application, but individually they do not best answer the question. Therefore, if answers A through F are valid answers, then answer G is obviously incorrect.

15

Manipulating Data in a Spreadsheet

Spreadsheets are wonderfully powerful tools, but only if you know how to enter, arrange, and manipulate data using their features, functions, tools, and commands. The power of a spreadsheet is probably best demonstrated through formulas and functions that allow you to calculate simple or very complex results and then arrange the data to provide the information you need.

In this chapter, we look at the different ways in which formulas, functions, sorting, and filtering can be used to calculate a result, sort data into a relative sequence, filter data to view data related to a single value, and project new outcomes. To understand formulas, sorts, filters, and the rest, we first need to review a few formula basics and how cells are referenced.

CERTIFICATION OBJECTIVE

Manipulate Data Using Formulas and Functions

3.1   Be able to sort data, manipulate data using formulas and functions and create simple charts.

Although Excel 2007 includes a wide variety of formulas for specific financial, statistical, mathematical, logical, and date and time calculations, a formula can also be a simple arithmetic function as well. Many worksheet calculations involve nothing more than simply adding, subtracting, multiplying, or dividing numbers or cell contents.

Before we get too deep into formulas and functions, we really should discuss the formats that can be used for numerical data in a worksheet. Although they are mostly formula or function proof, some formats can produce unexpected results when paired with other numerical formats. For example, you divide a short date field by a fraction and get a currency amount. The formats available by default in Excel 2007 are (listed in alphabetical order with no relative importance): Accounting, Currency, Fraction, General, Long date, Number, Percentage, Scientific, Short date, Special, Text, and Time. Table 15-1 shows examples of the data to which the more commonly used of these formats are applied and the result.

TABLE 15-1	Number Format	Data	Result
Examples of Excel 2007 Number Formats	Accounting	1234.56	$1,234.56
	Currency	–1234.56	$(1234.56)
	Long Date	1234.56	Monday, May 18, 1903
	Number	1234.56	1234.56
	Percentage	1.23456	123.456%
	Short Date	1234.56	5/18/1903
	Time	1234.56	1:26:24 PM

In any of the number formats, the number of decimal places can be controlled using the Increase decimals or Decrease decimals button on the Home tab of the Excel 2007 Ribbon or using the settings on the Format Cells dialog box.

Formula Basics

A formula is a mathematical statement that produces a calculated result. The result can be a conditional result, like true or false, or a value. Generally, spreadsheet applications indicate a formula with an equal sign (=) in the first position of an entry. The equal sign (or in some cases, a plus sign or a minus sign as well) indicates to the spreadsheet application that the characters that follow are a calculation or a comparison of some sort. Nearly all spreadsheet applications include a variety of formulas and functions that can be used for general, mathematical, statistical, engineering, and financial calculations, among others. However, before we get too deep into what formulas are typically available, we should first look at a basic arithmetic formula and the arithmetic operators involved, so that we have a general understanding of how a formula is constructed.

Arithmetic Operators

The formulas and functions (a function is a predefined and built-in formula) of a spreadsheet application are built around four basic arithmetic operators: addition (+), subtraction (-), multiplication (*), and division (/). Spreadsheets used these operators in the same way they are used to calculate a result manually. In addition to these four basic operators, two more operators are generally available: percentage (%) and exponentiation (^). Table 15-2 lists the arithmetic operators generally available in spreadsheet applications along with an example of how each is used.

TABLE 15-2	Operator	Action	Example
Arithmetic Operators Used in Spreadsheet Applications	+	Addition	=2+2, =C2+G7
	/	Division	=10/2, =A5/15
	^	Exponentiation	=2^2, =F5^3
	*	Multiply	=3*5, =R7*S4
	%	Percentage	=35%
	-	Subtraction	=10-3, =B10-F11

Operator Precedence

Spreadsheet applications use a specific priority or precedence for performing the actions of arithmetic operators. Certain operators have priority over other operators. The operators are actually divided into three sets: multiply and divide, add and subtract, and exponentiation. The percentage operator is applied separately after all other operations. The multiply and divide operations are performed first left-to-right on a whichever-comes-first basis, left to right. Then the addition and subtraction operations are performed in the same manner; followed by the exponentiation operation.

For example, you may have expected a result of 15 from the statement =15+6/3-2*3, but a spreadsheet application will evaluate this statement to 11. This is because the divide and multiply operations are performed first and then the subtraction and addition operations, in this order:

- 6/3 = 2
- 2*3 = 6
- 15+2 = 17
- 17-6 = 11

In effect, the formula was evaluated as if it were written as =15+(6/3)-(2*3) with the operations inside the parentheses performed first. Parentheses are used to alter the precedence of the operations. When an operation or statement is enclosed in parentheses, it is evaluated before other operations. In a statement with more than one set of operations enclosed in parentheses, like the example given earlier in this paragraph, the operations inside the parentheses are evaluated in order, left to right. After the parenthetical statements are evaluated, the standard operator precedence is applied to calculate a result.

Here's another example: =B4-A5*((D2/A8)+D16)-B7. To evaluate this statement, a spreadsheet performs the following steps:

1. The value in cell D2 is divided by the value in cell A8.
2. The result of Step 1 and the value in cell D16 are added together.
3. The value in cell A5 is multiplied by the result of Step 2.
4. The result of Step 3 is subtracted from the value in cell B4.
5. The value in B7 is subtracted is subtracted from the result of Step 4.

If parentheses are embedded inside other parentheses, like in the preceding example, the innermost embedded parenthetical operation is evaluated first.

Cell References

Virtually all spreadsheet applications use two types of cell references or addresses in formulas:

- Relative cell references
- Absolute cell references

A relative cell reference remains relative to a given worksheet position whenever it is copied or cut and pasted into a new location. An absolute cell reference remains constant to an exact worksheet location at all times. In addition, some spreadsheet applications, including Excel 2007, make an R1C1 reference available that can be used to reference the content of another cell using a relative offset. Each of these cell reference types is discussed in the sections that follow.

Relative Cell References

A relative cell reference, which is the default cell referencing method in spreadsheet applications, adjusts the cell addresses in a formula whenever the formula is copied to a new cell location. For example, if the formula =D12+E12 is entered into cell C12 and this formula is then copied to cell D15, the formula in cell D15 is =E15+F15 (see Figure 15-1). Why? When the formula =D12+E12 is copied to a cell D15, the relative offset from C12 to D15 is two columns to the left and two rows down from cell C12. When a formula containing relative cell references is copied to a new cell, the relative cell references inside the formula are adjusted for each of these distances. Likewise, if the formula in cell C12 (=D12+E12) is copied

FIGURE 15-1

The results of relative cell references for a copied formula

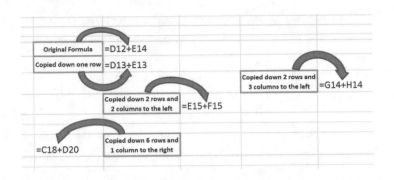

to cell C13, the relative reference offset is one row and the resulting formula in cell C13 is =D13+E13 (see Figure 15-1). The column references (D and E) remain the same because the reference offset is only in rows.

Let's check your understanding of relative cell references at this point. What would be the result if the formula =D12+E12 in cell C12 is copied to cell F14? Moving from cell C12 to cell F14, the formula is displaced three columns (C to F) to the left and two rows (12 to 14). If your answer is that the formula in cell F14 is =G14+H14, you're correct and seem to understand relative cell references. If your answer is incorrect, study Figure 15-1 to understand the results shown.

on the
job

Cell references aren't case sensitive when used in a formula. Most spreadsheet applications automatically raise the alpha characters to uppercase in a formula. The formula =a1+b1 is the same as =A1+B1 or =a1+B1 or =A1+b1.

Absolute Cell References

The primary difference between a relative cell reference and an absolute cell reference is that an absolute cell reference remains constant no matter how far it's moved. Another difference is that an absolute cell reference must be coded as such to differentiate it from a relative reference.

Converting a relative cell reference into an absolute cell reference requires a dollar sign ($) be placed before each of the cell reference components (column and row) that you wish to lock into an absolute reference. For example, the absolute cell reference $A$1 locks the reference absolutely to cell A1. Table 15-3 lists the three absolute cell reference variations that can be used to completely lock, lock only the row reference, or lock only the column reference.

TABLE 15-3	Absolute Cell Reference Type	Example	Description
Absolute Cell Reference Variations	Complete lock to absolute reference	$A$2	Row and column references are absolutely locked to cell A2
	Lock only the row reference	A$2	Row reference locked to row 2, but column reference remains relative
	Lock only the column reference	$A2	Column reference locked to column A, but row reference remains relative

As indicated in Table 15-3, placing a dollar sign before a cell reference component (column or row) converts that part of the cell reference into an absolute reference. Regardless of where an absolute (or partially absolute) cell reference is copied, the component(s) that are coded with a dollar sign are locked and aren't relatively adjusted. If either component of the cell reference is not coded as absolute, it remains relative and is changed when the reference is copied to a new location.

You have two choices you can use to encode an absolute cell reference: manually enter the dollar signs in a formula or place the insertion point in the cell reference and press the F4 key on the keyboard. The F4 key is a three-step toggle that steps through the three absolute reference variations, starting with the absolute cell reference lock.

Just to be sure you understand absolute cell references, if the formula in cell C12 is =$D$12+$E12 and this formula is copied to cell F14, the result in F12 is =$D$12+$E14 (see Figure 15-2). Notice that only the row component of the second element was a relative reference, which is why that portion of the cell references in the formula changed.

RICI References

The R1C1 cell reference isn't common to all spreadsheet applications. This cell reference style is a hybrid that combines elements of both relative and absolute

The result of copying a formula containing absolute cell references

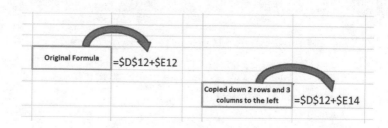

cell references. A spreadsheet application that provides for macro scripting or a programming language for creating custom macros, such as Visual Basic for Applications (VBA), will also support the use of the R1C1 reference style.

Entering and Modifying Formulas

The preceding sections described the syntax of a spreadsheet formula, which essentially defines how you enter a formula. Just to be sure, the first character entered for a formula is an equal sign (=) and the formula is entered immediately after it. However, from time to time, you may want to edit or change a formula after it has been entered. This process is basically the same as that used to enter the formula, but let's review a few of the basics.

A common feature of spreadsheet applications is the formula bar. Figure 15-3 shows the Excel 2007 Formula bar in which a formula can be edited or modified. To edit a cell formula, click the cell you want to edit and then make the changes needed in the formula bar. The same procedure is used to edit functions inserted into a cell. So, what is a function? Read on to the next section for that discussion.

Spreadsheet Functions

Perhaps the most valuable feature of any spreadsheet application is its collection of predefined and built-in functions. A function is a predefined formula that can be used to perform a specific calculation or action. In the sections that follow, the different types and categories of functions included with most spreadsheet applications are discussed.

Selecting a Function

Refer back to the Excel 2007 formula bar shown in Figure 15-3. Notice the *fx* symbol at the left end of the formula bar. Clicking this symbol displays the Insert Function dialog box, shown in Figure 15-4. On the Insert Function dialog box, you can search

FIGURE 15-3

The Excel 2007 formula bar

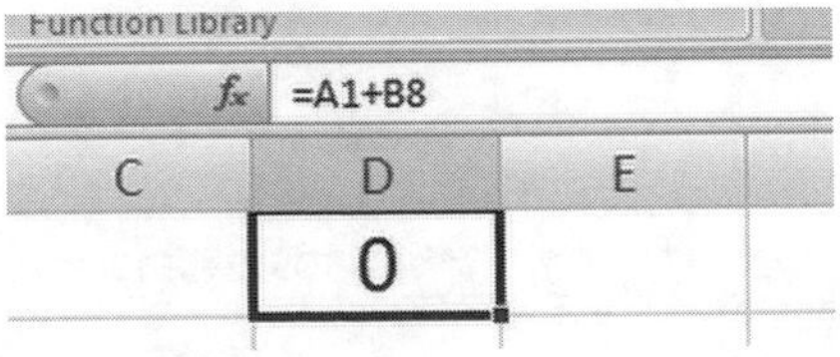

FIGURE 15-4

The Insert
Function symbol
and the formula
bar

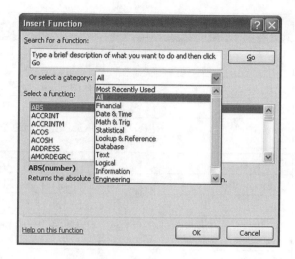

for or use the function categories list to find a specific function and then insert it on the formula bar. Figure 15-5 illustrates the results of selecting a function.

As shown in Figure 15-5, when a function is selected, its formula or function template is placed in the formula bar and the Function Arguments dialog box is displayed (see Figure 15-6). The Function Arguments dialog box then guides you through the process of selecting the cell or range of cells that are to be used as the arguments of the function.

Commonly Used Functions

Spreadsheet applications include a variety of functions that can be used to count, summarize, calculate, relate, or compare one or more values in a worksheet. Some spreadsheet applications have more functions than others, and if you need a specific set of functions, such as functions in categories to perform Financial, Statistical, Engineering, Mathematics, or other calculations, the number and variety of functions should be one of your criteria for selecting the spreadsheet application you'll use. Table 15-4 lists the more common function categories (see Figure 15-6) found in spreadsheets.

FIGURE 15-5

A function's
formula inserted
in the formula bar

TABLE 15-4	Category	Examples of Functions in This Category
Common Function Categories Included in Spreadsheet Applications	Cube	CUBEMEMBER, CUBESET, CUBESETCOUNT, CUBEVALUE
	Database	DAVERAGE, DCOUNT, DMAX, DMIN, DSTDEV, DSUM
	Date & Time	DAY, MONTH, NOW, TIME, WEEKDAY, YEAR
	Engineering	BIN2DEC, CONVERT, DEC2BIN, IMCOS, IMPOWER, IMPRODUCT
	Financial	IRR, FV, PMT, PV, RATE, YIELD
	Information	ISBLANK, ISEVEN, ISNUMBER, ISODD, ISTEXT, TYPE
	Logical	AND, IF, FALSE, NOT, OR, TRUE
	Lookup & Reference	CHOOSE, HLOOKUP, HYPERLINK, INDEX, MATCH, VLOOKUP
	Math & Trig	ABS, COS, EVEN, LOG, ODD, MULTINOMIAL
	Statistical	AVERAGE, COUNT, FDIST, FREQUENCY, MEDIAN, MODE
	Text	CHAR, CONCATENATE, FIND, LEFT, MID, RIGHT

It's doubtful that you would ever use all of the functions included in a spreadsheet application, but chances are that you will use one or two categories frequently. Every user has a different need, which is why such a wide array of function categories and functions are included in the spreadsheet.

FIGURE 15-6

The Function Arguments dialog box in Excel 2007

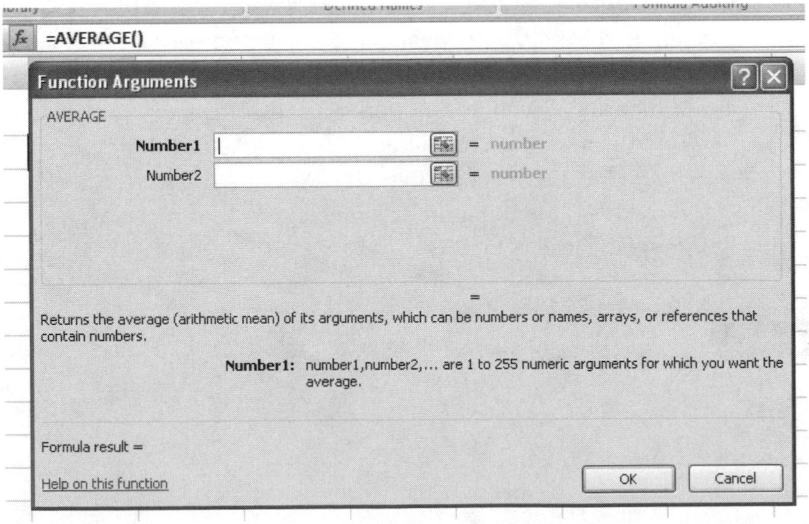

Another frequently used function in nearly all spreadsheet applications is the AutoSum tool. Represented in Excel 2007 with the mathematical symbol of sigma (Σ), this tool is available in the Editing group of the Home tab of the Excel 2007 Ribbon. To apply this tool, click into the cell in which you wish to place a total or a range of cells either above or the left of the selected cell, click the Sum icon, and then adjust the selection range automatically displayed by this function to group those cells you wish to include in the sum.

Common Formula and Function Issues and Errors

Functions can be very handy for specific calculations that involve fairly complex formulas. However, there are some issues, tips, and common errors that you should be aware of when using functions. The following sections outline some of the more common issues that can occur with the use of spreadsheet functions.

Literal Values vs. Cell References

Something to avoid when specifying a function's arguments is the use of literal values (such as 1, 123, or 12345) instead of cell references. For example, the AVERAGE function defines a relatively unlimited number of arguments (the actual limit is around 256).

The arguments of the AVERAGE function (and most other functions as well) can be entered in one of the following three forms:

- A literal value, such as =AVERAGE(12,10,45,83,2)
- A range of cells (the most commonly used argument for the AVERAGE function), such as =AVERAGE(A4:A35)
- A combination of cell references and literal values, such as =AVERAGE(A4:35,83,A2)

Entering literal values into a function, or even into a formula, removes the capability for the function or formula to be later used as part of a what-if simulation, because the values are hard-coded and don't change. However, if a single literal value is used, one that won't ever change, in combination with cell references, future calculations may still be valid.

Divide by Zero

A common occurrence, especially for formulas that involve division with a cell reference, is the divide by zero error. Whenever a cell contains the result "#DIV/0!" the dividend is either a null value or zero. While you are constructing a worksheet, this error can be a temporary issue until data is entered into the cells involved in the formula that include a division operation. In any case, however, a divide by zero error means only one thing: you tried to divide something by zero.

Circular References

A circular reference occurs whenever a formula involves its own cell in a calculation, directory or indirectly. For example, if the formula in cell D5 is =SUM(D1:D5), a circular reference error message is displayed (see Figure 15-7). Typically, a circular reference is caused by a data entry error, but in a case where you are attempting to execute an iterative calculation, you may need to change the formula settings for the spreadsheet to allow them. For most spreadsheet applications, iterative calculations are turned off by default.

Adding, Changing, or Removing Values

Before you remove one or more rows or columns or clear the contents of a cell or range of cells, be sure that the cells and especially the values in the cells aren't integral to a formula or function. After a row or column that was referenced in a formula or function is deleted, its reference is marked by the error indicator of "#REF!" This error condition tells you that a cell reference used in the formula or function in a particular cell is no longer available. However, as long as you undo the removal or deletion before you save the workbook, you can recover the original references. Otherwise, the formula or function must be corrected with the appropriate reference.

Inserting and Modifying Charts

The capability to create charts from the data in a worksheet is another important feature of a spreadsheet application. A chart is a representation of data in a graphical form that can be viewed for comparative or analytical purposes. A chart, which can only be as accurate as the data used to create it, provides a much better way to compare data, trends, and performance metrics than scanning the raw data in rows and columns.

FIGURE 15-7

The circular reference error message box displayed by Excel 2007

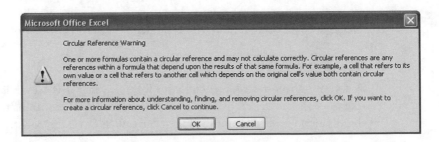

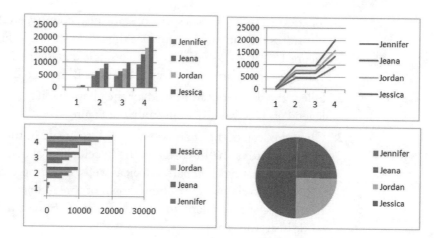

FIGURE 15-8

The four basic charts types supported by spreadsheet applications are column charts (upper left), line charts (upper right), bar charts (lower left), and pie charts (lower right).

Some spreadsheet applications offer more standard chart formats than others (for example, Excel 2007 supports eleven different chart types), but nearly all spreadsheet applications support four basic chart types: column, line, bar, and pie charts. Figure 15-8 shows an example of each of the four basic chart types.

Some chart types are better for comparing results, such as bar charts and column charts; some are better for evaluating trends, such as line charts; and others are great for showing proportion or percentage, such as a pie chart. The actual chart you use to depict data depends on two things: the data itself and the result you are trying to convey.

Creating a Chart in a Worksheet

The basic steps used to create a chart in a worksheet are essentially the same for almost all chart types. About the only preparation that needs to be made is to be sure the data to be used for the chart is oriented appropriately for the chart type to be created. Some chart types are specifically designed to use data that is arranged in rows, and some need the data arranged in columns.

Creating a chart in any of the more popular spreadsheet applications involves about the same steps as those used in Excel 2007, which follow:

1. Arrange the data to be used for the chart into the format the chart type to be created requires. Generally, data can be arranged into data series (each of which consists of a legend or title and its associated data values). A data series is typically arranged across a row with each cell (column) representing a unique time period (year, month, quarter, etc.), measurement (pounds, kilograms, feet, meters, miles, kilometers, etc.), event, or geographical

location (sales event, salesperson, state, city, country, etc.). Figure 15-9 illustrates the data used to produce the charts shown in Figure 15-8. In Figure 15-9, rows 2–5 each contain a single data series consisting of separate values for the quarters of a year in columns B through E.

2. Select the data series to be used for the chart, including both the data series legend and the values (as illustrated in Figure 15-9).

3. Click the icon of the chart type you wish to create in the Charts group (see Figure 15-10) of the Insert tab of the Excel 2007 Ribbon to display the chart gallery for that type of chart. Excel, as well as other spreadsheet applications, allows you to choose a two-dimensional or three-dimensional chart, and, in the case of a pie chart, an exploded view. The chart is created in the worksheet workspace.

4. The chart can be resized, repositioned, or edited as needed.

Formatting and Modifying a Chart

Virtually every part of a chart can be formatted or reformatted as you wish. There are two levels of formatting and modifications that can be performed on a chart: chart-level and content-level. Chart-level formatting means that you can change the chart type, chart title, color scheme, size, position, and even where the chart is located in the workbook. Content-level formatting and modifications are performed on the data, legends, and axis labels, as well as on the color of the bars, columns, lines, segments, and other chart elements.

Sorting and Filtering Worksheet Data

The data in a worksheet can be sequenced (sorted) on any of the data contained in one or more of its columns. The sort feature of a spreadsheet application can sort on any data type in the worksheet, including alphabetic data, numeric data, dates, or times.

FIGURE 15-9

Data arranged for use in producing a chart

	A	B	C	D	E
1		Qtr 1	Qtr 2	Qtr 3	Qtr 4
2	Jennifer	123	4566	4588	9277
3	Jeana	234	6512	6655	13401
4	Jordan	546	7531	7722	15799
5	Jessica	842	9542	9859	20243

FIGURE 15-10

A gallery of chart type variations provides for customization of a chart created in Excel 2007.

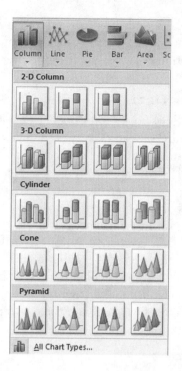

Another feature, loosely associated with sorting, is filtering. When a filter is applied to the data in a specific column, only the rows containing data matching the criteria of the filter are displayed. Spreadsheet applications perform filtering in slightly different ways, but the effect is the same. Excel 2007 creates sort and filter controls for each column that allow the data in the column to be selected, sorted, or both.

Sorting Data

Sorting the data in a worksheet or a portion of a worksheet allows you to order the data for ranking, sequence, or comparative purposes. Spreadsheet applications provide two primary options for sorting data: ascending order, which orders the data in a low-to-high (A to Z, 0 to 9, etc.) sequence, or descending order, which orders the data in a high-to-low (Z to A, 9 to 0, etc.) sequence. Some spreadsheet applications, like Excel 2007, also allow you to order cells based on cell formatting characteristics, such as cell color, font color, and even cell icons, if used.

The process used to sort data involves three basic steps: select the data to be ordered, define the sort criteria, and execute the sort. Excel 2007 offers three methods to perform a sort: a quick sort that can be performed from a pop-up menu, quick sorts on the Data tab, and using the Sort command button, which allows for the definition of fairly complex sort criteria with up to 63 sort levels.

Filtering Data

Filtering allows you to limit the data displayed to only that data meeting specified criteria. Filtering can be very useful when you are working with a large worksheet that contains a variety of related data values, such as an inventory, sales data, or even personnel or student data. For example, if a worksheet column contains product information for the products falling into a large number of product categories, filtering the data to show only one or perhaps just a few of the categories allows you to better view or analyze specific data groups.

Excel 2007 provides an AutoFilter feature that converts the column headings into separate filters. Figure 15-11 illustrates both the AutoFilters (the down arrows added to the heading of each column) and the filter menu that can be used to specify the filter to be applied to the column. When the filter is applied, the data on the entire row(s) of a qualifying column value is displayed.

What-If Simulations

After the budget, financial statements, inventory valuation, or even a list of the items in a collection is prepared (and saved) in a spreadsheet application, questions may arise concerning what would be the outcome of some future event, action, or value change on the data. A spreadsheet application is an excellent tool to use to quickly simulate the impact of changing one or more values in its key data.

FIGURE 15-11

The Excel 2007 AutoFilter feature converts each column into separate filters.

FIGURE 15-12

A worksheet
containing the
sales projections
of a company

	A	B	C	D	E	F
	A1		fx	Sales Forecast by Representative		
	Sales Forecast by Representative					
1	Sales Forecast by Representative					
2	Representative	Qtr 1	Qtr 2	Qtr 3	Qtr 4	Total
3	Camryn	$ 1,547	$ 14,214	$ 14,802	$ 30,563	$ 61,126
4	Carly	1,794	15,809	16,490	34,093	68,186
5	Evan	1,054	11,025	11,426	23,504	47,008
6	Jeana	234	6,512	6,655	13,401	26,802
7	Jessica	842	9,542	9,859	20,243	40,486
8	Jordan	546	7,531	7,722	15,799	31,598
9	Katie	2,782	22,187	23,242	48,211	96,422
10	Kevin	2,535	20,593	21,554	44,682	89,363
11	Lindsey	1,300	12,619	13,114	27,034	54,067
12	Markus	2,041	17,403	18,178	37,622	75,245
13	Robert	2,288	18,998	19,866	41,152	82,304
14	Shaun	123	4,566	4,588	9,277	18,554
15	Total	$ 17,086	$ 160,999	$ 167,496	$ 345,581	$ 691,162

Figure 15-12 shows a worksheet listing the sales projections for the sales
representatives of a company for an upcoming year. What if one or more of the sales
representatives were to leave the company in the third quarter? What would happen
to the sale projection if a replacement couldn't be hired? Figure 15-13 shows that by
changing the data associated with this scenario, the totals are changed automatically
through their formulas. The actions we have just performed on this worksheet are
the basic form of a what-if simulation.

FIGURE 15-13

A what-if
simulation
performed on the
sales projection
worksheet

	A	B	C	D	E	F
1	Sales Forecast by Representative					
2	Representative	Qtr 1	Qtr 2	Qtr 3	Qtr 4	Total
3	Camryn	$ 1,547	$ 14,214	$ 14,802	$ 30,563	$ 61,126
4	Carly	1,794	15,809	16,490	34,093	68,186
5	Evan	1,054	11,025	11,426	23,504	47,008
6	Jeana	234	6,512	6,655	13,401	26,802
7	Jessica	842	9,542	9,859	20,243	40,486
8	Jordan	546	7,531	7,722	15,799	31,598
9	Katie	2,782	22,187	23,242	48,211	96,422
10	Kevin	2,535	20,593	-	-	23,128
11	Lindsey	1,300	12,619	13,114	27,034	54,067
12	Markus	2,041	17,403	18,178	37,622	75,245
13	Robert	2,288	18,998	-	-	21,286
14	Shaun	123	4,566	4,588	9,277	18,554
15	Total	$ 17,086	$ 160,999	$ 126,076	$ 259,747	$ 563,908

on the
job

It is a best practice when getting set to perform a what-if simulation on a workbook that you open the workbook and then save a copy of the workbook. The new workbook may be something you wish to keep for later, in which case you'd carefully name the workbook and save it to an appropriate location. However, if the copy is only for a temporary what-if, you can name it "what-if" or "junk" or as you like.

Excel 2007 provides a special what-if analysis feature that can be used to perform this simulation. The What-If Analysis tool (located on the Data tab of the Excel 2007 Ribbon) can be used to define a what-if scenario, set a goal value, and specify the data to be analyzed.

CERTIFICATION SUMMARY

Formulas and functions provide users with the capability to perform simple as well as quite complex calculations, comparisons, and data organization and formatting actions. Formulas are user-defined actions that are based on standard arithmetic operations: add, subtract, multiply, and divide.

The data in an electronic spreadsheet worksheet can be arranged to suit the informational needs of the reader. The data can be sorted, filtered, and displayed graphically in the form of a chart.

✓ TWO-MINUTE DRILL

Manipulate Data Using Formulas and Functions

❏ A formula is a mathematical statement that produces a calculated result that can be a conditional result or a value. Spreadsheet applications indicate a formula with an equal sign (=) in the first position of an entry. A function is a predefined and built-in formula.

❏ Spreadsheet applications include formulas and functions that can be used for general, mathematical, statistical, engineering, and financial calculations.

❏ Formulas can include one or more of four basic arithmetic operators: addition (+), subtraction (-), multiplication (*), and division (/). Two other operators are also available: percentage (%) and exponentiation (^).

❏ Arithmetic operators are evaluated in a specific order of precedence. The operators are actually divided into three sets: multiply and divide, add and subtract, and exponentiate. The percentage operator is applied separately after all other operations. The multiply and divide operations are analyzed first as they occur left-to-right in a formula; the addition and subtraction operations are evaluated next; and then the exponentiation operation.

❏ Spreadsheet applications use two types of cell references or addresses in formulas: relative cell references and absolute cell references. A relative cell reference remains relative to a given worksheet position whenever it is copied to a new cell location. An absolute cell reference remains constant to an exact worksheet location at all times. In addition, an R1C1 reference is supported by some spreadsheet applications.

❏ Formulas are edited or modified on the formula bar. To edit a formula, click the cell and make the changes in the formula bar.

❏ A function is a predefined formula that can be used to perform a specific calculation or action. When a function is selected, its formula or function template is placed in the formula bar and the Function Arguments dialog box is displayed. Functions can be used to count, summarize, calculate, relate, or compare one or more values in a worksheet. Functions are typically defined in categories for Financial, Statistical, Engineering, Mathematics, and others.

❏ Avoid the use of literal values instead of cell references in a formula.

❏ Divide by zero (#DIV/0!) is a common error caused by the dividend in a division operation having the value of null or zero.

❏ A circular reference occurs whenever a formula involves its own cell in a calculation, directory or indirectly.

❏ A reference error (#REF!) occurs when a cell reference included in a formula is removed or cleared of its contents.

❏ A chart is a representation of data in a graphical form that can be viewed for comparative or analytical purposes. The four basic chart types are column, line, bar, and pie charts.

❏ Data in a worksheet can be sorted on any of the data contained in one or more of its columns. Sorting orders data in ascending order or descending order.

❏ Filtering limits the data displayed to only the data that meets specified criteria.

❏ A what-if simulation is used to analyze the impact of a key value change in the overall outcomes of a worksheet.

SELF TEST

The following questions are intended to help you be sure that you understand the material included in this chapter. Read the questions and the answer choices carefully.

Manipulate Data Using Formulas and Functions

1. Which of the following is an example of a relative cell reference?
   A. $B5
   B. B$5
   C. $B$5
   D. B5

2. Which reference element is locked in the cell reference A$1?
   A. Column A
   B. Row 1
   C. Column A and row 1
   D. All cells

3. In the formula =B2+D4 - C1*R4/A4^3+T4-S5, which operation is evaluated first?
   A. B2+D4
   B. C1*R4
   C. R4/A4^3
   D. T4-S5

4. What type of cell reference is $A$4?
   A. Absolute
   B. Relative
   C. R1C1
   D. Hybrid

5. On what feature of a spreadsheet workspace is a formula edited?
   A. Cell
   B. Status bar
   C. Formula bar
   D. Address bar

6. What is the term used for a predefined formula used to perform a specific calculation or action?
   A. Expression
   B. Statement
   C. Function
   D. Equation

7. If a formula references its own cell location in a calculation, what type of error or warning may be displayed?
   A. #REF!
   B. #DIV/0!
   C. #CALC!
   D. Circular reference

8. Which of the following are basic chart types found in nearly all spreadsheet applications?
   A. Bar
   B. Column
   C. Line
   D. Pie
   E. All of the above
   F. None of the above

9. True or False: A spreadsheet application is only able to sort data in an ascending sequence.
   A. True
   B. False

10. What spreadsheet action can be used to select and display only data that meets specific criteria?
    A. Sort
    B. Filter
    C. Query
    D. Table

11. What is the expression used to describe the use of a spreadsheet to simulate the impact of changing a key value in the data of a worksheet?
    A. Trial-and-error
    B. Projection
    C. Forecast
    D. What-if

SELF TEST ANSWERS

Manipulate Data Using Formulas and Functions

1. ☑ **D.** Relative cell references are the default cell reference in a spreadsheet.
   ☒ **A, B,** and **C** are incorrect. These are variations of an absolute cell reference. Answer A locks the column reference; answer B locks the row reference; and answer C locks both the column and row references.

2. ☑ **B.** The use of a dollar sign before either the column or row reference locks that portion of the cell reference.
   ☒ **A, C,** and **D** are incorrect. In the A$1 cell reference, column A is not locked, as it doesn't include a dollar sign. Cell references aren't a practical way to lock an entire worksheet.

3. ☑ **B.** In the default order of operation precedence, a multiplication or division, whichever occurs first left to right, is performed first in a formula.
   ☒ **A, C,** and **D** are incorrect. Answer A is an addition operation, which is lower in the operation precedence. Answer C is a division operation that would be performed second after the multiplication operation preceding it in the formula. Answer D is a subtraction operation that would follow the operations in the preceding choices.

4. ☑ **A.** The use of a dollar sign before either the column or row reference locks that portion of the cell reference and creates an absolute cell reference.
   ☒ **B, C,** and **D** are incorrect. Relative and R1C1 cell references don't include dollar signs. To my knowledge, there is no such thing as a hybrid cell reference.

5. ☑ **C.** The formula bar is used to enter, edit, or remove a formula from a cell.
   ☒ **A, B,** and **D** are incorrect. Although it may appear on a spreadsheet that a formula is being edited in its cell location, the formula bar is the actual site of the action. The status bar relates to the entire workbook and not formulas specifically. An address bar is a feature normally associated with a Web browser.

6. ☑ **C.** Spreadsheet applications contain a variety of predefined formulas for specific calculations that are called functions.
   ☒ **A, B,** and **D** are incorrect. All formulas consist of expressions; a formula may contain mathematical or algebraic statements; and while a spreadsheet will do mathematical calculations, you can't actually express an equation.

7. ☑ **D.** A circular reference is when you try to calculate a value for a cell that includes the cell itself.
   ☒ **A, B,** and **C** are incorrect. Answer A is displayed when a cell reference is no longer available; answer B is displayed anytime a value is divided by a null or a zero; and I made up answer C.

8. ☑ **E.** Nearly all spreadsheet applications support bar, column, line, and pie charts.
   ☒ **A, B, C, D,** and **F** are incorrect. While answers A through D are each correct, answer E is the best answer. Since there is a correct answer, answer F is incorrect.

9. ☑ **B.** Spreadsheet applications can sort data in an ascending or descending order. Some, such as Excel 2007, can also sort on certain cell characteristics.
   ☒ **A** is incorrect. Spreadsheet applications can sort in either ascending or descending order.

10. ☑ **B.** A filter allows you to list specific information from a worksheet that meets particular criteria.
   ☒ **A, C,** and **D** are incorrect. A sort action will place certain information together, but it does that with all of the information in the worksheet. A query is in effect a filtering action, but queries are more associated with database systems. A table can be defined in the worksheet, but it alone does not answer specific questions.

11. ☑ **D.** Spreadsheet applications are especially good at performing what-if analysis, which can be used to predict the outcome caused by a change in a key value.
   ☒ **A, B,** and **C** are incorrect. Answer A may be what is actually happening, but this isn't an official term for a what-if analysis. A worksheet can contain a projection or a forecast, and changing a key value on either is a what-if analysis.

16

Creating a Slide Show with Presentation Software

Presentation applications, such as Microsoft Office PowerPoint 2007, Corel Presentations, Open Office Impress, Apple Keynote, Google Presentation, and Zoho Show, among others, the success of presentation software is largely because of the ease with which a nontechnical user can create and show a computer-based slide presentation. For the IC[3] exams, you should have a good working understanding of how to create, edit, and manage a slide show using a presentation application. In this chapter, we'll use PowerPoint 2007, which is perhaps the most widely used of the presentation applications, for the examples. However, you'll find that essentially all of the presentation applications work pretty much the same. This chapter covers the processes used to create a new slide presentation, customize and manage its slides, and present the presentation.

CERTIFICATION OBJECTIVE

Creating and Formatting Simple Presentations

4.1   Be able to create and format simple presentations.

A basic PowerPoint 2007 presentation consists of a set of at least three slides: a title slide, at least one normal (topic) slide, and perhaps a summary slide. One characteristic that all of the slides in a presentation should share is consistency. This consistency should be visible in the fonts used, the use and placement of objects (such as illustrations), and the color scheme or slide theme used throughout the presentation. The difference between the different slide types is primarily in their layouts, which can be chosen directly from either the standard slide layout library or from the slide layouts included in a presentation template.

Creating a New Slide Presentation

When a presentation application is started, a new default slide presentation is opened in its workspace. When creating a new presentation, only one slide is absolutely required, but since most slide presentations include multiple slides, on average, let's discuss the processes used to create a three-slide presentation consisting of a title slide, a bulleted list slide, and an object slide.

Technically, any slide can have any layout you wish, but because the potential audience is more or less conditioned to a particular type and sequence of the slides in a presentation, the first slide in a presentation is typically a title slide. The default first slide in a new presentation is created with a title slide layout and the default slide format or theme. However, in those applications that open the first slide in a general format, we need to discuss slide layouts, themes, and presentation templates and how they are used to change the layout, format, and functions of a presentation's slides.

Slide Layouts

When a new presentation opens, the first slide is automatically placed in the slide workspace with the Title Slide layout and the default slide formatting, design, and theme applied (see Figure 16-1). Presentation applications typically support multiple slide layouts. For example, PowerPoint 2007 supports nine built-in slide layouts. In most presentation applications, you aren't limited to the built-in slide layouts, because each of these layouts can be customized and you can create new layouts as well.

To change the slide layout on a PowerPoint 2007 slide, you can choose from one of the nine built-in slide layouts available on the Layout gallery. As shown in Figure 16-2, PowerPoint 2007 has the following built-in slide layouts available: Title Slide, Title and Content, Section Header, Two Content, Comparison, Title Only,

FIGURE 16-1

An example of a PowerPoint 2007 Title Slide layout

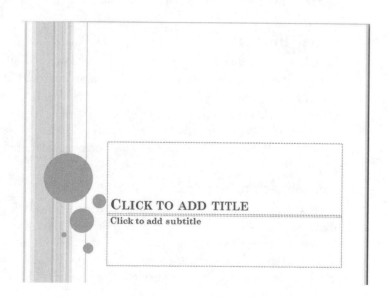

CLICK TO ADD TITLE

Click to add subtitle

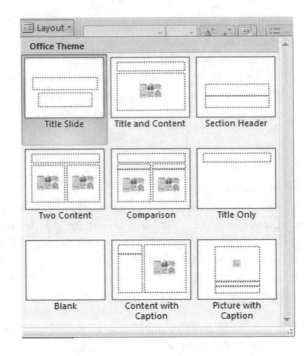

Blank, Content with Caption, and Picture with Caption. Each of these slides is designed to provide you with a slide layout to fit just about any slide-related purpose.

Slide Themes

A slide theme defines a set of customized slide layouts, fonts, and color schemes. In some presentation applications, slide themes are referred to as slide designs. In either case, a slide theme allows you to create slides that conform to a single color scheme and background graphic or illustration. PowerPoint 2007 provides a gallery of available slide themes that can be applied to a slide presentation to enhance its eye-appeal. Figure 16-3 shows the Slide Theme gallery of PowerPoint 2007.

Presentation Templates

A presentation template is a predefined presentation shell that includes a slide theme and slide layouts designed for a particular type of slide presentation. Presentation templates are saved as template files and can be opened when you start the creation of a presentation. PowerPoint 2007 includes six presentation templates, with many other templates available from Microsoft Office Online.

FIGURE 16-3

The Slide Theme gallery in PowerPoint 2007

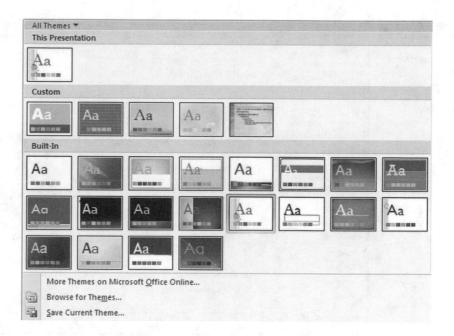

To start a new presentation using a template in PowerPoint 2007, the New Presentation option on the Microsoft Office button is used to display the New Presentation dialog box (see Figure 16-4) on which you can select the template you wish to use.

Add Content on a Slide

While it may be debatable, the content placed on each slide, along with any supporting graphics, tables, charts, or links, provides the value of the slides in a presentation. Some may disagree, claiming that the background, theme, and animations of the slide are what creates a presentation, but a slide presentation without a message is really not a presentation at all; it's more like an art slide show.

Templates and slide themes provide preset layouts that include text boxes and tools to assist you in adding art, animation, sound, and other types of objects to a slide. Any additional objects added to a slide should be used prudently and only in support of the message provided by the slide's text. Using PowerPoint 2007 as an example, the following sections explain the use and processes used to add content to

FIGURE 16-4

The PowerPoint 2007 New Presentation dialog box

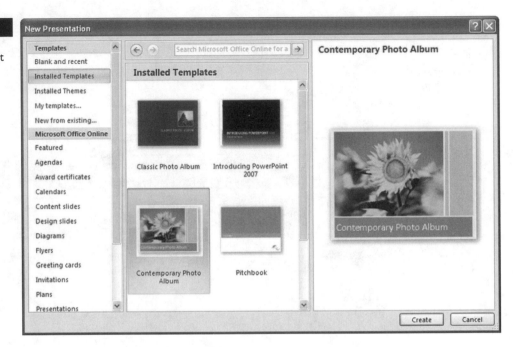

a slide. For the most part, content is added to a slide using the tools located on the Insert tab or the PowerPoint 2007 Ribbon.

Adding Text to a Slide   Text is entered on a slide in a text box, which can be added anywhere on the slide space. If you start with a blank slide layout, which is totally featureless, clicking the Text Box icon on the Insert tab changes the cursor into a text tool (that looks something like a sword). Using the text tool, click the mouse at the location on the slide where you wish to start the text box (don't worry, you can move it later if needed). Hold down the mouse button and draw the outline of the text box, creating it in the size and shape you need.

Once the text box is created, you can use its resizing handles to change its shape, rotate it, or move it to a new location on the slide space. Once you are satisfied with its size, shape, and position, you should enter the text you wish to place in the text box (the text box will disappear if you don't enter anything into it before starting another action).

Text entered into a text box on a slide can be formatted using essentially the same character and formatting tools found in Word 2007, including bulleted and numbered lists, bold, italics, underline, font, font size, color, and more. The text in a text box can also be manipulated in much the same way that text in a Word 2007 document is. Virtually all of the text manipulation tools used in Word can be used on text placed on a slide, including drag-and-drop, and cut, copy, and paste.

Using an Outline   When you create a slide presentation, the text you add to the slides, including the slide headings and the body text, automatically create an outline that can be viewed in the Presentation pane by selecting the Outline tab. If you have an existing Word document that you wish to use for the content of a slide presentation, opening the Word document in PowerPoint will create both an outline and slides from its content (each paragraph contained on a different slide).

You can create the outline yourself in the Outline view of the Presentation pane using the same entry rules as those used in Word 2007 outlines. The first line of text entered for a slide becomes its heading. Pressing the ENTER key opens a new slide, but if you press the TAB key, the new line is converted into a bulleted item under the preceding slide heading and each new line of text adds additional bulleted items on the slide until you press the SHIFT-TAB keys to move the control to a new slide.

Adding Bulleted or Numbered Lists   Text entered into any text box can be formatted into a bulleted or numbered list in much the same way text is formatted into either of these arrangements in a word processing application. To apply either numbers or bullets to text on a slide, select the text you wish to organize into a list and click either the Bullets or Numbers icon on the Home tab of the PowerPoint 2007 Ribbon. The TAB key can be used to demote a line of text to a second-level number or bullet, and SHIFT-TAB can be used to promote a list item to the next higher level.

Adding Graphic Objects   The slide space works essentially like a table top in that each object type added to the slide adds to the stack of items on the slide. Text boxes and object boxes stack on top of one another and can be ordered bottom to top to create the look and effect you desire.

To add a graphic to a slide, click the icon for the type of object you wish to add on the Insert tab of the PowerPoint 2007 Ribbon. Virtually any type of visible object you'd want to add to the slide has an icon on the Insert tab, including pictures, clip art, shapes, movies, sounds, and hyperlinks. Each of the different object type icons displays either a dialog box on which you can navigate to the object you wish to add or a gallery showing your choices for a particular object type. To add the picture, graphic, or object to a slide, click the filename or thumbnail of the object. Once the object is added to the slide, you can resize and reposition it as you wish. In the case of a sound file, however, the file's size has nothing to do with its playback properties.

You are prompted for one or more of the playback properties for movies, animations, and sounds, but static objects, such as pictures, clip art, and the like, are added directly to the slide without intervention. Animated or sound objects can be further customized using the Action icon that is enabled when these objects are added to a slide. Pictures, images, and other graphics can be stylized using the Picture Effects gallery that displays when these items are added to a slide, including edge borders, shadows, edge effects, and shading to add visual appeal to the graphic.

Saving a Presentation

For the most part, presentation applications save their files, as you'd expect, as slide presentations. However, some presentation software, such as PowerPoint 2007 and Corel Presentations to name only two, allow you to save files in a variety of different formats. In most presentation applications, the default file format is a slide presentation. In PowerPoint 2007 this file is a presentation file, which is saved with a .pptx filename extension. You can also save a PowerPoint 2007 slide presentation as a macro-enabled presentation (.pptm), a presentation that is compatible with previous versions of PowerPoint (.ppt), a PowerPoint slide show (.ppts), a PowerPoint template (.potx), a Microsoft XPS file, and even a Portable Document Format (.pdf) file.

Typically, a new slide presentation is named Presentation*N* (where *N* is a sequential number for each new slide presentation created during the current session), and when you save the slide show for the first time, you should assign the file a meaningful name to help you find it later.

Manage Slides

As you're preparing a slide show or editing an existing show to use again, there are some tools you can use to arrange, add, remove, and annotate the slides in the presentation. While other presentation applications have similar features, PowerPoint 2007 provides very good examples of each of these actions.

Arrange Slides

One of the features supported by PowerPoint 2007 is the Slide Sorter view. This view approximates the use of a light table to sort film slides in that it arranges the slides in rows. To move a slide from one location to another, meaning to change the sequence of the slides, requires only a simple drag-and-drop action. Figure 16-5 shows the Slide Sorter view.

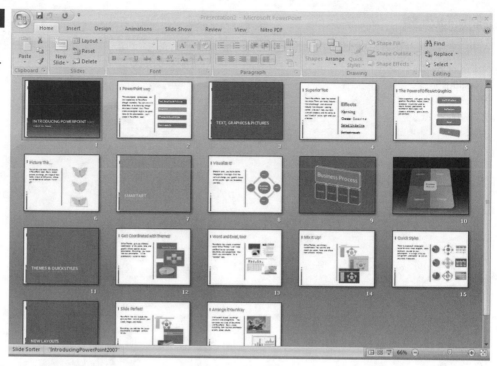

FIGURE 16-5

The PowerPoint 2007 Slide Sorter view

Add Slides

If you wish to add a new slide to a slide presentation, the best tool is the Presentation pane that is a part of the default normal view in PowerPoint 2007. As shown in Figure 16-6, clicking between two slides in the Presentation pane and performing one of three actions that can be used to insert (add) a new slide adds the new slide to the presentation. The three options you have to add a new slide are the keyboard shortcut CTRL-M, the New Slide button on the Home tab, and the New Slide option on the pop-up menu that appears when you right-click the insertion bar.

Duplicate a Slide

Although a template can set the theme and layout of a particular slide, on occasion you may want to copy a slide to use it as a sort of template for an individual slide later in a presentation. The process used to copy and paste a slide isn't a lot different from the copy and paste action in any application.

FIGURE 16-6

The insertion bar placed between two slides in the Presentation pane of PowerPoint 2007

To duplicate (copy) a slide within a presentation, right-click the thumbnail of the slide to be duplicated in the Slide view of the Presentation pane (on the left edge of the workspace) and choose Copy from the pop-up menu. Click in the space between the two slides where you wish to add the slide copy, right-click the insert cursor, and choose Paste from the pop-up menu. For more information on inserting a slide into a presentation, see "Arrange Slides" earlier in this chapter.

To duplicate a slide to a different presentation, copy the slide from its original presentation, activate the workspace of the other presentation, and then use the steps described in the preceding paragraph to add the slide to the presentation.

Remove Slides

Should you want to remove a slide from a presentation for any reason, you can do so by clicking the slide in either the Slide Sorter view or in the Presentation pane and pressing the DEL button on the keyboard. You can also remove a slide after selecting it by right-clicking the slide and selecting the Delete Slide option on the pop-up menu.

Annotate Slides

PowerPoint 2007 and other presentation applications provide the capability to add presenter notes. This is accomplished on a Notes Page view (see Figure 16-7). Information you wish to enter into the text box can be printed and used as a presenter's guide so that you don't forget any important information during the presentation, such as anecdotes, supporting data, and even an outline of the information related to each slide.

Slide Backgrounds

A slide presentation created from a template typically has an illustration, graphic, or color set for the background. However, if you wish to change the background of an existing presentation or want to set the background of a new slide presentation, virtually all presentation applications provide support to allow you to do so.

The background of a slide can be set to a solid color, a one- or two-color gradient (a gradual change from darker shades to lighter shades on a background), a picture, or

FIGURE 16-7

The PowerPoint 2007 Notes Page view

Click to add text

FIGURE 16-8

The Colors
gallery in
PowerPoint
2007

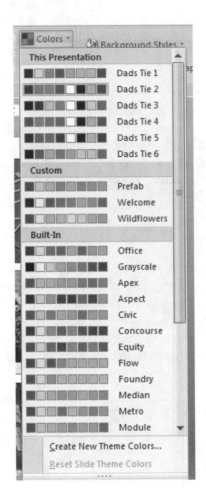

a graphic image. Like other presentation applications, PowerPoint 2007 provides the capability to set a color scheme for a slide, choose a background style that includes the active color scheme, as shown in Figure 16-8, and apply a variety of effects that apply to any text objects in the slide, such as bullets, numbers, or the like.

Slide Animations and Transitions

Slide animations and transitions can be used in a slide presentation to add some whimsy, fun, or even emphasis to a slide and to make the gap between slides a bit more interesting. Slide animations are motion effects that can be used when a portion of a slide, such as an item in a bulleted list, appears, is emphasized, or exits from view. On the other hand, a slide transition occurs between slides as one slide is removed from view and the next slide is displayed. The transition effect of a slide is seen as the slide is displayed. Transitions should be used consistently even though each slide can have a different transition. Mixing in too many transitions in a slide presentation can become distracting should the transitions become the focus of the presentation in place of the slides and their content.

PowerPoint 2007 provides a variety of slide *transition* effects. The default transition is actually No Transition, in which the screen darkens briefly between one slide and the next. The standard set of slide transitions available in PowerPoint 2007 are

- **Fade**   One slide fades out and the next slide fades in.
- **Wipe**   When you move from one slide to the next, the previous slide is covered with a black block, which is then directionally removed to reveal the next slide. The action of a wipe transition effect can be horizontal, diagonal, vertical, or based on a shape, such as a diamond, a circle, and more.
- **Push and Cover**   This effect is essentially a variation on the Wipe effect, with the difference being that the slide is pushed into view from the edge of the display, covering a black background.
- **Stripes and Bars**   Also called blinds and checkerboards in some presentation applications, this effect reveals a slide by giving the illusion that the stripes, bars, or checkerboard squares are rotating to reveal the slide.

Most presentation applications also provide a random transition option that can be used to apply any of the transitions available to the slides in a presentation randomly. Figure 16-9 shows some of the transition effects available in PowerPoint 2007.

In addition to the visual transition effects, sound effects can be applied that play during the transition. Transitions can also be controlled with timing, which is typically used when a presentation is shown on a kiosk or as an automatically advancing slide show.

Slide Animations

A slide *animation* is different from a slide transition. A slide transition effect takes place between slides, but slide animations occur while a slide is in view and are used to reveal, emphasize, or remove elements on the slide. The most frequently used slide animations are the effects that reveal, dim, or remove bulleted or numbered items.

FIGURE 16-9

The PowerPoint 2007 Transitions gallery

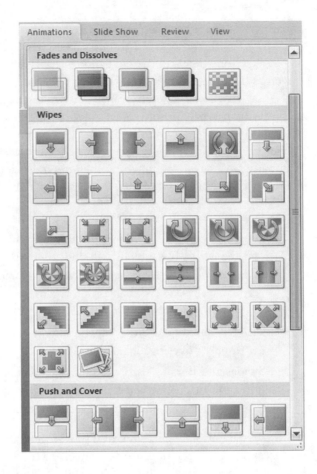

Most presentation applications provide a fairly wide variety of animation effects, but generally the animation effects available fall into three primary categories:

- **Fade** The action of the animation effects in this category applies the same effects as the Fade slide transitions to one or more elements of a slide with each element fading into view.

- **Fly In** Using this animation effect, a slide element moves into place from beyond any of the slide's edges using a variety of "flight" patterns.

- **Wipe** This animation applies the same effect as the Wipe slide transition to one or more elements of a slide.

FIGURE 16-10

A few of the options available for creating a custom animation in PowerPoint 2007

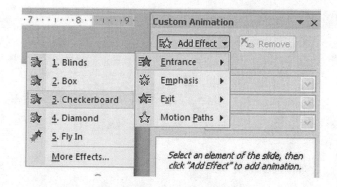

In addition, some presentation applications also allow you to create a custom animation in which you have more options for the animation of an element, such as including the speed of a fade or wipe, also called a dissolve in some cases, or drawing the path of a fly-in effect. Figure 16-10 shows the Custom Animation pane in PowerPoint 2007.

Animations are applied to one or more selected elements on a slide individually. In fact, each element on the slide, including bulleted or numbered items, text blocks, illustrations, graphics, and other objects, can have a completely different animation. However, as when choosing slide transitions, avoid overdoing animations, as they can distract the audience from your message.

Changing the Workspace

All presentation applications allow you to change the structure, content, and look of their workspace. PowerPoint 2007, which offers ten different workspace views, provides a very good example of how you can set the workspace to suit your activities. Every presentation application has a default or Normal workspace view. This is typically made up of a set of two or more windows or panes that allow you to navigate, edit, or view a presentation and its slides. Figure 16-11 shows the Normal workspace view of PowerPoint 2007.

PowerPoint 2007 provides six different variations on the Normal workspace view, each of which includes or excludes a feature or viewing pane to create a workspace layout suited to particular presentation creation or editing actions. Figure 16-12

FIGURE 16-11

The default
or Normal
workspace view
of PowerPoint
2007

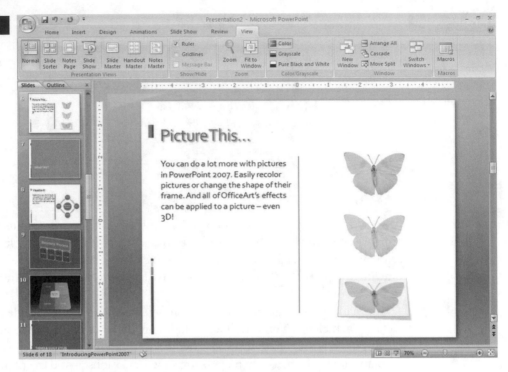

FIGURE 16-12

The available
workspace views
that can be set
as the default
workspace views
in PowerPoint
2007

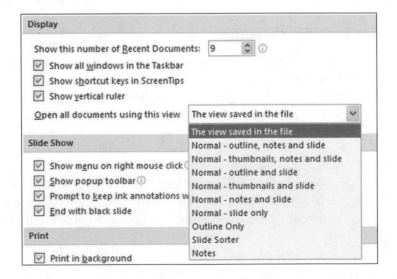

shows the list of available workspace views that can be used as the default view of the workspace. Notice the various options for the Normal workspace view.

As discussed earlier in the chapter (see "Arrange Slides"), another workspace view that is commonly available in presentation applications is the Slide Sorter view (shown earlier in Figure 16-5). This workspace view can be very handy for changing the order of the slides in a presentation. The Notes Page view, also shown earlier in Figure 16-7, is used to enter presenter notes for a particular slide.

Previewing a Presentation

To preview or rehearse a presentation while you are working on the presentation or after it is complete, all presentation applications include a mechanism to display the presentation's slides in full-screen view. Typically, this feature is named Show Slides, Slide Show, or Run Slides, depending on the application.

Some presentation applications also provide a viewer utility that can be used to preview a slide presentation outside of the main presentation software. This allows the slide creator to develop the slide presentation on a main station, such as a desktop computer, and travel with only the slides and the viewer. The benefit of an available viewer is that it eliminates the need for the presentation application used to develop the slide to be installed wherever the slides are to be presented.

Presenting a Slide Show

The reason you prepare presentation slides is to share them with an audience. Slides can be shared electronically in a file so that the audience can view them at their leisure, but the primary use of a slide show is to share information in support of a presentation or talk.

When you start a slide show in PowerPoint 2007, you have the choice of starting the slide show from the beginning, from the first slide, or from a particular slide in the presentation. Regardless of where you begin the slide show, the navigation methods remain the same. There are essentially five navigation actions that can be used when presenting a slide show:

- **Advance to the next slide**   There are three methods that are available to move from one slide to the next in sequence:
    - **Mouse click**   Clicking the active slide advances the slide show to the next slide in sequence.

- **Slide controls**   The transparent slide control panel that displays when you move the mouse over the lower-left corner of the active slide includes an arrow that points to the right. Clicking this control advances the slide show to the next slide in sequence.

- **Pop-up menu**   Right-clicking the active slide (or clicking the menu icon in the slide control panel) displays a pop-up menu that includes the Next command that advances to the next slide in sequence.

- **Back up to previous slide**   As with the advance controls, you can use either of two methods to back up to the slide before the active slide. Right-clicking the active slide displays a pop-up menu from which you can choose Previous, or you can click the left-facing arrow control in the slide control panel.

- **Jump to a specific slide**   In a presentation that contains slides for a variety of topics, a slide show can be easily tailored, either beforehand or on the fly, to a particular audience by jumping out of sequence from one slide to another. There are three primary ways to do this:

  - **Use hyperlinks**   Hyperlinks can be inserted into a slide and used to navigate and display documents, Web sites, and other remote information during a slide show. Hyperlinks can also be used to jump from one slide to another within a presentation or perhaps even to a slide in another presentation.

  - **Jump to a specific slide**   Right-clicking the active slide (or clicking the menu icon in the slide control panel) displays a pop-up menu; there, the Go To Slide tool that a list of all of the slides in the presentation in sequential order showing the title of each slide. To move to a particular slide, simply click its entry in the slide list.

  - **Create a custom slide show**   To reorder the slides for a particular presentation, you can create a custom slide show in which you select and save a custom order for the slides to appear.

- **End a slide show**   When the presentation is completed or should you wish to end the presentation at any point, right-click the active slide (or click the menu icon in the slide control panel) and choose the End Show command.

- **Run a slide show in a continuous loop**   One of the options on the Slide Show Setup dialog box is to run a slide show continuously until the ESC key is pressed on the keyboard. This feature is typically used for running slide shows unattended on a kiosk or display.

Although it's not exactly a navigational tool, the pencil icon on the slide control panel allows you to annotate and write on the active slide. Options for the type of writing tool to be used display on a pop-up menu. Any annotations made during a slide show can be saved, and if you have made annotations during a slide show, you are asked whether you wish to save these marks when you end the slide show.

Printing Slides

There are often multiple needs when printing the slides of a presentation. You may want full-page copies of the slides for reference purposes or documentation; you may want to print handouts to distribute to the audience so that they can make notes on each slide as the presentation is given; or you may want to print out any presenter notes you've added to the slides for use as a script to use during the presentation. PowerPoint 2007, along with other presentation applications, allows you to print a version of the slides for each of these purposes.

Figure 16-13 shows the PowerPoint 2007 Print dialog box. Notice in the Print What section that you can select what it is you wish to print, choosing from Slides, Handouts, Notes Pages, and Outline view (which prints the text of the slides in an outline form). When Handouts is selected, the Handouts section is enabled and you can choose the number of slides to be printed on each page: one, two, three, four,

FIGURE 16-13

The PowerPoint 2007 Print dialog box

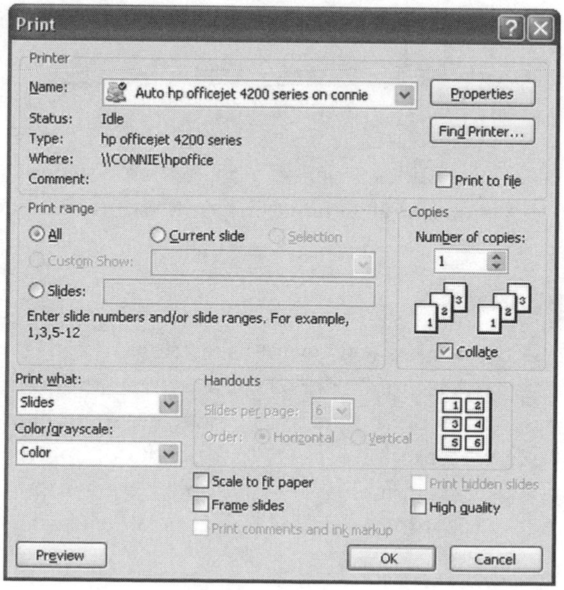

FIGURE 16-14

A Handouts print with three slides per page

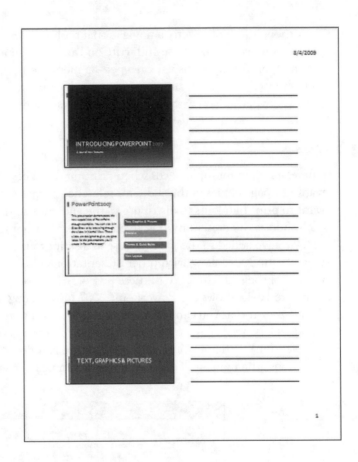

six, or nine slides per page, along with a note area for each slide. Figure 16-14 shows a print preview of a Handouts print with three slides per page.

Distributing Slides

On occasion, you may want to distribute a slide presentation on a network for others to view online or to use as a presentation themselves. Before you publish a presentation for others to use, there are some steps you should complete to ensure that a presentation is ready for distribution, protected, and finalized. These steps include checking the presentation for compatibility, any personal information, and source information, as well as possibly encrypting the presentation for security purposes. You can also limit who can access the presentation and restrict what those you have allowed to access it can do to or with the presentation.

PowerPoint 2007 provides tools to complete each of these steps. As shown in Figure 16-15, each of the tools needed to prepare a presentation for distribution is accessed through the Microsoft Office button and the Prepare selection. Once you have completed the preparation actions you wish to use, a presentation is ready for distribution. The sections that follow describe the actions used to prepare a presentation for distribution.

Check Presentation Properties

The properties of a PowerPoint 2007 presentation contain information that helps to identify and protect a shared presentation. As shown in Figure 16-16, this information includes the name of the author, the title of the presentation, its subject matter, category, status, keywords that can help to identify the presentation during a search, and any comments you wish to make to further identify or explain the purpose of the presentation.

FIGURE 16-15

The Prepare menu of PowerPoint 2007

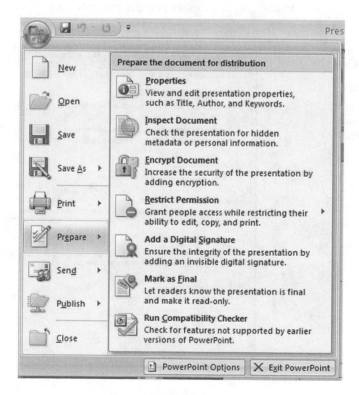

FIGURE 16-16

The Properties pane of a PowerPoint 2007 presentation

Document Properties ▾		Location: E:\Shared Presentations\template-and-transitions.pptx	* Required field ✕

Author:	Title:	Subject:	Keywords:	Category:	Status:
Doug McCracken	Textile Production in the United	Cotton Textile Production in the	cotton, textiles, production	Lecture slides	Final

Comments:
Copyright: Colgate University, Doug McCracken

Inspect a Presentation

To ensure that a distributed presentation doesn't contain any personal information or any extraneous data or content, PowerPoint 2007 provides the Document Inspector tool. As shown in Figure 16-17, you can select each of the content types you wish the inspection to find and identify. After the presentation is inspected, any content found in any of the selected inspection categories is flagged and can be easily removed.

Encrypt a Presentation

When you encrypt a presentation, you assign a password that you and other users must know to decrypt and open the presentation. After the password is assigned, the

FIGURE 16-17

The Office 2007 Document Inspector scans a PowerPoint 2007 presentation for the categories selected on its dialog box.

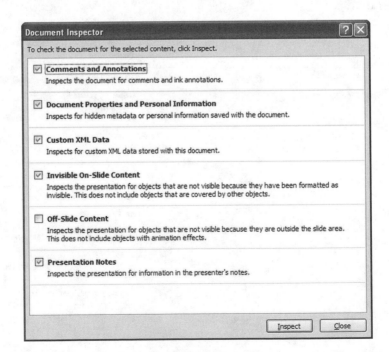

presentation file is encrypted, which means that only those users with whom you've shared the password are able to open the presentation.

Restrict Permission

This option is used when you want to restrict access to the presentation to only specific users or groups. The default permission setting is unlimited access, but if the presentation contains sensitive information or is intended only for certain users, you can set the restriction. However, the use of this option also requires a document management system be in use. In the Office 2007 environment, the Microsoft Information Rights Management (IRM) client must be available on your computer.

Digital Signature

A *digital signature* is a security protection device that can be applied to a presentation to add another level of security to encryption and access permissions. A digital signature is a small file issued by a certificate authority that is attached to a presentation to verify its source as trustworthy.

Mark as Final

A presentation that has been marked as final indicates to other users that the presentation is completed and is not being shared for review. When a presentation is marked as final, the status field in the document properties is changed to Final.

Run Compatibility Checker

The Compatibility Checker tool scans a presentation, looking for any features, formats, and other characteristics of the presentation that may not be compatible with an earlier version of PowerPoint. The PowerPoint versions that are the basis for the checking are the 97–2003 versions. Any conflicts found in the presentation that aren't supported in earlier PowerPoint versions are identified so that they can be eliminated or a more compatible feature or format can be substituted.

Publish a Presentation

Once a presentation has been prepared for distribution, you have a variety of distribution options you can use to share it with other users. As shown in Figure 16-18, the presentation can be placed on a CD for portability, placed on a document management server, added to a Microsoft Office SharePoint Server (MOSS) slide library, or placed into a new document workspace.

The PowerPoint 2007 Publish menu lists the distribution options for a presentation.

Creating an Effective Slide Show Presentation

A presentation created using a presentation application can be used to support a talk, speech, meeting, briefing, or lesson, in fact, any situation where visual support is needed or desired for spoken words or to convey a message on its own. The design, the layout, the content, and the manner in which it's presented determine the value of a slide show to the audience. The following are only a few of the issues you should consider when preparing a presentation:

- Clearly identify the topic or subject of each slide in the slide heading.
- Use graphics only to illustrate or demonstrate relevant information on a slide.
- Identify the presentation, the presenter, the date of the presentation, and any other pertinent information in the header or footer on each slide in a presentation.
- Apply a consistent layout to the slides to provide for a seamless transition from one slide to the next.

- Avoid the use of background, foreground, and text colors that can make a slide hard to read in certain rooms or on projectors with varying luminance.

- Use bulleted or numbered lists to present information that specifies or implies a sequence, but limit the number of bullets or numbered items on a single slide.

- Use tables and charts to illustrate the relationship of numerical data or trends.

- Avoid using too many different animations or slide transitions, as they can become distracting or take over a presentation, losing its primary message.

CERTIFICATION SUMMARY

Presentation editing applications allow users to create and display electronic slides to an audience. A full range of slide layout, design, editing, formatting, and management functions can be used to create, modify, change the order of, or remove slides from a presentation.

Presentation applications also provide a variety of tools that allow visual animation effects to be added to a slide show to help hold the audience's attention or to dramatize a particular point or two. The slides can be displayed as a slide show, printed, or shared across a network.

✓ TWO-MINUTE DRILL

Creating and Formatting Simple Presentations

❏ A basic presentation consists of a set of at least three slides: a title slide, at least one topic slide, and a summary slide. However, only one slide is required to create a presentation.

❏ The typical slide layouts available are Title Slide, Title and Content, Section Header, Two Content, Comparison, Title Only, Blank, Content with Caption, and Picture with Caption.

❏ A slide theme, which is also called a slide design, defines a set of customized slide layouts, fonts, and color schemes.

❏ A presentation template is a predefined presentation shell that includes a slide theme and slide layouts designed for a particular type of slide presentation. Presentation templates are saved as template files and can be opened when you start the creation of a presentation.

❏ By default, presentation applications save their files as slide presentations. Some presentation applications allow files to be saved in a variety of file formats, including presentation files, macro-enabled presentations, backward-compatible presentations, slide shows, templates, and portable document files. The default filename of a new PowerPoint 2007 presentation is Presentation$N$.

❏ The Slide Sorter view arranges a presentation's slides in rows to facilitate changing the sequence of the slides.

❏ Presentation applications provide the capability to add presenter notes to each slide.

❏ The background of a slide can be set to a solid color, a one- or two-color gradient, a picture, or a graphic image.

❏ Slide animations and transitions can be applied to individual slides. Slide animations are motion effects that are used to add action to a slide element for its entrance, emphasis, or exit. Slide animations commonly available include Fade, Fly In, and Wipe.

❏ A slide transition is seen when one slide is removed from view and the next slide is displayed. Slide transitions commonly available are Fade, Wipe, Push and Cover, and Stripes and Bars. Most presentation applications also provide a random transition option.

❑   A presentation application allows you to change the structure, content, and look of its workspace. PowerPoint 2007 provides six different variations on the Normal workspace view.

❑   A feature named Show Slides, Slide Show, or Run Slides, depending on the application, can be used to preview or rehearse a presentation.

❑   Slides can be printed in a variety of print layouts, including Slides, Handouts, Notes Pages, and Outline view. Handouts pages can include one, two, three, four, six, or nine slides per page.

❑   The properties of a presentation contain information to identify and protect a shared presentation, including the name of the author, the title of the presentation, its subject matter, category, status, keywords, and comments.

❑   To ensure that a distributed presentation doesn't contain any personal information or extraneous content, PowerPoint 2007 provides the Document Inspector tool.

❑   A presentation file can be encrypted and a password assigned that users must know to decrypt and open the presentation.

❑   Restrict Permissions are used when you want to restrict access to a presentation to only specific users or groups.

❑   A digital signature is a small file issued by a certificate authority that is attached to a presentation to verify its source as trustworthy.

❑   The Compatibility Checker tool scans a presentation, looking for any features, formats, and other characteristics of the presentation that may not be compatible with an earlier version of PowerPoint.

❑   A presentation can be distributed to a CD, placed on a document management server, added to a slide library, or placed into a new document workspace.

SELF TEST

The following questions are intended to help you be sure that you understand the material included in this chapter. Read the questions and the answer choices carefully.

Creating and Formatting Simple Presentations

1. What is the minimum number of slides that a presentation must contain?
   A. 0
   B. 1
   C. 2
   D. 3

2. What is the default slide layout applied to the first slide in a new PowerPoint 2007 presentation?
   A. Blank
   B. Comparison
   C. Title and Content
   D. Title Slide

3. What are the two names used for a defined set of color schemes, layouts, and fonts that can be applied to a slide presentation in a presentation application?
   A. Design
   B. Format
   C. Layout
   D. Theme

4. What term describes a predefined presentation shell that applies a set of slide designs and layouts typically intended for a particular type of slide presentation or audience?
   A. Boilerplate
   B. Sample
   C. Template
   D. Theme

5. What is commonly the default file format used when a new slide presentation is saved?
   A. Backward-compatible presentation file
   B. Macro-enabled presentation file
   C. Portable Document Format file
   D. Presentation file

6. What PowerPoint 2007 workspace view arranges slides in rows for editing and management purposes?
   A. Normal
   B. Outline
   C. Slide Show
   D. Slide Sorter

7. True or False: Presenter notes for each slide must be created in an external file.
   A. True
   B. False

8. True or False: The background of a slide is controlled by the slide layout and can only be changed by changing the slide layout.
   A. True
   B. False

9. True or False: A slide animation and a slide transition are different names for the same slide effects.
   A. True
   B. False

10. What are the slides per page options available when printing PowerPoint 2007 handout pages?
   A. Unlimited slides per page
   B. 1, 2, 3, 4, 6, or 9 slides per page
   C. 1, 2, 4, 8, or 10 slides per page
   D. 2, 4, 6, 8, or 10 slides per page

11. Which of the following data is not included in the document properties of a PowerPoint 2007 presentation file?
   A. Category
   B. Name of author
   C. Presentation title
   D. Subject
   E. Users allowed to access the presentation file

12. What PowerPoint 2007 tool can be used to check the document properties of a presentation file?
   A. Compatibility Checker
   B. Document Inspector
   C. Presentation Inspector
   D. Restrict Permission

13. What PowerPoint 2007 tool can be used to check a presentation file for compatibility to older versions of PowerPoint?
    A. Compatibility Checker
    B. Document Inspector
    C. Presentation Inspector
    D. Restrict Permission

14. What is the name used for a small file issued by a certificate authority that is attached to a presentation to verify its source as trustworthy?
    A. Digital signature
    B. Document properties
    C. Encryption
    D. Security license

15. To which of the following can a presentation be distributed?
    A. CD
    B. Document management server
    C. Slide library
    D. Document workspace
    E. All of the above
    F. None of the above

SELF TEST ANSWERS

Creating and Formatting Simple Presentations

1. ☑ **B.** A slide presentation must contain at least one slide.
   ☒ **A, C,** and **D** are incorrect. Answer A cannot be correct because a slide presentation must have at least one slide. Answers B and C are acceptable answers, but at minimum a presentation needs to have only one slide.

2. ☑ **D.** Unless you change its settings, the default first slide in a new PowerPoint 2007 presentation is a Title slide.
   ☒ **A, B,** and **C** are incorrect. You can set the layout of the first slide to any of the available slide layouts, but by default, meaning out-of-the-box (OTB), the layout of the first slide is the Title slide.

3. ☑ **A** and **D.** PowerPoint 2007 refers to a defined set of color schemes, layouts, and fonts as a theme, but other presentation applications and even earlier versions of PowerPoint call this a slide design.
   ☒ **B** and **C** are incorrect. Slide layouts are included in a slide theme, but slides don't exactly have a format, so answers B and C are incorrect.

4. ☑ **C.** A presentation template typically contains a prescribed set of slide designs, layouts, and themes designed for use when developing a presentation on a particular topic or to a specific type of audience.
   ☒ **A, B,** and **D** are incorrect. Answers A and B are terms not typically associated with a presentation or its slide. Answer D is one element that can be included in a slide template.

5. ☑ **D.** The default file format for a save presentation file is the editable presentation file format.
   ☒ **A, B,** and **C** are incorrect. These choices are valid file formats to which a presentation can be saved, but by default, the standard file format is the presentation file.

6. ☑ **D.** The PowerPoint 2007 view that most approximates the use of a "light table" on which slide can be sorted is the Slide Sorter view.
   ☒ **A, B,** and **C** are incorrect. While the PowerPoint Normal view does include the Presentation pane, the Slide Sorter is a much better tool for arranging slides. The Outline view displays the next of the presentation slides in an outline form, and the Slide Show view shows, well, the slide show.

7. ☑ **B.** Presenter notes can be added to each slide in a presentation.
   ☒ **A** is incorrect. The statement is false.

8. ☑ **B.** The background of a slide can be set individually for each slide or applied to all slides. The background design is independent of the slide layout.
   ☒ **A** is incorrect. The statement is false.

9. ☑ **B.** A slide animation affects one or more elements on a slide. A slide transition affects the action that occurs to display and remove slides from view.

   ☒ **A** is incorrect. The statement is false.

10. ☑ **B.** These are the selections available for the number of slides per page when printing handouts in PowerPoint 2007.

   ☒ **A, C,** and **D** are incorrect. It is virtually impossible to fit more than nine slides on a single print page and have them somewhat readable, so answer **A** is incorrect. The choices in answers **C** and **D** are also incorrect, as they don't match the actual options for slides per page on PowerPoint 2007 handouts.

11. ☑ **E.** The properties of a PowerPoint 2007 presentation doesn't include user permissions, but it does include the items listed in answers **A** through **D**.

   ☒ **A, B, C,** and **D** are incorrect. These items are included in the properties for a presentation and therefore are incorrect for this question.

12. ☑ **B.** The PowerPoint 2007 Document Inspector checks the presentation properties for personal information and comments that you may not want to share in a distributed presentation file.

   ☒ **A, C,** and **D** are incorrect. The Compatibility Checker examines a slide presentation for any features that may not be compatible with older versions of PowerPoint. There is no Presentation Inspector function in PowerPoint 2007. The Restrict Permission tool is used to limit who can access a distributed presentation file and what each user is allowed to do with the presentation.

13. ☑ **A.** The Compatibility Checker examines a slide presentation for any features that may not be compatible with older versions of PowerPoint.

   ☒ **B, C,** and **D** are incorrect. The Document Inspector checks the presentation properties for personal information and comments that you may not want to share in a distributed presentation file. There is no Presentation Inspector function in PowerPoint 2007. The Restrict Permission tool is used to limit who can access a distributed presentation file and what each user is allowed to do with the presentation.

14. ☑ **A.** A digital signature is a verification device in the form of a small file that is attached to a file that identifies and provides assurance of the originator.

   ☒ **B, C,** and **D** are incorrect. The document properties of a presentation file can be used to identify the creator of the presentation, its subject, category, and other information. Encryption can be applied to a presentation file to prevent an unauthorized user from viewing its contents. The term security license has no relationship to a presentation file.

15. ☑ **E.** The choices in answers **A** through **D** are distribution options for a slide presentation.

   ☒ **A, B, C, D,** and **F** are incorrect. While each of the choices in answers **A** through **D** is correct, answer **E** is the best choice. Answer **F** is wrong by elimination.

Part III

Living
Online Exam

Objectives Map: Living Online Exam

Official Objective	Study Guide Coverage	Chapter number
Identify that networks (including computer networks and other networks such as the telephone network) transmit different types of data	Transmitting Data	17
Identify concepts related to network communication (e.g. high speed, broadband, wireless (wifi), etc.)	Communicating on a Network	17
Identify fundamental principles of security on a network including authorization, authentication, and wireless security issues,	Securing a Network	17
Identify benefits of networked computing	Identifying the Benefits of Networked Computing	18
Identify the risks of networked computing	Identifying the Risks of Networked Computing	18
Identify the roles of clients and servers in a network	Identifying the Roles of Clients and Servers in a Network	18
Identify networks by size and type	Identifying Networks by Size and Type	18
Identify how to use an electronic mail application	Using an Electronic Mail Application	19
Identify different types of electronic communication/collaboration and how they work	Identifying Types of Electronic Communication	20
Identify the appropriate use of different types of communication/collaboration tools and the "rules of the road" regarding online communication ("netiquette")	Identifying Appropriate Uses for Electronic Communication	20
Identity information about the Internet, the World Wide Web and Web sites and be able to use a Web browsing application	The Internet, the World Wide Web, and Web Browsers	21
Understand how content is created, located and evaluated on the World Wide Web	Creating Content on the Web	22
Identify how computers are used in different areas of work, school and home	Computers at Work, School, and Home	23
Identify the risks of using computer hardware and software and how to use computers and the Internet safely, ethically and legally	Using Computers Safely and Ethically	24

17

Data
Communications
Basics

T he transmission of electrical signals over cable and through the air is the foundation of networking. However, without the capability to control and regulate these signals, data networking would be chaos. This chapter provides an overview and some detail into the types of signals that are transmitted along with how they are controlled, managed, and regulated. We look at the different cabling media, communications devices, and methods used to secure the transmission of data signals across the network.

CERTIFICATION OBJECTIVE

Transmitting Data

1.1.1   Identify that networks (including computer networks and other networks such as the telephone network) transmit different types of data.

The signals that are transmitted across a network are used to send a variety of data types, including text and numerical data, graphic images, video, sound, and multimedia. The signals that make up these data types can be transmitted virtually around the world. This means that a secure, reliable, and coordinated transmission system must be in place to assure not only that they are transmitted properly, but that the data that arrives at the requester (receiver) is error-free and complete.

To provide this assurance, a number of network components are required, including network media, internetworking devices, security methods, and the standards and protocols that provide the interoperability of these elements.

Digital vs. Analog Signals

A digital signal, regardless of whether it is transmitted on the internal bus structure of the motherboard and processor or across a network, represents the binary value of the data being transmitted. As a result, the signal pattern of the data consists of a series of high and low frequencies, as illustrated in Figure 17-1. On the other hand, an analog signal, also illustrated in Figure 17-1, is composed of multiple frequencies and amplitudes that represent many characteristics of the data being transmitted.

The frequency of a transmitted signal is, in effect, its identity. In the case of digital data, two primary frequencies are used for each data stream to represent the

FIGURE 17-1

A simplified depiction of digital (top left) and analog (lower right) data signals

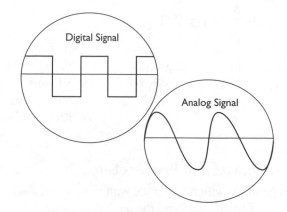

two binary values in the full range of frequencies that the transmitting device and the media support. However, analog signals are commonly used to represent the changes in pitch and volume of sound. Because the sounds a person can make can have quite a range in frequency (pitch) or amplitude (volume), it requires virtually the whole frequency spectrum of the media to transmit the sound accurately.

Today's networks are now essentially all digital, including a majority of the voice and multimedia traffic with one primary exception. That exception is the use of data modulators/demodulators, or modems for short, which translate (modulate) the digital signals of a computer into analog signals for transmission over the public switched telephone network (PSTN). A modem must also be placed at the receiving end of the transmission to reconvert (demodulate) the received signals back into digital form.

CERTIFICATION OBJECTIVE

Communicating on a Network

1.1.6   Identify concepts related to network communication (e.g., high speed, broadband, wireless [wifi], etc.).

The data communications technologies used on today's networks were essentially developed from the transmission methods used to send telephone voice signals from point to point. Before the full development of digital signals, all signals transmitted on the telephone network had to be converted to analog signals.

Data Communications Principles

Networks don't just happen; a great deal of planning, science, technology, and sweat must be brought together to enable even the simplest of networks to function properly. Three necessary building blocks must be in place before a network can operate. These required elements are protocols, media, and security. In the sections that follow, we discuss the first two of these necessities, with the third discussed later in the chapter.

Standards and Protocols

A *protocol,* which is defined by a standard, is a set of rules that are implemented by each of the devices and media that transmit data from its source to its destination. In order for the transmission to occur seamlessly, all of the devices carrying the signal must operate with the same protocols. The predominant set of protocols used for both local area networks (LANs) and wide area networks (WANs) is the Transmission Control Protocol (TCP)/Internet Protocol (IP) suite.

on the **ĵob**

A local area network (LAN) is a network of at least two nodes (networked devices) that operates within a limited geographical space to share resources, such as a company LAN or a home network. A wide area network (WAN) interconnects multiple LANs over a wide geographical space and operates to provide communications services to the local networks. The Internet is perhaps the best and most extreme example of a WAN.

TCP/IP contains an assortment of protocols each of which performs a specific task to support the transmission of data across a network. Table 17-1 lists the more commonly used data communications protocols in the TCP/IP suite.

TABLE 17-1	Commonly Used Protocols in the TCP/IP Suite
Protocol	**Application**
Domain Name System (DNS)	Conversion of named Internet locations to IP addressing
Dynamic Host Configuration Protocol (DHCP)	Consistent configuration of networked devices
File Transfer Protocol (FTP)	Transfer data from source to destination
Hypertext Transfer Protocol (HTTP)	Download and display Internet and Web content
Internet Protocol (IPv4 or IPv6)	Network addressing
Transmission Control Protocol (TCP)	Guaranteed transmission and receipt of data
User Datagram Protocol (UDP)	Nonguaranteed transmission of data

Networking Models

Perhaps the standard that has the most influence on other networking standards and protocols is the Open System Interconnect (OSI) standard. The OSI standard, which has been redefined in a variety of proprietary ways, was introduced when networking technologies were first being defined to provide a structure and to narrow the scope of networking standards and protocols.

The OSI model is defined in seven layers, which each layer defining one segment of operations that must occur in a network data communication. Table 17-2 lists the layers of the OSI model.

Another model that evolved from the OSI model is the TCP/IP model, which is commonly referred to as the IP mode. This model defines the functions of the seven-layer OSI model into five layers, shown in Table 17-3.

Regardless of the network model in use, the operations for a protocol or device must fall within the defined scope of a single network model layer. This helps to ensure that protocols and devices from different developers and manufacturers are able to communicate with each other; that is, they are interoperable.

Protocol Data Units

Data transmitted across a network must also conform to a format prescribed by the protocol in use. As data moves up or down the protocols and devices of each network model layer, the data is divided up into what are called protocol data units (PDUs) of varying lengths. The protocol or device on each layer adds a header or footer to the data that provides instructions to the corresponding protocol or device operating at the same network layer on the receiving end of the transmission.

TABLE 17-2	The Layers of the OSI Model	
Layer	**Title**	**Definition Scope**
1	Physical	Physical transmission media and devices
2	Data Link	Link setup and monitoring
3	Network	Network addressing and routing
4	Transport	Control and monitoring of data transmission
5	Session	Management and control of communications between devices
6	Presentation	Formatting data for transmission or use by user application; encryption
7	Application	Interaction with user software for access to network

TABLE 17-3

The Layers
of the TCP/IP
Networking
Model

Layer	Layer Title	OSI Layer Overlap
1	Physical	Physical
2	Link or Network Access	Data Link
3	Internet	Network
4	Transport	Transport and Session
5	Application	Session, Presentation, and Application

Table 17-4 lists the names of the data segments created on each layer of the IP networking mode and whether a header, footer, or both are added to the segmented units. As listed, transmitted data is passed by the user application to the Application layer as a block of data. With some restructuring, the data block is passed to the Presentation layer, where it's formatted for transmission, including encryption, if applicable, within its original data block. The Session layer receives the data block, extracts the destination and source addresses, and adds them and a few other data fields to a header. The header is then added to the data block in addition to the header added in the Presentation layer. Using information on the characteristics of the transmission link supplied by the Session layer, the Transport layer divides the data block into fixed-length segments and adds its header to each segment. The Network layer then creates packets that include the addressing and routing information for each. The Data Link layer then encapsulates frames from the packets for transmission. Finally, the Physical layer transmits each frame as a bit stream.

At the receiving end of the transmission, each bit stream is reconstructed into a frame based on the information in the frame's header and footer at the Data Link layer. The frame is converted back into packets, and using the information in

TABLE 17-4

The Protocol
Data Units
Created on Each
Layer of the OSI
Model

OSI Layer	PDU
Application	Data
Presentation	Data
Session	Data
Transport	Segment
Network	Packet
Data Link	Frame
Physical	Bits

the header of each packet, the data is formatted into segments and passed to the Transport model, and so on.

Data Communications Media

When we discuss network or communications media, what we're really talking about is the network cabling or the wireless transmission system. Media is a plural word; when we mean a single cable type or segment, we are talking about a medium. Network or communications media provide the means by which transmitted signals are carried on a network. In a wired LAN situation, the media are likely copper or perhaps even fiberglass or glass cabling. In a wireless network, the transmission medium is created by the radio frequency (RF) links between antennas.

Copper Media

The standard copper cabling used in networks is twisted-pair cable. Twisted-pair (TP) cable is inexpensive, easy to handle, and readily available. TP cable gets its name from its construction, in which the two copper wires in a wire pair are twisted around each other. Twisting the wires in pairs reduces the impact of cancellation between the two wires.

When an electrical signal is transmitted over a copper wire, some of the signal inevitably leaks out as electromagnetic interference (EMI). In addition, the copper wires can also absorb energy (EMI) from its environment. Depending on the strength of the signal and the amount of EMI present, this can interfere or override (cancel) the signal on itself and any other wires in close proximity. Twisting two wires around each other in a set pattern (twists-per-inch) helps to reduce the cancellation effect.

The most popular types of TP cable are unshielded TP (UTP) and shielded TP (STP). UTP wire, shown in Figure 17-2, as its name implies, doesn't include much

FIGURE 17-2

Unshielded twisted-pair (UTP) cabling

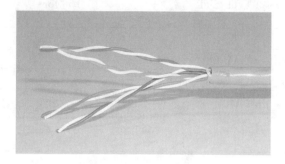

FIGURE 17-3

Shielded twisted-pair (STP) cabling

electromechanical interference (EMI) shielding. STP cabling (see Figure 17-3) and its variations of shielded and screened cabling, like screened TP (ScTP), have a wrapping of foil or metallic screening around the wire bundle and, in some versions, around each of the wire pairs as well. This shielding is added to protect the inner wires from EMI and cancellation effects.

TP Category Standards   TP cable is designated for a variety of voice and data uses by a standard specification that divides the various grades of TP cabling into a series of categories. Each category, or CAT, as they are commonly referred to, defines a specific number of wire pairs, a number of twists per inch, the bandwidth rating, the maximum segment length, and its recommended usage. Table 17-5 details the

TABLE 17-5   Twisted-Pair Cabling Category Standards

Cable Category	Cable Types	Wire Pairs	Bandwidth	Application
CAT 1	UTP	2	128 Kbps	Telephone, door bell, speaker wire
CAT 2	UTP	4	4 Mbps	Token Ring networks
CAT 3	UTP, STP	4	10 Mbps	10BaseT
CAT 4	UTP, STP	4	16 Mbps	10 Mbps Ethernet, 16 Mbps Token Ring
CAT 5	UTP, STP	4	100 Mbps	100BaseT
CAT 5e (enhanced)	UTP, STP	4	200 Mbps	1000BaseT
CAT 6	UTP, STP	4	600 Mbps	1000BaseT
CAT 7	STP	Multiple individually wrapped pairs	1 Gbps	Undefined

various TP wire categories defined in the current standards. The most common cable categories currently used in network cabling are CAT 5, CAT 5e, and CAT 6.

Ethernet Cabling Standards   Another commonly used coding scheme for TP cable is defined in the Institute for Electrical and Electronic Engineers Engineering (IEEE) 802.3 Ethernet standards. More commonly known as the Ethernet cable standards, this scheme includes coding for the nominal bandwidth, the transmission method, and the wire type. For example, 10BaseT refers to a cable that has a 10 Mbps bandwidth using baseband transmission over TP cabling. Table 17-6 lists the currently defined 802 cable standards for copper wiring.

TP Wiring Standards   The two basic standards covering network cable installation and termination in North America are the Electronics Industry Association/Telecommunications Industry Association (EIA/TIA) 568A and 568B. The primary difference between these cable standards is the sequence and placement of the color-code wire pairs in the terminated connectors (see "TP Connectors" later in this section), with the 568A standard configured for transmitting both data and voice (telephone) signals and the 568B standard carrying only data. However, internationally, the International Standards Organization/International Electrotechnical Commission (ISO/IEC) 11801 standard, which is based on the EIA/TIA 568 standards, is used.

Baseband vs. Broadband   Signals are transmitted over a network medium commonly using either baseband or broadband methods. Baseband refers to signal transmissions that use a single frequency range to carry a single signal stream. Broadband refers to signal transmissions that use multiple frequencies to transmit multiple signal streams. The "Base" reference in the Ethernet cable standards indicates that the network signals are transmitted one at a time over the medium. In a broadband transmission, the frequency spectrum of the medium is divided

TABLE 17-6

IEEE Ethernet Cabling Standards for Copper Cable

Cable Designation	Description
10BaseT	10 Mbps, baseband, TP wiring
100BaseT	100 Mbps, baseband, TP wiring
1000BaseT	1,000 Mbps (1 Gbps), baseband, TP wiring
10GBaseT	10 Gbps, baseband, TP wiring
100GBaseCR10	100 Gbps, baseband, copper wiring assembly

A sample of a
coaxial cable

into multiple channels, each of which can carry a separate signal stream, such as one channel each for voice, video, and data.

Coaxial Cable   Coaxial cable contains a single inner core wire that is encased in a layer of dielectric insulation, which is then wrapped by a wire mesh outer conductor and shield, all of which is then enclosed by a plastic sheathing. Figure 17-4 shows a sample of a coaxial cable.

Coaxial cable is typically used in situations where a more robust cable is needed where environmental conditions require it, such as damp, exposed, or relatively short vertical cable runs. Table 17-7 lists the common standard coaxial cable types and their uses. The "RG" in the cable type code of coaxial cable is a military term that stands for "radio guide."

Fiber Optic Cable

Fiber optic cabling (see Figure 17-5) is growing in popularity as a network medium. Although best suited for longer-run network segments, its use can provide a higher bandwidth throughput for any cable segment. In comparison to copper cabling (TP and especially coaxial cable), fiber optic cable has a much higher bandwidth.

Coaxial Cable
Types

Cable Type	Application
RG6	Analog cable television, digital satellite systems, and VCRs
RG11	Digital television, short-run network segments, designated as 10Base2 in Ethernet standards (the 2 refers to its maximum segment length of approximately 200 meters)
RG58	Security systems, video displays
RG59	Analog TV antennas, closed-circuit TV (CCTV)

FIGURE 17-5

A sample of multiple-strand fiber optic cable

Fiber optic cable is either single-mode or multimode. Single-mode cable carries a single signal, but over very long distances. Multimode fiber optic cable is capable of carrying multiple signals, but over shorter distances that are still longer than the requirements of most LAN network segment lengths. The fiber optic cabling used in networking is typically multimode cable.

Network Media Connectors

In order to connect to a networked device, all network media must be terminated with an appropriate connector, which is also referred to as a plug. The connectors used in a network are typically dictated by the connector types (jacks) available or supported by the devices being networked and, of course, by the type of media in use.

TP Connectors   The connectors used with TP cabling in a network are modular connectors that are generally classified as a group as registered jacks (RJ). The most commonly used connector for TP cabling is the RJ-45 connector (see Figure 17-6). Table 17-8 lists the more commonly used TP cabling connectors. Figure 17-7 shows the RJ-11 connector that is used for telephone connections over TP wire.

Coaxial Cable Connectors   Coaxial cabling, when incorporated into a network, is most commonly terminated with one of two primary connectors: a Bayonet Neill-Concelman (BNC) connector (see Figure 17-7) or an F-Type

FIGURE 17-6

An RJ-45 connector is the standard connector for TP cabling in a network.

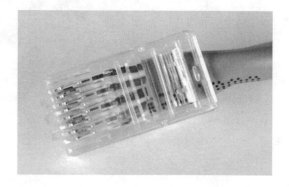

TABLE 17-8	Connector	Applications
	RJ-11	Telephone connections
Commonly Used TP Cabling Connector Types	RJ-31X	Interconnects security systems into a telephone system
	RJ-45	Standard four-pair TP cable connector in networks

connector (see Figure 17-8). BNC connectors are used in networking installations, and F-Type connections are used for coaxial cabling installed for video, sound, and security systems.

Fiber Optic Connectors   Fiber optic cable is becoming more common for home and business networks, especially integrated networks that include security, video, sound, and monitoring systems, for two reasons: its speed and bandwidth and as a hedge against future bandwidth requirements. A few of the more common fiber optic connectors used in networking installations are

- **Standard connector (SC)**   This connector, shown in Figure 17-9, is a push-pull snap-on and -off connector that is the connector currently specified by TIA 568 for both single-mode and multimode fiber cable.
- **Straight tip (ST)**   This is a commonly used connector for multimode fiber optic cabling.

FIGURE 17-7

A BNC connector is commonly used for coaxial cabling in network installations.

FIGURE 17-8

An F-Type connection is used on coaxial cabling in video and sound wiring.

- **Lucent connector (LC)**   The LC connector (see Figure 17-10) looks just like an SC connector but is one-half its size. The size of the LC is based on the size of the RJ-45 connector and is designated as a small form factor (SFF) connector for fiber optic cable.
- **Mechanical transfer (MT)**   This fiber optic connector is common on preterminated cables.

FIGURE 17-9

Male (top) and female (bottom) versions of the SC fiber optic connector

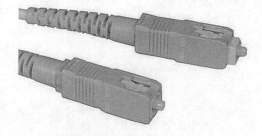

FIGURE 17-10

An LC fiber optic connector (Image courtesy of Trade Winners Net Marketing Co., Ltd.)

CERTIFICATION OBJECTIVE

Securing a Network

1.1.7   Identify fundamental principles of security on a network, including authorization, authentication, and wireless security issues.

Because networks transmit data using standard protocols and PDU formats, the data can be intercepted and interpreted by an external and unauthorized user, sometimes even if the data has been encrypted. Network security systems are often "best effort" methods that can protect the data from all but the most skilled and capable hackers.

Network security measures range from authorization and authentication to more sophisticated encryption systems. These security measures are aimed at allowing only authorized access to a network and the prevention of data being intercepted and interpreted. The next few sections provide a brief overview of the more commonly used security measures applied to networks.

Network Security Basics

The primary security measure applied to nearly all local networks is authentication and authorization. Authentication verifies that users, identified by a username and password, are who they say they are. The combination of a username and password uniquely identifies and verifies that the person entering these elements has been granted access to a local computer and the network to which it is connected. Authorization then determines what actions or accesses the authenticated user has been granted and limits his or her activities to only those activities.

Strong Passwords

The more a password resembles a common word, phrase, or series of numbers (such as a birth date), the easier it is for an attacker to crack. The use of a strong password is recommended for protecting against unauthorized access to a computer or a network. A strong password should appear to an attacker to be a random string of unrelated characters that has no apparent meaning.

The characteristics of a strong password include

■ **Length**   A longer password, one with at least eight characters, increases the number of character combinations exponentially. Each additional character in length added to a password continues to raise the number of possible character combinations to a level where the effort to crack the password is so high that it's not worth the effort. Many network operating system publishers, including Microsoft, Apple, and Novell, recommend an ideal length for a password of 14. For example, an eight-character password consisting of only alphabetic and numeric characters is over 30,000 times weaker than a 15-character password that includes the same character types.

■ **Character variety**   Just as the length of a password increases its robustness, the variety and combinations of character types, including upper- or lower-case alphabetic characters, numerical characters, and special characters, such as a question mark, at sign, asterisk, or the like, can add to the complexity and strength of a password. The characters included in a password, although seemingly unrelated, shouldn't create a pattern on the keyboard. A password should include characters located randomly about the keyboard to lessen its chances of being cracked coincidently. The password "theThirdofJune" is a far weaker password than "7h3T>1rd0fJun3."

■ **Being easily remembered**   The downside to a long password that is made up of apparently random characters is that it can be hard to remember. One way around this problem is to use a word or phrase that has meaning only to you. However, you should avoid using words, phrases, or number strings that others may know or that can be discovered easily. Actually, a completely blank password (meaning no password at all) is more secure that a short, easily detected password. Remember that passwords are supposed to be a secret that only you know.

Data Communications Security

Data transmitted over wires or through the air uses radio frequency (RF) signaling, which can be intercepted and interpreted. To prevent the transmitted signal from an unauthorized capture and interpretation, the data is typically encoded. Encryption is the most commonly used method to protect transmitted data, but security can also be applied through the communications devices in the network.

Security has become an important aspect for all types of networks, whether small networks in homes and offices or large international networks, such as the Internet. The primary source of network security is the TCP/IP suite of protocols, which includes utilities specifically designed to help create a secure network environment.

In a home or small office network, the device that connects it to a WAN for Internet access (Internet gateways, such as modems, bridges, and routers) provides security services that help to secure the devices attached to them. In addition, third-party software and hardware can be added to a home network to provide additional security.

Threats to a Network

To understand the need for security on a network, you should first understand the potential threats to a network. Most of these potential threats are possible because the Internet Protocol (IP), the addressing and access protocol of the Internet, doesn't include any mechanisms for authentication, meaning that it doesn't ask who or where is trying to access the device or network represented by a particular IP address.

Most attacks on a network typically are focused on making the network's router or primary server so busy that it can't provide a normal level of service to bona fide network traffic, which in effect shuts down the network. The most common network-borne threats to any network are denial of service and IP spoofing attacks.

A *denial of service (DoS)* attack is intended to deny service of an Internet gateway or router by occupying it with a stream of service requests of the type that the gateway or router must service above all other requests, internal or external. In a similar way, *IP spoofing* takes advantage of the fact that some networking devices support an access control list that contains the external source IP addresses that can be passed onto the internal network. An outside source can gain access to a network if any of the allowed IP addresses is discovered or if, as in a denial of service attack, the source can busy-out the gateway with a stream of random IP addresses.

Security Protocols

Typically, Internet service is acquired through an Internet service provider (ISP) that provides an IP address. This address is assigned through DHCP and will commonly be a different address each time the user connects to the ISP's network. While not intended as a security feature, changing the IP address frequently creates a moving target for a network hacker looking to invade a network.

NAT   Most Internet gateway devices support the Network Address Translation (NAT) service, including most dialup connections. NAT may be supported in the local device, which is common with most commercial internetworking devices that include routing capability, or through the ISP's router.

NAT translates the IP address assigned to a local connection into a generic IP address that is sent out on the WAN. Because evildoers only see the generic IP address, a specific network is protected because its actual IP address is unknown to them.

Internet Protocol Security   Internet Protocol Security (IPSec) secures transmitted packets at the Network (OSI) or Internet (TCP/IP) layer. IPSec applies encryption to a message packet in one of two ways: Transport mode, which encrypts only the payload (the portion of the packet containing data from the original data) of the packet, and Tunnel mode, which encrypts the entire packet, including its header and payload.

Firewalls

Some Internet gateways also provide basic firewall functions. A firewall, which works something like an access control list, performs packet filtering and denies access to the internal network from an unknown external source. A firewall can also filter network access requests based on the type of application, service, or action requested, such as browser requests, chat, e-mail, FTP, and so on.

Wireless Network Security

Essentially, the security systems used with wireless networking are about the same as those used with a wired network. The two primary wireless security systems are MAC (Media Access Control), or physical address, filtering, which works much like an access control list, and one of two encryption methods: Wi-Fi (Wireless Fidelity) Protected Access, or WPA, the currently recommended security protocol; or Wired Equivalent Privacy (WEP), a simple encryption method.

CERTIFICATION SUMMARY

A network provides a means of communications and the sharing of resources between two or more computers connected through a communications medium. Networks are able to transmit data in either analog or digital formats with separate standards and network models defining the processes used to control, manage, and monitor the transmission.

Protocols are a series of guidelines and rules that provide interoperability between networked devices by establishing the format of transmitted data and how data is transmitted between two points on a network.

The transmission media used in a network can be twisted-pair or coaxial copper cabling, fiber optic cabling, or even a wireless radio frequency medium. Specific types of security measures are implemented to provide for secure communications on each type of network media.

✓ TWO-MINUTE DRILL

Transmitting Data

❏ A transmitted digital signal represents one binary bit of data. The signal pattern consists of high and low frequencies. An analog signal uses multiple frequencies and amplitudes to represent data. Digital data transmits on two primary frequencies that represent binary values. Analog signals require a frequency spectrum to transmit sound and video data.

Communicating on a Network

❏ Modern networks are digital networks that transmit data, voice, and multimedia traffic. A modem, which translates between digital and analog signals, modulates digital signals into analog signals for transmission and demodulates received analog signals to digital form.

❏ A protocol is a set of rules that govern the devices and media used to transmit data. The most commonly used protocols for LANs and WANs are in the TCP/IP suite.

❏ The OSI Reference Model provides a networking structure and provides for media and device interoperability. The OSI model is defined in seven layers: Physical, Data Link, Network, Transport, Session, Presentation, and Application.

❏ Data transmitted across a network must conform to a format prescribed by the protocol in use. As data moves up or down the protocols and devices of each network model layer, it's divided into PDUs.

❏ Data transmitted over wires or through the air uses RF signaling that can be intercepted and interpreted. To prevent against unauthorized capture, data is encrypted. The primary source of network security is the TCP/IP suite, which includes utilities specifically designed to create a secure network environment.

❏ The standard copper cabling used in networks is TP cable that twists the strands in a wire pair around each other to reduce cancellation. The types of TP cable are UTP and STP. UTP cable doesn't include EMI shielding. STP and ScTP have a foil or metallic shielding around the wire bundle or around each of the wire pairs.

❏ TP cable is designated by a series of categories, with each category defining the number of wire pairs, twists per inch, bandwidth, maximum segment length, and usage. The cable categories used in network cabling are CAT 5, CAT 5e, and CAT 6.

❏ The IEEE 802.3 Ethernet standards define a scheme that includes coding for nominal bandwidth, transmission mode, and wire type, such as 10BaseT.

❏ The basic standards for network cable installation and termination in North America are EIA/TIA 568A and 568B. ISO/IEC 11801 is the international standard.

❏ Signals are transmitted over a network medium commonly using either baseband or broadband methods. Baseband transmissions use a single frequency range to carry a single signal stream. Broadband transmissions use multiple frequencies to transmit multiple signal streams.

❏ Coaxial cable contains a single inner core wire that is encased in a layer of dielectric insulation, which is then wrapped by a wire mesh outer conductor and shield, all of which is then enclosed by a plastic sheathing. Coaxial cable is used when a more robust cable is needed and for damp, exposed, or relatively short vertical installations.

❏ Fiber optic cabling has a much higher bandwidth than TP or coaxial cabling. Fiber optic cable is single-mode or multimode. Single-mode cable carries a single signal over long distances. Multimode fiber optic cable carries multiple signals over shorter distances.

❏ The most commonly used TP networking connector is the RJ-45 connector. Coaxial cabling is terminated with a BNC connector in networks. The common fiber optic connectors are SC, ST, LC, and MT.

Securing a Network

❏ The primary security measure applied to nearly all local networks is authentication and authorization. Authentication verifies users, identified by a username and password, are who they say they are. Authorization determines what actions or accesses the authenticated user has been granted and limits his or her activities to only those activities.

❏ The use of a strong password is recommended for protecting against unauthorized access to a computer or a network. A strong password should have a sufficient length, include a variety of characters, and be easily remembered.

❑ The potential threats to a network are focused on occupying a network's router or primary server so that a normal level of service is interrupted. The most common network-borne threats to any network are DoS and IP spoofing attacks.

❑ NAT translates the IP address assigned to a local node into a generic IP address sent out on a WAN. IPSec secures transmitted packets by applying encryption to a message packet in one of two ways: Transport mode and Tunnel mode.

❑ A firewall performs packet filtering and denies access to the internal network from an unknown external source.

❑ The primary wireless security systems are MAC address filtering, WPA, and WEP.

SELF TEST

The following questions are intended to help you be sure that you understand the material included in this chapter. Read the questions and the answer choices carefully.

Transmitting Data

1. What type of signal is represented in the following illustration?

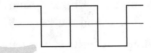

- A. Analog
- B. Digital
- C. Video
- D. Voice

2. What is the device used to convert digital signals to analog signals for transmission across a network?
- A. Firewall
- B. Internet gateway
- C. Modem
- D. Router

Communicating on a Network

3. What is the name for a set of rules that govern the actions of devices and media used to transmit data across a network?
- A. Guideline
- B. Model
- C. Protocol
- D. Suite

4. Which of the standard network models defines seven layers?
- A. DoD
- B. OSI
- C. TCP/IP
- D. None of the standard reference models define seven layers.

5. What is the third layer of the TCP/IP network model?

   A. Internet

   B. Network

   C. Physical

   D. Transport

6. What is the general name given to network message units as they progress up or down through a network model?

   A. Frames

   B. Packets

   C. PDUs

   D. Segments

7. What is the standard copper cabling type most often used in networks?

   A. Coaxial

   B. EMI

   C. Fiber optic

   D. Twisted-pair

8. What type of classifications are copper twisted-pair cabling grouped by based on the cable's characteristics?

   A. Categories

   B. EIA/TIA standards

   C. IEEE standards

   D. RJ groups

9. What is the IEEE standard that defines Ethernet and the use of copper cabling in a network?

   A. IEEE 11801

   B. IEEE 802.3

   C. IEEE 802.11

   D. Ethernet is not defined by an IEEE standard.

10. What are the basic standards used for network cabling installation and termination in North America?

   A. ISO/IEC 11801

   B. EIA/TIA 568a and 568b

   C. IEEE 802.3

   D. IEEE 802.11

11. What type of signal transmission uses a single frequency to carry a single signal stream across a transmission medium?
    A. Baseband
    B. Broadband
    C. Single-mode
    D. Multimode

12. What type of cabling is shown in the following picture?

    A. Coaxial
    B. Fiber optic
    C. Shielded twisted-pair
    D. Unshielded twisted-pair

13. What are the two most common styles of fiber optic cabling used in LANs and WANs?
    A. Single-mode
    B. Multimode
    C. Shielded twisted-pair
    D. Screened twisted-pair

14. What is the standard connector type used with twisted-pair cabling in a network installation?
    A. BNC
    B. F-Type
    C. RJ-45
    D. SC

Securing a Network

15. What are the two primary levels of security applied on a local computer to prevent unauthorized access to the computer and its network?

- **A.** Accounting
- **B.** Authentication
- **C.** Authorization
- **D.** Packet filtering

16. Which of the following is the best example of a strong password?

- **A.** #12345678!
- **B.** Blank
- **C.** S7r0n9P@5sw0r6!
- **D.** Ic3Rocks!

17. What is the primary source of security for network traffic transmitted across a TCP/IP network?

- **A.** IP
- **B.** IPSec
- **C.** TCP
- **D.** TCP/IP contains no security features.

18. Which of the following are common types of network attacks?

- **A.** Access control lists
- **B.** DoS
- **C.** IP spoofing
- **D.** MAC filtering

19. What is encrypted by NAT running in Transport mode?

- **A.** Footers and payload
- **B.** Footers only
- **C.** Headers and payload
- **D.** Headers only
- **E.** Payload only

SELF TEST ANSWERS

Transmitting Data

1. ☑ **B.** A digital signal represents only the two binary values in a digital data stream.
   ☒ **A, C,** and **D** are incorrect. Analog signals represent changes in data values, sound pitch, and volume and must use a full range of frequencies and amplitudes to do so. Video and voice signals are transmitted as either digital or analog.

2. ☑ **C.** A modem modulates and demodulates a digital signal into an analog signal or the reverse.
   ☒ **A, B,** and **D** are incorrect. A firewall is a digital network device that prevents unauthorized network traffic from gaining access to a network. An Internet gateway provides a link to the Internet or WAN provided by an ISP. A router is a digital network device that determines the best path network PDUs should take to reach their destination address.

3. ☑ **C.** Protocols define the rules of integration, interaction, and interoperability between networking software and devices.
   ☒ **A, B,** and **D** are incorrect. Protocols can include guidelines, but they are more rigid than that. A network model defines layers of network interactions on which protocols are specifically defined. A suite of protocols, such the TCP/IP suite, contain several protocols and utilities.

Communicating on a Network

4. ☑ **B.** The OSI network model defines seven layers: Physical, Data Link, Network, Transport, Session, Presentation, and Application.
   ☒ **A, C,** and **D** are incorrect. The DoD and TCP/IP models define five layers each, and because the OSI model does define seven layers, answer **D** is incorrect.

5. ☑ **A.** The third layer of the TCP/IP model is the Internet layer.
   ☒ **B, C,** and **D** are incorrect. The Network layer is the third layer of the OSI model. The Physical layer is the first layer and the Transport layer is the fourth layer of both the TCP/IP and OSI models.

6. ☑ **C.** The message units of all layers of a network model are referred to as protocol data units (PDUs).
   ☒ **A, B,** and **D** are incorrect. A frame is the PDU created at the Data Link layer. A packet is the PDU created at the Network or Internet layer. A segment is the PDU created at the Transport layer.

7. ☑ **D.** Twisted-pair copper cabling is by far the most commonly used network medium.

   ☒ **A, B,** and **C** are incorrect. Coaxial cabling is used in network installations for special purposes, such as vertical runs and audio/video cabling. EMI (electromagnetic interference) is not a cabling type, but rather an environmental hazard to copper cabling. Fiber optic cabling is not a copper cabling type.

8. ☑ **A.** Twisted-pair cabling is classified into categories (CATs) that specify the characteristics of specific cabling types.

   ☒ **B, C,** and **D** are incorrect. The EIA/TIA cabling standards (specifically the EIA/TIA 568A and 568B standards) specify the installation and termination of cabling. The IEEE standards (specifically the IEEE 802.3 standard) specify the use of copper cabling in Ethernet networks. The RJ (registered jack) standards include copper cabling connectors.

9. ☑ **B.** The IEEE 802.3 standard defines the use of copper cabling in a network running Ethernet technology.

   ☒ **A, C,** and **D** are incorrect. The 11801 standard is defined by the ISO/IEC. The IEEE 802.11 standard defines wireless networking. The IEEE does define the Ethernet standards.

10. ☑ **B.** The EIA/TIA 568a and 568b are the standards that define cable installation and termination in North America.

    ☒ **A, C,** and **D** are incorrect. The ISO/IEC 11801 standard is an equivalent standard used outside of North America. The IEEE 802.3 standards define cabling for Ethernet networks. The IEEE 802.11 standard defines wireless networking.

11. ☑ **A.** Baseband transmissions send a single signal across network media.

    ☒ **B, C,** and **D** are incorrect. Broadband transmissions send multiple signals across network media. Single-mode and multimode are types of fiber optic cabling.

12. ☑ **A.** The cable shown in the illustration is a coaxial cable.

    ☒ **B, C,** and **D** are incorrect. Fiber optic cabling is shown earlier in the chapter in Figure 17-5. Shielded and unshielded twisted-pair cables are shown in Figures 17-3 and 17-2, respectively.

13. ☑ **A and B.** The most commonly used fiber optic cabling types for network installations are single-mode and multimode.

    ☒ **C and D** are incorrect. Fiber optic cabling is not a twisted-pair cable.

14. ☑ **C.** The RJ-45 connector is the standard and most frequently used connector for network installations.

    ☒ **A, B,** and **D** are incorrect. The BNC connector is the standard connector for coaxial cable in a network installation. The F-Type connector is used for special-purpose network runs, such as audio/video connections. The SC connector is a commonly used connector for fiber optic cabling.

Securing a Network

15. ☑ **B and C.** Authentication and authorization verify the username and password and determine the access levels of the verified user.

    ☒ **A and D** are incorrect. In certain networks, what the user accesses is logged—logging is an accounting action common to ISP networks. Packet filtering is a security measure applied by a firewall or router to protect a network.

16. ☑ **C.** Because of its length, its mixture of special characters, upper- and lowercase letters, and numbers, of the passwords included in the answer choices, this is the most robust example of a strong password.

    ☒ **A, B,** and **D** are incorrect. While it includes special characters, the use of a sequence of numbers eliminates answer A as a strong password. Sometimes a blank password is too obvious to be guessed, but it is more insidious than strong. The password in answer D is not long enough to be considered a strong password.

17. ☑ **B.** IP Security (IPSec) is the primary security protocol used on a TCP/IP network.

    ☒ **A, C,** and **D** are incorrect. Answers A and C do not contain security features. Answer D is incorrect because IPSec is a part of the TCP/IP suite.

18. ☑ **B and C.** Denial-of-service (DoS) and IP spoofing are the most common general types of network attacks.

    ☒ **A and D** are incorrect. Access control lists (ACLs) and MAC filtering are security features that attempt to guard against network attacks.

19. ☑ **E.** NAT running in Transport mode encrypts only the payload of a packet.

    ☒ **A, B, C,** and **D** are incorrect. NAT running in Tunnel mode encrypts the entire packet, including any headers or footers attached to the packet.

18

Network Basics

CERTIFICATION OBJECTIVES

- Identifying Networks by Size and Type

- Identifying the Roles of Clients and Servers in a Network

- Identifying Benefits of Networked Computing

- Identifying the Risks of Networked Computing

✓ Two-Minute Drill

Q&A Self Test

Beyond the cabling, connectors, and protocols, a network provides a number of benefits that aren't available to standalone computers. A networked and internetworked environment is able to share resources; provide for better security; and facilitate cooperation, collaboration, and coordination to its users.

This chapter discusses these benefits along with the devices and network layouts that go beyond the basic infrastructure of the network to provide the connectivity necessary to fully realize the true worth of a network to its users and their organizations. There are some risks to a networked environment, as was briefly discussed in Chapter 17, but most can be prevented or avoided. In nearly all situations, the benefits of a networked environment outweigh the risks.

CERTIFICATION OBJECTIVE

Identifying Networks by Size and Type

1.1.5   Identify networks by size and type.

A *network* is an arrangement in which two or more computers are interconnected for the purpose of sharing resources. A network can vary in size and scope. It can service a single department, an entire company or organization, or, in the extreme, the entire world. In any situation, a network requires a certain type of arrangement (topology) and be designed and implemented with its purpose and the needs of its users as its priority. In the next few sections, the primary network topologies and how each topology is best suited to a particular type and size of network is discussed.

Network Topologies

A network topology is its layout. In effect, a network topology is a pattern in which networked computers and devices are arranged. In theory, each of the basic topologies loosely arranges network nodes into a particular shape or arrangement. However, in actual practice, the topology is more about how the cabling is arranged, which dictates the pattern of the connected devices.

There are essentially five network topologies that can be used in a network: peer-to-peer, bus, star, ring, and mesh. Each of these topologies is discussed in the following sections.

Peer-to-Peer Topology

A network must connect at least two computers or devices, and the *peer-to-peer* network, shown in Figure 18-1, is the most primitive of the network topologies. Two computers are directly connected through network media for the purpose of sharing resources. Each computer user controls the level of access available to the network peers (other users), which may not always be the most cooperative network environment. If additional computers are added to the peer-to-peer network, each additional computer is added by connecting to a network peer in a sort of daisy-chain fashion. A peer-to-peer network has a practical limit of 10–15 connected peers.

Bus Topology

A primary network cable, called a *backbone* (picture a fish skeleton), provides the main bus structure to the network. Any devices connecting to the network must connect into the backbone directly through a connecting device, such as a hub, switch (see "Connectivity Devices" later in the chapter), or tap. As illustrated in Figure 18-2, the backbone carries transmitted signals between network nodes. The extreme ends of the backbone must be terminated to prevent signals from bouncing back onto the medium. The bus topology is most associated with Ethernet networks, although a hybrid of the bus and star topologies is most commonly used.

Star Topology

The *star* topology (see Figure 18-3) connects network nodes directly to a signal source. In its earliest form, each networked device was connected through a dedicated cable to a server or communications processor. The advantage of the star topology

FIGURE 18-1

A simple peer-to-peer network

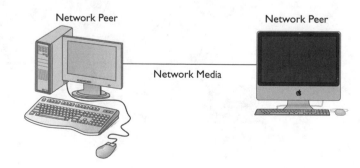

A bus topology

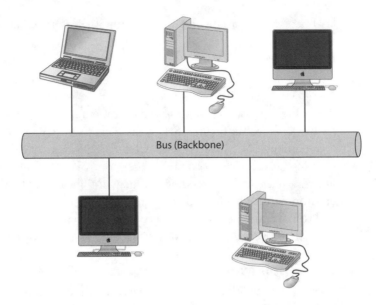

over a bus topology is that each device has dedicated bandwidth, which is shared on a bus structure.

Star topologies are very popular in Ethernet networks as a clustering arrangement. As illustrated in Figure 18-4, the bus topology and the star topology are combined to form a hybrid topology often referred to as a star-bus topology. The clustering device, typically a hub or switch (see "Connectivity Devices" later in the chapter),

A basic star topology

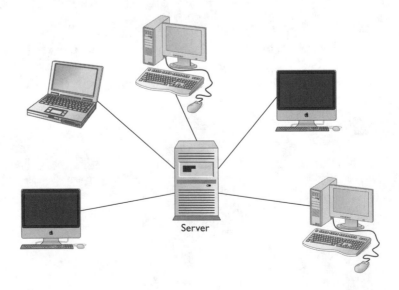

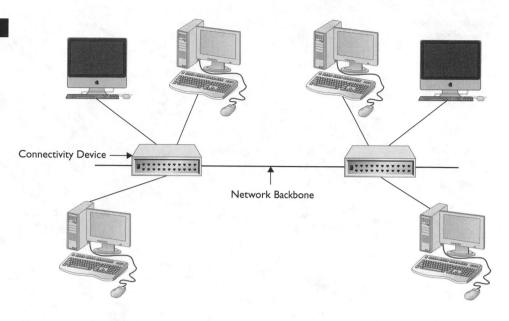

FIGURE 18-4

The star-bus topology hybrid is commonly used in Ethernet networks.

Connectivity Device →

Network Backbone

is connected to the network backbone, and each network node is connected to the network media through the clustering device.

Ring Topology

In the *ring* topology, introduced by IBM as the basic topology for its Token Ring network technology, the network backbone is arranged in a loop that is not always circular. Devices connect to the network backbone through devices called multiple-station access units (MSAUs), which are essentially smart hubs. As shown in Figure 18-5, the main ring (backbone) passes through the MSAUs to which multiple devices can connect to the network, much as in the star-bus topology.

By the nature of electrical signals and the network backbone, only a single signal can occupy the network media at any one time. This is a particular problem for bus and star-bus networks in that more than one networked device may attempt to transmit to the network at once, causing what is called a collision. Although Ethernet technologies have mechanisms to reduce the likelihood of a collision, they do still happen.

In a ring topology, as implemented in a Token Ring or Apple Token Talk network, only the device that has been designated as the active node, because the

The basic layout of a network using a ring topology

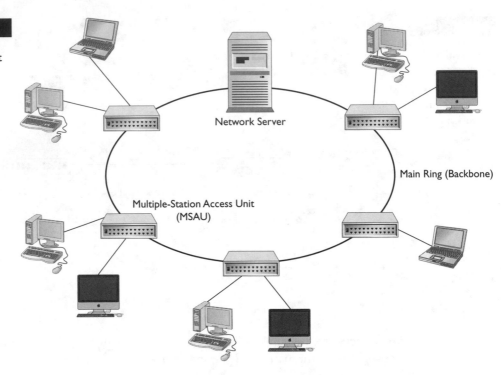

Network Server

Main Ring (Backbone)

Multiple-Station Access Unit (MSAU)

network server has assigned it a token, can transmit to the network, thus avoiding collisions.

Mesh Topology

In its most basic form, a mesh network topology is a peer-to-peer arrangement, except that each network node is directly connected to all other network nodes. As you can see in Figure 18-6, this network arrangement requires more network cabling than other network topologies. However, a mesh network has the benefit that, unless there is a complete catastrophic event, a node can communicate to another node, to which it may have lost connectivity, by passing through any nodes with which it still has connectivity.

Network Types

Essentially, there are only two types of networks: local area networks and wide area networks. However, there are a number of variations to these two basic types, each named and based on the area it's intended to serve. The more dominant of these network types are discussed in the sections that follow.

FIGURE 18-6

A mesh topology provides built-in redundancy.

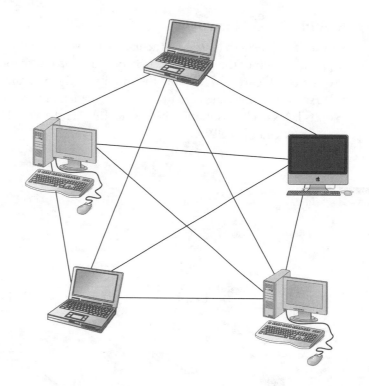

Local Area Networks

A *local area network (LAN)* is the most basic form of network. It must include at least two computers connected with a network medium and exist for the purpose of sharing resources. A LAN can be implemented on any of the five standard topologies (see "Network Topologies" earlier in the chapter) and need not be connected to any external network.

As its name implies, a LAN is a local network typically limited to a specific geographical area, such as a single home, department, business, or organization. Even if a LAN does connect to an external network, it's generally self-sufficient to support the resource sharing needs of its users.

A LAN can also host an intranet, which is an information and resource sharing system for network users connected to the local network. A LAN can also support an extranet, which allows external employees, suppliers, and even customers to connect to the network from outside the LAN. Some LANs also support secure, direct-link connections for authorized users, who connect via a WAN, to access network resources via a virtual private network (VPN).

Wide Area Networks

A *wide area network* (WAN) is actually a network of networks (a nexus) that provides each of the connected networks the capability to communicate with each other (see Figure 18-7). While the Internet is the best and biggest example of a WAN, a single business or enterprise can implement its own WAN to connect each of its LANs. The distinction between a LAN and a WAN is the larger geographical area serviced by the WAN.

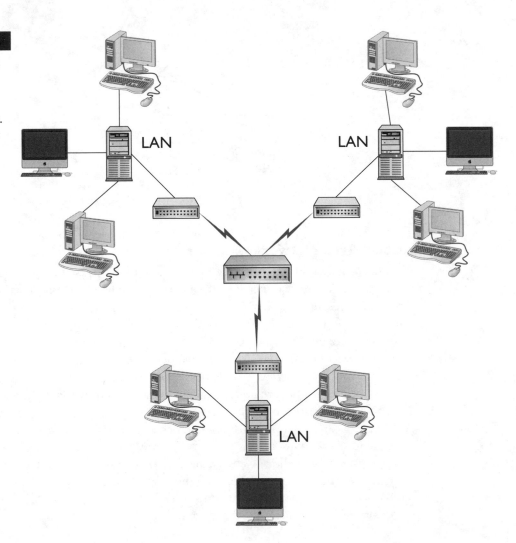

Personal Area Networks

A *personal area network (PAN)* is a limited-space network designed to provide connectivity between a computer and its peripheral devices for the flexible productivity of a single user. Typically, the devices of a PAN are connected through one form of cable-replacement technology or another, including radio frequency (RF) and infrared (IR), in the space of 30 feet (slightly less than 10 meters) or less.

Other Network Types

A few other network types are defined for specific usage or geographical spaces. A *campus area network (CAN)* is an interconnection of LANs in a specific and contiguous, geographical space, such as on a business or college campus. A *metropolitan area network (MAN)* provides network connectivity over an enlarged geographical area, such as in the downtown core of a city for business, government agencies, schools, libraries, and in some cases, even citizens.

Connectivity Devices

To achieve a desired level of performance, all but the simplest peer-to-peer and local area networks require the use of connectivity devices to provide certain levels of bandwidth, connections to local network media, and external connections as well. These devices, which are also called networking or internetworking devices, range from repeaters to routers, each of which performs a specific and essential network function.

Repeaters

At some point, all network media reaches an attenuation distance. Attenuation is the point at which a signal transmitted over a network medium begins to lose its signal strength and integrity. For example, the attenuation distance for a coaxial cable ranges from around 185 meters (about 607 feet) to approximately 500 meters (about 1,600 feet); twisted-pair cabling's attenuation distance is just under 110 meters (about 360 feet); and fiber optic cable, when used in an Ethernet network, has an attenuation distance of around 1,000 meters (or about 3,200 feet or two-thirds of a mile).

In the situation where a network media segment must extend beyond its standard attenuation length, a repeater can be installed. A repeater basically does what its name says; it receives the signal and re-energizes it so that it can be transmitted on the network beyond the attenuation length of the media.

Hubs

A network *hub* allows multiple devices to share the bandwidth of a network connection. At their most basic, hubs receive any incoming signals and pass them to any devices connected to them without enhancing the signal in any way. Hubs have evolved from their basic function to smart hubs and switches. These devices provide essentially the same function as a repeater, and some even include switching capabilities that send the signal out to one or more of its connected devices only when the signals are addressed to them.

Switches

A network *switch* can be compared to the function of a switchboard operator. An incoming signal is examined to determine if it is addressed to a device connected to one of the switch's ports (interfaces). If so, the signal is forwarded only to the addressed device. Switches also provide some buffering capabilities that allow them to enhance the signal strength and bandwidth. Figure 18-8 illustrates the placement of a network switch in a LAN.

Bridges

A *bridge* is essentially what its name suggests, a connection between two networks, often with dissimilar networking technologies or media. For example, a bridge can be used to provide an interconnection between a Token Ring network and an Ethernet network. A wireless bridge can also be used to span between two separate but adjacent buildings.

Routers

A *router* is the primary connection point between one or more LANs and a WAN. Routers have evolved to become very robust devices, with several network security and support capabilities, but their primary job is to determine the better path (meaning which of its ports is connected to the better path) for a network packet to take to best reach its destination.

Figure 18-8 illustrates a typical placement of a router in a LAN. The router is connected to any internal devices to provide access to an external network (WAN, Internet). The router serves the role of the Internet gateway in that it is the primary entrance and exit point for a LAN to reach outside networks.

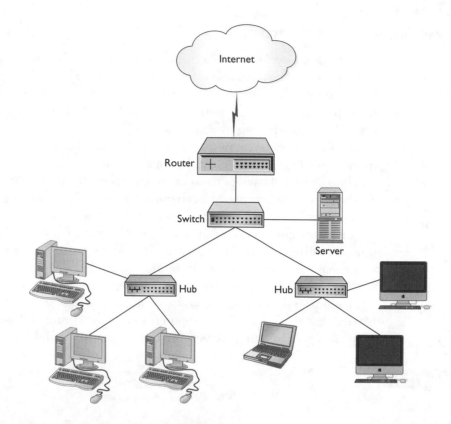

FIGURE 18-8

The connectivity devices commonly included in a LAN include one or more hubs to connect networked nodes to the network media.

CERTIFICATION OBJECTIVE

Identifying the Roles of Clients and Servers in a Network

1.1.4   Identify the roles of clients and servers in a network.

The majority of local networks are implemented as client/server networks, since servers are needed to service requests for resources or processing from network clients. While it's common to think of clients and servers in terms of hardware, they are both actually software. In fact, a single computer can be both a client and a server, depending on the software installed and its defined role to the network.

Client/Server Networks

One of the primary benefits of a client/server network is that shared resources can be centralized, making them readily available to any user who has been granted permission by the network administrators to access them. The resources shared on a client/server network can be almost anything that could be installed on each of the individual network clients separately, which of course would create redundancy and increase costs.

In effect, creating a network server requires only that the server software be installed on a network-connected computer. A networked computer can actually function as several types of network servers if the software for each server is installed. At the same time, any network computer can also be a network client, even if it functions as a network server in certain cases.

A network client, such as an e-mail client, is any locally installed software that interacts with a network server, such as a mail server, to request the resources it needs or to accomplish a task. For the most part, local network nodes are only clients typically, but as discussed in the preceding paragraph, they can also be network servers fairly easily.

Figure 18-9 illustrates the physical elements of a sample client/server network. Notice that two server-class computers have been configured as the primary network server (running the network operating system) and as a database server

FIGURE 18-9

The physical components of a client/server network

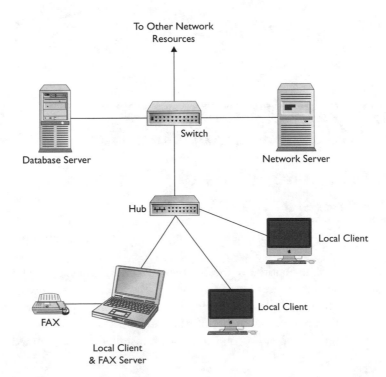

(running the database management system). Requests for network services, such as boot-up network configurations or logins, are requested by a client from the server, which responds with the requested data or performs the requested action. Requests for data from the network database are made by a client to the database server, which responds with the data requested.

Figure 18-9 also shows that one of the local computers serves as the fax server for the network. While this computer is primarily a local client, it also provides fax support to all other network computers, including the two designated servers, when requested.

CERTIFICATION OBJECTIVE

Identifying Benefits of Networked Computing

1.1.2   Identify benefits of networked computing.

The difference between working in a networked environment and working with a standalone computer is much like a team of very strong tug-of-war athletes competing against a single, frail person in a tug-of-war contest. The benefits of a networked environment far exceed the risks, especially if steps are taken to minimize the risks.

The Benefits of a Computer Network

A network exists to provide its users and organization with the ability to share resources, cooperate on activities, collaborate on projects, and coordinate use of shared resources and products. However, beyond the benefits inherent from a network achieving these goals, there are other benefits a home, business, or enterprise can realize from a computer network, including

- **Communications**   Users connected to a network have the capability to communicate by e-mail, by voice, and through shared documents and systems with other users who can be local, remote, or across the world.
- **Cost reduction**   Sharing networked devices, such as printers, fax machines, and disk storage, and Internet access reduces the number of these items to be purchased and maintained. A network also allows the computer support function in a business or enterprise to be centralized, creating a cost savings over multiple and distributed support functions.

■ **Error reduction** The number of errors made in data rises directly with the number of times the same data is entered. A networked environment that centralizes critical data stores can help to eliminate the number of times data is entered, stored, and accessed. Having accurate and readily available information can not only make network users more efficient, but can also provide a cost savings by increasing the accuracy of their work.

■ **Collaboration, cooperating, and coordination** The three Cs of networking allow network users, near or far, to collaborate on a document or project, cooperate in providing accurate data and work products, and coordinate on important correspondence, reports, and other published information.

■ **System maintenance** In an environment where every user has a standalone computer, backups must be created by physically visiting each workstation. As the number of computers increases, this can be a very costly activity in terms of both time and money. A networked environment facilitates backups, and other types of workstation maintenance can be performed from one central location, thereby reducing the size of the technical staff and increasing the effectiveness of the support function.

CERTIFICATION OBJECTIVE

Identifying the Risks of Networked Computing

1.1.3 Identify the risks of networked computing.

Computer networks also have risks, but generally the benefits outweigh the risks, if the proper and appropriate steps are taken to secure a network and properly train the network users and maintenance staff.

The Risks of a Computer Network

Unfortunately, there are risks involved with a computer network, but with the proper system configuration, security measures, and protocols, the risks can be minimized. Many of the risks are the result of external and internal threats, such as hacker attacks and unauthorized access to network resources, but the risks to a network can also be environmental, lost data, and operational failures due to improper maintenance and preventive measures.

Security Threats

Security threats to a network exist in a variety of forms such as weak passwords, viruses, and weak or nonexistent security measures. A network's password policy should require strong passwords that are changed regularly and frequently. Antivirus software should be installed on the network servers as well as their clients. The entry point to a network from external networks, such as a router, Internet gateway, or the like, should be secured with firewall services that protect the private, proprietary, or sensitive portions of the network. The security policies implemented by the network operating system and its clients should be configured at their most appropriate levels.

An unsecured network presents what amounts to an open door to hackers and other evildoers. Closing this door reduces the risk of outside attacks, avoids having compromised clients, and protects a network's resources.

Catastrophic Loss

Regardless of how secure a network may be, it is at risk from natural disaster and other catastrophic events that can either destroy the network and its devices or cause the loss of the data resources stored on the network. Natural disasters, like hurricanes, tornadoes, floods, and perhaps wildfire, not only disrupt the operations of a business or other types of organizations but can also destroy the computers, connectivity devices, and media of the organization.

In preparedness for catastrophic events, organizations should have a disaster recovery plan in place that has been tested. This plan should address the steps to be taken in the event of a catastrophic event to restore not only the network's functionality, but also the integrity of the data resources and the security measures of the network.

Internal Threats

The highest risk of an attack on a network comes from within the network's internal structure. Viruses, worms, compromised clients, and other types of network threats can gain a presence on a network client and then spread to other clients and even the network servers.

Viruses, worms, Trojan horses, and similar malware can enter a network via an e-mail message or downloaded file on a single networked computer and then spread to other computers, including the network servers. While this is much more common in a Windows operating environment, the threat is growing for UNIX, Linux, and Mac OS environments as well.

Another threat to a network is a compromised client. Regardless of how the client is compromised, whether by a stolen or computed password, malware, or perhaps even a disgruntled user or ex-employee, a compromised client can be a backdoor entry to a network that bypasses the security placed at the network's front door to guard against intrusion.

The potential risks to a computer network, including those described in this chapter, can be prevented using well-planned and executed maintenance, security, and training policies and programs. The Web has literally hundreds of sites that share examples and templates for the plans and policies that should be in place to provide a relatively risk-free network environment. One such site is the Computer Technology Documentation Project at www.comptechdoc.org.

CERTIFICATION SUMMARY

Networks are laid out and connected in one of five standard topologies—peer-to-peer, bus, star, ring, and mesh—to form local, wide, campus, metropolitan, and personal area networks. Local networks are primarily implemented as client/server networks. There are several risks and benefits for a networked environment, with the benefits exceeding the risks, if proper precautions are taken and security measures are installed.

✓ TWO-MINUTE DRILL

Identifying Networks by Size and Type

❏ A network is an arrangement in which two or more computers are interconnected for the purpose of sharing resources. A network can vary in size and scope. It can service a single department, an entire company or organization, or, in the extreme, the entire world.

❏ A network topology is a pattern in which networked computers and devices are arranged. There are five basic network topologies: peer-to-peer, bus, star, ring, and mesh.

❏ A network must connect at least two computers or devices. A peer-to-peer network is the most primitive of the network topologies. Two computers are directly connected through network media for the purpose of sharing resources.

❏ A bus topology is designed around a primary network cable or backbone that provides the main bus structure to the network. Devices connecting to the network connect into the bus through a connecting device, such as a hub, switch, or tap.

❏ The star topology connects network nodes directly to a signal source. The advantage of the star topology over a bus topology is that each device has dedicated bandwidth.

❏ In a ring topology, the network backbone is arranged in a loop. Devices connect to the ring through MSAUs.

❏ A mesh network connects each network node to all other network nodes providing the benefit that nodes can communicate to other nodes, even when direct connectivity is lost.

❏ There are two basic types of networks: a LAN and a WAN. A LAN must include at least two computers connected with a network medium and exists for the purpose of sharing resources. A LAN can host an intranet or an extranet.

❏ A WAN is a network of networks that facilitates the communications between the connected networks. The distinction between a LAN and a WAN is the larger geographical area serviced by the WAN. Other types of networks include PAN, CAN, and MAN.

❏ Networking or internetworking devices include repeaters, hubs, switches, bridges, and routers.

Identifying the Roles of Clients and Servers in a Network

❏ The majority of local networks are client/server networks. The benefit of a client/server network is that shared resources can be centralized.

Identifying Benefits of Networked Computing

❏ The benefits of networked computing include: enhanced communications, cost reduction, error reduction, collaboration, and simplified system maintenance.

Identifying the Risks of Networked Computing

❏ Security threats to a network include weak passwords, viruses, and weak or nonexistent security measures, catastrophic loss, and external and internal threats.

SELF TEST

The following questions are intended to help you be sure that you understand the material included in this chapter. Read the questions and the answer choices carefully.

Identifying Networks by Size and Type

1. Which network topology is most commonly associated with Ethernet networks?
   A. Bus
   B. Mesh
   C. Peer-to-peer
   D. Star

2. Which hybrid network topology is commonly used to cluster multiple devices onto the network backbone?
   A. Bus-mesh
   B. Ring-bus
   C. Star-bus
   D. Star-ring

3. What are generally defined as two or more computers connected via communications media for the purpose of sharing resources?
   A. Clients
   B. Hubs
   C. Networks
   D. Routers

4. What is the network type that is typically installed in a single department of a business?
   A. CAN
   B. LAN
   C. PAN
   D. WAN

5. Which network type is defined as a network of networks?
   A. CAN
   B. LAN
   C. MAN
   D. WAN

6. Which connectivity device is used to connect a local network to a WAN?
   A. Hub
   B. Network switch
   C. Repeater
   D. Router

7. What connectivity device is used to cluster multiple devices onto the network backbone?
   A. Hub
   B. Network bridge
   C. Network switch
   D. Router

Identifying the Roles of Clients and Servers in a Network

8. What is the commonly used name for a network in which network nodes request and receive services and data from another networked node?
   A. Client/Server
   B. Distributed
   C. LAN
   D. PAN

Identifying Benefits of Networked Computing

9. Which of the following is not a benefit that can be realized from a networked environment?
   A. Decreased data errors
   B. Improved collaboration
   C. Improved communications
   D. Increased operating costs

Identifying Risks of Networked Computing

10. Which of the following is not one of the risks that threaten a networked environment?
    A. Centralized system maintenance
    B. External intrusions
    C. Natural disasters
    D. Unauthorized access from an internal client

SELF TEST ANSWERS

Identifying Networks by Size and Type

1. ☑ **A.** Although most Ethernet network now use the star-bus hybrid, the bus topology has been identified with Ethernet networks from its beginning.
    ☒ **B, C,** and **D** are incorrect. Mesh networks are designed for network environments that require a high level of redundancy and reliability, but they are not specifically related to Ethernet networks. Peer-to-peer networks typically operate without a particular network technology. Star networks, in their basic form, are not used with an Ethernet network.

2. ☑ **C.** The star-bus topology hybrid is perhaps the most commonly used topology for Ethernet networks today.
    ☒ **A, B,** and **D** are incorrect. A bus-mesh network would be unnecessary overkill in a network. A ring-bus hybrid is a contradiction in basic topology definition and doesn't exist. A star-ring is a hybrid that is commonly used with ring networks.

3. ☑ **C.** The generic definition of a computer network is that stated in this answer.
    ☒ **A, B,** and **D** are incorrect. A client is a piece of software that runs on a networked device and requests services from server software running on, commonly, another networked device. A hub is a connectivity device used to cluster multiple devices onto the network media. A router is a connectivity device used to route outbound and inbound network traffic to its destinations.

4. ☑ **B.** A local area network (LAN) is the type of network installed in smaller geographical areas.
    ☒ **A, C,** and **D** are incorrect. A campus area network (CAN) interconnects LANs within a limited geographical area. A personal area network (PAN) is created by peripheral devices around a single computer. A wide area network (WAN) interconnects LANs over a wide geographical area.

5. ☑ **D.** A wide area network (WAN) interconnects LANs over a wide geographical area. A WAN is also defined as a network of networks.
    ☒ **A, B,** and **C** are incorrect. A campus area network (CAN) interconnects LANs within a limited geographical area. A local area network (LAN) is the type of network installed in smaller geographical areas. A metropolitan area network (MAN) is a limited-area WAN that provides connectivity to multiple LANs.

6. ☑ **D.** A router is typically the connectivity device used to interconnect a LAN to a WAN.
    ☒ **A, B,** and **C** are incorrect. A hub is a connectivity device used to cluster multiple devices onto the network media. A network switch is a connectivity device used to direct internal network traffic efficiently to its destination node. A repeater is a connectivity device used to overcome attenuation issues.

7. ☑ **A.** A hub is a connectivity device used to cluster multiple devices onto the network media.
☒ **B, C,** and **D** are incorrect. A network bridge is a connectivity device used to interconnect two dissimilar networks. A network switch is a connectivity device used to direct internal network traffic efficiently to its destination node. A router is typically the connectivity device used to interconnect a LAN to a WAN.

Identifying the Roles of Clients and Servers in a Network

8. ☑ **A.** A client/server network is made up of clients running on network nodes that request services and data from servers running on other network nodes.
☒ **B, C,** and **D** are incorrect. A distributed network, not discussed in this book, is a network that distributes workload and data across connected computers. A local area network (LAN) is the type of network installed in smaller geographical areas. A personal area network (PAN) is created by peripheral devices around a single computer.

Identifying Benefits of Networked Computing

9. ☑ **D.** Typically, a networked environment decreases operating costs by allowing expensive devices to be shared by network users and by centralizing the maintenance and support activities.
☒ **A, B,** and **C** are incorrect. These choices are all benefits of installing a networked environment.

Identifying Risks of Networked Computing

10. ☑ **A.** Centralized system maintenance and support is a definite benefit realized from a networked environment.
☒ **B, C,** and **D** are incorrect. These choices are all risks or threats to a network environment.

19

E-Mail Systems

- Using an Electronic Mail Application

✓ Two-Minute Drill

Q&A Self Test

T his chapter covers the features, usage, and management of an electronic mail (e-mail) client and how it's used to work with e-mail messages. It's very likely that you're already familiar with an e-mail client, such as Outlook 2007 or Outlook Express, but just to be sure you understand all of the capabilities provided by the more full-featured e-mail clients, you should study this chapter as a part of your preparations for the IC^3 exams.

CERTIFICATION OBJECTIVE

Using an Electronic Mail Application

2.2 Identify how to use an electronic mail application.

One of the very first applications used on what was to become the Internet was electronic mail (e-mail), and it has grown to be perhaps the largest single application in use today. If users know no other application, they use e-mail. The following sections cover this popular application, including its components, use, management, pitfalls, and security, all of which are important to know for the IC^3 exams.

Message Components

An e-mail message is made up of two basic components: the message header and the message body. Each part has a variety of elements that identify, address, communicate, and provide other information, such as the urgency of the message and its original sources. The following sections discuss each of these components.

E-Mail Addresses

The use of e-mail addresses has become so commonplace that we don't often think about what makes up these identifying codes. The formatting of an e-mail message is prescribed by the IETF for use with the Simple Mail Transport Protocol (SMTP), if the message is to be sent across the Internet.

An e-mail address has three components: a local-part, which contains the mailbox or user name of an e-mail client, the e-mail address separator (the at sign [@]), and a domain identity, which is used to look up the Internet address of the mail server on which the local-part is located. Figure 19-1 illustrates where in an e-mail message each of the parts is located.

FIGURE 19-1

The components
of an e-mail
address

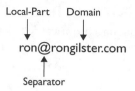

Local-Part   Domain

ron@rongilster.com

Separator

Message Headers

The *header* of an e-mail message contains a variety of information that identifies the sender, the addressee, the subject, and the origin date (the date the message was sent), along with some protocol-oriented and system-related data, which is prescribed by the Internet Engineering Task Force (IETF) for all standard-format e-mail messages (for more information on the fields in an e-mail message header, visit the IETF Web site at http://tools.ietf.org/html/rfc5322).

The fields that are commonly included in the header of an e-mail message are

- **Source address**   This field contains the e-mail address of the sender and optionally can include a sender's name or e-mail identity. This field is commonly known as the "From:" address.

- **Destination address**   This field contains the address of the intended recipient(s) of an e-mail message and optionally can also include the name or identity for each of the recipient addresses. This field is commonly called the "To:" address.

- **Subject**   This field contains an optional line of text entered by the message author to identify or summarize the contents of the message body.

- **Origination date**   This field contains the date and time the message was originated (sent) by the sender.

- **Carbon copy (Cc)**   This field contains the e-mail address and optional identity for any additional recipient(s) to which the message is also to be delivered. The term "carbon copy" refers to the days of typewriters when carbon paper was used to create additional information copies of letters, memos, and reports.

- **Blind Cc (Bcc)**   This field contains the e-mail address and optional identify of any additional recipients who are to received a blind (without the knowledge of the primary or Cc addressees) copy of the e-mail message.

- **Message ID code**   This field contains a unique identification code for each e-mail message. The code is generated by the e-mail client or the mail server to create an identity for the message as an active document.

■ **In-Reply-To**   This field references the message ID of the message that is being replied to or forwarded. The reference to the original message ID creates a link between the messages that helps to prevent the original message from also being forwarded to recipients of the reply or forwarded message.

Message Body

The *body* of an e-mail message is essentially a block of text, a graphic object, or any combination of the two. The formatting for a message body for transmission across a network is defined by the Multipurpose Internet Mail Extensions (MIME) standards that encode the content of the message body so that the receiving e-mail client can display the message as it was composed.

E-mail message bodies can be formatted in either American Standard Code for Information Interchange (ASCII) text (also called plain text) or in Hypertext Markup Language (HTML), depending on the capabilities of the e-mail client. Plain text messages are smaller and therefore faster to send, but some people prefer the aesthetics of HTML-encoded messages.

Composing and Sending E-Mail Messages

It has become almost second nature to create an e-mail message and sent it off to its addressees. However, because not every message you send is formatted exactly the same, nor do you wish them to be, there are some features common to e-mail clients (such as Outlook 2007 or WordPerfect Mail) that can be used to enhance the look or impact of a message.

After you have filled in the fields of the message header (From, To, Subject, and perhaps Cc or Bcc), you begin composing the body of the e-mail message. After entering the text or inserting graphics, tables, and other objects, the next step in sending an e-mail message is to click the Send button. However, there are a few other options and features you can use before you actually send the message to fully set the characteristics and transmission control for the message.

Although not all of the following features or options are offered by every e-mail client available, many do offer the majority of them in one form or another. The features and options available from the better e-mail clients (with the assistance of a compatible mail server) are discussed in the following sections.

E-Mail Delivery Options

You may wish to communicate the urgency or importance of a message to addressees of the message; or you may wish to set an expiration date after which the message contents are no longer valid; or you may want to delay the transmission of a message until a later time or date. To send a message immediately, there is nothing to do but click Send. However, if you wish to change the delivery options for the message, you can use one of the following features:

- **Delay delivery**   A fairly common feature of e-mail clients is the capability to set a future time or date for an e-mail (or all e-mails) to be delivered (sent). This feature can be dependent on a compatible mail server to delay the delivery of a single message, but typically, all e-mail messages can be delayed by the e-mail client alone.

- **Expiration date**   This option is not supported by all e-mail clients, but in those that do support it (such as Outlook 2007), a date can be assigned to a message that indicates when the contents of the message are no longer valid or in effect. In the Outlook 2007 mail client, an expired message is shown with strikethrough (~~strikethrough~~) applied to the message header.

- **Level of importance**   The default importance for an e-mail is generally Normal (Outlook 2007) or something to that effect. However, a message can also be set to High Importance (urgent) or Low Importance (not urgent) to let the recipient(s) know whether immediate action is required or not.

Formatting an E-Mail Message

The body of an e-mail message can be formatted in most e-mail clients in much the same way as a word processing document. Although the less full-featured e-mail clients may limit the formatting to plain text, the more full-featured clients are integrated with the word processing application of the application suite to which both belong. Outlook 2007 and WordPerfect Mail are two examples of these applications.

In these more full-featured e-mail clients, a user can format and style his or her e-mail messages using a variety of effects, styles, and both character and paragraph formatting. The formatting features and effects available (see Figure 19-2) can include the following:

- **Background color**   A solid, textured, or gradient background color can be applied to an e-mail message instead of a complete theme or stationery effect. If you want to colorize a message, setting the background color, especially on messages sent in HTML format, can reduce the overall size of the message.

- **Fonts**   Typically, the font sets available in the companion word processing application are available for use in an e-mail message.

FIGURE 19-2

An example of a formatted e-mail message

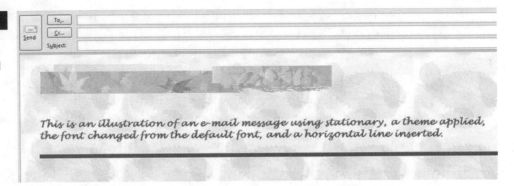

This is an illustration of an e-mail message using stationary, a theme applied, the font changed from the default font, and a horizontal line inserted.

- **Graphics and illustrations** Graphics and image files can be attached to an e-mail message if the intent is to transmit the file. However, if you wish to use a photograph, drawing, or image as the background to the message, you may do so.

- **Horizontal lines** Often it can be difficult to indicate a separation of different topics or thoughts in an e-mail message. Inserting horizontal lines can divide a message into independent parts.

- **Numbered or bulleted lists** An ordered or itemized list can be added to an e-mail message to organize its content.

- **Stationery** The background of a message can be set to a graphic, texture, or a solid or gradient color and a color scheme applied to create the effect of virtual stationery.

- **Symbols and equations** Although inserting an equation into an e-mail message is something done only in special cases, symbols, such as trademark (®), copyright (©), and style separators (❧ and ❧), can be inserted into a message. Not all e-mail clients can display these characters, so their effectiveness depends on the recipient's client.

- **Tables** A table can be inserted into an e-mail message to organize content that has two or more related elements for clarity.

- **URLs and hyperlinks** Although not technically a formatting feature, a URL (or multiple URLs) or hyperlink can be added into the body of an e-mail message should you need to reference a particular Web site, a particular document, or virtually any other addressable object. Embedded links are often a better way to share information than large attachments to a message. The security system of the e-mail server or client may strip attachments, rendering the purpose of the message void.

The one drawback to decorating an e-mail message with any of these effects or features is that the recipient may accept e-mail messages in plain text only, which eliminates most of the formatting applied to a message.

Message Attachments

Many of the security and virus risks for a computer involve e-mail attachments, but generally attaching a file to an e-mail and sending it to someone is safe. The types of documents that can be attached to an e-mail message and sent are commonly limited by the network administrators, but as long as you know what you can safely send, and the recipient is able to receive, there shouldn't be a problem.

Most e-mail clients give you three options for attaching files or documents to an e-mail message: attach a file, include an item, or attach an electronic business or address card. Commonly, each of these attachment types has its own tool or menu choice, such as the paper clip icon in Outlook 2007 that is used to attach a file to a message.

Incoming messages can also have documents or files attached to them, which can present a dilemma to the recipient. If the message to which the file is attached is from an unknown or untrusted source, it is generally a good idea not to open the attachment. Files attached to e-mail messages are the primary vehicle for viruses, malware, and worms to gain entrance to a computer and possibly a network. If the attached file is from a known and trusted source, the attachment can be saved or opened and read.

An attachment to an incoming message can be saved as a file, opened in an associated application's workspace, or deleted from the message. To save an attachment (or multiple attachments), click the attachment identities on the Attachments line of the message to select it (or them), right-click the selected file, and choose Save As. The Save As dialog box that opens is the same common Save As function used in all Office 2007 applications. Navigate to the folder in which you wish to save the attachment file and click Save.

An e-mail message attachment can be opened directly from the e-mail message by double-clicking its identity on the Attachment line of the message. Provided the file type of the attachment is associated with an application on the local computer, the attachment file opens in a workspace of the associated application. Not all attachments are safe, and you should be running a virus protection utility that in addition to scanning the incoming message also scans its attachments. Never directly open an attachment from a sender with whom you are not familiar.

Unwanted or untrusted attachments can be deleted from messages simply by clicking the attachment and pressing the DEL key on the keyboard. In some e-mail clients, especially those that don't open graphic files as a safeguard against viruses, the attachments may be only signature box art or the background graphic of a stationary theme. These types of attachments can be deleted even if you plan to keep the original message in your inbox.

Message Signature Blocks

Most of the better e-mail clients provide the capability to create and format a signature block that can be automatically or manually inserted at the end of an e-mail message body. In fact, some clients allow you to create more than one signature block with a different signature for different types of messages, such as one for business, one for friends, one for replies, and so on.

Send an E-Mail Message

The easiest part of composing and sending an e-mail message is to actually send the message. In almost every case, the e-mail client has a large Send button associated with the e-mail message window that begins the sending process.

The first thing that happens, provided it wasn't already done when the e-mail addresses were entered, is that the e-mail addresses are checked for format and validity. If the client is configured for these, the message may then be automatically scanned by a spellchecker and a grammar checker. If all is well, the e-mail message is transmitted and added to the Sent Mail folder, if this action is also configured.

When you send an e-mail message that contains sensitive, private, or confidential information, you should add additional security measures to the message to protect the information against hackers or inadvertent discovery by unauthorized individuals. E-mail messages containing sensitive information should be encrypted and probably protected with a digital signature and public-key cryptography.

Incoming E-Mail

Incoming e-mail messages are held in an inbox on the mail server until the client connects and requests to download them. Each e-mail client has one or more profiles associated with it that are used to identify it to the mail server and a particular mail box. Generally, e-mail clients request that e-mail messages be downloaded to the client inbox after the user clicks a Send/Receive button, but some e-mail clients can also be configured to automatically query the mail server at a certain time interval.

After incoming e-mail messages are downloaded to the client inbox, the user can open the message into a message window so that it can be read.

E-Mail Protocols

When e-mail is requested from the mail server by an e-mail client, one of two primary protocols can be used: one that downloads and clears the mail server inbox and one that downloads the contents of the mail server inbox and retains copies of the downloaded messages on the mail server.

The Post Office Protocol, or POP3 (indicating the third and current version of the protocol), requests that any messages in the user's mail server mailbox be sent to the e-mail client's inbox. After each message is downloaded, it is removed (deleted) from the mail server. This is the most commonly used e-mail protocol for stationary computers connected to a local mail server.

The Internet Message Access Protocol (IMAP) downloads the header information (From, To, Subject) of the messages in the mail server mailbox to the client inbox. The user can then choose which messages he or she wishes to download and those to be deleted. Unless the user requests that a message be removed from the mail server, the message is retained in the mail server mailbox. IMAP can be used with mail clients running on desktop computers, but it is more commonly used by clients running on mobile devices.

Managing Incoming Messages

The better e-mail clients provide a variety of features that can be used to automatically categorize, segregate, and classify incoming e-mail messages. For example, Outlook 2007 allows you to create a number of rules that are used to assign an incoming message to a particular folder or multiple folders based on the sender's information, the date of the message, the type of message, and even certain words in the message body or subject.

While these features can be very helpful in categorizing incoming messages so that you can deal with groups of messages separately, this is also the way that e-mail spam filters work. Certain e-mail addresses, IP addresses, words in the subject or message body, and more are used to identify and segregate suspicious e-mail. Some spam filters also automatically quarantine attachments on suspected tainted messages.

Messages that you wish to keep in the mail client can be saved to folders that you've created within the inbox. Figure 19-3 shows the Outlook 2007 Folder pane that contains both the standard and user-created subfolders of the mail client.

When new e-mail messages arrive in the Inbox folder, they are marked in boldface to indicate that they are unread or have not been viewed, which includes being displayed in a reading pane. After a message has been viewed, the boldface is removed to indicate that the message has been read.

Inbox messages can also be flagged for follow-up, categorized, or marked as unread using the commands available on the pop-up menu displayed by right-clicking a message. Flagging a message for follow-up allows you to set a due date for an action requested in the message or as a reminder to take a certain action. A To-Do list task is created for each flagged message in the e-mail client of each recipient of the message. Messages can be categorized either manually or automatically through a message rule. Categorized messages are listed separately by category in the Inbox. Should you wish to reread a message at a later time, you can mark the message as unread so that it remains in the Inbox.

Managing Messages in Folders

Any message, whether read or unread, can be moved to a standard or custom folder in the mail folders area using the Move To Folder command or using drag and drop. Using message rules, an incoming e-mail message can be automatically saved to one or more mail folders according to its source, content, size, and several other characteristics (as shown earlier in Figure 19-3).

Messages can also be moved and copied between mail folders, and for that matter, the mail folders themselves can be moved or deleted as well. Of course, e-mail messages in any folder, including the Inbox folder, can be deleted. As a safeguard, deleted messages are moved into the Deleted Items folder, which can be configured to empty each time the client is closed, or else it can be managed manually. Messages in the Deleted Items folder can be restored to a folder using the same process used to move any message between one folder and the next. To empty the Deleted Items folder, which means to permanently delete any messages in this folder, right-click the Deleted Items folder and choose Empty Deleted Items Folder from the pop-up menu. To remove the contents of any other folder, open the folder, select the messages you wish to delete, and then click the Delete icon or press the DEL key on the keyboard.

FIGURE 19-3

The Folder pane of Outlook 2007 showing the folders that can be used to manage e-mail messages

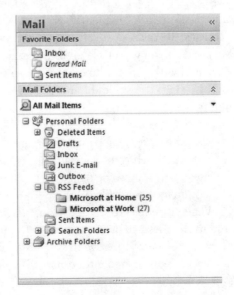

Sorting Messages

Like the column headings in Excel and Access, the column headings in the Outlook 2007 Inbox folder can be used to sort messages in either ascending or descending order simply by clicking the column heading you wish to use to order the messages in the folder. For example, clicking the From heading sorts the messages alphanumerically by the display name of the sender. If the heading you wish to use to sort the folder isn't included in the column headings, you can easily add any message property to the column headings and use it to sort the folder.

Searching for Messages

Outlook 2007 features a much more robust search capability than the previous versions of Outlook, such as Outlook 2003 and Outlook Express, which used a simplistic Find function to search through message headers and bodies for a word or simple phrase. The Search function in Outlook 2007 is a full keyword-in-context search tool that starts its search as you enter the criteria, narrowing down the search as you type. The Search in Outlook 2007 can also be customized to seek out only the messages you wish to return in the search results.

Backing Up or Archiving Messages

If your Outlook 2007 client is connected to a Microsoft Exchange Server account, your e-mail messages are automatically backed up into a personal archive file on the server. Otherwise, you must back up or archive your e-mail, appointments, contacts, and tasks to a personal folder file (.pst) stored on your computer's hard disk, a removable medium, or a network storage device.

Microsoft provides the Outlook Personal Folders Backup tool that can be used to create .pst files. This tool can be downloaded from Microsoft Office Online. You can also move your old or expired Outlook 2007 messages from the message folders to an archive folder using the Archive option on the File menu. Regardless of the method used, you should archive or back up your messages and mail folder contents regularly to ensure against losing important messages, contact information, and other e-mail client information.

Replying to a Message

E-mail messages often request or invite a response from its recipients. To respond to an e-mail message, you simply reply to it, which addresses the replying message to its sender and opens a new message space at the top of the received e-mail message. Some e-mail clients tag the lines of the original message along the left border with

">" (greater-than sign) characters or with a solid vertical line on the left side of the original message. In some clients, the original message is separated from the reply with a solid horizontal line. Typically, the prefix "RE:" is added to the beginning of the message subject to indicate that the message is a reply. After the reply message is entered, the message is sent using the same method used with a new message: clicking Send.

E-mail messages can also be sent to any recipient addresses listed on the Cc line along with the originator by clicking Reply To All. As with the Reply button, a reply message area is created, but the address lines include the sender and the Cc addressees or the original message on the Cc line.

The primary difference between a reply and a forwarded message is that any files or objects that were attached to the original message are not included on the reply. When you forward a message, by clicking Forward, you have the option of sending a complete copy (including any attachments of the original message) to other parties, which can, and usually does, include addressees who were not sent the original message. Like a reply, a forwarded message opens a message area above the original message for your message or comments, but the prefix "FW:" is added to the subject line to indicate that the message was forwarded.

Automatic E-Mail Responses

You can advise people who e-mail you when you are away from your computer for an extended period of that fact and include a message of when you'll be gone or will return. In e-mail clients, this feature is called an out-of-office assistant or a title to that effect. In Outlook 2007, this feature is available only to accounts supported by a Microsoft Exchange Server. To activate this feature, choose the Out Of Office Assistant link on the Tools menu and fill in the information on the Out Of Office Assistant dialog box that appears.

If your Outlook 2007 client is not connected to an Exchange server account, you can use an automatic reply message template to compose the message to be automatically sent to all, some, or only selected messages and then create a rule that controls to whom the auto-reply is sent.

Through the use of message rules and alerts, you can automatically reply to or display an alert for certain types or specific senders at any time. To create a message rule or alert, click the Rules And Alerts option on the Tools menu and fill in the criteria to define which messages are to be affected and the reply or alert message as needed.

Synchronize Mail Between Devices

Many handheld devices, such as personal digital assistants (PDAs), smart phones, handheld computers, netbooks, and portable computers, are able to interface with

Outlook 2007 using either third-party synchronization software or built-in proprietary applications. Depending on the device, e-mail messages, tasks, appointments, and even contacts can be downloaded or uploaded to synchronize Outlook and the device. This capability allows you to keep a portable device up-to-date with Outlook and vice versa. For example, if you wish to synchronize e-mail messages between a Blackberry device and your desktop computer's Outlook folders, you can use the Blackberry Desktop Software application that comes with that device.

Managing E-Mail Addresses

One of the more convenient features of most e-mail clients is the *address book,* which is also called a contact folder in some clients. The address book stores the e-mail addresses and other contact information, such as business and personal addresses, phone numbers, and the like. The address book of an e-mail client provides a means to manage e-mail addresses, including categorizing them into business or personal contacts. Figure 19-4 shows the Contacts folder of Outlook 2007.

Perhaps the primary purpose of the Outlook 2007 Contacts folder is to facilitate easy access to e-mail addresses when you are composing or forwarding an e-mail

FIGURE 19-4

The Outlook 2007 Contacts folder

message. When addressing an e-mail, clicking the To: or Cc: button in the message heading displays contacts stored in the Contacts folder (the address book in older Outlook versions and other e-mail clients), from which you can choose the contacts to whom you wish to send a message.

The Contacts folder can be managed like any other Outlook folder. Contacts can be added, edited, or removed to keep the contact folder up-to-date and accurate. To add a new contact, open the Contacts folder using the Contacts button in the Navigation pane and double-click an empty space in any of the Contacts folder's views. On the Contacts dialog box that displays, fill in the contact's information and then click Save & Close to add the contact to the folder.

E-mail addresses on e-mails received from someone not already in your Contacts folder can be added to your contacts. Right-click the e-mail address you wish to add to your contacts, choose Add To Outlook Contacts on the pop-up menu, and then fill in any additional information for the contact in the dialog box that displays (the dialog box is partially completed using the information available for the contact in the e-mail message).

Contact information can be modified by double-clicking the contact name in any of the Contacts folder views and editing the information as needed on the contact's record. Contact records can be deleted completely by selecting the contact record to be deleted and either pressing the DEL key on the keyboard or right-clicking the record and choosing Delete on the pop-up menu.

Another feature of most e-mail clients is that a mailing list or distribution list can be created from the contacts in the Contacts folder or address book. In general, the process used to create a mailing or distribution list is similar to that used in Outlook 2007. To create a distribution list in Outlook, right-click an empty space in the Contacts workspace and choose the New Distribution List option on the pop-up menu. On the Distribution List dialog box that displays, you can add contacts to the list from existing contacts, add completely new contacts to both the Contacts folder and the distribution list, and add notes to yourself about the group.

E-Mail Security and Spam

E-mail security is a two-way street. Not only do you need to protect against unsolicited messages and perhaps their evil cargo, but you also may need to secure outgoing messages containing sensitive or confidential information.

Spam and Unsolicited Messages

As mentioned briefly earlier in the chapter, e-mail messages and files attached to them are the main culprit for viruses, worms, and Trojan horses gaining access to a computer or network. For the most part, this maliciously intended software is attached to unsolicited e-mail that manages to get through any spam (junk e-mail and other unsolicited messages) filtering system in use, if any.

The best defense, besides installing a spam filter and antivirus software, is to not open any message from a sender you don't know. You also run the risk of infection if you are using a reading pane in the e-mail client's inbox. When a message is listed in the inbox of an e-mail client, only the heading information is displayed. However, if you view the message in a reading or preview pane, the body of the message must be opened, which can potentially activate any malware attached to the message.

Most e-mail clients offer you these further options for dealing with spam and unwanted messages:

- Incoming e-mail messages can be filtered and blocked if desired. Many e-mail clients, including Outlook 2007, provide a capability to scan and identify certain incoming messages as either junk or untrusted. In Outlook 2007, you have several options for filtering incoming messages, including setting the level of protection and message scanning you wish to have performed, identification of safe senders and recipients (people you e-mail who you don't want treated as unsafe senders) and blocked or suspicious senders, and also options to allow you to block any messages from certain top-level domains. The filtering applied to an incoming e-mail message scans not only the sender's handle but also the domain name used to send the message. This is accomplished by comparing the IP address of the sending domain to the domains listed in either the safe or blocked senders to filter out e-mail coming from a particularly suspicious mail server.

- Most e-mail clients, including Outlook 2007, the Mac OS Mail client, and Eudora, Penelope, and Thunderbird from Mozilla, allow for the creation of filtering rules that can be used to scan incoming e-mail messages for just about anything, such as the type of e-mail client used to create the message or the mail server that forwarded the message. Defining filters or rules can extend the default capabilities of the e-mail client's protection against unwanted messages. Of course, and it bears repeating, you should install an antivirus utility to scan all incoming and outgoing messages and attachments.

Outgoing Message Security

If the contents of an e-mail message are sensitive or confidential and you wish to keep it private between you and the recipient, special handling can be applied to the message to ensure its content isn't read by anyone intercepting the message. The two methods generally supported by e-mail clients are applying a digital signature to the message and encrypting the message's contents, including any attachment to the message.

Digital Signatures A digital signature is not to be confused with the signature block discussed earlier in the chapter (see "Message Signature Blocks"). A digital signature is a security device that is attached to a message that verifies the sender as being who he or she claims to be. In many ways, a message with a digital signature attached is like sending registered or certified snail-mail.

A digital signature is obtained from a certificate authority (CA) in the form of a digital security identification code. Once you have been issued a digital ID, it can be used to secure virtually any document sent across a network, including e-mail.

Encryption Encrypting an e-mail message transforms its readable text content into an encoded (unreadable) format that is based on a public security key. The recipient of the message uses a public key that matches the private key used to encrypt the message to decrypt (decode) the content back into its original, readable form.

CERTIFICATION SUMMARY

E-mail messages are sent and received by e-mail clients, using either the POP3 or IMAP protocol, through an e-mail server. E-mail is a convenient way to communicate across a network, but there are threats and risks, such as viruses and sensitive information being intercepted.

The primary function of an e-mail client is to compose, send, and receive e-mail messages. An e-mail client includes tools and features to manage messages and contacts, along with others to format and personalize e-mail messages.

TWO-MINUTE DRILL

Using an Electronic Mail Application

❑ An e-mail message is made up of two basic components: the message header and the message body. These components contain elements to identify, address, and communicate information.

❑ The formatting of an e-mail message is prescribed by SMTP.

❑ An e-mail address has three components: a local-part, the "@"address separator, and a domain identity.

❑ The header of an e-mail message identifies the sender, the addressee, the subject, and the origin date. The fields common to e-mail headers are source address, destination address, subject, origination date, Cc, and Bcc.

❑ The body of an e-mail message can contain a block of text, a graphic object, or any combination of objects. The format of a message body is defined by the MIME standards. E-mail message bodies can be formatted in either ASCII text or HTML.

❑ Many of the security risks for a computer involve e-mail attachments, but generally attaching a file to an e-mail is safe. E-mail clients provide three options for attaching files to a message: attach a file, include an item, or attach an electronic business or address card.

❑ A signature block can be automatically or manually inserted at the end of an e-mail message body.

❑ Incoming e-mail messages are held in an inbox on the mail server until the client connects and requests to download them. After incoming e-mail messages are downloaded to the client inbox, the user can open the message into a message window so that it can be read. Two primary protocols are used: POP3 and IMAP.

❑ The address book stores the e-mail addresses and other contact information, such as business and personal addresses, phone numbers, and the like. The address book provides for the management of e-mail addresses.

❑ E-mail security involves both protecting against unsolicited messages and securing outgoing messages.

❑ A spam filter and antivirus software provide defense against unsolicited and potentially harmful messages.

❑ Two methods that can be applied to secure an outgoing message are digital signatures and encryption.

SELF TEST

The following questions are intended to help you be sure that you understand the material included in this chapter. Read the questions and the answer choices carefully.

Using an Electronic Mail Application

1. Which of the following is typically the folder into which new e-mail messages are received?
   A. Calendar
   B. Contacts
   C. Inbox
   D. Tasks

2. What are the two primary components of an e-mail message?
   A. Body
   B. Footer
   C. Header
   D. Signature Block

3. What is the protocol used to carry e-mail messages on a network?
   A. HTML
   B. HTTP
   C. POP3
   D. SMTP

4. Which of the following is not an element of an e-mail address?
   A. @
   B. Domain identity
   C. E-mail client identity
   D. Local-part

5. Which of the following address elements is used to send an e-mail message to an addressee that is hidden from all other recipients?
   A. Bcc
   B. Cc
   C. From
   D. To

6. What are the two most commonly used text standards in e-mail message bodies?
   A. ASCII
   B. HTML
   C. HTTP
   D. POP3

7. What is the most commonly used vehicle for transmitting a virus to a computer?
   A. E-mail address blocks
   B. E-mail bodies
   C. E-mail headers
   D. E-mail message attachments

8. True or False: An e-mail signature block and a digital signature are essentially the same thing.
   A. True
   B. False

9. What are the two primary protocols used to retrieve e-mail messages from a mail server?
   A. HTTP
   B. IMAP
   C. POP3
   D. SMTP

10. What feature is common to e-mail clients and can be used to manage e-mail addresses and contact information?
   A. Address book
   B. Calendar
   C. Inbox
   D. To-Do list

11. What two actions can be used to secure outgoing e-mail messages?
   A. Composing brief, nondescript messages without attachments or inserted objects
   B. Applying a digital signature
   C. Applying encryption
   D. Sending messages only to well-known addressees

12. What software can be used to scan incoming e-mail messages for inappropriate content?
   A. Malware
   B. Spam filter
   C. Junk mail
   D. Antivirus

SELF TEST ANSWERS

Using an Electronic Mail Application

1. ☑ **C.** Incoming e-mail is received into the Inbox of the mail client.
   ☒ **A, B,** and **D** are incorrect. E-mail clients may provide a Calendar or appointments feature, but incoming messages are not received directly into this feature. The Contacts or address book folder is used to manage and maintain a library of e-mail contacts but doesn't receive incoming e-mail. A Tasks folder is not common to all e-mail clients, and even where it does exist, it doesn't receive incoming messages.

2. ☑ **A** and **C.** An e-mail message has two commonly used components: the message header and the message body.
   ☒ **B** and **D** are incorrect. Not all e-mail clients add a footer to an e-mail message, and a signature block is an identification feature that can be inserted into a message body.

3. ☑ **D.** The Simple Mail Transfer Protocol (SMTP) is used to transmit e-mail messages across a network.
   ☒ **A, B,** and **C** are incorrect. The Hypertext Markup Language (HTML) is used to compose some e-mail messages. The Hypertext Transfer Protocol (HTTP) is used to transfer Web pages across a network. The Post Office Protocol (POP3) is used to transfer incoming messages from a mail server to a client.

4. ☑ **C.** Because standard formatting standards, such as MIME, the identity of the e-mail client is not needed.
   ☒ **A, B,** and **D** are incorrect. These elements are each a part of the standard e-mail address.

5. ☑ **A.** An e-mail address in the blind carbon copy (Bcc) address element is hidden from all other recipients of the message.
   ☒ **B, C,** and **D** are incorrect. The carbon copy (Cc) address element is used to send information copies of a message to other addresses, all of whom see the address of these recipients. The From address element contains the e-mail address of the sender. The To address element includes the e-mail addresses of the primary recipients.

6. ☑ **A** and **B.** The American Standard Code for Information Interchange (ASCII) and the Hypertext Markup Language (HTML) are the most commonly used message text formatting standards.
   ☒ **C** and **D** are incorrect. The Hypertext Transfer Protocol (HTTP) is the protocol used to transfer HTML-coded files across a network. The Post Office Protocol (POP3) is used to request and transfer e-mail from a mail server to a client.

7. ☑ **D.** Attachments to e-mail messages are frequently used to transmit viruses.
☒ **A, B,** and **C** are incorrect. These message components are sent in plain text and are poor vehicles for hiding programming statements, such as a virus.

8. ☑ **B.** This statement is false. A signature block is a text element that can be inserted into a message body for identification purposes only. A digital signature is obtained from a certificate authority (CA) and can be attached to a message for security purposes.
☒ **A** is incorrect. The statement is false.

9. ☑ **B** and **C.** The Internet Mail Access Protocol (IMAP) and the Post Office Protocol (POP3) are the protocols used to transfer messages between an e-mail client and a mail server.
☒ **A** and **D** are incorrect. The Hypertext Transfer Protocol (HTTP) and the Simple Mail Transfer Protocol (SMTP) are protocols used to transfer messages across a network.

10. ☑ **A.** E-mail clients include an address book or Contacts folder in which e-mail addresses and other contact information can be managed.
☒ **B, C,** and **D** are incorrect. A Calendar or an appointment book is a feature of some e-mail clients. The Inbox of an e-mail client is used to manage received messages, but not necessarily the e-mail addresses of the senders. A To-Do list or tasks list is included in only the more full-featured e-mail clients.

11. ☑ **B** and **C.** Applying either a digital signature or encrypting a message, or both, are methods that can be used to secure an outgoing e-mail message.
☒ **A** and **D** are incorrect. While these actions are good practices for e-mail use in general, they aren't particularly secure.

12. ☑ **B.** A spam filter, which is commonly included in an antivirus package, scans incoming messages for certain words, symbols, or phrases to segregate or block inappropriate messages.
☒ **A, C,** and **D** are incorrect. Malware is a type of malicious software that can infect a computer. Junk mail is the type of incoming messages that a spam filter seeks to identify or block. An antivirus package protects against viruses and other malicious software; it often includes a spam filter, which is a better answer.

20

Communicating/
Collaborating over
a Network

- Identifying Types of Electronic
  Communication

- Identifying Appropriate Uses for
  Electronic Communication

✓ Two-Minute Drill

Q&A Self Test

T here is no doubt that electronic communications have revolutionized human communications over the past twenty years or so, opening up fast, efficient, and effective ways for people to communicate with one another and to collaborate on projects in ways that heretofore were unthinkable.

For the Internet and Computing Core Certification (IC^3) exams, an understanding of the use of the Internet and other forms of networked communications as a means of interaction and collaboration is a must. You need to understand the different ways that people can communicate, collaborate, and cooperate using electronic communications, as well as the benefits and risks involved. Finally, you should also know how to safely use electronic communications and the "rules of the road," acceptable use policies, and best practices that support and enhance its use. This chapter discusses each of these aspects of electronic communications and how it can be applied not only to improve your interactions with other people, but to make you more productive as well.

CERTIFICATION OBJECTIVE

Identifying Types of Electronic Communication

2.1 Identify types of electronic communication/collaboration and how they work.

A list of electronic communications types is almost never complete. There are far more types of electronic communications than most people can remember or even think of. In the next few sections, we discuss a few of the more commonly identified types of electronic communications, some of which you should recognize and perhaps some you won't find familiar.

Types of Electronic Communications

Most people assume that the term "electronic communications" refers to electronically transmitted data, such as is used to send an e-mail, talk on a telephone, send a fax, or send a text message. However, electronic communications can also include electronically produced visual messages as well, such as digital video billboards, the scoreboards and video displays at a stadium or ballpark, and highway warning reader boards.

In the context of the IC³ exams, electronic communications, which are also called computer-mediated communications (CMC), refer to the services that provide voice, data, and image transmissions. So, let's focus on just this part of electronic communications.

Much of the electronic communications services that are emerging today involve the use of the Internet in some form. Over the years, the separate networks that were used individually to send voice, data, or image transmissions are seemingly merging into one large communications network. However, while its capabilities weren't as robust as they are today, the plain old telephone service (POTS) and the public switched telephone network (PSTN) systems essentially provided a universal communications network that is still in use for a significant part of electronic communication traffic.

While the telephone has been and still is a major form of electronic communications, let's focus on the electronic communications that are network-based. The major types of electronic communications within this group of services are

- **Blogs and social networking Web sites** Although rarely real-time or interactive, blogs (Web logs) and social networking Web sites, like MySpace, Facebook, Twitter, and LinkedIn, provide a means of electronic communications that allow you to post messages, comments, and articles for other site users to post a response. Discussion forums are a form of social networking, but they are typically used to get answers to real and often work- or task-related questions.

- **Computer-based teleconferencing** Broadband communications provides the capability to transmit and receive data, voice, and images at virtually the same time. Not only can you see and speak with someone down the hall, across town, across the country, or around the world, but you can share and collaborate on documents and images at the same time, all from your computer.

- **Disaster recovery** In the event of a natural disaster, electronic communication may be the best means, if not the only means, available to restore computing services to a business, organization, or school. Backups saved on remote storage sites using an Internet connection can be retrieved and restored on a computer when physical backup media may be compromised. In many situations, the use of electronic communications to restore a system is likely a faster method as well.

- **Electronic mail** Perhaps the most common type of electronic communications is e-mail. Although we don't typically think of e-mail as being anything special and most likely not as a type of electronic communications, it certainly is both these things. However, e-mail has become a much faster way to communicate with other people on just about anything at just about any time.

- **Internet telephony** Services such as Vonage, Skype, and Speakeasy provide an alternative to carrier-based and regulated telephone services, such as the phone company provides. Some of these services offer what amounts to a normal telephone service package, and others merely provide a supported link over which voice and video can be transmitted across the Internet. Even the cable television companies are now providing this type of service.

- **Text and instant messaging** Beginning with the ICQ (I seek you) protocol, text messaging has rapidly become a preferred way to communicate with others on the Internet or cellular telephones. There is only a subtle difference between text messaging and what is today called instant messaging. That difference is that text messaging requires you to know the other person's phone number or Internet address. Instant messaging (IM) involves registration on an IM service, such as Microsoft Live Messenger, Yahoo! Messenger, Google Talk, or Meebo.

Electronic Collaboration

Electronic collaboration at its most basic level is two or more people discussing, developing, creating, or reviewing a common entity. In effect, when two people are engaged in a discussion, whether synchronous (interactively) or asynchronous (noninteractively), on a common topic, document, image, or other form of object, they are collaborating.

Virtual Team Space

Collaboration can occur on any of the electronic communications types or services discussed in the preceding section. The collaborative discussion can be held via a telephone, a teleconference, e-mail, or perhaps even through forum or blog posts. Each of these instances would be an informal collaborative interaction.

More formal collaborations are supported by specialized software that creates a virtual team space (VTS). A VTS is an asynchronous, secure workspace in which networked team members, regardless of their geographical locations, can independently or cooperatively collaborate on a project. The specialized software that supports VTS collaboration is generically called groupware.

The advantages of a VTS collaborative environment include the elimination of travel expense, the avoidance of interruptions of other assigned duties and responsibilities, and the availability of input and feedback from the team members. However, there are also disadvantages as well. Conflicts can arise, as in any situation with differing opinions or personalities. Some team members may not be as familiar with the groupware software as others and may be reluctant or unable to contribute as much as they could in a face-to-face situation. The success of a groupware-based VTS environment especially depends on the availability of active technical support.

Collaborative Software Tools

The tools and features of groupware software are often divided into project management tools and collaboration management tools. Table 20-1 lists the more commonly used features and tools that are included in each of these groups.

Participant Identification

In asynchronous collaborations, such as using e-mail or messaging, the participants are relatively easy to identify. However, in a synchronous collaborative session, such as an interactive voice and video session, some form of control must be used. In Web-based applications, such as WebEx or NetMeeting, the session organizer or administrator assigns each authorized participant a password that is entered to gain access to the session.

Typically, a user in a collaborative session must be granted permission by a system administrator or group leader to participate in sessions, sometimes at specific levels or in types of collaborative sessions. In some cases, a user is assigned a handle, a username, and a globally unique identifier (GUID), or in other cases, users just use their e-mail addresses. As session participants join the session, by logging in, requesting entrance, or clicking a specific hyperlink, their identity is listed in a participants list, commonly with other identifying information such as their location or title.

A session participant wishing to "have the floor" can click a button or enter a particular code phrase that signals that the participant has "raised a hand." The session moderator then activates the participant to contribute to the collaboration.

TABLE 20-1	Collaborative Management Tools (CMT)	Project Management Tools (PMT)
Collaborative Management and Project Management Tools Found in Groupware Software	Electronic calendar	All CMT tools
	Workflow event manager	Time and cost accounting tools
	Knowledge management system	Revision control
	Online personal productivity software	Project management software
	Instant messaging	Document management system
	Video conferencing	Reporting and publishing tools
	Telephony	

Benefits and Risks of Electronic Communication

Electronic communication has its advantages and disadvantages, but with the right precautions in place, the advantages can outweigh the disadvantages or risks. The advantages and disadvantages of using electronic communication are explained in the following sections.

Advantages of Electronic Communication

The general advantages of using electronic communication include the following:

- **Speed of exchange**   While they don't have the real-time speed of a face-to-face or voice-to-voice exchange, some types of electronic communications can approximate a live conversation using the speed of the network to carry out a dialog, whether it is a voice or electronic message exchange, such as e-mail or instant messaging.

- **Flexibility**   Because a variety of electronic communication types can be used in a collaborative session, the form of the communication can be selected to suit the needs of a collaborative session.

- **Enhanced participation**   Collaborators are able to participate on an equal basis, to have immediate access to relevant information, and to archive the session media for later reference.

Disadvantages and Risks of Electronic Communication

There are a number of disadvantages and risks inherent in the use of electronic communication, many of which come from using a networked environment. However, some of the disadvantages are unique to electronic communication, including

- **Permanence**   Once an e-mail or any other form of written message is sent, it is typically unrecoverable. Most forms of electronic communications can be archived, and what is said (received) can be saved. Like the magazines in a doctor's office, text messages, postings to blog sites or social networks, and e-mails may end up being read by any number of unaddressed and unintended readers.

- **Voice**   E-mail and messaging can't capture voice inflections or tone, so humor, irony, sarcasm, and even sincerity can be lost or misunderstood, causing confusion, anger, or the risk that the message will be disregarded altogether. Hasty responses caused by a misunderstanding of a message's intent (voice) can change a serious dialog into something else altogether. Teleconferencing can overcome this risk, but at a much higher cost.

■ **Diversity of audience**   Even in face-to-face communications, regional, cultural, or personal differences between a speaker and a hearer can impair understanding. Electronic communication can exacerbate these problems, making it difficult to bridge differences in outlook in the course of a relatively short dialog.

■ **Lack of supporting documents**   Purely electronic communications, such as voice or video teleconferencing, don't typically create a paper trail of a dialog. Some applications are able to record the session and be used to produce a transcript, but this feature isn't as common as it probably should be.

The quality of an electronic communication can be impacted by technology failures, glitches, and even the ethics or morals of a message's sender. The following is an incomplete list of the risks that can impact electronic communication.

■ **Equipment failures**   If the connection is lost due to an equipment or service failure during a teleconference or Web video conference, the electronic communication session is interrupted for as long as it takes to restore service. In situations where the participants are located in several different time zones or have other pressing commitments, this can be catastrophic to the success of the conference.

■ **Application failures**   Application software can fail. Although this is uncommon, if the primary application facilitating an electronic communication should freeze, lock up, or crash, the communication session ends. An e-mail client could fail to send or receive messages (although this is most likely a connection issue); rules on the e-mail server cause message attachments not to be forwarded; a communication server crashes; the format of a message may be unsupported by the communication client (such as HTML formatted e-mail messages being sent to a recipient who uses an e-mail client that can only display plain text messages); or the lack of virus protection software results in a downloaded virus. All electronic communications are subject to equipment and application failures.

■ **Inappropriate messages or content**   There can be a fine line (although companies are attempting to clearly define the differences) between professional and nonprofessional (informal or personal) communications. A significant amount of many companies' network bandwidth is lost to informal communications, which unfortunately include junk mail or spam, fraudulent offers, hoaxes, and chain letters.

- **Unethical use of electronic communication** With the use of text messaging, instant messaging, and social networking services, electronic communications can be used for a variety of unethical, or perhaps even illegal, purposes, such as encrypted messages between terrorists and criminals, quick messages between students taking tests requesting or supplying answers, or spoofing messages that attempt to gather personal information from users.

- **Inappropriate use of e-mail addressing** The use of the Reply All option and the inappropriate use of the To:, Cc: and Bcc: addressing lines on an e-mail message can create privacy issues. Entering the e-mail addresses of all addressees on any of the addressing lines of an e-mail message or using the Reply All option has two primary issues: the recipients all know that the message was sent to a number of people; and the e-mail addresses of the recipients are available to all addressees. Using the Bcc: address line for large group mailings hides the e-mail address of all other addressees and the fact that the message was sent to several recipients.

In addition to the risks in the preceding list, e-mail servers or clients may not provide for guaranteed delivery of e-mail messages to the addressees or provide a delivery failure notification to the sender. Some e-mail systems will simply drop an e-mail message that cannot be delivered for any reason other than a bad address. And, there is always the threat that a message may be received garbled or incomplete.

CERTIFICATION OBJECTIVE

Identifying Appropriate Uses for Electronic Communication

2.3 Identify the appropriate use of different types of communication/collaboration tools and the "rules of the road" regarding online communication ("netiquette").

Just like in everyday interactions with people, when you use electronic communications to interact with other users on the Internet and Web, there are certain "rules" of good conduct that you should observe. Beyond politeness and courtesy, although they are important, you should understand that not everyone, especially around the world, may follow the same customs or use the same style of speech as you (as outlined in the preceding section).

Netiquette

The word *netiquette*, a combination of the words network and etiquette, covers the guidelines and best practices that should be followed in an electronic communication to conduct a meaningful and appropriate conversation. There are several versions of netiquette available on the Web, most of which pertain to e-mail and instant messaging, but in general, the guidelines that should be followed in e-mail or electronic talk are

- **Ownership** Be sure you know who "owns" the e-mail being sent and received. In many business situations, the owner of the network also owns any communications conducted on it, which can, and should, limit the subject matter of your conversations.

- **Security** Always assume that messages sent across the Internet are not secure. You should never write anything into a message that you wouldn't write on a snail-mail postcard.

- **Copyright** Know and understand copyright rules and laws. What may be permissible in your location may not be okay in the recipient's location. If you forward or repost a message, don't change its wording or content, assuming you have permission from the sender to forward the message in the first place.

- **Chain letters** Chain letters are highly discouraged on the Internet, and their senders can have their network access revoked by a local administrator or an Internet service provider (ISP). If you receive a chain letter, you should notify your network administrator or ISP.

- **Flames** Never respond in anger or respond to angry messages (flames) you receive. It's best to be very conservative in what you send out and to be tolerant of what you receive.

- **Addressees** Before responding to a message, be sure that you are the primary addressee. If you are a Cc addressee, you were sent an information copy and may not have been the person from whom help or assistance was sought. Also be sure you know who a message you send is actually going to; a distribution list or group name, while very convenient, may include addressees you don't wish to include.

- **Identity** Always identify yourself in messages, so that the recipients know who sent the message and from where. Always include a subject line on a message that really reflects the content or purpose of the message. However, avoid lengthy signature blocks that include graphics and fonts that the recipients' e-mail clients or messaging software don't support.

■ **Message length** Messages should be kept as short as possible. If a message must be longer than 100 lines, the work "Long" should be included in its subject line. Each line of the message should be limited to less than 65 characters. Some message servers have a limit on the size of a single message, and most have a limit on the total size of a recipient's mailbox. So, don't send messages with very large and uncompressed attachments, as they may never be seen by the addressee. Attachments should be limited to fewer than fifty thousand (50,000) bytes. Both you and the recipient are paying for the communications service carrying your message, so be as brief as possible.

■ **Timely responses** Respond to all appropriate messages in a timely manner. Remember that the sender is often waiting for your response or some other means of verifying that you received the message, may have answers to any questions posed, or may not be the person to whom the message should have been sent. Message senders can set options to request a confirmation that a message was delivered and read, as well as setting the priority of the message for quicker response.

■ **Spelling and grammar** To ensure that your message is understood and taken seriously by a recipient, use a spelling and grammar checker to scan the message body (and subject line in some cases) before the message is sent.

■ **E-mail attachments** Some mailbox services don't allow large attachments on e-mail messages, and you should avoid sending an attachment larger than one megabyte (1MB) when possible. Use a file compression utility, such as WinZip or 7-Zip, to reduce the size of the file if necessary. If a file you wish to attach to an e-mail message can be accessed through a hyperlink, you should insert the hyperlink in the message and not attach the file.

■ **E-mail privacy** Avoid sharing the e-mail addresses of other people on an e-mail message or posting another person's e-mail address on a public site, poster, or flyer without their permission. Nor should you forward an e-mail message containing another person's e-mail address to somebody the original sender may not know or trust.

■ **E-mail graphics** Not all e-mail clients are able to or configured to display embedded graphics, sound files, or animations in a message. Text-only e-mail clients are not able to display graphics at all, so you should check with recipients to verify whether graphics will display or not on their clients.

Perhaps it's intuitive, but you should scan all outgoing messages and any message attachments for viruses to guard against transmitting a virus to unsuspecting user. Many e-mail clients, including Outlook 2007, can be set to prevent the downloading of any linked graphics or objects included in an e-mail message, as these are the vehicles most commonly used to transmit viruses.

In addition to the publicly posted netiquette rules, your company, organization, or school may have its own set of system and network policies and guidelines for courteous and cooperative usage by all users. Regardless of the rules, procedures, or guidelines of your company or school, electronic communications are subject to many local, state, and national laws, which must also be followed.

Acceptable Use Policies

Virtually all subscriber networks, interactive Web sites, or electronic communication systems have a published acceptable use policy (AUP) or a fair use policy. An AUP defines what authorized users of the network or service are allowed to do, what they are not allowed to do, and what constitutes an acceptable use of the network, service, or Web site.

AUPs are generally based on the security policies of the host service, network, or site, which is why users are often asked to sign or click an acceptance check box or button before they are permitted to access any resources. AUPs also serve to reduce the legal exposure of the host service, network, or site by informing users what actions would be considered illegal or unacceptable.

The primary portion of an AUP is typically a user code of conduct that describes the netiquette; language; illegal activities; and warnings, cautions, and restrictions on the types of information that should and should not be shared on the host. The AUP also defines the potential consequences that could be suffered should a user violate the conditions of the AUP. Typically, this is limited to a loss of access, but it could include civil or criminal legal actions. AUPs must conform to local, state, and national telecommunications laws, rules, and regulations and include a statement that acknowledges this requirement.

CERTIFICATION SUMMARY

Electronic communications have become an important part of personal and business communications. E-mail, text and instant messaging, voice communications, teleconferencing, interactive meetings, and social networking and blog Web sites are used to conduct conversations, collaborative sessions, and team and project meetings.

Person-to-person and group collaborations are facilitated by electronic communication services. These collaborative sessions can be conducted between participants, who are located down the hall or around the world either in an asynchronous offline way or in interactive online sessions.

Electronic communications have their advantages and disadvantages, but if used properly and following the acceptable use policies and netiquette, the risks are minimized.

✓ TWO-MINUTE DRILL

Identifying Types of Electronic Communication

- ❑ The major types of electronic communications within this group of services are blogs and social networking Web sites, computer-based teleconferencing, e-mail, Internet telephony, and text and instant messaging.

- ❑ Electronic collaboration is two or more people discussing, developing, creating, or reviewing a common entity. Collaboration can occur on any electronic communications types or services.

- ❑ The advantages of electronic collaboration include the elimination of travel expense, avoiding interruptions in other duties, and the availability of input and feedback from the team members. The disadvantages include conflicts that can arise because of personal philosophy, understanding, cultural differences, or unfamiliarity with software. Collaboration over electronic communications services is very dependent on the availability of technical support.

- ❑ In a synchronous collaborative session, some form of participant control must be used. The session organizer or administrator assigns each authorized participant a password that is entered to gain access to the session. Users are assigned a username that identifies them to the other participants.

- ❑ The advantages of electronic communications include enhanced participation, flexibility, and speed of exchange. The disadvantages of electronic communications include diversity of audience, permanence, and voice.

Identifying Appropriate Uses for Electronic Communication

- ❑ Netiquette refers to the guidelines and best practices that should be followed in an electronic communication to conduct a meaningful and appropriate conversation. These guidelines cover areas of addressees, chain letters, copyright, flames, identity, message length, ownership, and security.

- ❑ An acceptable use policy (AUP) defines what authorized users of the network or service are allowed to do, what they are not allowed to do, and what constitutes an acceptable use of the network, service, or Web site.

SELF TEST

Identifying Types of Electronic Communication

1. Which of the following is not a common type of electronic communication?

   A. E-mail

   B. Groupware

   C. Instant messaging

   D. Post-it notes

2. Two or more individuals who are discussing, developing, creating, or reviewing a document or project using a type of electronic communications are engaged in what type of activity?

   A. Collaboration

   B. Coordination

   C. Teleconferencing

   D. Text messaging

3. When individuals engage in a discussion using electronic communications, what disadvantages or risks are possible?

   A. Cultural differences

   B. Disagreements due to personal philosophies

   C. Limited knowledge of the communications vehicle that can restrict participation

   D. All of the above

   E. None of the above

4. What is perhaps the primary resource that must be available to ensure effective electronic communications?

   A. Common philosophies

   B. Synchronous communications

   C. Technical support

   D. User training

5. So that the participants in a synchronous electronic communications session can identify the other participants of the session, what must each participant be assigned?

   A. Location code

   B. Message type

   C. Security code

   D. User identity

6. Which of the following is a disadvantage of electronic communications?
   A. Diversity of audience
   B. Enhanced participation
   C. Flexibility
   D. Speed of exchange

Identifying Appropriate Uses for Electronic Communication

7. The guidelines and best practices that should be followed in an electronic communication to conduct a meaningful and appropriate conversation are called
   A. Net-courtesy
   B. Netiquette
   C. Net-manners
   D. Net-nicety

8. An agreement provided by a network, service, or Web site that outlines and defines what users are allowed and disallowed from doing is called an
   A. Acceptable use policy
   B. Fair use policy
   C. General user agreement
   D. Legal use agreement

SELF TEST ANSWERS

Identifying Types of Electronic Communication

1. ☑ **D.** Primarily since Post-it notes are not electronic, they are generally not considered to be electronic communications.

   ☒ **A, B,** and **C** are incorrect. E-mail, groupware, and instant messaging are all types of electronic communications.

2. ☑ **A.** When two or more individuals work together by any means, hopefully they are collaborating.

   ☒ **B, C,** and **D** are incorrect. Typically, collaboration includes coordination, but teleconferencing and text messaging are electronic communications methods.

3. ☑ **D.** All of the choices given in answers A through C are risks and disadvantages to any electronic communication session. However, none of these answers is correct on its own.

   ☒ **A, B,** and **C** are incorrect. Because there is more than one disadvantage given in these choices, none is a correct answer by itself. Answer E is just wrong because there is a correct answer.

4. ☑ **C.** The availability of technical support and user help is essential to effective and efficient electronic communications.

   ☒ **A, B,** and **D** are incorrect. Common points of view and philosophies can enhance a collaborative session, but they are often hard to achieve. Synchronous communications aren't essential to conducting a collaborative session, and user training would be very nice, but it isn't always available.

5. ☑ **D.** A user identity can be a name, handle, e-mail address, or some other identity that lets the participants in an electronic communication know with whom they are interacting.

   ☒ **A, B,** and **C** is incorrect. Location codes, message types, and security codes can be included with a participant's identity, but they aren't common to all electronic communications types.

6. ☑ **A.** Cultural and other differences can create misunderstandings and conflict in a collaborative session.

   ☒ **B, C,** and **D** are incorrect. These choices are considered to be advantages to electronic communications.

Identifying Appropriate Uses for Electronic Communication

7. ☑ **B.** The generally accepted rules and guidelines for how one conducts himself or herself in an electronic communications session are called netiquette.

   ☒ **A, C,** and **D** are incorrect. These choices are terms I made up, as far as I know.

8. ☑ **A.** Virtually all networks, services, and Web sites that provide information, communications, or interactivity require users to acknowledge or sign an acceptable use policy.

   ☒ **B, C,** and **D** are incorrect. A fair use policy is another term used for an acceptable use policy, but it is also a guideline used with copyrights. The choices given in answers C and D are terms I made up and, even if they do exist, aren't correct.

21

The Internet
and the Web

The Internet and the World Wide Web (WWW) have together provided a virtually boundless source of information, communications, and other resources to users everywhere. Although most people think of the Internet and the WWW as a single thing, they are actually separate entities. One, the Internet, is a vast network of networks on which the other, the WWW, is able to link a variety of information sources together to create a logical pathway through the Internet's resources.

This chapter discusses the differences between the Internet and the WWW and how each contributes to the success and continued expansion of the other. Included in this discussion is a look at the anatomy of the WWW, or the Web as it's more commonly called, and how users are able to navigate through the information maze it creates.

CERTIFICATION OBJECTIVE

The Internet, the World Wide Web, and Web Browsers

3.1   Identity information about the Internet, the World Wide Web and Web sites and be able to use a Web browsing application.

The Internet and the World Wide Web (Web) are two fully distinct structures that work together to create a symbiotic system that appears to be a single entity. However, the Internet can exist without the Web, but the reverse is not true. In the sections that follow, these differences are explained, with the focus on the Web and its operational components.

The Internet

For the IC^3 exams, you really don't need to know the history and developmental timeline of the Internet. However, you should know enough about the Internet to be able to clearly differentiate it from the World Wide Web. Toward that end, let's take a look at the basic infrastructure of the Internet and then move on to how it serves as the arterial system of the Web.

A Network of Networks

When defined in terms of the various types of network structures, the Internet is basically a wide area network (WAN). It is, without a doubt, the single largest WAN in the world, by far. In fact, it is such a large WAN that it should be called a super WAN, a nexus (a network of networks), an interconnected network or internetwork, or just the Internet, for short.

Even though it involves a lot of software that facilitate the interconnections, the Internet is basically a physical structure. Network devices connect local networks to communication lines that connect to more powerful network devices that connect to larger communication lines, and so on. Yes, without the software (protocols) in the network devices, the Internet would certainly not function, but the physical connections of the communication media and the networking devices create the pathways (circuits) over which the electrical signals of user messages travel. See Chapters 17 and 18 to review the concepts of networking and the relationship of hardware and software in a networked environment.

Another way to view the Internet is in terms of a more logically oriented concept, which says that the Internet is one extremely large network that consists of a number of subnetworks, including the Web subnetwork, e-mail subnetworks, file transfer subnetworks, voice communication subnetworks, and more. Regardless of which view you wish to use, both are correct: one is just a physically oriented view, and the other a more logically oriented view. In either case, the Internet is the foundation communications network that provides the infrastructure, through its cabling, network devices, and protocols, required by each of the subnetworks to operate.

Internet Terminology

The Internet has grown to the point that it has merged into society and its cultures. As a result, certain terms have entered the language and you should have an understanding of these terms for the IC^3 exams. The more common Internet-related terms you should know are

- **IP address** The Internet Protocol defines internetwork addressing. The current standards define 32-bit (IP version 4 [IPv4]) and 128-bit (IP version 6 [IPv6]) addressing schemes. Each node (down to a computer on a local network) is assigned an IP address for use on the Internet.

- **Router** This networking device is used throughout the Internet to direct message traffic to the better of the available options on the interconnected communications links, which in many instances is the next upstream or downstream router.

■ **TCP/IP (Transmission Control Protocol/Internet Protocol)**   This is a suite of protocols that provide the processing rules and guidelines to transmit and receive messages across the Internet to and from destination addresses and sender addresses.

The World Wide Web

The World Wide Web, or Web, is the primary vehicle used to navigate around the Internet and all of its resources. The Web is just one of the various subnetworks that operate on the Internet, but it is safe to say that it is by far the most active of the Internet's subsystems.

The Web was developed in 1989 by Tim Berners-Lee and Robert Cailliau, who thought there should be a way to link from one informational resource to another without the tedium of entering the direct Internet address of each file, document, or object they and other users wished to view. The mechanism they developed—one that allows a Web user to move from one Web page to another relatively seamlessly—was embedding hypertext links, or hyperlinks, that included direct Web address links to other pages that related to the topic of the file in view.

Hyperlinks

Hypertext links, which were conceived by Ted Nelson and implemented by Douglas Englebart (who also invented the mouse), contain the uniform resource locator (URL) of a referenced Web page (see Figure 21-1) that includes the identification of the resource type, which is typically identified by the protocol used to move it across the Internet, such as HTTP or FTP (file transfer protocol), the name of the host or server on which the referenced item is located, and the domain identity of the site.

Hypertext links, or *hyperlinks*, are embedded into the coding of a Web page and contain a link to a location in the same page or to a document, file, Web site, or other resource located on the same server (host) or a remote host. Clicking the hyperlink emits a request that the referenced item be downloaded and displayed.

FIGURE 21-1

The components of a Web URL

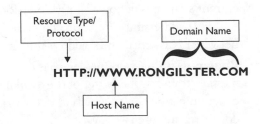

Web Browsers

Along with the concept of using hyperlinks to connect related documents, Web pages, and other types of transmittable resources came specialized software that is able to download a file and interpret its Hypertext Markup Language (HTML) and scripting (such as Visual Basic, JavaScript, and others) or structuring (Extensible Markup Language [XML]) coding schemes to display the content of the file as designed. This software is used to browse the Web, hence its name: *Web browser*.

The most popular Web browsers in use today are Internet Explorer from Microsoft, Firefox from Mozilla, Opera from Opera Software, Safari from Apple, and Chrome from Google. For the most part, all browsers perform the same basic functions, but each of the different browsers adds enhancements for security, add-in support, archiving, blog editors, and more to differentiate itself from the other browsers available.

A Web browser is the user's window to the Web and the Internet. Users issue requests for downloadable content, view the content, and interact with Web sites, and more. It is not required that users wishing to access content on the Web or Internet know how to code a Web page; they only need to know the URL of the content they wish to view.

Web Terminology

The Web, like the Internet, has merged into society, its culture, and its language. And like the Internet, the Web has given rise to a terminology that has become commonplace and, in many instances, a part of the common language. In addition to the terms discussed in the preceding sections, you should have an understanding of these terms for the IC^3 exams:

- **ActiveX** ActiveX modules are common function applets that can be executed by a Web browser to perform tasks; they include downloaders, PDF file viewers, movie players, and more.

- **Digital certificate** A digital certificate is an electronic identity card that is issued by a certification authority (CA) to guarantee the validity of a person or company on the Internet.

- **Download** This term is used to describe the action of requesting and receiving a file from another networked computer.

- **Home page** This is the Web page displayed when a browser is first opened. All browsers have a default home page assigned, but this can be easily reconfigured by the user.

- **HTML** This is the most commonly used coding language used for Web-based content. Its coding is interpreted by HTTP and the browser to properly display the content of a downloaded file.

- **HTTP**   This is the protocol used to transfer Web-based files from one networked computer to another. HTTP also instructs the browser on how the file should be displayed.

- **Internet service provider (ISP)**   An ISP is a company that provides subscribed users with a connection to the Internet through dialup, cable, telephone line, or satellite connections.

- **Podcast**   A podcast is one or more video or audio files that can be downloaded or streamed by a Web browser or a handheld device for playback. Its name is derived from the Apple iPod device.

- **Really Simple Syndication (RSS)**   RSS refers to a variety of content feeds from Web sites that are frequently updated, such as blogs, news, and audio or video sites. RSS feeds can be played back on a local device using an RSS reader or aggregator.

- **Secure Sockets Layer (SSL)**   Now known as Transport Layer Security (TLS), this security protocol is used to encrypt communications at the Transport layer to provide an end-to-end secured link.

- **Web browser**   This is a software program that is used to send requests for downloadable content, interpret the coding of the content, display the content of the downloaded file, and support the user's interaction with the content.

- **Web cache**   A Web cache is used by ISPs to improve the response time for its subscribers. A Web cache service captures and stores any Web site requested by users of a particular network so that its content can be provided to the requesting user without the need to download the entire file from its source; only the portions of a Web page that have changed since it was captured, if any, are downloaded to the cache server.

Internet and Web Content Types

Since nobody actually owns the Internet or the Web, the types of content and files that can be made available on the network are virtually unlimited. However, in the interest of commonality and interoperability, U.S. government agencies have stepped in to provide a form of standardization and control to what would otherwise be an even more chaotic situation. The Internet Corporation for Assigned Names and Numbers (ICANN) operates a variety of agencies, committees, task forces, and authorities under a contract from the U.S. Department of Commerce.

Content Types on the Internet and Web

The Internet Assigned Numbers Authority (IANA) is the ICANN agency that assigns and monitors the allocation of IP addresses, domain names, content and media types, and several other Internet-related numbers, standards, and other Internet and Web assignments. To ensure commonality and universal compatibility, the IANA maintains a registry of the media types and content encoding schemes in use, which is available to all users over the Web. IANA lists nine primary media and content encoding types that are used on the Internet:

- **Audio**   This group includes the Motion Pictures Experts Group audio formats (MPEG and MP3), Windows Media Audio (WMA), RealAudio (RA), and waveform (WAV) files.

- **Human-readable**   This group includes formats for text and Web page source code, such as Cascading Style Sheets (CSS), text files in comma-separated value (CSV) format, HTML, and XML.

- **Image**   This group includes the image file formats, such as the Graphics Interchange Format (GIF), the Joint Photographic Experts Group (JPEG) format, the Portable Network Graphics (PNG) format, the Tag Image File (TIF) format, the Scalable Vector Graphics (SVG) format, and the Windows icon file format (ICO).

- **Message**   This group contains a single HTTP message format.

- **Multipart**   This group includes Multipurpose Internet Mail Extensions (MIME) formats for text e-mail, HTML e-mail, and digitally signed or encrypted files.

- **Multipurpose files**   This group includes JavaScript, binary data streams, Electronic Data Interchange (EDI), ZIP file compression, and extensible HTML (XHTML) files.

- **Non-standard**   This group includes file formats and encoding schemes not otherwise classified into another group, such as Digit Video Interactive (DVI) video files; PHP encoding (PHP once stood for personal home page, but now it's just PHP); Adobe Flash; and the Stuffit (SIT), Roshal Archive (RAR), and tape archive (TAR) compressed file formats.

- **Vendor-specific files**   This group contains file formats specific to a particular content provider, such as Oasis' OpenDocument text and OpenDocument spreadsheets; Microsoft's Excel, PowerPoint, and Word formats; and Mozilla's XML user interface language (XUL).

- **Video**   This group includes video content file formats, such as MPEG-1 video, MP4 video, QuickTime, and Windows Media Video (WMV).

Types of Web Sites and Pages

Web pages, the most common file type on the Internet, generally contain human-readable text, audio, video, images, and scripting content types. However, a Web site can include a variety of Web page types, as differentiated by their file extensions. Table 21-1 lists some of the more common Web page filename extensions found on the Web.

Regardless of the file format or encoding method used to construct it, a Web page can serve a variety of different purposes or site types. The primary Web site or page types that exist are

- **Application-based Web site** A Web site of this type (Microsoft Live, Google Docs, and Zoho are examples) provides access directly to a variety of applications, including word processing, spreadsheets, and more.

- **Blog site** A Web log (blog) could also be used as a portal site, but it's primarily designed to display contributed content in a chronological sequence.

- **E-commerce site** This type of site is essentially a storefront on which users can browse through products and make purchases. These "click-and-order" sites, such as Amazon.com and other retail sites, are quite common on the Web.

- **Forum site** Similar to a blog site, this type is primarily designed to support question and answer forums on specific topics to which users and the site host can contribute.

TABLE 21-1

Filename
Extensions
Commonly Seen
on the Web

File Extension	File Format Type
.asp/.aspx	Active Server Pages
.cfm	ColdFusion Markup Language file
.css	Cascading Style Sheet
.htm/html	HTML file
.htmls	HTML server-side code
.php	PHP file
.ssi	HTML with server-side includes
.swf	Shockware Flash file
.vrml	Virtual Reality Markup Language file
.xht	Extensible HTML file
.xhtml	XML/HTML file

- **Identity site**   Slightly larger than a micro-site, an identity site could be classified as a mini-site. This type of Web site typically has from five to seven pages and is primarily used by individuals and small businesses or organizations who wish to establish a homepage presence for friends or clients.

- **Map and geographical imaging site (GIS)**   A Web site along the lines of Google Maps, MapQuest, or Yahoo! Maps provides the capability to view a map of or to a particular location. Perhaps the best-known GIS site on the Web is Google Earth, which provides satellite imagery of the Earth down to a single house or street in many locations.

- **Micro-site**   This obviously smaller Web site contains only one or two Web pages and is typically used for redirection, sign-up or opt-in pages, or the like.

- **Portal site**   This type of Web site contains a variety of content types and is designed to be a point-of-destination site that users could use as their personal home page, such as Yahoo!, Google, MSN, and more. Portal sites typically provide a number of different ways for users to interact with the various content types included.

- **Social networking site**   Such a Web site provides users with the ability to create a profile page and then post their thoughts, status, and just about anything else they'd like to share with the connections or friends who also subscribe to the service. The more popular social networking sites are MySpace, Facebook, and Twitter.

Web Page Components

There are two schools of thought when considering the essential components of a good Web page or site: those that believe the layout of the page is the most important aspect and those who believe that the content is more important that the layout. Although often discussed separately, each of these component approaches plays a crucial role in the success and effectiveness of a Web site or page.

Web Page Layout   When designing a Web site that is to have more than a single Web page, consistency is the underlying key to success. Each of the pages of the Web site should have essentially the same layout and visual effects. Graphics, such as logos, top of the page (banner) images, and other images included on each page should have the same exact location to provide a smooth transition between pages.

The standard design layout of a Web page contains three parts that can be included in its layout, depending on the purpose of the page. The three Web page parts are the banner, sidebar, and body. The banner and the sidebar are optional, but the page must have a body. The banner, if included, is generally at the top and can extend from side to side completely and usually contains a logo or graphic along with text identifying the page or the person, company, or organization presenting the page. The sidebar is typically used for navigation links but can be on either side of the page (or even included as a footer across the bottom of the page, if desired). Figure 21-2 illustrates the general layout of a standard Web page.

A Web page should be designed and laid out in much the same way that a magazine or newspaper advertisement would be. In order for a Web page to have what is called "stickiness," or the ability to hold a viewer's interest, it must be designed with that objective in mind. The design issues that must be considered are the font (including font face, color, and size) to be used, the size and placement of graphics or animations, and how to effectively minimize the amount of text on the page without minimizing its message.

Web Page Content   A Web page must be carefully planned around its purpose, its vision, and its overall presentation, which means that its content must also support its general design. There are several content components that can be included in a Web page to achieve its purpose efficiently. Some of the more popular components found on Web pages are

- **Forms**   Figure 21-3 shows a simple Web page form, like one used by viewers to contact the site host or Webmaster, to subscribe to a site or a newsletter, or to register for a contest.

FIGURE 21-2

A standard layout for a Web page

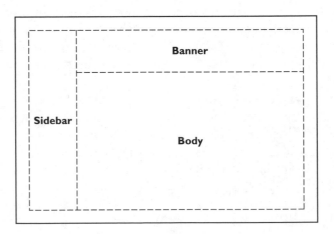

FIGURE 21-3

An example of a
Web page form

- **Frames**   Although no longer in vogue, Web page frames can be used to keep a viewer on a particular page even though the viewer selects a link to an off-site URL. Frames allow you to control each of the parts of a Web page separately and display new content into a particular part or frame.

- **Graphic hyperlinks**   Photographs, clip art, images, and other graphic content can be inserted into any part of a Web page for illustration, logo, or informational purposes. Graphics inserted into a Web page can also be configured with a hyperlink so that when a viewer clicks a graphic, the browser downloads the linked page or file.

- **Horizontal bars**   HTML includes a command tag that can be used to insert a horizontal bar into a Web page to separate parts of its content.

- **Image maps**   Using the same general effect of a graphic hyperlink, an image map allows for multiple hyperlinks to exist on an image. For example, a common use of an image map is a map of the United States on which a hyperlink is anchored to an outline of each state.

- **Interactive elements**   A Web page can include several types of interactive objects, such as buttons, text boxes, radio buttons, check boxes, and pull-down lists. These objects allow a user to start an action (submit a form), enter data (enter a name into a Name text box), choose from alternative values (choose a size or color, for instance, or answer a survey question using a radio button or check box), or choose from a preset list of values (choose a state name from a pull-down list).

- **Tables**   Perhaps the most common organizational feature used on a Web page is a table that is defined as a structure with individually specified header, rows, and cells that can vary in both width and height to contain whatever content is being organized.

- **Text hyperlinks**   By far, the most common element in a Web page is a hypertext link. Unless a Web page contains no links to other pages or sites, the Web page contains at least one text hyperlink.

Web Browser Security Settings

Most of the popular Web browsers (see "Web Browsers" earlier in the chapter) come with default settings and configurations that serve the needs of a vast majority of all users. However, there are situations where, for a variety of reasons, you may need to change the default settings. Most typically, the security settings of a Web browser are customized for compatibility with the security policies of your company, organization, or family.

Not only can changing the security settings in a Web browser help you to prevent unwanted Web pages, pop-up or drop-down windows, and other forms of unwanted content from displaying, they also help to avoid browser script attacks that may be embedded in a Web page you download.

Typically, the options to block pop-ups (and other forms of page-initiated content) are available on the Web browser's Tools, Options, or Settings menu bar selection. Figure 21-4 shows a sample of the Tools and Preferences menus for the Opera Web browser. Configuring these settings to block unwanted pages and windows can provide the first line of security to a Web browser.

In the Internet Explorer Web browser, security is configured in security zones, as shown in Figure 21-5. The Internet zone can be configured to limit the actions of

FIGURE 21-4

The Tools and Preferences menus in the Opera Web browser

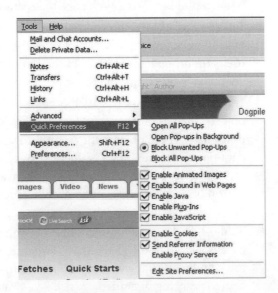

FIGURE 21-5

The Security tab
of the Internet
Explorer Tools
option

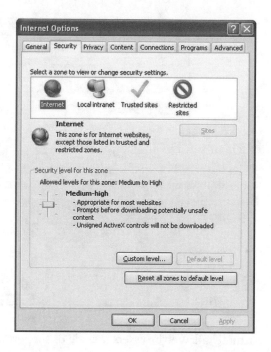

downloaded Web pages from outside the local network; the Intranet zone is configured
for content downloaded from within the local network; the Trusted Sites option allows
you to list the Web sites you believe you can trust to provide content that is free from
any security or virus issues; and on the Restricted Sites option, you can list those Web
sites that you believe bring malware, viruses, and security threats to your computer.
Other Web browsers provide similar security and content protections, although each
has a different look and navigation. In contrast to Opera (see Figure 21-4) and Internet
Explorer (see Figure 21-5), Firefox has a slightly different group of settings to control
security and content permissions, as shown in Figure 21-6.

Navigating the Web

The purpose of a Web browser is to provide a user with a specialized tool to
download Internet, Web, and intranet content and to navigate from one Web site
to another using a hyperlink, a user-entered URL, or an IP address. To download a
specific Web page, the URL of the page is entered into the Navigation or GoTo bar
of Web browser. As long as the hyperlink (a URL embedded in the code of a Web
page), URL, or IP address entered is valid and all of its components are correctly
spelled with the component separators in the right places, the Web browser requests
the content from the Web server located at the address represented by the URL,
downloads it, interprets its coding, and displays the content.

FIGURE 21-6

The Tools/
Options dialog
box of the Firefox
Web browser

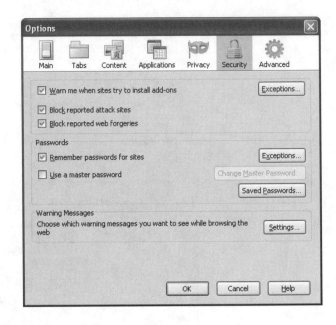

Virtually all Web browsers include or support a standard set of browsing features, including

- **Back and forward**   While browsing the Web, users can move backward to a previously viewed page or move forward to one that has already been viewed using the Forward and Back buttons or menu links of the browser.

- **Bookmarks or favorites**   Web browsers also provide the capability to create a list of bookmarks or favorites sites, which are typically sites that the user frequently visits or links the user wishes to keep handy. Adding a link to the list of bookmarks or favorites can be done within the browser and, in some operating systems, from the desktop as well, by clicking the Bookmarks or Favorites menu bar option and selecting the Add command. Some browsers, for example Internet Explorer, allow bookmarks and favorites to be categorized into folders or groups. Favorites can be moved between folders or groups using a menu option for organizing the bookmarks or favorites. To jump to a Web page from the list of bookmarks or favorites, click the Bookmarks or Favorites menu selection and then click the page you wish to open. A bookmarks or favorites list can also be shared as an attachment to an e-mail message or uploaded to a social networking or information sharing Web page. A sharable file of a bookmarks or favorites list can be created using the Export function that is typically located on the File menu bar option's submenu.

■ **Find**   Rather than scrolling down through a Web page in an attempt to locate specific information, you can use the Find command to search for the word or phrase for which you're looking. The Find command is typically located on Edit menu bar option's submenu.

■ **History**   Depending on the configuration and settings of a Web browser, the browser keeps from zero to 999 days of your browsing history. The browsing history can be used in myriad ways, but perhaps the most common use is to revisit a site for which you have forgotten the URL. To view the history in the Internet Explorer browser, you can use the shortcut keys CTRL-H, display the Explorer bar and choose History, or click the History icon at the top of the screen. With the History displayed in the Explorer bar, you can click the page you wish to open.

■ **Home page**   The term home page really has only one meaning, the first page viewed, but, in practice, a browser can be configured to display a certain Web page when it opens or you can move to a Web site's home page using a hyperlink (typically this link is named "Home") that points to the home page of the site. Clicking the home page button or menu command in a Web browser immediately displays the Web page configured as its home page.

■ **New window or tab**   Users also have the option of keeping a Web page active (and not covered up by another page) by opening a new browser window or, in many of the newer browser versions, opening a new browser tab. In either case, the new window or the new tab can be selected by clicking into the new window or clicking the new tab. On a tabbed browser, each tab can contain a different Web page that can be made the active page of the browser simply by clicking the tab. To close a tab or a browser window, click the "X" symbol of an active tab or click the Close button of the window. If more than one tab has been added to a browser, when the user attempts to close the browser window, a prompt displays that asks whether only the active tab is to be closed or all of the tabs.

■ **Refresh/reload**   The view of a Web page can be refreshed (reloaded) to update any objects on the page that may have changed or to fix the display if it becomes garbled.

■ **Web Search**   Most of the more popular Web browsers also support a built-in search capability that allows the user to specify a search engine (such as Google, Dogpile, Ask, Yahoo!, or Bing) to be used as the default.

Working with a Browser

Once a Web page is displayed in a browser, there are a number of actions you can do to use or save all or some of its information. The best way to save all of a Web page's information (including its hyperlinks) is to save the file on the local computer. However, you can also copy some of the page's information (being mindful of copyright laws and plagiarism), print the page, or download or save a linked file or object on the page.

Copy Web Page Elements

Unless a Web page is protected against its content being copied, which is becoming more and more common, you can select the text, objects, and elements on the page and paste them into another document. To copy some or all of a Web page's content, use the mouse to select the content to be copied, right-click the selected area, click Copy from the pop-up menu, and then paste the copied content into a word processing document, presentation slide, spreadsheet, HTML editor, or text document.

Save Web Page Elements

Individual objects, such as tables, graphics, and links, can be saved as individual files using the Save Target As command on the pop-up menu that displays when you select and then right-click a Web page element. The Save Target As command, which allows you to specify the location and name of a file saved to a storage medium, is the most commonly used way to save a file referenced on a Web page with a hyperlink. Right-click the hyperlink and choose Save Target As to open the Save As dialog box.

Print a Web Page

Some Web pages provide a hyperlink that can be used to display a print-ready (printer-friendly) version of the page. If you wish to print a Web page and a printable version is not available, consider that all of the visible content on the displayed page will be printed, including any graphics (although animations typically print as still image). To print a Web page, you can choose the Print function of the File menu bar selection or you can use the keyboard shortcut of CTRL-P.

Change Browser Settings

Every browser application has a wide range of settings that users can use to create a personal Web browsing experience. Some of the browser's settings control its display (and more important, what is to be displayed and not displayed), others set the security level of the browser, and yet others control the color scheme of the browser, the browser's home page, and more.

Some browsers, like Internet Explorer, cluster the majority of the settings onto one or two primary dialog boxes, while others, such as Opera, split up their settings onto multiple single-focus dialog boxes. Perhaps the most important of these settings are the security settings, which allow you to set the level of security (and trust) for each of the network source types from which you download Web pages, such as the Internet, an intranet, a specific list of trusted or not-trusted pages, sites, or domains. Another security option is the control of cookies.

Virtually every Web browser allows the user to designate at least one startup or home page that is to be displayed when the browser opens. This home page, also called the default page, is designated on the Internet options or preferences dialog box of the browser. Some browsers allow multiple home pages that are assigned in a priority scheme and displayed should any of the higher-priority pages not be available.

Cookies

A browser or Hypertext Transfer Protocol (HTTP) cookie is a small data file that is stored on a user's computer (meaning hard disk) by the coding of a Web page. The data inside a cookie file typically includes information about the parts of a Web site a user visited, the user's preferences (such as which products the user viewed), the contents of an electronic shopping cart at the end of a session, or a profile of the user.

There are two basic types of cookies stored on users' computers: first-party cookies and third-party cookies (the user is considered to be the second party). A first-party cookie is created by the Web page being viewed and is "owned" by the publisher of that page. A third-party cookie is created by someone other than the displayed page's publisher. For example, if you view a retail Web site, such as Amazon.com or Tower .com, a first-party cookie is generated to track your movement around the site, the items you viewed, and the items you place into its shopping cart. This information is intended to help the site better serve you in the future. However, should you download a Web page that contains advertising banners, which are downloaded by the page from a remote server, the banner server is likely to create a third-party cookie. This cookie would be used to store profile information about you should you click the banner and visit the Web page of the advertiser.

Most of the better browsers provide settings to block all cookies, including both first-party and third-party cookies, to block third-party cookies only, to display a prompt before creating a cookie, or to accept all cookies, which can be somewhat risky. Some browsers also support the concept of *leashing,* which is a rule-based form of blocking cookies. Leashing allows third-party cookies only if the triggering link is associated with a first-party cookie.

Web Browsing Issues

Of course, the most common error that occurs on the Web is caused by the URL being either misspelled or constructed with erroneous data, such as with the wrong top-level domain (.com, .edu, etc.). However, there are a number of other problems that can occur during a Web browsing session, including

■ **Browser version**   Unfortunately, not all Web content is written for or kept up-to-date with the latest browser versions. On the other hand, some Web content, created for the latest version of a particular browser, may not be backward compatible with older browser versions. In either of these cases, some page content may not display properly or a new Web-based application may not function as it should when viewed through an older browser version.

■ **Garbled text**   This condition is typically caused by an improper font substitution. Some Web pages are designed with infrequently used or generally unavailable fonts. A browser attempts to overcome this problem by substituting a font that closely approximates the unsupported font. On occasion, the substituted font may not display properly, resulting in what appears to be garbled text.

■ **Page Not Found errors**   Table 21-2 lists the most common of the HTTP error messages and their causes that can be encountered on the Web. All of the 400-series error codes indicate a problem caused by a resource request, and the 500-series error codes indicate a problem at the host server. In addition to the error messages listed in Table 21-2, there are also error messages, some of which are standard to all browsers and some of which are unique to specific Web browsers, that include such actions as bad file request, Internet connection unavailable, and the like.

■ **Plug-in or add-in version**   What could be seemingly a browser version problem could very well be caused by the version of a required browser plug-in or add-in, such as Adobe Flash or Sun Microsystems' Java. Some Web content requires a certain browser plug-in to display or run certain types of content. Before you resort to more drastic measures, such as re-installing the browser application, you may want to download the latest version of a required browser plug-in.

■ **Pop-up pages**   Pop-up pages are typically smaller Web pages that are displayed because of either a user request or as a result of something a user did on a particular Web page. All Web browsers include a pop-up blocker due to the heavy use of pop-ups by advertisers attempting to get their product, company, or message in front of users' eyes. There are some helpful or valid reasons for using a pop-up window, such as help information, to install downloaded applications, and to view a graphic in a larger image. However, most pop-ups are advertisements and most are not generated by user request. If the browser's pop-up blocker is enabled, any pop-up windows are blocked, including good ones.

■ **Slow or interrupted page loading**   Most likely this condition is caused by a break in the Internet connection rather than something on the local computer. If in the middle of downloading a Web page, the network connection is lost (if only for a brief moment) or the network must renegotiate the connection, the result is that the download seems much longer than usual or the download stops altogether. Another cause, although much less common these days, is that the Web server from which the file is being downloaded could just be very slow.

■ **Spoofing and phishing sites**   For obviously nefarious reasons, some Web sites are published for the sole purpose of gathering information from users to be used for identity theft or other forms of fraud. A spoofing site is one that masquerades as a legitimate site, such as a bank or credit card company, and induces users to confirm their profile information by recreating it. A phishing site is a Web site that is fishing for personal information from users who believe the site to be authentic and are willing to comply with requests for personal information. Some phishing sites (and e-mail messages) also try to induce users to fall for get-rich-quick schemes or requests to help an unfortunate (and totally fictitious) person by sending money.

	Error Code	Error Message	Cause
TABLE 21-2 Common Web Browser (HTTP) Error Codes and Messages	401	Unauthorized Request	A valid username and password was not entered.
	403	Forbidden/Access Denied	An attempt was made to access a restricted directory or file for which a password or specific permission is required.
	404	File Not Found	The URL entered or included in a hypertext link is misspelled or no longer exists.
	500	Server Error	The server hosting a service is unable to respond due to an internal error.
	503	Service Unavailable	The server hosting a requested Web site is either too busy or is experiencing an interruption in service.
	504	Gateway Timeout	The requesting gateway (router) timed out due to non-response from the host server.
	505	HTTP Version Not Supported	The version of HTTP used to make the request on the host server is not supported.

CERTIFICATION SUMMARY

The Internet and the World Wide Web (the Web) are two distinct and separate structures that can be used to share resources. The Internet is a network of networks and essentially is composed of the physical components that interconnect local networks and their resources. On the other hand, the Web is a logically interlinked network of resource locations and services.

Internet and Web resources are identified uniquely with an Internet Protocol (IP) address, but the Web also uses a user-friendly Uniform Resource Locator (URL) to address a specific site, page, or other file. Access to Internet and Web resources is facilitated through networking devices, such as routers and Internet gateways.

Security is an important setting on a Web browser and it should be carefully considered and configured to provide an appropriate level of security to a local network and its nodes.

✓ TWO-MINUTE DRILL

The Internet, the World Wide Web, and Web Browsers

❑ The Internet is the single largest WAN in the world, that is, an interconnected network of networks. The Internet is basically a physical structure.

❑ The Internet consists of a number of subnetworks, including the Web subnetwork, e-mail subnetworks, file transfer subnetworks, and voice communication subnetworks. The Internet provides the infrastructure for these subnetworks, through its cabling, network devices, and protocols.

❑ Important Internet-related terms are IP address, router, TCP/IP, and the World Wide Web (Web).

❑ The Web is the primary vehicle used to navigate around the Internet and all of its resources.

❑ The Web is used to link from one informational resource to another on the Internet.

❑ A hypertext link contains the URL of a Web page that identifies a resource type, the name of a host or server, and a domain identity.

❑ A Web browser is specialized software used to download a file and interpret its HTML or scripting code to display the file's content. A Web browser is the user's window to the Web and the Internet. The popular Web browsers are Internet Explorer, Firefox, Opera, Safari, and Chrome.

❑ The IANA is the ICANN agency that assigns and monitors the allocation of IP addresses, domain names, content and media types, and several other Internet-related numbers, standards, and other Internet and Web assignments. IANA lists nine primary media and content types: audio, human-readable, image, message, multipart, multipurpose, non-standard, vendor-specific, and video.

❑ A Web site can include a variety of Web page types, including Active Server Pages (.asp/.aspx) and HTML (.htm/.html), and have a specific purpose, such as a blog site, an e-commerce site, a forum site, an identity site, or a portal site.

❑ The components of a Web page or site include its layout and its content. Consistency is the key to success on a Web site. The standard design layout of a Web page contains a banner, a sidebar, and a body. The banner and the sidebar are optional, but the page must have a body.

❑ A Web page can include one or more content components, including forms, frames, hyperlinks (graphic, text, or image map), horizontal bars, and tables.

❑ The security settings of a Web browser are customized for compatibility with the security policies of your company, organization, or family. The security settings of a Web browser can prevent unwanted Web pages, pop-up or drop-down windows, and browser script attacks.

❑ When using a Web browser, the navigation bar, a built-in search capability, and support for other Internet and browser protocols are important. Web browsers keep a history of the Web sites visited and a list of favorites or bookmarks.

❑ The most common Web browser error is caused by misspelled URLs. HTTP error messages can display to indicate a common browsing issue. The 400-series error codes indicate a problem caused by a resource request and the 500-series error codes indicate a problem at the host server.

SELF TEST

The Internet, the World Wide Web, and Web Browsers

1. The Internet is essentially the biggest _____ area network in the world.
   A. Campus
   B. Local
   C. Metropolitan
   D. Wide

2. Which of the following is not a major subnetwork of the Internet?
   A. File transfer
   B. Intranet
   C. Voice
   D. Web

3. What is the internetworking device that is the primary means of interconnections on the Internet?
   A. Hub
   B. Repeater
   C. Router
   D. Switch

4. Which of the following is not a component of a URL?
   A. Domain identity
   B. Host name
   C. IP address
   D. Resource type

5. What is the mechanism used to interconnect and create the pathway around the Web?
   A. HTML
   B. HTTP
   C. Hypertext link
   D. TCP/IP

6. What agency is contracted by the U.S. government to assign and monitor the allocation of IP addresses, domain name, content and media types, and other Internet-related numbers and standards?

   A. HTTP

   B. ICANN

   C. IEEE

   D. IETP

7. Which of the following is not a commonly used filename extension for a file containing a Web page?

   A. .aspx

   B. .cfm

   C. .docx

   D. .html

8. Of the standard Web page layout components, which is the only component that must be included in the design of a Web page?

   A. Banner

   B. Body

   C. Corner

   D. Sidebar

9. What is the Web page content component that is frequently used to gather information about a viewer?

   A. Form

   B. Frame

   C. Image map

   D. Table

10. True or False: The default security settings of a Web browser are preconfigured to handle every level of security situation encountered by any and every user.

    A. True

    B. False

11. What common Web browser feature can be used by viewers to create and save a list of frequently visited or favorite URLs?

   A. Bookmarks

   B. Cookies

   C. History

   D. Security settings

12. What is generally the source of a Web browser error when a 500-series error message is displayed?

   A. User

   B. Local computer

   C. Local network

   D. Remote server

SELF TEST ANSWERS

The Internet, the World Wide Web, and Web Browsers

1. ☑ **D.** The Internet is the ultimate wide area network, consisting of a network of networks.
   ☒ **A, B,** and **C** are incorrect. A campus, local, or metropolitan area network has a limited geographical space and would not be expansive enough to provide worldwide interconnection.

2. ☑ **B.** An intranet is a subnetwork of a local area network.
   ☒ **A, C,** and **D** are incorrect. These options are each a subnetwork of the Internet, among others.

3. ☑ **C.** Routers provide the interconnected communications that forward Internet message traffic from its source to its destination.
   ☒ **A, B,** and **D** are incorrect. Hubs, repeaters, and switches are generally local area network devices, although some switches are robust enough to be used as WAN devices.

4. ☑ **C.** While a URL is translated into its corresponding IP address by the Domain Name System (DNS), the human-readable form of a URL doesn't contain the IP address.
   ☒ **A, B,** and **D** are incorrect. These choices are all parts of a URL construction.

5. ☑ **C.** While the answer choices given for this question are all Web communications elements, the primary mechanism of the Web is the hypertext link.
   ☒ **A, B,** and **D** are incorrect. HTML, HTTP, and TCP/IP are essential to the Web as it exists today, but the mechanism that creates the Web is the hypertext link.

6. ☑ **B.** The Internet Corporation for Assigned Names and Numbers (ICANN) is the agency that is contracted by the U.S. Commerce Department to administer the names and numbers used on the Internet.
   ☒ **A, C,** and **D** are incorrect. HTTP is the primary protocol of the Web; the IEEE is a trade society of electrical and electronics engineers; and the IETP is the engineering task force that administers and controls Internet standards.

7. ☑ **C.** The filename extension .docx is the Word 2007 default filename extension.
   ☒ **A, B,** and **D** are incorrect. The filename extensions .aspx, .cfm, and .html are commonly used filename extensions for Web page files.

8. ☑ **B.** A Web page must have a body, and the other elements listed are all optional.
   ☒ **A, C,** and **D** are incorrect. A Web page can include a banner, or a sidebar, but only a page body is required.

9. ☑ **A.** Web page forms are commonly used to gather information from a viewer, including contact information, registrations, and the like.

   ☒ **B, C,** and **D** are incorrect. Frames are used to display linked content within a dynamic page; an image map is a form of graphic hyperlink; and a table is used to organize and present page content, including a form, if desired.

10. ☑ **B.** While a browser's default security settings address most of the common security issues on the Web, your network administrator or your own personal preferences are most likely not reflected in the default settings.

    ☒ **A** is incorrect. It is not logically possible for the default security settings of a browser to address every possible security situation.

11. ☑ **A.** Named either Favorites or Bookmarks, this is a user-managed feature that allows a viewer to create and manage a list of frequently visited sites.

    ☒ **B, C,** and **D** are incorrect. Cookies are reference entries saved to a local system to keep login, navigation, or preferences data about how the viewer interacted with a site. A Web browser's history function retains none, some, or all of the sites visited by the viewer. The security settings don't retain information about the past, except for lists of sites that the user wishes to allow or deny.

12. ☑ **D.** The 500-series of HTTP error codes are used to indicate a possible problem with the remote server or host.

    ☒ **A, B,** and **C** are incorrect. The 400-series of HTTP error codes can indicate a problem with the local computer or the local network servers. However, just about any error code or message can apply to errors made by the user.

22

Working with Content on the Internet

W eb pages and Web sites must be coded, programmed, or formatted specifically for how potential viewers are to see the page or site in their Web browsers. Web content, on the other hand, can be added to a page as a part of its programming, or uploaded by viewers as a blog entry, a comment on a social networking page, or as a Wiki page contribution. This chapter discusses the different coding schemes used to create a Web page, and how viewers add content to a Web page.

CERTIFICATION OBJECTIVE

Creating Content on the Web

> 3.2   *Understand how content is created, located, and evaluated on the World Wide Web.*

Within the IC³ objective covered by this chapter, there is a lot to be discussed: how a Web page is created using Web protocol–compatible markup and scripting languages; how to use a search engine to locate content on the Web and a quick look at how search engines work; how to know if information found on the Web can be trusted; how to avoid copyright and plagiarism issues with Web content; what a Web browser does with downloaded files to display them; how a Web page is uploaded to a Web server; and how to print a document from a Web browser.

As you can see, our seemingly simple exam objective covers a lot of information. Each of these topics is discussed in the sections that follow.

Creating a Web Page

For the most part, Web pages are created using one of two primary coding schemes:

■ Hypertext Markup Language (HTML)
■ Scripting languages

While HTML remains the most popular coding scheme for creating Web pages, scripting languages, such as JavaScript and VBScript, are becoming more popular. Each of these Web page coding schemes is discussed in the sections that follow.

Using HTML to Create a Web Page

To fully explain HTML would require another whole book. However, for the IC³ exams, you really don't need to be an expert at HTML, but you do need to have a general understanding of its structure, syntax, and usage. So, to that end, let's look at the basic structure of an HTML page, the syntax of HTML statements, and a few examples of how its major content elements, specifically a list, a table, and a form, are created.

A variety of HTML editor software is available, some for a fee and some free for download. However, in this case, you do get what you pay for. HTML editors are classified as either a text editor or a WYSIWYG (What You See Is What You Get) graphic interface editor. WYSIWYG editors allow you to see the results of a Web page as it's created, where a text-based HTML editor typically provides only coding support.

The Structure of an HTML Page

The HTML coding used to create a single Web page is structured into three primary elements: the page itself, a header, and the body of the page. Each of these elements is defined in HTML inside of a specific container. The HTML page is defined in an <html> . . . </html> container. The <html> tag starts the container and the </html> tag ends the container. This syntax (<*tag*> . . . </*tag*>) is consistently used throughout HTML to define a variety of container elements.

The header for an HTML page is defined inside the <head> . . . </head> container, which is placed inside the page container along with the body container. The page body is defined inside the <body> . . . </body> container. The following code segment demonstrates the minimum HTML coding required to create a Web page that includes a title and a line of text in its body:

```
<html>
     <head>
          <title>Success on the IC3 Exam</TITLE>
     </head>
     <body>
          This Web page is dedicated to success on the IC3 exam.
     </body>
</html>
```

Figure 22-1 shows the Web page created by this HTML code as it is displayed in a Web browser. Notice that the title entry is displayed on the top bar of the browser and, if the browser supports multiple pages, like Firefox in this case, on the page's

FIGURE 22-1

The sample
HTML code
displayed in a
Web browser

This Web page is dedicated to success on the IC3 exam.

tab as well. The unformatted text included in the body of the page displays at the top left of the page by default.

To format the body of a Web page, a variety of elements can be programmed into the page, such as a bulleted or numbered list, a table, pictures, images, and hypertext links. In addition, if the page is intended to collect user information, like on a registration or contact page, a form can also be programmed into the page. Figure 22-2 shows an example of a simple Web page form.

Web Page Scripting Languages

There are several scripting languages that can be used to create entire Web pages or to embed a routine into an HTML document to accomplish a task that HTML itself can't do. For the IC[3] exams, we can concentrate on the latter use for scripting languages. In the next few sections, we look at the more popular scripting languages used to enhance the capabilities of an HTML Web page, specifically JavaScript and VBScript.

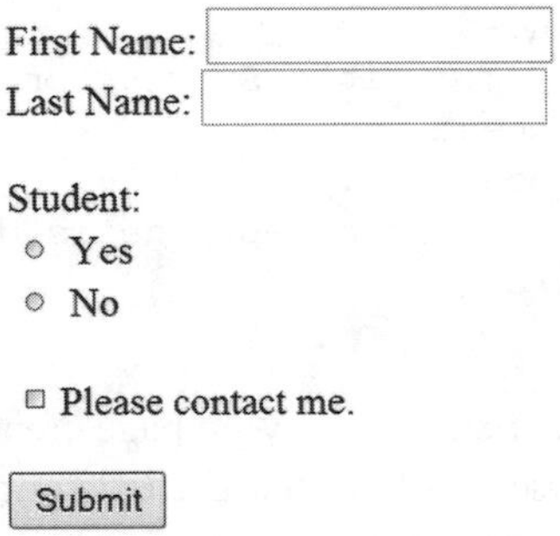

FIGURE 22-2

An example of a
simple Web page
form

First Name: [   ]
Last Name: [   ]

Student:
   ○ Yes
   ○ No

   ☐ Please contact me.

[Submit]

JavaScript   First of all, JavaScript is *not* a derivative of the Java language. Actually, it was developed by Netscape and was originally called Mocha and then LiveScript. The name change to JavaScript occurred in 1995 when Netscape added Java support to its Netscape Navigator browser to help promote that product.

The primary advantage of using JavaScript in an HTML Web page is that JavaScript can access data from other objects on the page. For example, if after a viewer has entered certain values, such as a postal or ZIP code, you wish to automatically look up the viewer's city and state, a JavaScript routine can access the value in the postal or ZIP code field and perform the lookup, perhaps in a database or embedded list, and display the information in the correct fields.

JavaScript is more like a true programming language than HTML, and some knowledge of programming techniques and logic development is required to create a successful routine. However, the Web is host to a vast array of special-purpose routines that can be used as examples or, where permission is granted, embedded directly into your HTML page.

The following code segment is a very simple JavaScript routine embedded in an HTML page:

```
<html>
<body>
<script type="text/javascript">
document.write("This is a simple JavaScript function");
</script>
</body>
</html>
```

This example also shows how a JavaScript routine is embedded into an HTML page. The <script> . . . </script> container can be inserted in either the header or the body of an HTML page, depending on what the routine does or when it is to be invoked.

VBScript   Like JavaScript, VBScript (short for Visual Basic Scripting Edition) has the capability to access other objects within the same Web page or, using SQL commands, from a database. The major difference between VBScript and JavaScript is that VBScript can be directly embedded in HTML code, whereas JavaScript must be defined within a script container.

The following code sample shows a simple example of VBScript embedded into an HTML page:

```
<html>
    <body>
        <script type="text/vbscript">
            document.write("This is a simple VBScript
            function")
        </script>
    </body>
</html>
```

If you compare the VBScript example to the JavaScript example in the preceding section, you should notice that they are virtually identical. That's true for these simple examples, but in more complex routines, their differences are apparent.

Server-Side vs. Client-Side

Web sites and pages can be provided from either a server-side or client-side source. A server-side operation preprocesses the script language of a Web page and sends out HTML data to be displayed on the requesting client (browser). If the requested page is a static Web page, meaning that it has no dynamic content, such as data from a database, very little, if any, preprocessing is needed.

If the requested content is a dynamic Web page that contains content that must be retrieved, calculated, or configured specifically for the requesting client, then the scripted Web page must be preprocessed by the server before the page is transmitted to the client. Server-side Web page operations save time on the client by sending the immediately displayable coding of the requested page to the client browser. On the other hand, in client-side Web page operations, the browser performs the interpretation, data lookup (such as a cookie), and formatting of the Web page.

Web Page Content

Web page viewers are able to contribute content to a variety of Web page types, such as Web logs (blogs), Wiki sites, and social networking sites. Viewers can also download and view content from video and audio sites, as well as upload content for other viewers to see or hear.

Blogs

A *Web log*, or *blog*, site is typically created and managed by an individual or organization who regularly posts information in the form of a commentary, opinion piece, or article to the page, to which viewers can add comments relating to the discussion. Blogs are categorized by their content or their intended audience. Some of the more common types of blogs are

- **Personal blogs**   This type of blog is often a public diary or journal from the blog's creator or a public forum that allows viewers to keep the world informed of their activities, such as Twitter.com.

- **Organizational blogs**   This type of blog, which is also called a corporate blog, can be intended only for the employees, customers, or supplies of a company or corporation, but some are also public. Some companies use this type of a blog as a form of institutional advertising and public relations, but for the most part they are used for improving organizational communications internally and externally.

- **Media-specific blogs**   Blogs that are specifically designed for sharing video content, such as YouTube.com and others, are referred to as v-logs. Other media-specific blogs may share links to recommended sites for others to use (linkblogs) or function as sites to which art and drawings (sketchblogs), photographs (photoblogs), or a variety of mixed media or content (tumbleblogs) can be posted.

- **Subject- or genre-specific blogs**   It's safe to say that a majority of the personal blogs on the Web are generally focused on a particular topic or type of discussion, such as politics, travel, education, art, music, or fashion.

Creating a blog is a relatively simple task. The primary requirement is a personal or company Web site on which the blog can be hosted. Then you only need to download the blog site pages (and programming) to your site from any number of providers (most are free). Alternatively, you can create an account on a blog hosting site. From that point on, what type of blog you have is strictly up to you.

Wiki Sites

Wiki is a Hawaiian word for quick, and the first Wiki site was named WikiWikiWeb, as a play on World Wide Web. A *Wiki* is essentially a database of text and graphic content that can be edited by the public in an effort to provide the best of conventional wisdom to viewers and contributors. Like a blog site, a Wiki is typically built up from an initial posting on a particular topic and the comments, corrections, or edits that are contributed by other viewers.

Any Web viewer can start a Wiki. In fact, several free Wiki starter sites are available on the Web to assist you in doing so.

Proprietary Sites

Perhaps the most common Web sites on the Internet are published for a business, company, organization, college, or school. These sites are published to provide information or to promote and provide retail or wholesale activities for one or more products or services. Businesses, individuals, and schools create their Web sites using one form of Web design and programming language, tool, or service or another. Some develop their own Web sites, and others contract with a Web development company or an advertising company, or else perhaps they have one or more students or interns create their sites.

Social Networking Sites

Social networking sites, just like social networks that are outside of the Web, attract groupings of individuals who share a common interest, such as a hobby, politics, or vocation. Some social networking sites, like MySpace and Facebook, allow users to connect to their friends and family to share information about their life, activities, and interests. Other social networking sites, like LinkedIn, are aimed at allowing individuals to make business or occupational connections and share discussions, ideas, and personal information.

Participants on a social networking site create a personal profile and connect to friends and family to create their social network. Viewers of the profile page can then post comments, links, art, and more to the profile page for the creator. Although Twitter was mentioned earlier as a type of activity blog, it is also a social networking site where you can keep your friends or the world up-to-date on your detailed activities, should you wish to do so.

Although only a few social networking sites tend to make the news, there are literally hundreds of such sites, which, it's fair to say, means that there is likely a social networking site for virtually any individual and his or her unique interests.

Search Engines

Today's users tend to take search engines for granted, not thinking about how they may operate. For the IC^3 exam, you really don't need to be a search engine expert, but you should have some basic knowledge of how at least a Web search engine finds context-related sites for any given search criteria.

Web Search Engines

There are literally hundreds of Web, selection-based, and meta-search engines that can be used on the Web and Internet. The most popular type of search engine in use today is the Web search engine.

A Web search engine creates a database of Web content and provides a list of sites meeting the viewer's criteria using three steps: Web crawling, indexing, and searching. In the Web crawling process, a spider (an automatic Web browser that seeks out and follows every hyperlink it encounters) returns information about the content found on each link, which is analyzed for possible indexing. If the page is determined to be searchworthy, it is indexed. When a viewer enters search criteria into the search engine to look for certain content, the search engine searches its index for matching information.

Search engines like Google, Yahoo!, and Bing are Web search engines that also store a portion of each Web page included in their indexes to provide a faster response to their users.

Selection-Based Search Engine

A *selection-based* search engine, like KallOut (see Figure 22-3), is one in which the search engine is available outside of the Web browser. In a selection-based search engine, highlighting a word or phrase in any document pops up the search tool from which a variety of search sources can be accessed using just the mouse.

Meta-Search Engines

A *meta*-search engine (also called a metacrawler), such as Dogpile and Vivisimo, sends search criteria to several search engines and then compiles the results into a single listing of available sources for the search criteria. Figure 22-4 shows the results of a search performed in Dogpile.

FIGURE 22-3

The KallOut selection-based search engine can be operated only using the mouse.

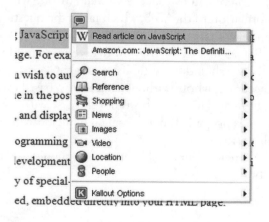

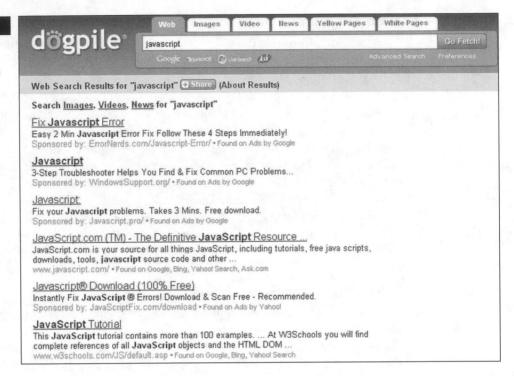

FIGURE 22-4

A meta-search engine compiles search results from several search engines.

The Quality of Information on the Web

The Internet and Web are information explosions. There is information available on just about any subject you can possibly think of. However, not all of the information available is necessarily good, but then, neither is most of the information bad. The quality of the information available on the Internet and Web is more or less a judgment call by you, the viewer. Anyone with an Internet access can publish information to the Web, which raises the question of how much of the information on the Web is good information.

Before we can discuss how to determine if information on the Web is good or valid, we should first establish just what "good" information is. Good information is accurate, whole, without subjectivity, based on first-hand or verifiable authority, and timely. However, this is not the case with all of the information on the Web. Some is not only bad, but some is maliciously bad, loaded to the Web to provide misinformation.

There are four considerations you should use to verify the quality and validity of information found on the Web:

- **Identify the source** If you are unable to identify the original source of information, you probably should not be using the information, no matter how much it may help you. Also verify the level of the source's expertise on the subject or topic of the information.

- **Objectivity** How objective is the source of the information? If you are looking for information about the benefits of gun control, you'll probably not find it on the National Rifle Association Web site.

- **Timeliness** Was the information published at a time when the types of information you are seeking was available? Have new developments occurred since its publication?

- **Veracity** Can the claims or discussion points made in the information be verified? Anyone can have an opinion and that may be what you want, but if you need authoritative and accurate information, you should be able to verify its claims.

If an information source, including one from the Web, is able to meet all four of these criteria, then the information is reasonably reliable. However, when in doubt—throw it out.

Copyrights, Trademarks, and Plagiarism

One surprising fact to most users is that everything, excluding nothing, on the Web and Internet is copyrighted. The originator, creator, artist, composer, poet, author, and any other kind of visual or audio content owns the copyright on anything he or she creates the instant the piece is completed. It really doesn't need to be published to fall under the protection of copyright laws—it only has to exist.

Copyrights

Anyone who copies all or part of a document, graphic, image, or sound object from the Internet or Web without first obtaining the written permission of the copyright owner is committing *copyright* infringement. Rationalizing the use of even a small picture under the guise that "they won't mind" is still a crime, which can be punishable by law. The Napster case and a few individuals who downloaded music without permission have demonstrated that there are companies and government agencies willing to prosecute copyright offenders.

Therefore, the bottom line is that an item on the Web marked with the © symbol is definitely copyrighted. However, even if it doesn't have this symbol or a copyright rights statement, someone still holds the copyright to the item, which is most likely not you.

Trademarks

A *trademark* is protected like a copyright, but in this case the protected item is a word, phrase, or image that has been registered with the U.S. Patent and Trademark Office as an identity for a particular company or organization. Using a company's trademark without permission is a trademark infringement, which can be cause for civil court litigation by the trademark's owner.

Trademarks are generally indicated with a small symbol to indicate the level of protection it has. Table 22-1 lists the three most commonly used trademark symbols in advertising and on the Web.

Plagiarism

The dictionary defines plagiarism as using or closely imitating the words or thoughts of another person and representing them, directly or indirectly, as your own words or thoughts. In other words, if you copy someone else's words without giving the original author credit, you are committing plagiarism.

Plagiarism has been and continues to be a problem in colleges and universities. However, new Web-based services like Plagiarism.org and Copyscape.com are able to detect plagiarized work fairly easily, especially if the copied work was on the Web.

Plagiarism is also a growing problem on the Internet and Web. After a Web site is published, its content, if not protected, can be copied and pasted into another Web site or a document. Tools like the Right HTML Protector (www.rightfiles.com) can protect the content, including text, graphics, e-mail addresses, and even embedded script, from being extracted from a Web site.

TABLE 22-1	Use/Symbol	Meaning
Trademark Symbols	Trademark ™	Unregistered trademark
	Service Mark SM	Unregistered service mark
	Trademark ®	Registered trademark or service mark

Ethical Internet Publishing

Anyone with an Internet connection and an opinion can post anything they wish to the Web. While this statement is totally true, there are some ethical and respectful behaviors you should consider before publishing content to the Web, including

- **Abstention from libelous statements** Libel is a harmful statement against a person or group that is published in a fixed medium, such as print, a graphic image, or an electronic broadcast. If deemed to be injurious or published with malicious intent, libel can lead to a criminal or civil tort action by the offended party. Even in countries with a guaranteed freedom of speech, one cannot intentionally malign someone without truth and the facts to support one's accusations. Suspicions, rumors, or gossip should not be published to the Web.

- **Regard for privacy** The privacy of others should be respected at all times. There is a danger in sharing too much personal information (about yourself or anyone else) on the Web. The primary danger is that, in general, nobody really has total control over who can view or use any information published to the Web. What may seem like a great prank or joke at the time may in the end damage someone's public image and reputation beyond repair.

- **Respect for others** Within reason, everyone is capable of publishing their opinion to the Web. Regardless of how you may agree or disagree with published opinions, you should refrain from personal attacks on others because of their opinion, just as you want your opinions to be respected. Online harassment or bullying is fast becoming criminally unlawful around the U.S., not to mention that you could lose any rights you may have on certain Web sites or your ISP account.

- **Factual content** There are some questions you should ask yourself about information being published to the Web:
  - Is the information relevant?
  - Are the information and its source reliable?
  - Is the information valid (factual)?
  - Is the information free from unidentified bias or libelous statements?
  - Are any opinions included in the information clearly identified as such?
  - Is the information presented in a respectful manner, including its content, wording, and tone?
  - Is the information appropriate for the audience of the Web site to which it is published?

If your answer is no to any of these questions, you should rethink and rework the information until the answers to all of these questions is yes.

Downloading and Uploading Content on the Web

Using a Web browser by entering in a URL and clicking the Go or Find button downloads the content located on the server addressed by the URL. Many browsers also support uploading content or files to remote servers. However, there are other ways to download information from the Web, and the most popular way to do so, after browsers of course, is the use of a File Transfer Protocol (FTP) client.

FTP, as its name states, is a TCP/IP protocol designed to perform reliable file transfers from one computer to another over the Internet. Using an FTP client, such as WS_FTP, FileZilla, or SmartFTP, allows the user to easily connect to a remote server and download or upload data from his or her computer to the remote computer. Many Web browsers also incorporate support for FTP; for instance, Internet Explorer, Fetch, Firefox, and Opera each provide FTP support for both downloads and uploads from and to FTP servers.

CERTIFICATION SUMMARY

A Web page is created using either a markup language (HTML) or a scripting language (JavaScript or VBScript). The coding in a Web page file is interpreted by a Web browser and displayed according to the coding in the file.

Web pages are stored on Web servers and can be either client-side or server-side pages. A *client-side* page has no special processing required and can be easily processed and displayed by a Web browser. A *server-side* page typically contains some dynamic content that needs to be preprocessed before its coding instructions are transmitted to the Web browser.

HTML defines a page with two major sections: head and body. The body contains the coding that defines how the page is to display. A Web page file can also contain scripting that has the capability to access objects on the Web page and retrieve data from external sources.

Search engines, which can be Web crawlers, selection-based engines, or meta-search engines, are used to locate content matching search criteria on the Web.

The quality of the information on the Web must be determined by the viewer. The source and validity of information on any Web site must be verified by the viewer.

Copyright laws, along with the protections afforded trademarks, protect the works of individuals, companies, and organizations publishing to the Web. Plagiarism is when the works of an individual are copied and represented as the works of another person.

✓ TWO-MINUTE DRILL

Creating Content on the Web

❑ For the most part, Web pages are created using one of two primary coding schemes: HTML and scripting languages. HTML is a markup language that defines the characteristics of text, graphics, and links that are to be displayed on a Web page.

❑ An HTML page contains three primary elements: the page itself, a header, and a body. HTML components are defined in containers. Three of the most commonly used HTML page components are lists, tables, and forms.

❑ The primary advantage of using scripting languages in an HTML page is that script statements can be used to access data from other objects on the page.

❑ Web sites and pages can be provided from either a server-side or client-side source. A server-side operation preprocesses the script language of a Web page and sends out HTML data to be displayed on the requesting client (browser). If the requested page is a static Web page, meaning that it has no dynamic content, such as data from a database, very little, if any, preprocessing is needed.

❑ A Web search engine operates in three steps: Web crawling, indexing, and searching. A selection-based search engine can be operated only using a mouse. A meta-search engine sends search criteria to several search engines and compiles the results into a single listing of available sources.

❑ Four considerations should be applied to verify the quality and validity of information found on the Web: identify the source, check the objectivity, check the timeliness, and verify the validity of the information.

❑ Everything on the Web and Internet is copyrighted. The originator, creator, artist, composer, poet, author, and any other kind of visual or audio content owns the copyright on anything he or she creates the instant the piece is completed.

❑ A trademark is a word, phrase, or image that has been registered with the U.S. Patent and Trademark Office as an identity for a particular company or organization.

❑ Plagiarism is using or closely imitating the words or thoughts of another person and representing them as your own.

❑ FTP can be used to transfer files from one computer to another over the Internet.

SELF TEST

Creating Content on the Web

1. What are the two primary coding schemes used to create a Web page?
   A. HTML
   B. HTTP
   C. Scripting language
   D. Visual Basic

2. Which of the following is not a primary Web page element?
   A. Body
   B. Footer
   C. Header
   D. Web page

3. In what syntax structure are HTML statements enclosed?
   A. Containers
   B. Functions
   C. Scripts
   D. Tags

4. Which of the coding schemes that can be used to define the characteristics of a Web page has the capability to access other objects within the Web page?
   A. Headers
   B. Scripts
   C. Tables
   D. Tags

5. What is the term applied to Web pages that must be preprocessed before HTML code is sent to a Web browser by the host server?
   A. Client-side
   B. Local host
   C. Remote host
   D. Server-side

6. In which step of its operating process does a Web search engine organize and categorize the information it has collected?

   A. Crawling

   B. Indexing

   C. Meta-search

   D. Searching

7. True or False: All data on the Internet and Web has been verified and is valid.

   A. True

   B. False

8. What percent of the content on the Web should be considered as copyrighted?

   A. 50%

   B. 60%

   C. 90%

   D. 100%

9. What is the term used for a word, phrase, or image that is used as a part of the identity of a company or organization?

   A. Copyright

   B. Corporate identity

   C. Logo

   D. Trademark

10. Which of the TCP/IP protocol suite can be used to reliably transfer files over the Internet from one computer to another?

   A. FTP

   B. HTTP

   C. IP

   D. TCP

SELF TEST ANSWERS

Creating Content on the Web

1. ☑ **A** and **C.** HTML is the most commonly used Web page language, but scripting languages, like JavaScript and VBScript, are also popular.

   ☒ **B** and **D** are incorrect. HTTP is the primary transfer protocol used to transmit Web pages across the Internet, and Visual Basic (not the scripting version) is not a commonly used programming language on the Web.

2. ☑ **B.** Web pages do not define a footer by default.

   ☒ **A, C,** and **D** are incorrect. The basic structure of an HTML page includes containers for the body, the header, and the whole page itself.

3. ☑ **A.** HTML statements are defined inside opening and closing tags that delimit a container.

   ☒ **B, C,** and **D** are incorrect. Functions are typically single-purpose routines in a scripting language. A script is an HTML container in which scripting functions are defined. Tags are used to define the beginning and end of an HTML container.

4. ☑ **B.** Scripting languages, like JavaScript and VBScript, are able to access the data or other objects included in a Web page.

   ☒ **A, C,** and **D** are incorrect. HTML headers include containers that define, identify, and characterize a Web page. An HTML table can be used to organize related information or provide a structure to align Web page content. Tags are used to define the beginning and the end of an HTML container.

5. ☑ **D.** Server-side pages are preprocessed before they are transmitted to a Web browser client to be displayed.

   ☒ **A, B,** and **C** are incorrect. Local host and remote host refer to the source and destination nodes of transmitted data. Client-side Web pages typically don't require preprocessing before they can be displayed.

6. ☑ **B.** After a Web search engine's Web crawler (or spider) gathers URLs for inclusion in the search engine's database, the next step is to index the information so that it can be quickly found and displayed.

   ☒ **A, C,** and **D** are incorrect. Crawling is the step in which a spider is used to find and qualify new Web content. Meta-search is a type of search engine that transmits search criteria to multiple search engines. Searching is the act of applying a search engine to locate the information that meets specific criteria.

7. ☑ **B.** The Web doesn't have an inherent service to verify and validate Web content. Viewers must perform this task themselves.

☒ **A** is incorrect. The statement is false.

8. ☑ **D** is correct. Without specific knowledge to the contrary, you should consider all Web content to be copyrighted.

☒ **A, B,** and **C** are incorrect. Virtually all Web content should be considered to be copyrighted.

9. ☑ **D.** A trademark, whether registered or not, is used by a company or organization as a part of its public identity.

☒ **A, B,** and **C** are incorrect. A copyright is a protection for all published works. A corporate identity is the results of the trademarks and other identifying information a company publishes to the public. A logo could be used as a trademark, but there is no guideline that a trademark must be a logo.

10. ☑ **A** is correct. FTP is the standard TCP/IP file transfer protocol (hence its name) for transferring files over the Internet.

☒ **B, C,** and **D** are incorrect. HTTP is used to transfer and interpret HTML files across the Internet. IP and TCP are the primary addressing and transport protocols of the TCP/IP suite.

23

Computers at Home, Work, and School

T o say that computers are everywhere and used in just about all aspects of daily life for much of the world is a gross understatement. Over the past twenty-five years, computers have become so commonplace that they are essentially integrated into our lives in much the same way pencils, writing paper, telephones, and libraries have been over the years. This chapter looks at the ways in which computers have been integrated into the workplace, the schoolhouse, and our homes and the benefits that they provide in each of these instances.

CERTIFICATION OBJECTIVE

Computers at Work, School, and Home

4.1   Identify how computers are used in different areas of work, school and home.

Computers, and more specifically information technology, is used to collect, analyze, and evaluate information in a wide range of work, school, and home applications. As a result of its ever-expanding communications technologies, the computer is now a catalyst to the interaction of society in building social communities that extend beyond those available to individuals in the past.

The computer, meaning the one on your desktop or the portable you carry around, is only a small segment of the total computer technological environment that exists today. In the next few sections, we look at the impact the computer makes on our daily lives and how we benefit from its use.

Computer Technology

To fully understand what is referred to as computer technology, we must have some knowledge of the history of the computer. The full history of the computer dates back into ancient times beginning with devices like the Chinese abacus, pattern-making machines, and early versions of calculators. What these early devices were able to do, although fairly remote from the multitasking and multiprocessing capabilities of today's computers, was consistent with the most basic functions of any computer—analyzing inputs to produce outputs.

Through the course of its history, the computer has evolved from a mechanical device that was used to perform a single task to an analog device that was used to solve problems and perform relatively complex calculations to today's fully digital device that is fully integrated into productivity, control, communication, entertainment, and still more of our daily lives.

Computer Technology Generations

The history of the computer and computer technology, the advancements in science and engineering that enable a computer to be applied to more and more tasks and processes, is categorized into a series of generations. Each generation is defined by the amount of computer technology available at the time, with major advancements causing movement to a new generation. The generations through which computer technology and the computer have advanced are

- **Mechanical devices generation**   This generation spans a period of about three hundred years and includes the mechanical devices that were able to perform high-level numerical calculations, including the human-operated difference engines developed in the period that began in the early 1600s and lasted until about the mid-1900s.

- **First generation**   This generation is also called the first electronic generation because electricity and electronic components were applied to increase the capabilities of the computing devices that were developed between the late 1930s and the early 1950s. The advancements in computer technology that occurred during this time culminated in the use of the ENIAC computer (the first commercial application of a computer) by the U.S. Census Bureau and by the UNIVAC to correctly predict the outcome of the 1952 election.

- **Second generation**   With the advent of the transistor, which replaced the vacuum tubes of the first generation, the computer became smaller, faster, and easier to operate. In addition, second-generation computers also had the capability to store programs and data, which lead to the development of programming languages like the Common Business-Oriented Language (COBOL) and Formula Translating (Fortran) languages in the mid to late 1950s.

- **Third generation**   Depending on how you look at it, the third computer technology generation may actually have been the first generation of the computer technology we know today. During the time span from the early 1960s to the early 1970s, integrated circuits, more powerful programming languages, and operating systems were developed or vastly improved.

- **Fourth generation** Some "experts" believe we are still in the fourth generation of computer technology that began in the mid-1970s. The hallmark of this generation is the personal computer, which is still evolving to some extent. Computer technology has continue to advance throughout this period, and the computer is applied to more and more tasks and processes all the time.

From a purely objective point of view, the computer is already "invented," and the advancements that have been made since the 1970s have been essentially refinements and improvements that extend computer technology to solve additional problems.

Computer Technology Applications

It's hard to imagine what life would be without the computer. Unless you are a member of an indigenous tribe that has not ventured outside of the jungle or been integrated into modern society, the computer is pervasive in just about every aspect of your life. However, it wouldn't be much of a surprise to see even remote and seemingly isolated natives with cell phones.

Think for a minute what it would be like if the ultimate computer worm or virus were able to shut down every computer in the world all at once. For most, there would instantly be no telephone service, certainly no television (now that the conversion from analog to digital television has taken place in the U.S.), absolutely no electrical power (unless you have an electrical generator), and the list goes on and on.

Computer Technology in the Workplace While many people still believe that the world would be a better place without computers, it's hard to argue with the benefits computer technology has brought to virtually every industry, educational pursuit, and daily life. The following is a list of only a few of the areas in which computer technology is used today:

- **Banking** The banking industry has always been an early adopter of computer technology. In the beginning, the computer provided a faster means of processing transactions and performing accounting for banks and other financial institutions, but the banking industry has continued to be an aggressive user of computer technology, as evidenced by online banking, the automatic teller machine (ATM), and many other customer-related services.

- **Entertainment** In addition to computer-based games, game consoles, interactive television, and digital video recording devices, computers play a large role in the creation of animated and mixed-media movies, recordings, and schemes for sharing personal videos and information.

- **Law enforcement** The computer has a central role in communications, information retrieval, investigation, and management activities of police, probation departments, and correctional agencies around the world.

- **Manufacturing** Computerized robotics allow manufacturers to consistently assemble products and to plan, monitor, and control the production and status of products.

- **Medicine** Computer technology has advanced the field of medicine primarily by automating the menial tasks that required much of medical professionals' time and providing for a variety of services that physicians, surgeons, nurses, and medical administrators can use to provide better and more accurate care to patients. Some of the areas in which computer technology is used in medicine are diagnosis, information management, patient monitoring and tracking, and enhanced laboratory testing.

- **Transportation** Computerized sensors in automobiles monitor engine and other system status, assist in the control of a vehicle and braking, and manage the deployment of safety equipment. Sensors along a highway can measure the weight of a truck or a train car and determine if highway or safety laws are being violated. The air traffic control system is assisted by computerized analysis of radar and weather conditions to protect passengers and equipment.

- **Weather forecasting and tracking** Satellites communicate with earthbound computers to track, predict, and monitor weather conditions on earth, enabling agriculture, defense, aeronautical, and shipping industries to plan and carry out their operations. Computerized sensors also help to detect catastrophic weather conditions, earthquakes, and volcanic action. Satellite communication systems also provide support for Global Positioning System (GPS) tracking of GPS-enabled devices, including automobiles, emergency vehicles, cell phones, some computers, and several other types of electronic devices.

In addition to automating the processes of industry, computer technology has also changed the way we work. Workers are able to work from home to avoid the commute to the office, a practice called telecommuting. Workers who travel on business can connect to the home office network through virtual private networks (VPNs) and work as if they are at the office on their desktop computer.

Computer Technology in School Computers and computer laboratories are commonplace in today's schools. Computers in the schools are used for interactive learning, research, analysis, and the application of specialized software as a part of a student's training for the workplace.

Computers are central to virtually every part of the daily routines of instructors and students. They provide information resources to help students research for a paper; they help teachers update their knowledge in the areas they teach; they help the teacher manage student records; they help the student learn industry- or task-specific software, such as computer-aided drafting (CAD), electronic circuit analysis, and network design and implementation, as well as foreign languages, art, and science.

One of the fastest growing segments of education is online learning. Place-bound students, who are unable to attend what are now called residential or on-ground courses for a variety of reasons, including transportation as well as economic, cultural, and physical issues, are able to participate in an online class toward achieving a high school diploma or a college degree. In addition, a wide range of continuing education courses are available on the Web on what seems to be virtually any subject area.

Computer Technology at Home Home automation is slowly gaining popularity in newer homes that incorporate home theater systems, environmental control systems, distributed audio and video systems, and security systems. Many homes now have multiple-station computer networks and wireless communications.

However, one of the biggest impacts computers are making in today's homes is the general availability of the Internet. The Internet has effectively removed the barriers of geography to let users create social networks to share their activities, their thoughts, their pictures, and as much of their lives as they wish. Information resources abound and the opportunity exists to search for and find information on just about any topic.

By incorporating computer technology, many home appliances, including refrigerators, stoves, ovens, microwaves, and more, are able to notify their owners when service is required, when a filter needs to be changed, or when dinner is ready. Likewise the homeowner is able to start the oven, send a message to the screen on the refrigerator, and soon, retrieve the shopping list prepared by the computer built into the refrigerator.

Adaptive and Assistive Computer Technology

Another area in which computer technology is benefiting society is through the devices, mechanisms, and software tools designed to assist people who are physically challenged, disabled, or disadvantaged. Through the use of adaptive and assistive technologies, physically disabled individuals can overcome their limitations to lead productive lives, both at home and on the job.

Adaptive Technology   Adaptive technology devices are generally designed for a specific area of need or disability. The major focus areas for adaptive technology devices are

- **Vision impairment**   Products designed for individuals with vision impairment are categorized into two groups: those for people who have completely lost their sight (total blindness) and those for individuals who suffer eye problems but still have some of their sight (partial blindness).
  - **Products for total blindness**   These include talking watches, calculators, computers, and a variety of measuring devices, like scales, thermometers, crossing signals, and more. A talking computer has speech synthesis software that reads the screen and performs text-to-speech translation that sounds out the letters, numbers, and words as they are typed or scanned.
  - **Products for partial blindness**   These tools, generally called accessibility tools, are used to enlarge the image of a computer display so that text and images can be viewed clearly.
- **Hearing impairment**   Computer technology allows broadcasters and film makers to provide closed captions on television and movies using a high-technology form of speech recognition. Speech recognition software can also be installed on portable computers to perform speech-to-text translation in classroom, business, and home situations. In addition, the text messaging capabilities of cell phones, although not specifically developed for disabled individuals, provide a mobile communications system for the hearing impaired.
- **Speech impairment**   Text-to-speech technologies allow individuals who have completely or partially lost their speech to enter what they wish to say on a computer and have the computer speak for them. Speech-impaired individuals can also take advantage of text messaging on cell phones.
- **Mobility impairment**   Quadriplegics, paraplegics, and individuals who are missing a limb or hand or have lost the ability to control their limbs or hands have a variety of computerized wheelchairs, computer keyboards, joysticks, hand and foot switches, and sip-and-puff control devices to enable them to control their movement and enter text on a keyboard.

CERTIFICATION SUMMARY

Computer technology has radically changed how society works, plays, and learns over the past twenty years. The computer has become a part of everyday life. Many industrial processes and applications are computerized. Students have a wealth of information resources and can learn online. In the home, the computer can provide, in addition to communications and access to information resources, the capability to monitor and control the home environment. Adaptive and assistive technologies are used to improve the lives of disabled or disadvantaged individuals.

✓ TWO-MINUTE DRILL

Computers at Work, School, and Home

❑ Computer technology has evolved through five generations: the mechanical devices generation, and four (first through fourth) generations that began in the 1930s and extend through today.

❑ Computer technology benefits virtually every industry, educational pursuit, and daily life, including banking, entertainment, law enforcement, manufacturing, medicine, transportation, and weather forecasting and tracking.

❑ Computer technology has changed the way we work: workers are able to telecommute, and traveling workers can connect to the home office network through VPNs.

❑ Computers in the schools are used for interactive learning, record-keeping, research, analysis, and the application of specialized software as a part of a student's training for the workplace.

❑ Home automation allows homeowners to incorporate home theater systems, environmental control systems, distributed audio and video systems, and security systems. Many home appliances, including refrigerators, stoves, ovens, microwaves, and more, are able to notify their owners when service is required, when a filter needs to be changed, or when dinner is ready.

❑ People who are physically challenged, disabled, or disadvantaged are benefited through the use of adaptive and assistive technologies, including devices and software to help those with vision, hearing, mobility, and speech impairments.

SELF TEST

Computers at Work, School, and Home

1. What is generally considered to be the current generation of computer technology?
   A. Mechanical devices generation
   B. Second generation
   C. Third generation
   D. Fourth generation

2. What part of society benefits from computer technology?
   A. Business
   B. Education
   C. Medical
   D. Homeowners
   E. All of the above
   F. None of the above

3. What mechanism can an employee who is traveling away from the home office use to connect to the office's local network?
   A. VPN
   B. Intranet
   C. Extranet
   D. None; security policies typically prevent outside users from connecting to a local network.

4. Which of the following learning methods is based on computer technology?
   A. Athletics
   B. Mathematics
   C. Online learning
   D. Reading

5. What home appliances are beginning to incorporate computer technology as a means of interaction with the homeowners?
   A. Refrigerators
   B. Ovens
   C. Microwave ovens
   D. Digital frames

    E. All of the above

    F. None of the above

6. True or False. Computer technology is used to provide, enable, or extend the capabilities of a physically challenged, disabled, or disadvantaged person.

    A. True

    B. False

SELF TEST ANSWERS

Computers at Work, School, and Home

1. ☑ **D.** Most computer technology experts agree that the evolution of the computer and computer technology is in its fourth generation.

   ☒ **A, B,** and **C** are incorrect. The mechanical devices generation spanned the 1600s to the early 1930s. The second and third generations included the development of the first analog computers and later the first electronic computers.

2. ☑ **E.** There is literally no parts of society that is not affected by computer technology in some way.

   ☒ **A, B, C, D,** and **F** are incorrect. The choices in A through D are each areas in which society benefits from computer technology, but none of these answers is the best answer on its own. Since essentially A through E are correct choices (with E the best choice), F is definitely wrong.

3. ☑ **A.** Remote employees can connect to the company's local network through a VPN.

   ☒ **B, C,** and **D** are incorrect. A traveling employee may wish to connect to a company's intranet or extranet, but a VPN is used to make the connection. The answer given in D is completely false.

4. ☑ **C.** Online learning has provided educational services and resources to students who are place-bound.

   ☒ **A, B,** and **D** are incorrect. Computer technology has contributed benefits to each of these areas. Online learning is generally the vehicle that helps to make remote learning possible.

5. ☑ **A, B,** and **C.** Many models of these home appliances are network-ready and have the capability to communicate with the homeowner.

   ☒ **D, E,** and **F** are incorrect. Digital picture frames have not yet been made to be network-ready, which eliminates E as a correct answer and voids F.

6. ☑ **A.** Computer technology has vastly improved the capabilities and, in many cases, the quality of life for disabled individuals.

   ☒ **B** is incorrect. The statement is false.

24

The Risks and Disadvantages of Computers in Society

Unfortunately, along with the benefits gained from using a computer, there are some risks, threats, and problems that are also involved. For the most part, the risks and threats can be relatively minor, but if ignored or not properly addressed, they can become major problems. This chapter discusses the ways that can help you create a safe, ethical, and (very important) legal environment for the use of a computer.

CERTIFICATION OBJECTIVE

Using Computers Safely and Ethically

4.2   Identify the risks of using computer hardware and software and how to use computers and the Internet safely, ethically and legally.

In order to avoid the risks and threats that are inherent to the use of a computer, there are a variety of actions that you must take to mitigate or avoid threats and to defend your computer and yourself. Depending on your particular situation and where you use a computer, some of the following actions are more or less important to creating a physically and logically safe, ethical, and legal environment, in which you can use your computer in a relatively risk-free way. The actions you should take to ensure a risk-free and carefree computing environment are

- Maintain a safe working environment.
- Safeguard against software threats.
- Restrict access to sensitive information.
- Protect your privacy while online and avoid e-commerce hazards.
- Use computers ethically.
- Dispose of computers and peripherals responsibly.

Each of these actions and what it entails is discussed in the sections that follow.

Maintaining a Safe Working Environment

A safe working environment is of course one in which you are physically safe, not only from things falling on you and being attacked, but from injuries caused by using a computer. Extended use of a computer can cause injuries to your neck, shoulders, arms, wrists, hands, and eyes if you don't follow the guidelines for how to arrange your body when you are at the computer.

Purchasing Computer Equipment and Furniture

The U.S. Occupational Safety and Health Administration (OSHA) has published guidelines for safe computing that includes how to purchase the proper types of computer peripherals and furniture and how to sit and work on a computer. When purchasing a computer, its peripherals (especially the monitor, keyboard, and mouse), and the furniture on which you and the computer sit (especially desks and chairs), you should consider the following issues:

Purchasing computer peripherals

- Monitor:
  - **The size of the display screen** Monitors should have at least 15-inch displays.
  - **The angle of the display** The angle of the display should be easily adjustable.
  - **Type of monitor** The monitor's overall size and type should be appropriate to the amount of workspace available. Flat-panel monitors take up much less room on a workspace.
- Keyboard:
  - **Type and style of keyboard** A keyboard that is separated from the display is best for prolonged usage. For example, the display and keyboard on a portable computer are not recommended for extended use. If comfortable, choose an ergonomic keyboard design that doesn't include wrist rests.
  - **Wrist rests** Separate wrist rests can be positioned to provide for neutral wrist positions and should be made of a gel-type material, conform to the shape and contours of the front edge of the keyboard, and be at least 1.5 inches deep.
  - **Adjustability** The keyboard should include feet or risers that allow you to raise or lower its height from the workspace surface and to change the angle of the keys.

Purchasing workspace furniture

- Desk or workspace surface:
    - **Dimensions**   The depth of the work surface should allow for the monitor to be placed 20 inches from your eyes and have a total depth of at least 30 inches. The height of the work surface should be adjustable between 20 and 28 inches for seated work activities.
    - **Clearance under the work surface**   The desk or table should provide at least 15 inches of clearance for your knees and 24 inches for your feet, with an overall clearance of at least 20 inches.
    - **Work surface finish**   The work surface should have a matte finish with a highly grained or patterned surface to avoid glare and to provide for the use of an optical mouse without a mouse pad. Avoid using glass surfaces altogether.
    - **Workspace lighting**   The lighting on the work surface should be adjustable to allow for brighter lighting for working with printed materials and lower light when you are interacting solely with the display.
- Chair:
    - **Height**   The height of the chair seat should be adjustable and provide for an adjustable range of at least 16 inches.
    - **Backrest**   The backrest should be at least 15 inches high and 12 inches wide. Avoid chairs on which the backrest can only be tilted forward or back. The backrest should be fully adjustable.
    - **Armrests**   The armrests on a chair should be removable and not fixed in position either vertically or horizontally.
    - **Load**   If the user weighs more than 275 pounds, purchase a special chair designed for this load.

Working with a Computer

The furniture's characteristics and the placement of the computer and its peripherals must support the safety and health guidelines to avoid any potential harm or injury to its user. These guidelines include the following recommendations:

- Body position:
    - **Head and neck**   The head and neck should be held upright in line with the torso, meaning they should not be bent back or leaned forward.

The head and shoulders should always be parallel to the display (not turned or twisted to one side).

- ■ **Torso** The trunk of the body should be vertically perpendicular to the floor or leaning back slightly using a proper backrest.

- ■ Arms and hands:

  - ■ **Upper arms and elbows** The upper arm and elbow should be held closely to the body.

  - ■ **Forearms** Forearms should be at 90 degrees with the upper arm. If this angle is more than 90 degrees, the keyboard is too far away. If the angle is less than 90 degrees, the keyboard is too close.

  - ■ **Wrists** Wrists should be in-line and straight with the forearms and not bent up or down or held at an angle toward either side. The wrists should not rest on a sharp or hard edge. Repetitive motions with hands, wrists, and arms should not be performed for extended periods to avoid what is called repetitive motion disorder or repeated strain injury.

  - ■ **Thighs and lower legs** The thighs should be parallel to the floor and the lower legs held perpendicular to the floor with the thigh slightly higher than the knees.

  - ■ **Feet** The feet should be flat on the floor or placed on a stable footrest.

The proper arrangement of equipment; the use of appropriately safe seating, furniture, lighting, and ergonomic injury prevention devices (such as wrist pads and anti-glare monitor screens); and the use of periodic breaks and rest periods can help to ensure a safe and injury-free workplace.

Safeguarding Against Software Threats

As discussed in Chapter 7, there are a number of software threats that can harm your computer and data. Viruses, malware, worms, Trojan horses, and more can invade your computer from a variety of sources.

The primary way that these software threats can invade your computer is by being downloaded in a Web page, as an embedded element in an e-mail attachment, or on an infected diskette or CD. Your best defense against these threats is to install and regularly update antivirus software that includes Web page, e-mail, and file scanning. Regular scanning of your computer and its data with a robust antivirus or anti-malware program can help to prevent the infection of your computer. For more information on software threats and antivirus software, see Chapter 7.

Restricting Access to Sensitive Information

In addition to antivirus and malware protection software, another safeguard you can install on your computer is a software firewall. A software firewall (as opposed to a hardware firewall that is an internetworking device that is typically installed at the gateway to a network) limits or prohibits access to your computer and its resources and data.

Protecting sensitive information on a computer or network can also involve the extra layer of protection that is afforded by applying encryption to sensitive data files and requiring passwords to access certain folders or files. Application software, such as word processors, spreadsheets, database systems, and some e-mail clients, support encryption of document files and the requirement of a password.

Another way to look at restricting access to sensitive information is to shield or perhaps limit inside users from accessing or viewing outside information. Although the majority of content on the Web is protected under the right to free speech in the U.S. Constitution, as a parent or guardian, you may not want children under a certain age to view some content or expose themselves to the potential danger of online predators. The same may be true for a business' employees or a schools' students.

Through the use of proxy servers and parental control applications, certain Web pages, Web sites, and Internet domains can be restricted from access specifically. Web filtering utilities can also be applied to scan downloaded Web pages for certain words, content, and in some cases, graphics. Beyond the technical means available to restrict access to undesirable content, the next best remedy is an aggressively enforced acceptable use policy (AUP) that is fully understood by the user in terms of its restrictions, allowances, and repercussions. To enforce an AUP to the point that restricted content is not accessed by users most likely requires the presence of a monitor to closely examine the content being downloaded, such as a teacher, parent, or supervisor.

The enforcement of restricting policies that govern the use of e-mail or the downloading of Web content is rooted in making every user understand what information is considered personal and what information is considered the property of the business or school. As a rule of thumb (and under the law in most states), any use of a company- or school-owned computer is considered to be the property of the equipment owner. Inherent in the right of ownership is the right to restrict the use of the equipment.

Protecting Your Privacy and Avoiding E-Commerce Hazards

The Internet and Web are not essentially private worlds. To protect your privacy while working online, you should make certain practices and policies an integral part of how you use the Web and Internet. We all want to believe that when we share private information on the Web, it will be kept private, just as many sites assure us. However, there are limits to the extent that our data and information can be kept private, so we need to protect ourselves.

The following are some of the best practices you can use to protect your privacy on the Web and Internet:

- **Personal information** In the Setup or Preferences tools of your Web browser (and in any software application that can share documents over the Web):
    - Don't use your real name; enter a nickname or pseudonym instead.
    - Don't enter your e-mail address; leave it blank.
    - Don't share any other personal information that is not required.
    - Only share required personal information on sites you know and trust.
- **Cookies** A cookie is a small file of data that is stored on your computer, sometimes temporarily but in many cases permanently. The purpose of a cookie for most sites is to store login information for use the next time you visit a site. For the most part, these cookies are completely safe and harmless. However, there are cookies that record what pages you opened and perhaps which products or objects on a site you viewed so that you can be targeted for follow-up marketing, such as spam. Some of the best practices to use with cookies are:
    - **Allow cookies** Unless you wish to enter a username and password each time you visit any registered site, you should enable cookies in your browser's setup.
    - **Enable cookie management** Most of the more popular Web browsers include some form of cookie management that you can configure to display every cookie request for acceptance or denial, which can become tedious over time. However, if you wish to avoid sharing personal information with untrusted Web sites, you should consider taking this step.
- **Neutral e-mail address** With the virtually unlimited number of free e-mail accounts, you can easily set up a "main" e-mail address that is given out to only friends, family, and others you can completely trust; a "nickname" e-mail address that you use to register for contests, newsletters, and the like; and a "junk" e-mail address that you use when you must on unknown and untrusted Web sites. If nothing else, you will unclutter your main e-mail inbox this way.
- **Social networking** One of the easiest ways to get personal information about you is from a publicly available social networking profile. Unless you truly know a person and have good reasons to trust them, you probably

shouldn't add them to your friends, contacts, or connections, as the case may be. Limit the amount of information you provide to the general public. Your true friends likely know all they need to know anyway.

- **E-mail at work**   E-mail sent or received on a computer in your workplace is the property of the company or organization for which you work. In fact, some companies monitor the e-mail of their employees. Don't send personal e-mail from a work-related e-mail account, and keep your private files at home or on your portable computer and not your work computer.

- **Spammers**   Never reply directly to spam e-mail ever, not even to tell them to remove your e-mail address from their list or following their unsubscribe instructions, as this never accomplishes that but typically serves to add your e-mail address to even more spam lists.

- **Secure sites**   Never provide sensitive personal information, such as a credit card account number, to an unsecure site. Most browsers have a symbol on the status bar to indicate whether the site is secured or not. This symbol is a closed padlock, unbroken key, or the like. The URL of a secured site will also contain HTTPS as its resource component.

- **Privacy policy and service seals**   If a site has a privacy policy available, read it. Some privacy policies don't offer much in the way of privacy, regardless of their names. Also look for certification seals, such as those from the Better Business Bureau, TRUSTe, and others. These indicate that the site subscribes to a stringent third-party or industry privacy and security policy.

- **Encryption**   If you must share personal information by e-mail, you should encrypt the message. Software or services, like Pretty Good Privacy (PGP) and Anonymizer, can be used to protect transmitted information.

The Ethical Use of Computers

Organizations like the Computer Professionals for Social Responsibility (CPSR) and the Computer Ethics Institute publish whitepapers and articles of the ethics best practices for using a computer. In fact, the Computer Ethics Institute has developed "the Ten Commandments of Computer Ethics" (cpsr.org/issues/ethics/cei/).

In general, ethics are the rules of right and wrong that should govern the conduct of individuals, companies, and society. In business, ethics are typically defined by employers and schools for individuals or trade associations for companies. Ethics aren't laws generally. In fact, ethical rules and guidelines often come before laws that require certain actions. For this reason, ethics violations often go unpunished, with exclusion being the only punishment for an unethical individual.

On the Internet and Web, ethics require the observance of copyright and trademark laws, user agreements, and acceptable use policies (AUPs), along with the ethical recognition of ownership and permitted use. On the desktop (which is intended to include portable computers as well) and a local network, the observance of software licenses, data ownership, permitted access, and professional written speech is the subject of most ethics guidelines.

Disposing of Computers and Peripherals Responsibly

The circuits and components of computers and many of their peripheral units contain significant amounts of lead, mercury, cadmium, and other toxic heavy metals. Because of these materials, a computer and its peripheral devices, especially cathode ray tube (CRT) displays, should not be disposed of like general trash or garbage. It's estimated that electronic devices, including computer devices, account for as much as 70 percent of the toxins in public landfills.

The U.S. Environmental Protection Agency (EPA) and its equivalents in other countries, as well as a growing number of states, have issued guidelines and regulations that govern the disposal of computer equipment or e-waste. Some states, like California, Maine, and Washington, have passed stringent e-waste recycling laws that set up recycling centers to which the public can take their computers and peripherals for disposal at no charge.

A safe way of recycling a computer is to give it to someone who has use for it or to donate it to a charitable organization or a school that is in need for computing devices. However, when you give away a computer, you should takes steps to protect your privacy and information and to avoid violating any copyright laws or licensing agreements by erasing the data and programs from its hard disk drive and other internal storage media.

Something else that can be recycled or at least reused is your knowledge of computer hardware and software. As a professional with the IC3 certification, you should seek out opportunities to share your knowledge and skills with others in your school, workplace, or community.

Keeping Abreast of Technology Advances

In order to continue to use and apply computing and electronic communication hardware, software, and services effectively and efficiently, you need to stay as current as you can on their latest and greatest technological advancements.

Although this may seem like a daunting task, there is a simple four-step process you can use to keep as current as possible:

1. Talk to any technologically aware friends, co-workers, or family you may know about the latest trends or have them explain how something works or is done.

2. Seek out television or radio reports, specials, or shows that feature new developments, or new uses for existing technology, or how-to demonstrations.

3. Seek out newspapers, magazines, Web pages, or books that feature articles on new technology and its usage, especially the science and technology sections. Manufacturers regularly provide a "What's new" page on their Web site, which can be an excellent source for new technology information.

4. Visit local electronics stores to see what's new and speak with a customer service or a sales representative to learn more about any new technology being offered. If you can, visit any electronics or computing conferences or trade shows in your vicinity and speak with the factory reps about their products.

CERTIFICATION SUMMARY

Using a computer has its safety, ethics, and legal issues as well. Knowing how to safely use a computer to avoid injury is important. Equally important are the ethics guidelines, rules, and regulations that govern the courteous, considerate, and professional use of a computer.

TWO-MINUTE DRILL

Using Computers Safely and Ethically

❑ There are some risks, threats, and problems with the use of a computer. These risks and threats can be minor, but if not properly addressed, they can become major problems.

❑ The actions you should take to ensure a risk-free and carefree computing environment are to maintain a safe working environment, safeguard against software threats, restrict access to sensitive information, protect your privacy while online and avoid e-commerce hazards, use computers ethically, and dispose of computers and peripherals responsibly.

❑ To avoid injuries to your neck, shoulders, arms, wrists, hands, and eyes, you should follow the guidelines established for the purchase and safe use of a computer.

❑ OSHA has published guidelines for safe computing that include how to purchase the proper types of computer peripherals and furniture and how to sit and work on a computer. These guidelines include purchasing computer peripherals and workspace furniture and safely using a computer.

❑ Viruses, malware, worms, Trojan horses, and more can invade your computer from a variety of sources. Your best defense against these threats is to install and regularly update antivirus software that includes Web page, e-mail, and file scanning. Another safeguard you can install on your computer is a software firewall.

❑ Protecting sensitive information on a computer or network involves the use of encryption and passwords.

❑ To protect your privacy while working online, you should safeguard and restrict the sharing of personal information, e-mail addresses, and social networking information. You should also use neutral e-mail addresses and understand the ownership and ethics rules surrounding the ownership of information in the workplace.

❑ On the Internet and Web, ethics require the observance of copyright and trademark laws, user agreements, and acceptable use policies (AUPs), along with the ethical recognition of ownership and permitted use. On the desktop (which is intended to include portable computers as well) and a local

network, the observance of software licenses, data ownership, permitted access, and professional written speech is the subject of most ethics guidelines.

❑ Computers and peripheral devices contain significant amounts of lead, mercury, and cadmium, and other toxic materials. The EPA has issued guidelines and regulations that govern the disposal of computer equipment or e-waste. Some states have e-waste recycling laws that set up recycling centers to which the public can take their computers and peripherals for disposal.

SELF TEST

Using Computers Safely and Ethically

1. Which of the following is not generally considered to be a threat from the use of a computer?

A. Injuries caused by unsafe computer use

B. Overly secure personal information

C. Software threats

D. Unauthorized access to sensitive information

2. True or False: To avoid injuries to your neck, shoulders, arms, wrists, hands, and eyes, you must purchase a notebook computer.

A. True

B. False

3. What U.S. government agency issues guidelines for the proper use of a computer to avoid injuries?

A. CPSR

B. EPA

C. OSHA

D. PGP

4. What should be installed and used regularly to avoid the threat of viruses, malware, worms, or Trojan horses?

A. Firewall

B. PGP

C. Antivirus software

D. AUP

5. Which two of the following are typically used to protect sensitive information?

A. Encryption

B. File compression

C. Misnamed folders

D. Passwords

6. Who is typically the owner of e-mail sent or received on a workplace computer?

A. The company or organization

B. The recipient

    C. The sender

    D. The worker

7. What computer usage practice involves observing copyright laws, user agreements, AUPs, and information ownership?

    A. Computer citizenship

    B. Ethical computer use

    C. Good neighbor policies

    D. Netiquette

8. What toxic metals are found in a computer and its peripheral devices?

    A. Cadmium

    B. Calcium

    C. Lead

    D. Mercury

    E. All of the above

    F. None of the above

SELF TEST ANSWERS

Using Computers Safely and Ethically

1. ☑ **B.** Secure personal information is actually a goal of good computer management.
   ☒ **A, C,** and **D** are incorrect. Injuries, software threats, and accessing sensitive information are threats to a computer system.

2. ☑ **B.** Avoiding injuries to your body that result from working on a computer involves using the right furniture and positioning your body, arms, and hands properly.
   ☒ **A** is incorrect. If used for extended periods of time, a notebook computer could actually cause injuries.

3. ☑ **C.** The Occupational Safety and Health Administration (OSHA) issues guidelines and regulations that recommend the safe use of a computer.
   ☒ **B, C,** and **D** are incorrect. The CPSR makes recommendations on the ethical use of a computer; the EPA is the government agency that oversees the environment, including the proper disposal of a computer; and PGP is an open-source e-mail security system.

4. ☑ **C.** Antivirus software protects a computer from external software threats.
   ☒ **A, B,** and **D** are incorrect. A firewall is a physical protection device that keeps unauthorized users from gaining access to a network or computer; PGP is an open-source e-mail security system; and an AUP defines the acceptable use of a computer, network, or software.

5. ☑ **A and D.** The use of encryption and passwords helps to secure sensitive information against theft or unauthorized use.
   ☒ **B and C** are incorrect. File compression saves disk space but doesn't always protect the data, and putting a file in a misnamed folder is a low-level step to hiding a file, but search functions can defeat this action easily.

6. ☑ **A.** Anything done on a company's or a school's computer is generally its property.
   ☒ **B, C,** and **D** are incorrect. To an extent, the recipient may own an incoming message, but not if it is received on the recipient's office computer. The sender may own an e-mail message, but only to the point the message is sent. A worker on a company computer owns nothing on the computer.

7. ☑ **B.** Computer ethics involve the fair use of copyrights, agreements, and other guidelines that define what should and should not be done.
   ☒ **A, C,** and **D** are incorrect. Computer citizenship and good neighbor policies, if there are such things defined, would also fall under computer ethics, as netiquette definitely does.

8. ☑ **A, C,** and **D.** These metals and others are the reasons that computer and other electronics equipment should be disposed of properly.
   ☒ **B, E,** and **F** are incorrect. While there may be traces of calcium in a computer, calcium is normally not a toxic mineral. Since calcium is wrong, **E** is also wrong. Because there are three correct answers, **F** is definitely wrong.

A

About the CD

The CD-ROM included with this book comes complete with MasterExam and the electronic version of the book. The software is easy to install on any Windows 2000/XP/Vista computer and must be installed to access the MasterExam feature. You may, however, browse the electronic book directly from the CD without installation. To register for the bonus MasterExam, simply click the Bonus MasterExam link on the main launch page and follow the directions to the free online registration.

System Requirements

Software requires Windows 2000 or higher and Internet Explorer 6.0 or above and 20 MB of hard disk space for full installation. The electronic book requires Adobe Acrobat Reader.

Installing and Running MasterExam

If your computer CD-ROM drive is configured to auto run, the CD-ROM will automatically start up upon inserting the disk. From the opening screen you may install MasterExam by clicking the MasterExam link. This will begin the installation process and create a program group named LearnKey. To run MasterExam use Start | All Programs | LearnKey | MasterExam. If the auto run feature did not launch your CD, browse to the CD and click on the LaunchTraining.exe icon.

MasterExam

MasterExam provides you with a simulation of each of the three actual exams. The number of questions, the type of questions, and the time allowed for each are intended to be an accurate representation of the exam environment. You have the option to take open book exams, including hints, references, and answers; closed book exams; or a timed MasterExam simulation.

When you launch MasterExam, a digital clock display will appear in the bottom right-hand corner of your screen. The clock will continue to count down to zero unless you choose to end the exam before the time expires.

Electronic Book

The entire contents of the Study Guide are provided in PDF. Adobe's Acrobat Reader has been included on the CD.

Help

A help file is provided through the help button on the main page in the lower left-hand corner. An individual help feature is also available through MasterExam.

Removing Installation(s)

MasterExam is installed to your hard drive. For best results removing programs, use the Start | All Programs | LearnKey| Uninstall option to remove MasterExam.

Technical Support

For questions regarding the content of the electronic book or MasterExam, please visit www.mhprofessional.com or email customer.service@mcgraw-hill.com. For customers outside the 50 United States, email international_cs@mcgraw-hill.com.

LearnKey Technical Support

For technical problems with the software (installation, operation, removing installations), please visit www.learnkey.com, email techsupport@learnkey.com, or call toll free at 1-800-482-8244.

INDEX

INTERNET AND
COMPUTING CORE
CERTIFICATION

SETTING THE STANDARD

IC³ ...WHAT IS IT?

IC³, or the Internet and Computing Core Certification program, is a global training and certification program providing proof to the world that you are:

- Equipped with the needed computer skills to excel in a digital world.

- Capable of using a broad range of computer technology - from basic hardware and software, to operating systems, applications and the Internet.

- Ready for what the work employers, colleges and universities want to throw your way.

- Positioned to advance your career through additional computer certifications such as CompTIA's A+, and other desktop application exams.

IC³ ...WHY DO YOU NEED IT?

Employers, Colleges and Universities now understand that exposure to computers does not equal understanding computers. So now, more than ever, basic computer and Internet skills are being considered prerequisites for employment and higher education.

THIS IS WHERE IC³ HELPS!

IC³ provides specific guidelines for the knowledge and skills required to be a functional user of computer hardware, software, networks, and the Internet. It does this through three exams:

- **Computing Fundamentals**
- **Key Applications**
- **Living Online**

By passing the three IC³ exams, you have initiated yourself into today's digital world. You have also given yourself a globally accepted and validated credential that provides the proof employers or higher education institutions need.

Earn your IC³ certification today - visit www.certiport.com/ic3 **to learn how.**

CERTIPORT™
Lifetime advancement through certification.

Certiport is a registered trademark of Certiport, Inc. in the United States and other countries.

INTERNET AND
COMPUTING CORE
CERTIFICATION

CERTIFICATION ROADMAP

Whether you are seeking further education, entering the job market, or advancing your skills through higher ICT certification, IC³ gives you the foundation you need to succeed.

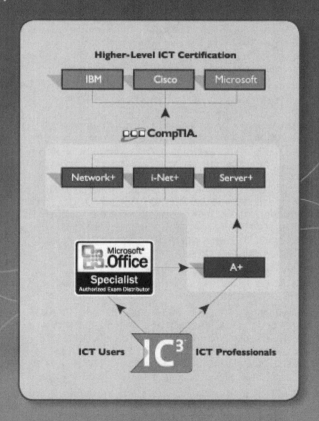

CERTIPORT

www.certiport.com/ic3

LICENSE AGREEMENT

THIS PRODUCT (THE "PRODUCT") CONTAINS PROPRIETARY SOFTWARE, DATA AND INFORMATION (INCLUDING DOCUMENTATION) OWNED BY THE McGRAW-HILL COMPANIES, INC. ("McGRAW-HILL") AND ITS LICENSORS. YOUR RIGHT TO USE THE PRODUCT IS GOVERNED BY THE TERMS AND CONDITIONS OF THIS AGREEMENT.

LICENSE: Throughout this License Agreement, "you" shall mean either the individual or the entity whose agent opens this package. You are granted a non-exclusive and non-transferable license to use the Product subject to the following terms:

(i) If you have licensed a single user version of the Product, the Product may only be used on a single computer (i.e., a single CPU). If you licensed and paid the fee applicable to a local area network or wide area network version of the Product, you are subject to the terms of the following subparagraph (ii).

(ii) If you have licensed a local area network version, you may use the Product on unlimited workstations located in one single building selected by you that is served by such local area network. If you have licensed a wide area network version, you may use the Product on unlimited workstations located in multiple buildings on the same site selected by you that is served by such wide area network; provided, however, that any building will not be considered located in the same site if it is more than five (5) miles away from any building included in such site. In addition, you may only use a local area or wide area network version of the Product on one single server. If you wish to use the Product on more than one server, you must obtain written authorization from McGraw-Hill and pay additional fees.

(iii) You may make one copy of the Product for back-up purposes only and you must maintain an accurate record as to the location of the back-up at all times.

COPYRIGHT; RESTRICTIONS ON USE AND TRANSFER: All rights (including copyright) in and to the Product are owned by McGraw-Hill and its licensors. You are the owner of the enclosed disc on which the Product is recorded. You may not use, copy, decompile, disassemble, reverse engineer, modify, reproduce, create derivative works, transmit, distribute, sublicense, store in a database or retrieval system of any kind, rent or transfer the Product, or any portion thereof, in any form or by any means (including electronically or otherwise) except as expressly provided for in this License Agreement. You must reproduce the copyright notices, trademark notices, legends and logos of McGraw-Hill and its licensors that appear on the Product on the back-up copy of the Product which you are permitted to make hereunder. All rights in the Product not expressly granted herein are reserved by McGraw-Hill and its licensors.

TERM: This License Agreement is effective until terminated. It will terminate if you fail to comply with any term or condition of this License Agreement. Upon termination, you are obligated to return to McGraw-Hill the Product together with all copies thereof and to purge all copies of the Product included in any and all servers and computer facilities.

DISCLAIMER OF WARRANTY: THE PRODUCT AND THE BACK-UP COPY ARE LICENSED "AS IS." McGRAW-HILL, ITS LICENSORS AND THE AUTHORS MAKE NO WARRANTIES, EXPRESS OR IMPLIED, AS TO THE RESULTS TO BE OBTAINED BY ANY PERSON OR ENTITY FROM USE OF THE PRODUCT, ANY INFORMATION OR DATA INCLUDED THEREIN AND/OR ANY TECHNICAL SUPPORT SERVICES PROVIDED HEREUNDER, IF ANY ("TECHNICAL SUPPORT SERVICES"). McGRAW-HILL, ITS LICENSORS AND THE AUTHORS MAKE NO EXPRESS OR IMPLIED WARRANTIES OF MERCHANTABILITY OR FITNESS FOR A PARTICULAR PURPOSE OR USE WITH RESPECT TO THE PRODUCT. McGRAW-HILL, ITS LICENSORS, AND THE AUTHORS MAKE NO GUARANTEE THAT YOU WILL PASS ANY CERTIFICATION EXAM WHATSOEVER BY USING THIS PRODUCT. NEITHER McGRAW-HILL, ANY OF ITS LICENSORS NOR THE AUTHORS WARRANT THAT THE FUNCTIONS CONTAINED IN THE PRODUCT WILL MEET YOUR REQUIREMENTS OR THAT THE OPERATION OF THE PRODUCT WILL BE UNINTERRUPTED OR ERROR FREE. YOU ASSUME THE ENTIRE RISK WITH RESPECT TO THE QUALITY AND PERFORMANCE OF THE PRODUCT.

LIMITED WARRANTY FOR DISC: To the original licensee only, McGraw-Hill warrants that the enclosed disc on which the Product is recorded is free from defects in materials and workmanship under normal use and service for a period of ninety (90) days from the date of purchase. In the event of a defect in the disc covered by the foregoing warranty, McGraw-Hill will replace the disc.

LIMITATION OF LIABILITY: NEITHER McGRAW-HILL, ITS LICENSORS NOR THE AUTHORS SHALL BE LIABLE FOR ANY INDIRECT, SPECIAL OR CONSEQUENTIAL DAMAGES, SUCH AS BUT NOT LIMITED TO, LOSS OF ANTICIPATED PROFITS OR BENEFITS, RESULTING FROM THE USE OR INABILITY TO USE THE PRODUCT EVEN IF ANY OF THEM HAS BEEN ADVISED OF THE POSSIBILITY OF SUCH DAMAGES. THIS LIMITATION OF LIABILITY SHALL APPLY TO ANY CLAIM OR CAUSE WHATSOEVER WHETHER SUCH CLAIM OR CAUSE ARISES IN CONTRACT, TORT, OR OTHERWISE. Some states do not allow the exclusion or limitation of indirect, special or consequential damages, so the above limitation may not apply to you.

U.S. GOVERNMENT RESTRICTED RIGHTS: Any software included in the Product is provided with restricted rights subject to subparagraphs (c), (1) and (2) of the Commercial Computer Software-Restricted Rights clause at 48 C.F.R. 52.227-19. The terms of this Agreement applicable to the use of the data in the Product are those under which the data are generally made available to the general public by McGraw-Hill. Except as provided herein, no reproduction, use, or disclosure rights are granted with respect to the data included in the Product and no right to modify or create derivative works from any such data is hereby granted.

GENERAL: This License Agreement constitutes the entire agreement between the parties relating to the Product. The terms of any Purchase Order shall have no effect on the terms of this License Agreement. Failure of McGraw-Hill to insist at any time on strict compliance with this License Agreement shall not constitute a waiver of any rights under this License Agreement. This License Agreement shall be construed and governed in accordance with the laws of the State of New York. If any provision of this License Agreement is held to be contrary to law, that provision will be enforced to the maximum extent permissible and the remaining provisions will remain in full force and effect.